THE PHONY WAR

1939–1940

By the Same Author

THE DAY AMERICA CRASHED
EDITH AND WOODROW

For Children

GROWING UP MASAI
THE BIRDMAN OF ST. PETERSBURG

Tom Shachtman

The Phony War

1939–1940

AN AUTHORS GUILD BACKINPRINT.COM EDITION

AN AUTHORS GUILD BACKINPRINT.COM EDITION

Published by iUniverse.com, Inc.

For information address:
iUniverse.com, Inc.
5220 S 16th, Ste. 200
Lincoln, NE 68512
www.iuniverse.com

Originally published by Harper & Row

ISBN: 0-595-16072-7

Printed in the United States of America

For Carol and Andy

Contents

Acknowledgments

Looking at the documentation of any aspect of World War II is a formidable task because of the mountains of documentation which have been amassed since the war. For their aid in cutting channels through these mountains I wish to thank Chris Connelly, Gudrun Dalibor, John Lord, my wife Harriet Shelare, Yvette Molineux, and Harris Colt of The Military Bookman. I received assistance beyond the ordinary from the following libraries: the National Archives (Washington); the New York Public Library, New York University Library at Washington Square, CUNY Graduate Center Library and YIVO Institute (New York); the Public Records Office and Imperial War Museum (London); and the libraries of the Sorbonne (Paris). I am grateful to the New York Public Library for granting me the special facilities of the Wertheim Room for private study. For their guidance and enthusiasm I wish to thank Mel Berger, E. T. Chase, Roger Jellinek, and Frances Lindley. Their efforts notwithstanding, what errors remain in the manuscript are mine alone.

Foreword

Germany invaded Poland on September 1, 1939, and the campaign ended roughly three weeks later. On May 10, 1940, Germany invaded France and the Low Countries. The time in between the defeat of Poland and the invasion of the West—about eight months—has been known ever since in the United States as the phony war, in England as the phoney war or the bore war, in France as *la drôle de guerre*, and in Germany as *der Sitzkrieg*. The names are not only wonderfully characteristic of their respective cultures, but are also significant because they show that people were deeply puzzled by this strange period that was both war and not war.

The phony war was hardly a time of nothingness. It was a period of fearful gestation, one that shaped the debacle that followed and was key to the character of the remainder of World War II in Europe.

During this period, Russia extended her dominance over large areas of the Baltic and the Balkans, and won a war with Finland. Stalin and Hitler became allies for a time and then edged toward becoming enemies. In Germany, Hitler took the direction of the war away from the military; the strategy for overrunning the West was fundamentally altered and an unforeseen invasion of Norway was executed. In Poland, a stark reign of terror was established. In France, governmental strength was dissipated and the army was fatally misdirected. In England, the torch passed from Chamberlain to Churchill, and resources were gathered which would see the country through the coming blitz. And in the United States, Franklin Roosevelt's near-moribund administration was reinvigorated, and America moved from isolation toward involvement in the European war.

To put the phony war into perspective, I have started this narrative with the summer of 1939 and have ended with the early summer of 1940—a period of about a year in which to chronicle the transition from complacent if uneasy peace to full belligerency on both sides of the conflict. To give it human dimension, I have used the words and actions of major figures as documented in contemporary accounts and papers, and those of some representative though unknown people, culled from their diaries. Between the major figures and the minor ones is a gulf of enormous proportions, a gulf thrown into clear light by the events of the phony war era. It was a time during which the small-mindedness of those with great responsibilities in the democratic states resulted in misfortune for millions. It was a time when politicians and generals on all sides demonstrated their inability to cope with the magnitude of the forces unleashed by war.

It was a gray era, full of illusions, in which much that was important was hidden. Denis Barlone, one of the unknowns, characterized it as a period of "dormant war" in which the soldiers of his French division felt "useless" and longed for release. These are modern feelings, and, indeed, except in the countries violated by the German and Russian armies, the phony war resembles nothing so much as a period of repressed but subtly violent cold war—which is perhaps the best reason for examining it afresh today.

Tom Shachtman
New York City

They resolved to leave means neither of ingress or egress to the sudden impulses of despair from without or of frenzy from within. The abbey was amply provisioned. With such precautions the courtiers might bid defiance to contagion. The external world could take care of itself. In the meantime, it was folly to grieve or to think.

—EDGAR ALLAN POE,
The Masque of the Red Death

... honor pricks me on. Yea, but how if honor prick me off when I come on? how then? Can honor set-to a leg? no. or an arm? no. or take away the grief of a wound? Honor hath no skill in surgery, then? no. What is honor? a word. What is in that word, honor?... air. A trim reckoning!—Who hath it? he that died o' Wednesday. Doth he feel it? no. Doth he hear it? no. Is it insensible, then? yea, to the dead. But will it not live with the living? no. Why? detraction will not suffer it:— therefore I'll none of it: honor is a mere scutcheon: and so ends my catechism.

—SHAKESPEARE,
Henry IV, Part I

This is a phony war.

—SENATOR WILLIAM E BORAH

part one

PRELIMINARIES

⫷≈⫸

July 1939 to
September 1939

1

Parties

In the early summer of 1939, the United States of America held a party. A New York suburban swamp called Flushing Meadows was transformed into "The World of Tomorrow." Beneath a symbolic trylon and perishphere, 100,000 visitors daily walked, or rode on buses and golf carts, to see the exhibits.

The 1939 World's Fair was America's way of bidding farewell to the Depression and of imagining the future. The most popular exhibit was the General Motors Futurama. It offered a trip through the mechanized, hygienic, efficient world of far-off 1960. Then fourteen-lane turnpikes would crisscross the country, allowing cars to go at fifty, seventy-five, or one hundred miles per hour in perfect safety. In high-rise cities, inhabitants would be suffused with culture and would enjoy many helpful commercial products. The happiest people would be those who lived in one-factory farm villages which would raise their own farm products and turn out one small industrial item.

At General Electric's Steinmetz Hall, there were five-million-volt lightning charges; twenty locomotives starred in *Railroads on Parade*; there was a Frank Buck Jungleland, a parachute jump, a bobsled ride, and midget cars. Visitors might cadge free long-distance phone calls, free stamps, free French lessons, free electric trouser pressings, and free food samples ranging from the exotic to the ersatz. At Billy Rose's Aquacade, Johnny Weissmuller and Eleanor Holm swam while forty-eight statuesque ladies, one for every state, lined the stage.

Many countries had pavilions at the fair. The Soviet building was vastly impressive. Outside, a large red marble column was topped by a statue of a Soviet worker grasping a red star. Inside, there was a twenty-ton model of the Palace of the Soviets and a mirrored mock-up of the Moscow subway. Italy's building had a bas-relief of Marconi and an outdoor waterfall. Belgium's pavilion held a statue of King Albert I, one of the heroes of the Great War. It was encrusted with 2,800 diamonds. People cried with delight at the gargantuan excesses of Sweden's smorgasbord, in which a half-empty dish disappeared into a kitchen on a revolving table and emerged filled.

One day in June, the fair had important visitors. Great Britain's King George VI and Queen Elizabeth were escorted through the fair by President Franklin Delano Roosevelt. The king paid a dutiful visit to the British pavilion, with its rare copy of the Magna Carta, but he had more fun at other exhibits.

After visiting the fair, the royal couple accompanied the Roosevelts up the Hudson River to Hyde Park, where a picnic was held. Young Franklin D. Roosevelt, Jr., brought two hot dogs to the royal couple. "My, it looks awfully good," the queen said to the president. "How do you eat it?"

"You take it and hold it and aim it and start pushing and chewing," the president directed. Beer was supplied for washing down the hot dogs. Later Mrs. Roosevelt reported in her newspaper column that the butler had slipped with a trayful of drinks and had splashed George VI's trousers. Other newspaper reports suggested that Roosevelt was spending so much time with English royalty in order to boost his own diminishing popularity. The president joined a crowd in singing "Auld Lang Syne" and "For He's a Jolly Good Fellow" as the king and queen boarded a train.

In Washington, to which the president returned, the New Deal was showing its age. Roosevelt had taken office in 1933, at the darkest period of the Depression. For the past six years he had championed economic and social changes which went deeper and were more daring than any the nation had ever experienced. But now the country seemed to have lost its zeal for such reforms, although recovery from the economic nadir was still slow and incomplete. Ten million were still unemployed. Farms had been salvaged from the ruin of the Dust Bowl, but many farmers felt they were now doomed to existing on permanently subsidized prices for their products. Welfare programs, which had helped millions, were beginning to look like continual doles. Newspapers were saying that Roosevelt had lost his initiative for change. It was assumed he would not dare run for a third term, since a deep tradition forbade such an attempt. A third term was too much like a crowning—anathema to a democratic people. When the subject was mentioned in a poll, over 50 percent of the people queried said they would not vote for Roosevelt under any circumstances should he try for a third term.

Congress stood ready to adjourn after a long session in which the legislators had been openly hostile to the president. Men still smarting from Roosevelt's opposition in the 1938 congressional elections had beaten him in the field of economic policy (he could no longer devalue the dollar at will) and social policy (the WPA was to be immediately curtailed), and were currently battling him on his proposed legislation to reform America's neutrality statutes.

Events in Europe in the past year had convinced Roosevelt that war was in the wind. In September of 1938, Hitler had signed an agreement at Munich to take over a portion of Czechoslovakia but to leave the rest of that country untouched; in March of 1939, he had forced his way into the Czech territory he had pledged to leave alone. Immediately afterward, Great Britain had given a military guarantee to Hitler's next likely victim, Poland. Should Hitler invade Poland, the guarantee said, England would declare war. Because of the danger of war, Roosevelt had argued all spring that America's neutrality statutes had to be changed. He himself had signed them into law in 1935, but the climate had been different then, both at home and abroad. Congressional committees had investigated the causes of American intervention in the Great War, and the American public had come to believe that American financiers and arms sales had enmeshed the United States in that war. As a consequence, there had come the drastic neutrality statutes that forbade the United States to sell arms to any belligerent once war was declared. It was hoped that this would keep the country out of any future wars. Roosevelt believed that if war broke out now, the current statutes would actually favor those who had arms (Hitler) at the expense of those who didn't have them (Britain, France, and Poland). Changing the law so that America could sell arms to the democracies might deter Hitler and prevent war.

American isolationists disagreed with Roosevelt's reasoning. They believed that the United States was safe behind its two oceans and would suffer should it become involved in Europe's quarrels. Over a holiday weekend, when a hundred Democratic members of the House of Representatives went home early, the Republican members stayed and rammed through an amendment to Roosevelt's neutrality reform bill. This amendment would allow the sale of airplanes so long as they were for peaceful uses, but would embargo "arms and ammunition." In Roosevelt's mind, this nullified the reform completely. He was stymied in the Senate as well. A reform bill was in the hands of the Foreign Relations Committee. The votes there were about evenly split, and when Roosevelt tried to exert pressure to get the bill through, his past came back to haunt him. Two wavering Democratic senators, Walter George of Georgia and Guy Gillette of Iowa, both favored neutrality reform, but Roosevelt had opposed them in 1938. Now they got even. By a vote of 12 to 11 the FRC refused to pass the bill, and the reform was dead in the Senate. Roosevelt did not blame the Democrats who had struck back at him, but he complained bitterly about the isolationist

Republicans to his friend, Secretary of the Treasury, Henry Morgenthau, Jr.:

> I will bet you an old hat that . . . when [Hitler] wakes up and finds out what
> has happened, there will be great rejoicing in the Italian and German
> camps. I think we ought to introduce a bill for statues of [Senators] Austin,
> Vandenberg, Lodge, and Taft . . . to be erected in Berlin and put the swas-
> tika on them.

Congress adjourned. When the legislators returned, it would be winter.
Roosevelt predicted that war would already have started by then—his
guess was September 10—and that the people's representatives would
already have their minds set on getting themselves re-elected in the
1940 contests.

In Paris at the beginning of July, it was *la grande semaine*, a week
of parties to which the rich annually devoted their attention. United
States Ambassador William Bullitt gave a ball for the Yale Glee Club.
President of France Albert Lebrun gave a dinner for the young Emper-
or and Empress of Annam. English Ambassador Phipps's ball in the
Charot mansion at Versailles was visited by rain, and guests were unable to traipse through the garden, which had been planted by Edward
VII in 1903. They had to make do with the magnificence of the mansion
itself, originally given to Pauline Borghese by Napoleon. The rain was
blamed on sunspots.

On the final night of the Longchamps racing season, the events
took place under arc lights and in the presence of twenty-two orches-
tras, ballet troupes, wrestlers and vaudeville teams, and 100,000 people.
Lady Mendl gave a gala that night for a select 750 guests—a circus with
trained horses, dogs, and elephants. Photographers snapped pictures of
the Bullitts, the Lebruns, the Emperor and Empress of Annam, Eve Cu-
rie, Douglas Fairbanks and Mary Pickford, the brothers Rothschild, and
the Duke and Duchess of Windsor. The Princess of Kapurthala wanted
to ride an elephant, but the beast refused; nonetheless the princess of
the country of the thousand and one nights said it was like the thousand
and second. A mysterious, impossibly beautiful woman passed among
the diners, alone and silent. Was she the celebrated heroine of a pas-
sionate affair that had ended badly? Whispers begat whispers until
Match found out that she was "unfortunately, married."

The Count of Beaumont's costume ball called for guests to come as
characters from Racine's plays—it was the dramatist's three hundredth
birthday. The first prize went to Maurice Rothschild as the Sultan Baja-
zet; on his turban he wore his mother's diamonds, and on his sash other
family trinkets that had been made by Benvenuto Cellini. Not to be
outdone, Mrs. Louise Macy rented a long-dusty mansion, temporary
furniture, kitchen facilities, and plumbing, and told her guests to come

wearing diadems and tiaras. Elsa Maxwell, a guest, said it was one of the most successful parties she never gave.

A most important party was given by Ambassador Jules Lukasciewicz at the new Polish embassy, the mansion of the Princes of Sagan, on July 4. In the garden on a perfect night, an arc lamp threw shadows of the sphinx and rainbows on a marble balustrade while an orchestra played polonaises. Some guests came from a banquet of the Franco-British Association: France's foreign minister, Georges Bonnet; commander in chief of the armed forces General Maurice Gustave Gamelin; and England's secretary for war, Leslie Hore-Belisha. At the banquet, it had been emphasized that the democracies' spiritual force was backed by the largest army in the world (the French), the largest navy in the world (the British), and by their combined air forces, which were also the world's largest. The presence of the distinguished trio at the Polish embassy was noted for its political significance.

"*Bravo, Luka, pour votre joli danzing,*" a guest said to the host. It was a pun on Danzig, the Polish free port with an overwhelmingly German population. Just that day *Le Temps* had quoted Danzig's Nazi newspaper as saying, "The return of Danzig to the Reich is decided. It is the Führer who will fix the date." Danzig was sure to be the focal point of the coming crisis between the democracies and Hitler.

"Mazurka!" a voice cried at three in the morning. Luka kicked off his shoes and socks and lined up a handful of his attachés; opposite them came Mme Artur Rubinstein, the wife of the celebrated pianist, and several other renowned beauties. With the ambassador leading, the dancers went through the formal figures, and then began to improvise as the music swelled. Fireworks spangled the sky and mixed with the dawn. An observer said to a journalist, "It is scarcely enough to say that they are dancing on a volcano. For what is an eruption of Vesuvius compared to the cataclysm that is forming under our very feet?"

The author of this dour remark was Paul Reynaud, minister of finance. He was sixty-one, small, athletic, cocksure, cultured, and moneyed. He had all the requisites for being one of the chosen handful attempting to manage the confused behemoth of the Third Republic. One hundred fifty years after the taking of the Bastille, France was still in the hands of a ruling clique. Reynaud had been born wealthy. He had been educated in the proper schools; he served in the Great War as an officer and received the proper decorations. The war over, his law degree in hand, he married the daughter of the wealthy and influential head of the Paris bar and went into politics. He sought election from the affluent Right Bank district of Paris that contained the Bourse, the stock exchange. He won his first election in the early 1920s, and from then on his seat was a sinecure. He moved easily among the men of finance, and they knew he would act in their best interests.

Reynaud was a member of the Chamber of Deputies, but the real power lay in the cabinet ministries. The legislative chambers rarely did more than occasionally topple a government. When this happened, there would be a cabinet shuffle: some names would be dropped, more would be shifted and rearranged. A new cabinet would be approved, and the legislators would settle back into torpor.

On those reshuffled lists, Paul Reynaud's name began to appear among the second-level appointments, but he did not rise to the first rank. He was a man of the right, a conservative without a major party behind him. He was blocked. He acquired a mistress, the powerful and ambitious Countess Hélène de Portes, a dynamic, outspoken, and wealthy woman with a circle of friends as influential as they were conservative. In the 1930s, she advanced Reynaud's cause, and he edged up slowly.

But another's cause was also being advanced by a titled mistress. He was Edouard Daladier. She was the Marquise de Crussol. Daladier had been born a poor provincial, a baker's son. He had served in the trenches and there had won his officer's chevrons. He was a history teacher, and became a leftist mayor and then a legislator from his home region of the Vaucluse. His personal appearance was the opposite of Reynaud's: he was large and sloppy and had a florid face.

In the early 1930s, Daladier had once been premier, briefly. Then he was eclipsed by Léon Blum, a remarkable leader. Blum was a Jew as well as a socialist, but nevertheless became premier of France as head of the Popular Front, a coalition of Radical Socialists, Socialists, and Communists. He introduced the forty-hour week and compulsory arbitration of wage disputes; he nationalized the Bank of France and the French munitions industry. Daladier, as a leader of the Radical Socialists, served in Blum's cabinet until conservative opposition rose to topple Blum's government. Daladier scrambled into another government of leftist persuasions, and then it, too, fell, and Daladier was the next logical premier. It was then March of 1938, a moment after Hitler had marched into Austria and, in a bloodless coup, linked up that country with Germany. Daladier, as a gesture to the conservatives and to national unity, took into his cabinet Paul Reynaud and five other men of the right.

Six months after he took office, Daladier faced a crisis. At Munich, Daladier (and British Prime Minister Neville Chamberlain) gave in to Hitler's territorial demands on Czechoslovakia in order to avert war; he came back to Paris expecting to be lynched, and was lionized. But behind the scenes, the conservatives demanded that the country prepare for war. In a cabinet shuffle, Reynaud emerged as a strong man, the minister of finance. He showed quickly what he could do. With the help of his conservative backers, he began to revitalize the nation's economy, in the process trampling under many concessions the workers had won under Blum, among them the forty-hour week and the right to collective bargaining. So that adequate war matériel could be produced,

Reynaud insisted that people work six days a week and not make so much noise about wage settlements. Meanwhile Hélène de Portes intensified a lifelong feud with Daladier's mistress: she circulated rumors that Daladier was beginning to stink of absinthe. The Marquise de Crussol fired back: Reynaud wouldn't mind a neofascist government and was trying to exert pressure to get around the divorce laws so he could ditch his wife and marry de Portes. Relations were strained between Reynaud and Daladier. At the culminating party of *la grande semaine*, the 150th anniversary of the taking of the Bastille, the *Quatorze Juillet*, the premier and the finance minister hardly spoke to one another.

By midnight July 13, crowds had begun to gather in Paris. The sky was bright, and the stargazers had thermoses of tea and mulled wine to drink as they sat on cushions and portable chairs, on curbs and in trees and on balconies. Some had harmonicas and accordions, and there were dancing and singing in the streets. From every conceivable place, tricolors and British Union Jacks hung, fraternally mixed. At dawn of the fourteenth, 300,000 people were around the Etoile at the head of the Champs Elysées. There had been nothing like it since Paris had acclaimed the American president as Wilson *le juste* in 1918. The day's celebration was to be the grandest and most awesome display of military might ever seen on earth.

In the air there was an enormous throbbing noise as a seemingly endless sky parade of airplanes roared past barely a thousand feet above the crowd. There were 315 airships flying by at a steady 175 mph—French Blochs, Breguets, Liore-Oliviers, as well as British Blenheims, Wellingtons, Hurricanes, Spitfires, Hampdens. They made an awesome sight.

So did the marching men, row upon row, thirty thousand strong, each man the representative of a hundred who could be mobilized to fight behind him. Bearing witness to the virility of the French Empire were Madagascan, Senegalese, and Indochinese *tirailleurs*; Chasseurs Alpins, with skis, ropes, and rifles; desert spahis on Arab stallions; Zouaves; the cadets of Saint-Cyr, with white-plumed kepis; and for the first time on European soil since the Great War, the bearded men of the Foreign Legion, who marched ax in hand. There were motorized units, enormous guns drawn by horses, and only medium tanks, since the heaviest would have caused cracking in the venerable Paris streets. In a gesture of undying friendship and alliance, middle-ranking officers of the British and French armies had taken to exchanging the top buttons of their tunics. Onlookers cheered the Grenadier Guards, the Scots, the Irish, and the Coldstream Guards, and the Royal Marine Band.

Television cameras, outside for the first time in history, transmitted the historic event to the handful of receivers in the country. On the reviewing stand were phalanxes of cabinet officers, parliamentarians, and dignitaries from all over, among them King Carol of Rumania and

President Roosevelt's mother. For this day and these hours, the Paris parade was the center of the world.

Hat in hand, Premier Edouard Daladier gave what everyone said was a beautiful speech. He told the crowd that it had made great sacrifices, and that

> today you are receiving the first fruits. The army which you accalimed ... is the guardian of your liberties. ... We have made an immense effort to assure the salvation of peace and liberty. We will pursue it without tiring and with that tenacity which animated our great ancestors.

The speech and the parade, all agreed, gave an unmistakable warning to Adolf Hitler to keep his distance.

On the podium watching the parade was Winston Churchill. He was sixty-four and had been out of the British cabinet ten long years, during which he had been kept going by his tongue and his pen. He was working on his *History of the English-Speaking Peoples;* his collection of newspaper articles, *Step by Step*, in which he argued for a more aggressive policy toward the totalitarian states, was becoming a best seller. He had been one of the few who dared to denounce the 1938 agreements at Munich as a sellout that would lead to Hitler's takeover of all Czechoslovakia. Now, in light of all that had happened in the past few years, Churchill seemed touched with the wisdom of Cassandra; people were taking him more seriously than they had for a decade. His friend Desmond Morton had written to Churchill, when he read *Step by Step:*

> Many years on historians will read this and ... wonder ... what devil of pride, unbelief, unselfishness or sheer madness possessed the English people that they did not rise as one man, depose the blind guides ... and call on you to lead them to security, justice, and peace. There is a Polish proverb about the Poles themselves: *Madry Polak po szkotzie,* or "Wise is the Pole after the event." The English electorate is growing more Polish daily.

Churchill had been correct often enough to awaken a public clamor for him to have a place in the government. A half-dozen papers, including the Communist *Daily Worker* and the liberal *Manchester Guardian*, advised Prime Minister Neville Chamberlain to forget his differences with Churchill and bring him in from the cold.

Neville Chamberlain was past seventy and, though few knew it, dying of cancer. He agreed that Churchill was brilliant, but believed him to be equally bullheaded and frequently dead wrong, full of fantastic ideas that passed into and out of his brain in a week. Chamberlain believed Churchill's influence in the councils of government would be disruptive: here was Churchill calling for a tough stance and war if necessary, while Chamberlain's own government had devoted itself to staying out of war. Chamberlain refused to take Churchill in, and he tried to recess Parliament. Churchill said Hitler would take this as a sign of weakness. Chamberlain won anyway, Parliament recessed, and Churchill fumed. He put his frustrations into a transatlantic radio speech. It was holiday time, he told Americans, and he felt a hush of suspense and fear coming over Europe:

> Listen! No, listen carefully; I think I can hear something—yes, there it was quite clear. Don't you hear it? It is the tramp of armies crunching the gravel of parade-grounds, splashing through rain-soaked fields, the tramp of two million German soldiers and more than a million Italians—"going on maneuvers"—yes, only on maneuvers!... After all, the Dictators must train their soldiers, they could scarcely do less in common prudence, when the Danes, the Dutch, the Swiss, the Albanians—and of course the Jews— may leap out at them at any moment and rob them of their living-space, and make them sign another paper to say who began it.

In mid-August Churchill set out to visit the Maginot Line. He had wangled an invitation to do so during the *quatorze juillet* parade. As with everything French, the Maginot had to be approached obliquely. First Churchill had to eat wood strawberries soaked in wine at lunch with General Alphonse Georges and the British MP and former general Sir Edward Spears. Then, in company with the generals, he could visit the line's sections near the Rhine.

The Maginot Line was a state of mind as much as it was the most advanced technological military achievement on earth. The designers believed it to be a vision of the future, but it was a product of the past. Preliminary studies for it began as the Great War ended. One of the lessons of that war was that advancing troops could always be stopped by trenches with adequate firepower—that is, by a good defense. Ten years later, when this idea had already been superseded by new ones, construction of the greatest trench of all time began. It took another ten years before *le trou*, as the troops called it, was complete.

In the public mind the Maginot Line was impregnable, a continuous wall reaching from the English Channel to the Mediterranean to protect France from invasion. It was, in reality, not so extensive—it went only from the south end of Belgium to the north end of Switzerland. It was discontinuous—a series of fortified barracks, antitank barriers, mine fields, and remotely controlled charges to blow up bridges and railroad junctions. Near Turcoing-Roubaix and Valenciennes, for example, there were gaps, for these were industrial cities and it was impractical for guns and forts to replace the industry there. There was no real wall in the southeast of Belgium at all, for Belgium would be on the side of the Allies when a war came. The lack of an extension of the line past Belgium worried some, but not the highest-ranking military authorities. Marshal Philippe Pétain, hero of Verdun, told an investigating committee in 1934, "Beginning at Montmédy are the Ardennes forests. They are impenetrable.... As this front would have no depth the enemy would not deploy there, If he should we shall close the pincers as he emerges from the forests. This sector, therefore, is not dangerous."

This reasoning was accepted. An extension to cover the Belgian Ardennes was never built.

The line was in three regions, each differently defended. Near the frontier and the railroad tracks were *maisons fortes*, small reinforced barracks from which troops would emerge to slow the advancing Germans, to blow up bridges and crossings, and to give warning to the rear defenses. A mile or two back were *avant-postes*, concrete blocks with heavy guns, where permanent garrisons slept with their weapons and were protected by antitank barriers. Behind these were bigger defense structures, the casements. Below ground, these had two tiers, one a firing chamber and the other the living quarters for twenty-five to thirty-five men. In front was a large ditch swept by automatic grenade launchers. Each casement had a diesel generator and a support system. In between casements were "interval troops" equipped with field artillery, who were to move wherever necessary to fight the invaders.

Three to five miles farther back were the fortresses. These were immense and came in pairs. Although separated by thousands of yards, the pairs had overlapping fields of fire; one could protect its partner, and if one was hit, the other could still function. The largest fortress had two thousand men, and guns that could fire at targets up to seven and a half miles away; most were smaller, and their guns reached two and a half to three miles. Between each pair of forts was an underground command post with buried telephone lines, an underground railroad, an infirmary, kitchens, a supply depot, a self-contained generator, and self-acting fireproof doors. Inside the forts, there were ultraviolet rooms for sun-starved soldiers and extra-high air pressure to prevent poison gas from seeping into the rooms. Psychological tensions were kept minimal by having all the men in one fort come from the same area, and by allowing the men to plant ten thousand rosebushes above the forts.

Churchill saw all these details, many of which were off limits to other visitors. During the day the group would drive through charming Alsatian villages, where the small houses were painted robin's-egg blue with cherry-colored shutters. During the nights they would talk war. They would debate the possibility of fog, natural or man-produced, or of parachute attack, or how the tank obstacles would hold. Not a man believed the Allies would get through the fall without war. Soldiers stood ready to blow up bridges. Churchill later summed up the visit:

> What was remarkable about all I learned on my visit was the complete acceptance of the defense which dominated my most responsible French hosts, and imposed itself irresistibly on me. In talking to all those highly competent French officers, one had the sense that the Germans were the stronger, and that France had no longer the life-thrust to mount a great offensive. She would fight for her existence—*voilà tout!* ... In my own bones, too, was the horror of the Somme and Passchendaele offensives.

The Germans were, of course, far stronger than in the days of Munich.

Hermann Göring had seen the Great War too, but it seemed to hold no horrors for him, not in 1939. The war had made him a national hero, a flying ace emblazoned with decorations. He had taken over the squadron of Manfred von Richthofen, the "Red Baron," after the leader's death; and he had gone on to glory. In the postwar days he was tall, lean, erudite, with a taste for beautiful women and fanciful clothes.

He used his celebrity to make money in the ruinous inflation of the early 1920s, which was when he joined forces with Adolf Hitler. A stalwart of the Nazi party, badly wounded in the Beer Hall putsch of 1923, he escaped to Austria and then to Sweden while Hitler went to jail. In Sweden he married a rich woman; he also became addicted to morphine and ran to fat. At his 1928 reunion with Hitler, he weighed three-hundred pounds, and his taste for power and high living had grown with his corpulence. He became an easy target for cartoonists, but that only increased his celebrity. In 1933, when Hitler became chancellor, Göring was the titular head of the Reichstag. Shortly thereafter, he was involved in the infamous Reichstag fire.

For many in Germany in the 1930s, Göring seemed the one man in the band of strange fanatics to whom people could still look for sanity. On the radio he was conversational and could be understood. As the head of German reindustrialization, he put people back to work, and many were grateful for that. By the late 1930s, he appeared to be indispensable. It was bruited about that if the Nazis were somehow kicked out, Göring would remain. He supported Hitler, but made certain distinctions known. To him, Jews were not criminals or scum; he liked artists, even cultivated them, and would not censor their output; he had a sense of humor; he was not afraid of wretched excess. Aristocrats were his friends; he had acquaintances in many countries; he was a man of the world.

Nonetheless Göring participated wholeheartedly in Hitler's bloodless triumphs of the 1930s. Just before Munich, he brainwashed the French air attaché so effectively that the whole French government accepted the invincibility of the Luftwaffe. That helped push Daladier's pen at Munich, which in turn strengthened Göring's idea that the Third Reich could achieve its territorial goals without war. The British Empire, which he studied, had been put together more by power plays than by war. Göring hoped (as Hitler did) that the Third Reich would one day be as powerful as Great Britain, and that the two countries would share the leadership of the world. Thus, in the summer of 1939, he believed war with England was unnecessary and avoidable.

On July 6, Göring gave a party to rival those of the Paris social season. It took place at Karinhall, his country estate, named for his Swedish wife (deceased). Ninety minutes outside Berlin, Karinhall was in the national forest of which he was the national huntsman. The grounds were stocked with deer, pheasant, and other game. His private zoo was on the grounds; often he would frolic in the tub with his lion cubs. The main house contained paintings by Rubens, Rembrandt, and El Greco, which had been given him by Jews grateful for his help in their leaving Germany. Karin's ashes lay in a small Greek temple, which, when one entered it, was automatically illuminated so that a spotlight shone on a bust of Karin on a slowly revolving turntable.

That night, Karinhall was gleaming, and Göring, in a white and gold silk uniform with a red sash across his stomach, cut a startling figure. Many guests were from the film and theater circles of Berlin and Vienna, some of them friends of the second Frau Göring, Emmy. It was known that the Görings were not so straitlaced or socially backward as other Nazi functionaries, and the actresses wore revealing gowns of silver and gold. In general, the guests were of the upper crust. They laughed over such drollery as the advice in the *Völkischer Beobachter* on "Kisses in the Summertime":

> In order to achieve success in kissing, the man must observe the following rules. Leave at least one of the woman's nostrils free because she must breathe. Pencils and fountain pens should be removed beforehand from the breast pockets. Alcohol has a bad taste. Take off the hat, because it will fall off in any case. Do not ask whether you may kiss her, because any decent girl would naturally answer no. For women, be sure that your lips feel soft. Leave hairpins, bosom brooches, heavy or knitted clothing, jewelry that scratches, and non-kissproof lipstick at home. Do not expect every kiss to presage matrimony; otherwise you will miss all the fun. Do not try to be a Garbo, but comb your hair so that the man will not have trouble afterward in removing it from his coat.

At the party, the guests danced in the large main hall, rode the private railroad over the grounds, and accepted champagne from servants dressed in hunting breeches, while Göring stayed in the library awaiting a visitor. When that visitor arrived, driven from the airport in a Luftwaffe staff Mercedes, he was shown immediately into Göring's presence. Birger Dahlerus was a Swedish businessman and the employer of Göring's stepson, a man who had often been helped out by Göring. It had occurred to Dahlerus, since he knew both Göring and certain highly placed people in England, that he might act as a go-between to prevent the two countries from going to war. He had just come from London.

"What have you learned from the Englishmen?" Göring asked him.

"They tell me that if you attack Poland," Dahlerus reported, "they will stand by their guarantee."

"Nonsense." Göring scoffed at the idea that the British might actually back up Poland. "They're just bluffing."

"I don't think they're bluffing," Dahlerus said. "If you attack Poland, there will be war."

Dahlerus's observations worried Göring, and he asked the Swede to set up for him meetings in neutral countries with representatives of the British government to see if together they could head off war. Göring informed Hitler of these contacts, though he didn't provide the Nazi leader with details. Hitler didn't mind the overtures. He didn't want war with England over Poland, either.

Two photographs of troops of the Soviet Union appeared in the world press that summer. One was of Russian soldiers in the upper reaches of Mongolia being shamefacedly shorn bald by Japanese barbers. They had been captured in the border war, which had been going on for some time. In the other photograph, a battalion of Russian soldiers, fully dressed and equipped, held their rifles high as they marched in perfect order and without breaking ranks through a chest-high lake.

Joseph Stalin would have found nothing to laugh about in these photos. Both the Red Army and the U.S.S.R. were in the process of a long evolutionary change and the photos showed it.

Nearing sixty and the absolute ruler of his country, Stalin wished to extend the Russian state to include territories once ruled by Peter the Great. A generation had passed since the Revolution, and consolidation of the Revolution's gains within the country had been achieved. Now the leader of the Russians must reach out for more. Stalin's current five-year naval plan was modeled on Peter's plan; so was his insistence on the development of Russia eastward into the Siberian wastes. As a young man, Stalin had defended Peter's city, Petrograd, against the White Russian general Nikolai Yudenich. That experience had taught him that he needed territory—in the Baltic, and perhaps in the Balkans, where oil was becoming important.

Unfortunately Stalin had another Russian leader on whom to base his behavior. "There cannot be a ruler without terror," one of Ivan the Terrible's men said. "Like a steed under the rider without a bridle, so is a realm without terror." Stalin agreed. After Lenin died in 1924, the troika of Stalin, Kamenev, and Zinoviev had ousted Trotsky and sent him into exile. By the early 1930s, Stalin has pushed the other two aside and emerged as sole dictator. The writer and editor Nikolai Bukharin, in those days a confidant of Stalin, wrote of him:

> He is unhappy at not being able to convince everyone, himself included, that he is greater than everyone; and this unhappiness of his may be his most human trait; perhaps the only human trait in him. But what is not human, but rather something devilish, is that because of this unhappiness he cannot help taking revenge on people, on all people but especially those who are in any way higher or better than he.

In the early 1930s, the image of Communist Russia stood quite high in the eyes of the liberal world. Russia was trying a grand economic and social experiment, while the capitalist countries of the West were in decline and depression. If there were a trickle of killings in Russia, most liberals in the West were willing to overlook them as perhaps necessary to the accomplishment of complete regeneration.

Then came Stalin's purges. In the first of them, those men who had been close to Lenin were arrested and charged with conspiracy and murder. They included Zinoviev, Kamenev, Bukharin, and others of the men who had made the Revolution. After a series of "show" trials during which they confessed, they were executed. Although the Russian public seemed convinced of the defendants' guilt, many foreign observers who had been sympathetic to Communist ideals were not convinced, and some began to drift away from the red banner.

A second purge took place in 1937. After a one-day secret trial, it was announced that Marshal Mikhail Tukhachevsky and six other generals had been convicted on charges of spying for Germany and had been shot. After this the secret police under Nikolai Yezhov executed 35,000 army men, nearly all of them officers, among them seventy-five of the eighty members of the Supreme Military Council. By mid-1938, the army was virtually leaderless. "If only," Boris Pasternak is reported to have said, "someone would tell Stalin about it." In the third and last purge, Yezhov and the secret police were the victims. Within five years about 100,000 people had been killed and between seven and fourteen million had been sent to forced-labor camps. The army had been purged on the pretext that the generals were spying for Germany. Particular emphasis had been placed on cleaning up the Ukraine, which had aligned itself with Germany in 1917. The purge of the secret police was justified on the grounds that Fascists had infiltrated them.

In Stalin's view, Germany was blocking Russia's territorial wishes and since Hitler had taken power Stalin's priority had been to prepare a road-block to Germany's expansion. He pushed the armaments industry to develop 2½ times faster than industry as a whole; he increased the army's size to 4.2 million while purging its leaders. When civil war broke out in Spain Stalin aided the leftwing against Franco, whose forces were fighting with extensive German aid, and encouraged France and England to perceive communism as a last bastion against fascism.

In reaction to the Anti-Comintern Pact signed in 1936 by Germany, Italy, and Japan, Stalin proposed to Britian and France that they unite with the U.S.S.R. to form a common front against Germany. There were many in the West who wanted such an alliance. French and British generals who had observed Red Army maneuvers in 1936 had come away impressed. But that had been before the trials and the purges. After the purges, Britain and France no longer considered Russia a fit partner for an alliance. Yet in 1938, Stalin proposed that Britain, France, and Russia unite with Czechoslovakia and prepare a combined military plan should Germany invade Czechoslovakia. But then came

Munich, a meeting to which Stalin was not invited. At Munich, Britain and France thought they had preserved peace in Europe.

Stalin struggled to understand Munich. The conference seemed to have been held as if the U.S.S.R. did not exist. It made no sense to him, unless he interpreted Munich to mean that the democracies had promised Hitler a free hand in the East if Hitler agreed to halt his demands on the West. "One might think," Stalin said, "that the districts of Czechoslovakia were yielded to Germany as the prize for her undertaking to launch war on the Soviet Union." When, a few months later, Hitler marched into what remained of Czechoslovakia, Stalin was not surprised. The very next day his foreign minister, Maksim Litvinov, proposed mutual military talks among the U.S.S.R., Britain, France, Poland, and Rumania.

England stalled and instead signed a pact with Poland. Another slap in Stalin's face. Yet he tried again, calling, on April 17, 1939, for the democracies to sign a mutual assistance pact with Russia which would guarantee the independence of Finland, Estonia, Latvia, Lithuania, Poland, and Rumania—from the Baltic to the Balkans. Chamberlain didn't answer. He was unwilling to agree to defend Finland, since by doing so he might offend Hitler. Patient, still knowing his ultimate goals and his immediate requirements, Stalin in the summer of 1939 requested Britain and France to send military negotiators to Moscow to discuss mutual defense—and simultaneously he put out feelers to Germany.

In a far-reaching, bitter speech, Stalin told the Soviet Presidium his vision of the future. War was coming; war between Germany and Russia, a costly and sanguinary conflict. The war would last for years and weaken both states to exhaustion. After a stalemate, after millions of souls had died, when both belligerents were defeated, the jackals would come. The British and the French and even the Americans would roll in and easily pick up the spoils. He foresaw nothing but catastrophe. It was not upon them yet, but it was approaching with great speed. At this late hour, he could promise but one thing: he would do everything in his power to prevent this vision from coming to pass.

2

Pact with the Devil

In a room of the lavish Spiridonyevka Palace in the fifteenth-century walled city called the Kremlin, three groups sat at a large round table to negotiate an Anglo-French-Russian military agreement. It was mid-August of 1939. Admiral Sir Reginald Aylmer Ranfurly Plunkett-Ernle-Erle-Drax, first naval aide to King George VI, had been all but retired when given this mission. General· André Doumenc was a brilliant staff officer who knew mobile forces and was commander of the Lille military district, but was not a member of France's Supreme War Council. Across the table from them was Marshal Kliment Voroshilov, Soviet defense commissar and one of the two top military men in the Soviet Union.

The negotiations were as slow as the summer. Drax and Doumenc had come to Moscow by boat and train, not by plane, and their governments had instructed them not to make too much progress or give in on anything. London and Paris were convinced that Stalin would eventually have to sign with the West in order to keep Hitler from his doorstep. If the Russians didn't come around, the attitude was, as Chamberlain put it in a letter to his sister, "I should not feel our position was greatly worsened if we had to do without them."

Stalin wasn't fooled. There were too many loose ends and unanswered questions in the negotiations. Where were the ranking military men, General Maurice Gamelin and Sir William Edmund Ironside? Why had Drax no proper credentials? "I regret my bluntness," Voroshilov said on August 14, "but we soldiers must be forthright in what we say." The scheme for military cooperation to stop Hitler if he attacked Poland or Rumania was not yet clear:

> Do the French and British General Staffs think that the Soviet land forces will be admitted to Polish territory in order to make direct contact with the enemy in case Poland is attacked? . . . Is it proposed to allow Soviet troops across Rumanian territory if the aggressor attacks Rumania?

Voroshilov knew all about those countries' fears that the Red Army would linger too long and take over large areas, but Rumania and Poland must nonetheless agree to let the Russians in to assist them, or, Voroshilov said, "further conversations will not have any real meaning." He insisted that Drax and Doumenc wire London and Paris to pressure Warsaw and Bucharest to obtain "exact and unequivocal" answers to his questions. In the meantime, the marshal said, he was going duck shooting.

The salon at the Berghof, Hitler's mountain retreat above Obersalzberg in the Bavarian Alps, was a large room. It was sparsely furnished with oversized objects: a sideboard ten feet high by eighteen feet long; a twenty-foot-long table; a massive clock with a bronze eagle; a grand chest concealing phonograph speakers; paintings by Titian and members of his school, and a landscape of ancient Rome; a huge fireplace with red stuffed chairs before it and an uncomfortable low sofa that seated eight abreast. An immense picture window could be mechanically raised or lowered and gave a view of awesome chasms and peaks beyond.

From this vacation house, Hitler issued instructions on what to do with Russia. Since last winter the two dictatorships had been talking; a trade agreement was in the works, but trial balloons about a far more extensive pact had not yet led to anything. For the past thousand years European wars had begun in September, once the harvests were in. In the spring, Hitler had laid plans for a September 1 invasion of Poland. To keep that timetable, he now believed he must have a pact with Russia, and soon, else the date would slip and the autumn rains would begin and his armies might become stuck in the Polish mud, which had mired would-be conquerors of Poland from Napoleon to the Bolsheviks. It was maddening how the Russians were dallying and flirting with the Allies. They insisted that a trade agreement be signed before talking about more serious matters—so Hitler made some concessions, and Moscow softened. On August 19, the trade pact was signed. Next day Hitler sent a personal note to Stalin: "A crisis may blow up any day" between Poland and Germany; therefore would Stalin please receive Foreign Minister Joachim von Ribbentrop within three days to iron out and then sign a mutual nonaggression pact. Hitler knew Stalin could read between the lines that Germany was ready to make substantial concessions in order to have a free hand in attacking Poland.

After sending the message, Hitler was near collapse. He couldn't sleep. He called Göring after midnight and worried over Stalin's reaction. He became impatient at delays in transmission and translation. He was agitated through August 21's late breakfast, the leisurely walk to the forest teahouse, the sunlit afternoon's small talk, the walk back to the large house. He sat at a long table for dinner, a young woman at either elbow, eating vegetarian dishes while the others had soup, meat, and wine or Fachinger mineral water. During the meal, one of the waiters—an SS man in white vest and black trousers—handed him a note. Young Albert Speer, Hitler's architect, remembered:

> He scanned it, stared into space for a moment, flushed deeply, then banged on the table so hard the glasses rattled, and exclaimed in a voice breaking with excitement: "I have them! I have them!" Seconds later, he had already regained control of himself. No one dared ask any question and the meal continued.

The note was Stalin's telegram inviting Ribbentrop to Moscow to sign a pact that would be "the "foundation for eliminating the political tension and for the establishment of peace and collaboration between our countries." Hitler passed the note around. Later his entourage watched a newsreel of Stalin reviewing a military parade; Hitler expressed his satisfaction that the enormous display of military might on the screen was now neutralized.

Next morning the senior military officers of the Reich flew or drove to the Berghof, dressed in civilian clothes so that the gathering would appear to be a tea party and go unnoticed by the press. Their limousines wound up the road blasted through the rocks, went past confiscated forests and church lands, to enter the retreat through a bronze portal and a marble hall damp from the moisture at the mountain's heart. About fifty men got onto the polished brass elevator and rode up 165 feet to wait in the great hall. At noon Hitler entered, placed his notes on the grand piano, and began to speak.

He was fifty and at the height of his powers; it was best that war should come now rather than in five years, when both he and Mussolini would be older. Germany's decisiveness rested on him alone, and "yet at any moment I might be struck down by a criminal or lunatic." His unshakable will was the difference between the new Germany and the rotten democracies of the West, the "worms" he had bested at Munich. England and France had no such personalities, but they were rearming and in several years might prove dangerous. He would guarantee his audience, however, that neither country would intervene in the short, localized Silesian war he planned. The Allies wouldn't even be able to mount a successful blockade, because the Reich's needs would now be provided for by Russia.

He had pursued wisps and hints toward this ultimate political triumph for some time. He had given a "particularly cordial" welcome to the Russian ambassador at the turn of the year; he had followed this with low-level talks; then, in May, he had seen a definitive sign. The news that Litvinov, a Jew married to an Englishwoman, was being replaced by Vyacheslav Molotov, a man who preferred dealing with the dictators, struck him "like a cannonball." After this he had pursued the quarry relentlessly, and now it was his. The trade pact would bring grain, cattle, coal, wood, lead, zinc, and oil. A nonaggression pact would guarantee a dream of German militarists for seventy years: a war to be fought on only one front. "Now I have Poland just where I want her!" Hitler's voice dropped as he concluded: "I am only afraid that at the last moment some *Schweinhund* might put to me a plan for mediation."

After a buffet lunch, Hitler continued; outside, a storm could be seen gathering over the mountains. Complete destruction of Poland's armies was the objective of the invasion, which would begin in four days, on August 26:

> I shall give a propagandist reason for starting the war—never mind whether it will be plausible or not. The victor will not be asked afterwards whether he told the truth or not. In starting and waging a war it is not right that matters, but victory! Close your hearts to pity! Act brutally! Eighty million people must obtain what is their right.

Göring rose to assure Hitler that all would do their duty. General Heinrich von Brauchitsch, commander-in-chief of the army, admonished his officers, "Gentlemen, to your stations!" There was no one in the room who questioned either the objective or the methods of the coming invasion.

There is the story of the Oriental executioner who dreamed of the perfect execution: with one swift stroke, he would sever his victim's head so neatly that the victim would feel nothing. The day for an execution arrived, the sword was raised and then swung. The victim appeared intact and chided the executioner for not having done his work. The executioner bowed low, and said to the victim, "Please nod."

The Nazi-Soviet alliance was such an executioner's stroke. The very idea of such an alliance overturned all prior notions about the two dictatorships. Many countries had predicated foreign policies on the belief that Soviet might would continue to balance German aggressiveness, and vice versa, and they themselves would be allowed to exist peacefully within the balance of power. That hope was now at an end. In Japan, which was at war with Russia, the government fell; in Finland, the government shook; in Estonia, Latvia, Lithuania, Rumania, and Yugoslavia—all with borders touching the Soviet Union—governments trembled and began hurried meetings. They did not know their necks had already been severed.

President Roosevelt came back from a fishing vacation when he learned of the pact. He had known of its imminence for a few weeks from an intelligence source in Moscow. He had tried to delay the swing of the ax by sending Stalin a message that signing with Germany would only postpone the day when the Reich would inevitably attack Russia, but that signing with the Allies would "have a decidedly stabilizing effect in the interest of world peace." His note was ignored. Without a word about the United States coming into any future conflicts, it was meaningless to Stalin.

Just as meaningless were a series of Roosevelt messages to Poland, Germany, and Italy sent at this time. These urged negotiations and delay before war; presidential adviser Adolf Berle characterized them in his diary as having "about the same effect as a valentine sent to somebody's mother-in-law out of season." One went to King Victor Emmanuel of Italy, who had no power in a country ruled by Benito Mussolini.

Once Benito Mussolini had been the world's leading Fascist, a man to whom even citizens of the democracies had given grudging respect, a man who had lifted Italy out of the doldrums in the early 1920s and who had set an example of efficiency in a state. Many had admired Mussolini's verve and style. Of late, however, the Duce was growing more corpulent, more dissolute, and less zestful. His mind had lost its sharpness. The change had begun eighteen months before, when Hitler had sought to annex Austria to Germany. Up until this time, Mussolini had been the elder statesman and Hitler the young upstart. Mussolini had strong ties with Austria, and objected to Hitler's plans. Hitler issued orders to his troops that if Italian forces actually came to Austria's aid, the whole operation was to be halted. Meanwhile he continued to wheedle and cajole. At last the Duce agreed to the *Anschluss* as a magnanimous gesture to a kindred soul—and forever lost the upper hand.

Six months later, at Munich, Mussolini had arranged the agreement by which Hitler annexed the Czech Sudetenland; when Hitler broke the agreement by marching into the rest of Czechoslovakia, Mussolini was mortified by the betrayal. As a sop to honor, Hitler offered him the Pact of Steel, which required consultation between their countries before major policy moves and strict alliance in war; should one partner not want to go to war, the alliance could be broken. Mussolini signed it, saying, "We cannot change policies, because after all we are not prostitutes." And he told Hitler Italy would not be ready for war until 1943.

The Russian bear was seeking dominion over the Adriatic and Balkan areas adjacent to Italy. Mussolini had been edging closer to the West because of the Russian threat. Now came the news that his partner, Germany, was signing a great pact with Russia—without telling him—and was preparing to go to war against Poland, the ally of the democracies. Despite talking about war for seventeen years, Italy was unprepared. Economically, "autarchy," which was supposed to make the country into a self-supporting unit, had not worked. Italy didn't have the right mix of products to pull it off, and Mussolini's adventures in the last few years had been costly. He had sent many troops and planes to fight in the Spanish Civil War, had conquered Ethiopia, and had tried to absorb Albania. In Italy itself, corruption was rampant. At military demonstrations, mock planes were passed off as real; trusted ministers salted away fortunes that were to have been spent on armaments. Mussolini had done nothing about it. Now the results confronted him.

Count Galeazzo Ciano, Mussolini's son-in-law and foreign minister, and the ambassador to Berlin, Bernardo Attolico, both advised the Duce to break the Pact of Steel. By invading Poland, Hitler might well explode the conflict into a world war if the democracies, as expected, lived up to their guarantees. And in a world war the democracies might try to get at Germany through Italy and the Mediterranean. Italy would suffer. Mussolini worried about his loyalties. "If there had not been a precedent in 1914 [when Italy had reneged on a promise to join Germany], I would tear up the alliance." One minute he would say how good it would be to march at Hitler's side, to make war speeches and to reap victories; the next minute he dreaded the disaster that might engulf Italy; then again he talked about setting up another Munich and emerging as the hero of the peace. His associates whispered that it would not be reason that would decide the Duce's actions, but the flip of a coin.

The news of the Nazi-Soviet pact went through Paris like an electric shock. Daladier was immensely sad. He had feared it would happen; he had issued gas masks to deputies leaving for vacation; he had importuned Lukasciewicz at the last moment to get Warsaw to yield on allowing passage to Russian troops. Nothing had worked. Reluctantly Daladier ordered an *alerte* and began the first stages in the cumbersome mobilization of the world's most powerful army.

He convened a meeting of the Supreme War Council. On one side of the council were hard-liners Paul Reynaud and Georges Mandel, who thought war with Germany was inevitable and who wanted it prosecuted with vigor. On the other side Foreign Minister Georges Bonnet and former premier Camille Chautemps wanted to prevent war at all costs, even if that meant wriggling out of the alliance with Poland. Daladier, a centrist, was minister for war as well as premier, but had largely ceded power in military matters to Gamelin, the country's ranking soldier.

Maurice Gustave Gamelin was sixty-seven. From an old military family of the Alsace, he had spent his lifetime in the service, having graduated from Saint-Cyr twenty-three years before the Great War had begun. In that war he had been a competent divisional commander, a disciple of Joseph Joffre. Small, impeccably dressed, given to clasping his hands in front of him when he talked, Gamelin was a man who discoursed equally well on philosophy, Italian painting, and theoretical military problems. He was fond of pointing out that the French General

Staff now had more battle and high command experience than had its German counterpart. The Germans respected Gamelin. Reynaud disliked him; he thought Gamelin "might be all right as a prefect or a bishop, but he is not a leader of men."

At the meeting, Daladier asked Gamelin three questions: Could France remain inactive while Poland was attacked? What means had France of opposing the Germans? And what measures should be taken now to prepare for war?

Gamelin's answers were astounding. Last spring he had told Poland that France would attack Germany in substantial force within fourteen days of mobilization if Germany attacked Poland. Today he insisted that in the early stages of the conflict the French army could do little against Germany except tie down a number of German units on the French border. Like everyone else, Gamelin had been counting on Russia as an ally in the event of war, though he had made no move during the summer to push through the Anglo-French-Russian talks to a satisfactory conclusion. Daladier asked how long Poland could hold out against Germany. Until spring, Gamelin suggested, at which time combined British and French forces could repulse a German attack on the West—however, France must not hope for victory in any but a long war. France would be unable to take the offensive against Germany before 1941–1942.

Gamelin reasoned that the Germans would move quickly into Poland and, without the Russians to stop them, would finish their business there and then turn west with the full power of their forces. He did not explain the dichotomy of arguing that Poland could stay alive until spring but that Germany would win a quick victory in Poland and then be ready to turn and face the West.

The first question was still unanswered: Could France remain inactive if Poland was attacked? Gamelin had already implied his answer: yes. But it was a question of honor, and after many years of equivocation and appeasement, the French now took a firm stand. If Poland was attacked, France would go to her rescue. For Daladier, there would be no more Munichs. Even so, the premier agreed that Bonnet could continue to explore possible mediation by Mussolini. Meanwhile the machinery of mobilization was to grind on.

The cabinet room at 10 Downing Street was in that part of the house first inhabited by an illegitimate daughter of Charles II and given to Sir Robert Walpole as a residence for the first lord of the Treasury in 1732. It was long, narrow, and high; on the sides were mahogany bookcases; saber-legged upholstered chairs surrounded a long table; at each minister's place were a blotter of worn leather with the gilt seal of the Treasury, a water carafe, and glasses. In this room on August 22—while Hitler was addressing his generals—Chamberlain met his cabinet in "grave circumstances." Halifax told the assembled group, in a masterpiece of understatement, that the Nazi-Soviet alliance had taken most of the senior people in the government by surprise. The American source in Moscow had reported to Washington the possibility of such a pact, but the information had been sent from the United States to London by slow boat and had then been mishandled and delayed. The cabinet had difficulties deciding what information to trust on any matter. Just the other day a secret request had come from Göring for a direct conference with Chamberlain. Plans had been laid for "a dramatic interlude" which involved Göring flying to Chequers for a clandestine meeting, but nothing further had been heard from the air marshal.

Intelligence said German forces were massed on Poland's borders. A year ago they had been massed on Czechoslovakia's borders and war had been averted. Poland was the fifth-greatest military power in the world, with two-thirds of its population under thirty, and able to mobilize an army potentially larger than that of France. Alongside Poland's army, the British forces were puny, and no plans had been made to send English soldiers to Poland or to send the Royal Air Force either to Poland or to strike against Germany proper, even though the air force was far from small. In fact, contingency plans for going to Poland's aid had never been drawn up.

Without openly confronting this fact, Chamberlain's cabinet went into action. It pushed Parliament for an emergency powers bill, put the fleet on alert, opened recruiting stations, and stopped the flow of gold out of the country. Chamberlain also wrote a letter to Hitler, believing peace might still be salvaged if he could scare Hitler out of attacking Poland by threatening Germany with the British Empire's potential for waging a prolonged conflict. He disregarded information that the German invasion date had been set and that troops had moved into position, and preferred to believe that perhaps he and Hitler could make another deal. But first there had to be a mailed-fist threat. Chamberlain's letter said, in part, "Whatever may prove the nature of the German-Soviet agreement, it cannot alter Great Britain's obligations to Poland, which H.M. Government have stated in public repeatedly and which they are determined to fulfill."

Hitler's intercepts picked up this letter as it was transmitted to Ambassador Nevile Henderson for eventual delivery. Hitler issued word that "Case White," the invasion of Poland, would begin at 4:30 A M on August 26, unless countermanded by August 25. Most units were only two days' march from their appointed destinations; nearly three thousand trainloads of troops were on the move. Hitler also drafted a formal reply to Chamberlain's letter before Henderson arrived at noon August 23 to deliver it.

A career diplomat who had not spent more than a few months at a time in England since 1905, Nevile Henderson had been in Berlin as ambassador since 1937. He prided himself on his fluency and accent in speaking German, on his sympathy with the German people, and on his cordial relations with the hierarchy. Yet he had not seen Hitler since March, and had been warning London for some time that a crisis would come in mid-August. Now it was here. Henderson faced Hitler in the salon at the Berghof, under the enormous picture window. Hitler described the pact with Russia, not yet even concluded, in glowing terms. Then with studied rage he told Henderson that Britain had "poisoned" the atmosphere with her guarantee to Poland, which would make a peaceful settlement impossible.

Henderson answered that Chamberlain was Hitler's friend; there was proof of it in Chamberlain's continued refusal to take Winston Churchill and other noted warmongers into his cabinet. Morever, "It is their influences that are responsible [for the war fever in London]. It isn't the British people who are anti-German—it comes from behind, from propaganda, directed by Jews and anti-Nazis."

Hitler said he had always sought friendship with England, but perhaps had been wrong in doing so. The meeting adjourned so that Hitler could ostensibly compose a reply to Chamberlain's letter. When Henderson returned and got that response, he read it and quickly ordered the embassy's papers packed for transport to London and prepared to go with them. Hitler's position appeared immovable.

Baron Ernst von Weizsäcker, state secretary in the German Foreign Office, got a moment alone with Hitler after Henderson had gone. Weizsäcker had flown down with Henderson, who was an old friend; he now told Hitler that the democracies were at the end of appeasement, that Chamberlain's talk of war would rally England behind him, and that the excursion into Poland by Germany would mean world war. Hitler claimed he could keep the war localized, but, Weizsäcker noted in his diary, he now said he could fight a general war as well. After Weizsäcker left, Hitler wandered the terraces of his mountain retreat, waiting for word from Moscow.

Joachim von Ribbentrop was at the Kremlin knocking back vodka toasts with Stalin and Molotov. During the Great War, Ribbentrop had been a regimental commander of no particular distinction. An aristocrat, he turned his prestige into profits during the postwar inflation through a hedge in wines and liquors, commodities for which people were willing to pay nearly any price. He capped his business career by marrying a Heinkel champagne heiress, then entered the foreign service at middle level. As ambassador to London he had managed to alienate the British government. Hitler liked him, however, and in February of 1938 he was appointed foreign minister. Rich, vain, arrogant, and short-tempered, Ribbentrop did exactly what Hitler told him to do. In Moscow, his secret instructions were simple: to give the Russians whatever they wanted in exchange for their pledge not to interfere in Poland. Negotiations took less than a day. Then there was a party. At it, Ribbentrop recalled a joke going around Berlin: "Just you wait. One of these days Stalin himself will join the Anti-Comintern Pact!" Stalin laughed, gave Ribbentrop a bear hug, and drank the Führer's health. The innocuous text of the nonaggression pact was released to the press, while the protocol which described how the Baltic and Balkan states were to be carved up between the two signatories remained a closely held secret.

During dinner at the Berghof, Hitler received word that the pact had been signed, and he regaled his dinner companions with the story of what happened when Goebbels announced the pact at a press conference in Berlin: the foreign correspondents had been fatalistic. A British reporter had said, as the bells began to ring outside, "That is the death knell of the British Empire." The bar of the Hotel Adlon, where the correspondents liked to gather, emptied: they were all rushing for the borders. As he listened, Albert Speer thought of Hitler as more like a god than a man, one who quelled all doubts, "like a hero of ancient myth who unhesitatingly, in full consciousness of his strength, could enter upon and masterfully meet the test of the wildest undertakings."

Out on the terrace of the Berghof, they could see a rare natural spectacle, the northern lights gleaming over the mountains, not their usual green but the deepest red. Speer was chilled:

> The last act of *Götterdämmerung* could not have been more effectively staged. The same red light bathed our faces and our hands. The display produced a curiously pensive mood among us. Abruptly turning to one of his military adjutants, Hitler said: "Looks like a great deal of blood. This time we won't bring it off without violence."

After flying to Berlin, Hitler welcomed Ribbentrop home next day with a gala. "Stalin is just like you, mein Führer," Ribbentrop gushed. "Extraordinarily mild—not like a dictator at all!" As von Brauchitsch noted in his diary that night, the date and time of the invasion were now fixed and "everything is to roll automatically."

Before the pact Poland wasn't sure what was coming. Her summer military exercises had been held with live ammunition and produced an impressive number of casualties. Since the takeover of Czechoslovakia, Hitler had been pointing to trouble over Danzig; beyond that was the historic inevitability of the coming conflict. The unsatisfactory boundaries between Germany and Poland had been set at Versailles: Poland lay between the body of Germany and the German province of East Prussia. The two "halves" of Germany were separated by the Polish Corridor leading to the sea. Danzig was the capstone of this corridor, an "international city" filled with Germans, though effectively under Polish control.

On the other hand, Poland was a near-dictatorship, and one that had professed admiration for the Nazi state. Among the handful of colonels who ran the country, Józef Beck was the foreign minister. He had served under Marshal Józef Pilsudski in the Great War; and in the fight against Russia afterward, he had helped to drive back the Bolsheviks from the gates of Warsaw. From such experiences the colonel had learned to hate Russians. During the early 1920s, he was an intelligence officer stationed in Paris, but he managed to get himself kicked out of France in 1923 for selling documents relating to the French army. He became assistant foreign minister in 1930, and foreign minister in 1933. For the past six years Beck had been moving Poland away from its traditional alliance with France and toward accommodation with Germany. The Polish government was autocratic, elitist, anti-Communist, and anti-Semitic, just as the Nazi government was.

The Nazi-Soviet pact came as a profound shock to Poland and to Beck. It left the country with only two choices. Poland could fight Germany or yield. Reluctantly, and with great languor, the officials began to mobilize the Polish army. Rumors began to circulate that Beck and the colonels might yield both Danzig and the Corridor to Germany, so peace could be maintained. Mobilization was not too hasty, so as not to provoke the Nazis.

In Germany, many people understood the shape of things to come and did what they could about them.

In Munich, Elspeth Rosenfeld and her husband, Siegfried, hurried through a thunderstorm up the steps of the train station. The place was packed with rain-drenched people, mostly Jews trying to get out of the country. Else was a social worker, the daughter of a Jewish doctor and a Lutheran mother; Siegfried was a Jewish lawyer. For six years they had been chased from city to city while Siegfried's practice was destroyed. They had tried to emigrate. Only Else's Lutheran relatives had been able to escape to Argentina last year, and in the spring of this year the couple's son and daughter had got exit visas to England. Just yesterday, in the midst of the mounting certainty of war, an exit permit had come, but for Siegfried alone. They had had a terrible argument, because he had not wanted to go without Else; finally she convinced him that, since he was in greater danger, he should leave and she would follow when she could.

The station was bedlam. Siegfried went to buy a ticket, while Else sat with the luggage. An elderly Aryan porter befriended her; guessing that her husband was leaving alone, he became solicitous and even offered to have Else live with his family if things became difficult. He stayed with them both until it was time for Siegfried's departure and then gave them a card with his name and address. It was a blessing to find a non-Jew who was still kind. Siegfried couldn't find a seat on the jammed train. He sat on his trunk and waved at Else as the train pulled away. She didn't know if she would ever see him or any of her family again.

Some trains were pulling into Germany. On one of them was Ruth Andreas-Friedrich, who was returning to Berlin from a trip to Scandinavia. She noted the scared faces of the recruits who were boarding other trains to go toward the east. Like some of her friends, Ruth had gone out of the country more than once this summer in order to take fur coats, jewelry, and money to exiled Jewish friends.

Ruth and her circle—intellectuals, artists—had money and connections and the means of making their livelihood abroad, but they had chosen not to emigrate. She was a writer, an editor, a child of the Germanic culture. She wanted to remain where she had grown up; someone, she and her friends would say to one another, someone must have the decency to remain. In Berlin, Ruth noted shortages of wool, fats, soap, shoes, and meat. Clothes could not be laundered properly because the factories that did such work were shorthanded—the workers had been sent to build the Siegfried Line. It was obvious to Ruth and her friends that the Nazi-Soviet pact meant war. As Ruth noted in her diary, all the people who had been even halfheartedly against Hitler

> have been certain that the "Thousand Years' Reich" would wind up in a war sooner or later—a war that Germany was bound to lose. We've had six years to get used to the idea. Now the end with its horrors seems almost more bearable to us than the horror without end.

Foot soldier Wilhelm Prüller was an ordinary youngster of twenty from Vienna. During the summer he was called up on maneuvers and never got sent back home. Now he was with a reserve unit a few miles from the Polish border. When the Nazi-Soviet pact was announced, he found his thoughts racing, going in a circle, "as if they wanted to turn a huge millstone. Everything on edge. And the feeling that we're in this place: painful when you think of home. The most wonderful feeling as well, though, of manly and loyal devotion to duty."

Prüller kept a diary for his young wife, Henny, and their months-old daughter, Lore. He kept it because he was not allowed to write letters home just then. He also carried a talisman about his neck, Lore's desiccated umbilical cord, wrapped in his leather dog tag. The diary was a sort of totem with him. He wrote in it that if war should come, the Poles wouldn't be able to withstand the German attack, and with the Siegfried Line impregnable and the Baltic controlled by the German fleet, neither England nor France would be able to save Poland. Hitler's "brilliant stroke of strategy" had got the Russians out of the picture, and, all in all,

> the situation is highly satisfactory for us, and it's unthinkable for us, too, as the greatest European power, to sit back and watch the persecution of the

Volkdeutsche [ethnic Germans in Polish territory] without doing something. It is our duty to rectify this wrong, which cries to Heaven. If we fight, then we know that we are serving a rightful cause. . . . We know, however, that the Führer will do all he can to avoid war.

Werner von Fritsch, also stationed near the Polish border, was not so certain Hitler would stay out of war. As former commander in chief of the Wehrmacht, he was in a better position to make such a judgment. From 1933 to 1938, Fritsch had helped Hitler build the German army. Under his guidance it became a cadre of professionals capable of expansion into a great force with the addition of recruits. Little by little the cannon fodder came in as the army increased in size. Marching into the Rhineland in 1936, the Wehrmacht was still small; a year later it paraded in columns so numerous that it had sent Mussolini into raptures over the wonders Hitler had wrought.

In early 1938, a crisis arose. For a long time von Fritsch and the highest officers had resisted Hitler's pressure to make the army an instrument of party power. In January 1938, a scandal surfaced involving von Fritsch's superior, Field Marshal Werner von Blomberg, minister for war. Blomberg married a woman with a shady past, and von Fritsch personally carried to the Führer the army's demand for Blomberg's resignation. A few days later, Hitler had von Fritsch on the carpet, and confronted him with a man who swore Fritsch had been involved in a homosexual blackmail incident.

Von Fritsch contemplated suicide; he was talked out of it by friends who said it would be seen as an admission of guilt; his friends also persuaded him not to challenge to a duel SS chief Heinrich Himmler, who had uncovered the "evidence." Von Fritsch resigned. Taken together with Blomberg's resignation, this gave Hitler total control of the army. Days later, he marched into Austria.

Von Fritsch expected his trial to be a kangaroo court, but the charges against him were proved false (a man named Frisch had been involved) and von Fritsch was cleared. But he was not restored to his rank as commander in chief; instead he was given honorary command of a horse-drawn artillery regiment. At the dinner celebrating his installation, von Fritsch said, "A soldier is a soldier, nothing more, so he must always be ready to serve. He must do so unquestioningly and with an absolute disregard for self, come what may." The good Prussian militarist, he maintained this façade for the public, but told his secret diary:

Either the Führer sees to it that law and order prevail again in Germany . . . and that people like Himmler and Heydrich get their deserts, or he will continue to cover for the misdeeds of these people—in which case I fear for his future. . . . Perhaps he personally begrudges me that I dented his aura of infallibility by being acquitted.

Though senior military men begged Hitler to give von Fritsch command of an army group because he was too good a soldier to waste, Hitler refused; and as war grew closer, von Fritsch lived a monastic life directing his regiment's training. His charges were little more than boys with no battle experience, hardly soldiers at all; he worried over their unreadiness. The country might bowl over Poland in a quick war, but after that? All the high-ranking military men in Germany agreed the Reich could not withstand a long war; the Russian pact might mean a quick victory, but could the conflict be kept localized? They believed not. Von Fritsch told friends he would nevertheless go into the fray gladly, "if only as a target."

Adolf Hitler spent August 25 in his new Reichschancellery in Berlin. Speer had designed and built it in less than a year, keeping 45,000 workmen going round the clock. It had four hundred rooms, was in the baroque style, with yellow stucco and gray stone, and with tall square columns framing the entrance. Visiting diplomats would drive through heavy gates into a court of honor, walk up an outside staircase, and be ushered by liveried servants through great doors and a small reception room into a series of opulent halls. The first had a mosaic of gold and gray designs in the marble. In the wall opposite the entrance was a large portal presided over by bronze and stone eagles clutching swastikas; this gave onto a magnificent marble gallery 480 feet long, twice the size of the Hall of Mirrors at Versailles. Eventually one would come to the chancellor's study, a room with outsized chandeliers, a pastel knotted carpet, statues of Wisdom, Prudence, Fortitude, and Justice looking down from four gilded panels over four doors, and—on Hitler's desk— an inlay of a sword half drawn from its sheath. "Good, good," Hitler said to Speer on seeing this last detail. "When the diplomats sitting in front of me at this desk see that, they'll learn to shiver and shake."

This day the Chancellery was a beehive. In the early morning, a letter dictated over the phone to Rome told Mussolini of the negotiations with the Russians; the Nazi-Soviet pact "must be regarded as the greatest possible gain for the Axis." Hitler warned Mussolini obliquely that the attack on Poland would come at any moment, and asked his partner to please be understanding about this. By noon, no response had been received. Hitler began to eat lunch. Ambassador Nevile Henderson was announced. Ambassadors of fully accredited countries were presented with a roll of drums and occasionally with the music of their anthems played by a full band; this day Henderson got only drums.

In contrast to his rage of two days before, Hitler assumed his most sincere and rational aspect for this meeting. What he wanted, he told Henderson, was "to pledge himself personally to the continued existence of the British Empire." After he settled Poland's hash—the pact with Russia would enable him to do so, he said—he would commit the Reich to support the Empire. Inasmuch as the British Empire included

40,000,000 square kilometers and the Reich a mere 600,000, Hitler felt
justified in asking for a slice of Poland that was more German than
Polish. After he got it, he would help England dominate the world;
should the British reject his magnanimous offer, there would be a war
"bloodier than that of 1914."

The offer was less outlandish than it appeared. The Chamberlain
government had suggested something similar the previous summer in a
clandestine meeting between the German ambassador in London and
Sir Horace Wilson, a close confidant of Chamberlain's. Wilson had outlined an Anglo-German partnership to divide the world. But Wilson
was known to be sympathetic to the Nazi government, and so perhaps
the offer had not been totally in earnest or genuine. It is unlikely that
Henderson knew much about it. Hitler's August 25 offer was made as
much to dazzle the British and to gain time as for any other reason. He
meant to have his war.

The Italian ambassador, Bernardo Attolico, had been waiting in the
antechamber while Hitler met with Henderson. Suddenly he received a
message from Rome canceling his instructions, and he left. Hitler was
alarmed. Ribbentrop phoned Ciano, but the Duce and his son-in-law
were at the beach. It was 2:45 P.M. Hitler and Ribbentrop closeted themselves for seventeen minutes. Dozens of people lined the halls, waiting.
At 3:02, a composed but pale Hitler opened the door and announced,
"Case White." Word for the invasion to begin at 4:30 A M next day was
transmitted to every station of the German war machine.

Later in the afternoon, information came that an actual Anglo-
Polish pact was about to be signed in London. This was a bad shock to
Hitler, his adjutants noted; evidently his gambit to Henderson had
failed. He would not be able to split England from Poland. He exploded when the French ambassador, Coulondre, arrived, and he ex-
pounded anew on Polish "atrocities" against the *Volkdeutsche*: private
German planes had been shot at, ten thousand people had been mis-
treated, six had been castrated. Coulondre responded by saying France,
too, would stand by her commitments to the Poles.

After Coulondre left, Ribbentrop panicked. Hitler must halt the invasion. Hitler hesitated. He asked Wilhelm Keitel, chief of the OKW,
the planning unit, whether the invasion could be halted. Keitel said
there was time but just barely. Ambassador Attolico was announced,
bearing Mussolini's formal response to Hitler's morning letter. It was
another rebuff, and one that struck Hitler like a bombshell. If Hitler
went to war, the letter said, "I inform you in advance that it will be
opportune for me not to take the *initiative* in military operations in view
of the *present* state of Italian war preparations of which we have repeatedly and in good time informed you."

Italy could, however, intervene if Germany delivered enough military supplies and raw materials "to resist the attack which the French

and British would predominantly direct against us." Stymied, Hitler told Attolico brusquely to have Mussolini quantify these demands, and he would see what could be done.

When Attolico had gone, Hitler tried to cancel the attack. The men who could transmit the orders could not immediately be found, and there followed some hours of frantic searching for them. By mid-evening, troops were already on the move. At nearly the last moment, the orders were sent. They succeeded in reaching most, but not all, of the attacking units, and the invasion was stopped.

Late at night, as was his habit, Hitler telephoned Göring to inform him of all this. The airman asked if this was to be a definitive aborting of the invasion or merely a temporary halt. The whole plan was collapsing under pressure of the Italian cave-in and the English standfast. Hitler told Göring, "I will have to see whether we can eliminate British intervention."

3

Last Days of Silence

A cross section of the information coming in to the upper echelons of the German government on the morning of August 26 showed that the situation was not so bad as Hitler's estimate.

Polish newspapers reported the unusually high level of German incidents near the border. It does not seem to have occurred to anyone high up in the Polish military that these incidents were the result of a few German units not having got Hitler's order to stop operations the previous evening. Most of the invading Germans, who had been in civilian clothes, had been massacred.

On the other hand, German intelligence reported losing track of three Polish ships during the night; these were, they later discovered, on their way to join the British navy, the Poles having decided their own navy was too small to withstand Germany's in case of war. German intelligence still reported great unreadiness in the Polish defense lines, and great ignorance of exactly what Germany was planning. Intelligence was also trying to assess what the rest of the world might do if there was an invasion. From Washington, military attaché Friedrich von Bötticher wrote that most Americans didn't want the United States involved in a European war. Further,

> besides lack of trained personnel, the deficiency of stocks of up-to-date war equipment is a decided weakness of the American army and after the outbreak of war it cannot be expected that units will be ready for use outside America in less than a year. Similarly, the air force will not be in a position to dispatch substantial units to an overseas theater of war for twelve months.

Bötticher added that the Allies were becoming disgruntled at delays in delivery of supplies from the United States. With such information in hand, Hitler could afford to neglect a letter from President Roosevelt which contained a renewed plea for negotiations and the assurance that

President Ignacy Moscicki of Poland had indicated his willingness to talk.

News from France was also good for Berlin. An editorial in the morning's *L'Action Française*, a royalist paper read by many in the French military, questioned whether Frenchmen should be ready to die for Danzig, and claimed that Georges Mandel and Paul Reynaud were pulling strings to get France into a war because they were

> Jews or friends of Jews . . . in closest contact with the powerful Jewish clique in London. . . . If today our French people allow themselves to be slaughtered unsuspectingly and vainly at the will of forces that are English-speaking Jews or at the will of their French slaves, then a French voice must be raised to proclaim the truth.

The editorial was sent to Berlin by the German embassy. It was also noted that Premier Daladier had that day suppressed two leading Communist papers. A letter from Daladier reminded Hitler that they had both been front-line soldiers in the last war and knew at first hand war's terrible nature: "If the blood of France and Germany flows again as it did twenty-five years ago, each of the two peoples will fight with confidence in its own victory, but the most certain victory will be that of destruction and barbarism."

Though Daladier went on to say that France would uphold her commitments to Poland, Hitler told Keitel that the letter indicated the French were not serious about going to war.

Mussolini's shopping list arrived that morning. "The minimum that the Italian Armed Forces need . . . in order to sustain a *twelve-month* war," wrote the Duce, was 150,000 tons of copper, 220,000 tons of sodium nitrate, large quantities of coal, steel, oil, molybdenum and other rare metals, and 150 flak batteries. Hitler concluded that the list had been designed to be exorbitant, to provide Mussolini with an excuse for not entering the war as his ally. When Attolico added a demand that all the supplies be delivered before the onset of hostilities, Hitler knew the list was unrealistic.

Nevertheless, he wrote back saying he would try to deliver, but not on Attolico's schedule, in order to take away Mussolini's excuse for inaction. Italian neutrality would be as good as Italian belligerency: with Italy neutral, Germany could retain the raw materials and still have its southern flank protected. The Allies could not gamble on Italy's steadfastness and risk transferring troops from southern France or warships from the Mediterranean. Hitler asked Mussolini not to reveal his decision to stay out of the war and to support Germany spiritually. Ciano observed that for the Duce confronting the truth was difficult. He had to choose between his sense of honor (which urged him to go to war at Hitler's side) and his good sense (which would keep Italy out of a war for which she was unprepared). As usual, Mussolini compromised:

he would stay out, await deliveries which might never come, and he wouldn't tell anyone what he was doing.

England's next move seemed for a time to hang on Birger Dahlerus. After seeing both Chamberlain and Halifax, the Swede had a frustrating day getting back to Berlin because of canceled flights. In Berlin, he couldn't find Göring, who had entrained for a tour of forward airfields. Dahlerus sped after him in a car, intercepted the train, and on board handed Göring a letter from Halifax which suggested that the English were willing to step back from the brink and negotiate a settlement. Göring and Dahlerus raced back to Berlin with the letter. It was after midnight when they met Hitler in the Chancellery office. There Dahlerus found himself on the receiving end of a tirade: Hitler's offers had been continuously spurned by the British, and his overwhelmingly superior forces were going to win the coming war. He would build "U-boats, U-boats, U-boats," and "airplanes, airplanes, airplanes," and would "disintegrate my enemies! War doesn't frighten me! The encirclement of Germany is impossible now; my people admire and follow me faithfully. If there are privations ahead for the German people, then let it be now—I will be the first to starve and set my people a good example."

Dahlerus thought he was listening to a "completely abnormal person." Eventually Hitler calmed down and outlined his negotiating demands, which were the same ones he had given to Henderson: the return of Danzig, a corridor through the Corridor so the two "halves" of Germany would be connected, the return of Germany's overseas colonies. In exchange he guaranteed to support the British Empire. Dahlerus was given a Luftwaffe plane to fly all this to London.

Next morning Hitler was confronted with an argument for peace from an unexpected source. Military economics experts under Georg Thomas had made graphically illustrated statistical analyses which clearly demonstrated the Allies' great military and economic superiority. Eventually the democracies, augmented by the United States' military and industrial power, would outgun Germany. Keitel presented this argument timidly; he distrusted the information. Hitler brushed it aside, for he had heard Thomas's gloomy predictions before, and reiterated that the West would not go to war over a Poland they knew they could not save. The date oı the invasion was rescheduled for August 31; the delay would mean only that more troops would be closer to the front and therefore available for the campaign.

A haggard and sleepless Hitler met the Reichstag deputies, his nominal legislative superiors. The day before, he had canceled three meetings with them; now he told them he was for peace, but if war came he would fight "with the most brutal and inhuman methods" to achieve victory. "If any one of you believes that my actions have not been inspired by my devotion to Germany, I give him the right to shoot me down."

Colonel Hans Oster, chief of staff of the Abwehr, the intelligence agency, was slim, of modest height, an intellectual, the devout son of a clergyman, and the very model of a cavalry officer. To many in these troubled times he was the representative of all that was good in the German character. He loathed Nazism. He had served under Werner von Fritsch and had been incensed at the general's treatment. Unlike most others who had been similarly outraged, Hans Oster had decided to do something about it. He had dedicated his life to the overthrow of Adolf Hitler. His views were shared by Weizsäcker and Erich Kordt of the Foreign Ministry; Carl Goerdeler, the former mayor of Leipzig; Georg Thomas; and Colonel-General Ludwig Beck, former chief of staff of the Wehrmacht. Abwehr chief Wilhelm Canaris was with them in spirit if not often in deed.

In the summer of 1938—a year earlier—these men had designed a takeover of the government. Beck's men would arrest Göring, Goebbels, Himmler, Heydrich, and other top Nazis; and Hitler would be secretly assassinated. After a short interval, the army would transfer power to a new civilian government, possibly with Goerdeler at its head. While Hitler shouted at Czechoslovakia and threatened war, the conspirators convinced themselves that the Germans did not want war and would support a coup. But then Beck made a wrong move. He protested against marching the army to the Czech border, and when Hitler overruled him, Beck resigned. Had his resignation been made publicly and in the midst of the crisis—say while the Munich conference was going on—the world might have seen that the army was not solidly behind Hitler, and everything might have been different. But it was badly timed and was kept secret at Hitler's request. The coup didn't happen, and the Munich accord did.

Plans were then shelved, because Germany was too happy with the bloodless victory to support a coup. For the past year Oster had been trying to get Franz Halder—Beck's replacement as chief of staff—into the opposition camp. He had succeeded. Halder had agreed to give the order to begin the coup over his military switchboard, but he kept saying the time was not yet ripe. Three days earlier Halder had been ready to move, but then had come the sudden halt in Hitler's invasion plans, and the momentum slowed. After the invasion was rescheduled, Oster could do little. Perhaps that was because he—and Halder and every other officer—was on the horns of a dilemma known only to honorable men. During peacetime it might be legitimate to depose an evil head of state; that was, simply, revolution. But to depose a head of state during wartime was, just as simply, treason. And none of the conspirators thought of themselves as traitors.

Denis Barlone—in his forties, single, graying, his officer's uniform out of fashion—felt echoes of the Great War all about him. On the train going toward the Maginot Line the French officers talked only to one another, and the *poilus* complained of having to leave the harvest before it was in. Everything and everyone moved mechanically, with no elation, no zeal. The soldiers' attitude was, Barlone wrote in his diary, "if one has to go—of course one will go, and return home to peace and quietness after having given Hitler a good drubbing. The men's great hope is that Hitler will be assassinated because, for the time being, they separate Hitler in their minds from Germany."

For Barlone, however, Hitler was the latest embodiment of a German people who had sought domination for generations, a man leagued with Mussolini and Japan "like gangsters in an attempt to plunder two rich and prosperous nations": England and France.

At Toul, Barlone took command of a "hippo" unit, the horse transport company of the Second North African Division. He also took possession of the bulky *Journal de Mobilisation*, which told him what to do each day, what stores to draw, how to dispose of them. A similar book existed for each unit. Everything had been planned in fantastic detail. Apart from a few like himself, the soldiers were young. That was to be expected. France had lost so many sons in the Great War that the country had not really recovered. That loss defined France's military posture: defense. This time there would be no *poilus* advancing toward fortified trenches across fields of machine-gun fire. Barlone had survived such assaults; he had been lucky. Now France's war plans called for conserving one of the most basic of all resources in war—men.

Barlone wound his way through the small village to the cottage of Mother Maquin, an old lady with innumerable nieces and nephews living in the area. She importuned him until he lent her his valet and a few other soldiers to shake her plum trees, which for the first time in four years were loaded with mirabelles that had to be harvested, war or no war. Barlone ate so many plums he was ill. Lying on his bed, which Mother Maquin seemed to have used for a flea-breeding ground, Barlone worried for France because the country had no war aims:

> We have more than enough colonies, we know that our land is safe from invasion, thanks to the Maginot Line; no one has the least desire to fight . . . for Poland, of which 95 Frenchmen out of every 100 are completely ignorant and unable to find on a map; we have no belief that Hitler will hurl himself on us after having swallowed up the little nations, one by one. We tell ourselves that having obtained what he wants, he will leave us in peace.

No such illusion was harbored by Leo Lania, a newspaperman who had fled Austria when the Nazis came in. On this last summer weekend he roamed the streets of his adopted city, Paris, with his antennae aquiver. At the Renault plant on the outskirts, workers grumbled that they would be doing all the fighting while the upper classes took advantage of the war to cancel the gains labor had obtained under Blum.

They pointed out that while men from aircraft and tank factories had already been mobilized, plants which made highly profitable consumer goods were still fully staffed.

At a party Lania heard women in couturier gowns complaining of heavy traffic on the roads from the Riviera; men wearing officers' uniforms talked of their sinecures in reserve regiments. The rich guests saw parallels between Mussolini and Napoleon, and hoped that the Duce could be wooed away from Hitler's side; then Italy, France, and Spain would join in a Catholic (and possibly royalist) coalition to secure the south of Europe. According to them, the socialist ex-premier Léon Blum, a Jew, had wrecked France during his administration and gotten them into their present fix.

Lania's restlessness took him to the Russian restaurant the Yar, where he heard the White Russian émigrés complain of being betrayed by the Nazi-Soviet pact. They had counted on Hitler to keep Stalin at bay. In the Champs Elysées, men were putting sandbags at the base of monuments, but gray military trucks hurrying about seemed more theatrical than real.

On Monday morning, Lania headed for the offices of the war ministry to volunteer for the army. On Rue Saint-Dominique a great sight greeted him: thousands of men from dozens of nationalities standing in line four abreast, eager to fight for France. Among them were the Russians from the Yar, and his friends the German refugees who formed the nucleus of the French film industry (Lania had recently completed a script for a producer, which would now have to be shelved). He met three Jewish soccer players from Vienna and a jockey who had escaped from Austria before the *Anschluss*. There was also a tall, blond, blue-eyed fellow who had spent two years in Dachau. All had stories to tell; all had been aimless, dislocated, without a sense of belonging. Now they had a task, the defense of France and the destruction of Hitler. It was worth dying for.

But when darkness fell the line hadn't moved much. Lania would have to come back the next day. He started home. The streetlamps, covered with dark-blue paint, barely glowed and were invisible from more than a few feet away. Buses were no longer running at night, and cars were allowed only one blue-covered headlight. Paris, city of light, was dim. Dark ghosts moved in the streets, groping their way toward homes in which shades were drawn. Not until people got inside could they take their gas masks from their shoulders. Young mothers stood in semi-dark hallways discussing how to get the children to evacuation centers when the time came. It couldn't be long now.

At night in Warsaw, the Polish bombers and fighters flew over the city maneuvering, aided by great searchlights which sent their pale shafts into the air. During a practice blackout, the swords of light against the shrouded city fascinated one resident, an English novelist married to a Polish count. After living here for many years, she felt she was almost Polish. She had come to love the country. Warsaw was a beautiful fairy village: the horse-drawn drays rumbled down cobbled streets; the painted bronze leaves of the Chopin monument were indistinguishable from the falling bronzed leaves of the giant hornbeam and lime trees. She had gone daily to write in the park of the Royal Palace, the Aleja, which surrounded a sixteenth-century bathhouse made of thousands of tiles, no two of which were alike. Earlier in August, she had sent her corrected proofs back to England. Now thousands of horses were billeted in the park, and in other gardens people dug trenches for shelter. The cynical said they were for graves.

It was interminably hot; normally the rains turned all roads to mud, but not this year. Her husband, a businessman and an engineer, suggested that they drive to their summer house and close it up; he expected to be mobilized at any moment. Along the road, she observed, under a blazing sun:

> The golden corn was falling under strong strokes of the scythe; the peasant women, half of whom we knew and all of whom knew us at least by sight, with their bell-shaped skirts swinging and the coloured kerchiefs tied round their heads dark and stained with sweat, were striding up and down the laid swathes gathering and binding; behind them the children, the dogs, the geese of the Commune and a few gypsies gleaning, drinking tepid water from bottles, laughing, quarreling and dashing the sweat from their faces.... Among the workers, a whole regiment of sappers, naked to the waist, white dust showing in queer patches on their broiled red skin, were flinging up barbed-wire entanglements. Every few yards or so steel posts were being driven into the ground. As soon as a post went in a dozen or so sappers ran along from the last one with what seemed the obscenest looking garlands of barbed wire and festooned it to at least the height of a man's head.... For as far as the eye could see it stretched away into the peaceful green country. The storks walked about as usual, taking no notice.

Some troops were marching. There were field kitchens, tanks, cattle, and a few groups of peasants moving on the roads. One of the peasants said he could now be killed with a clear conscience, as his four sons were mobilized and he had sold his horse to the army. Unfortunately the army had not given him cash, only a payment voucher. The novelist and her husband were upset when the peasants around their cottage kissed their sleeves in the old way and asked for guidance. They could give none.

In the evening, fourteen-year-old Sala Kaminska—pretty, red-haired, green-eyed, and Jewish—listened to the radio voices coming through the night air to Lask, a small town near the Grabia River in the south of Poland. Sala had had a most enjoyable summer swimming in the river, roaming in the fields; this fall she hoped to go to the gymnasium and learn how to teach Hebrew to small children.

The Kaminskas rented an apartment above the Catholic locksmith Petrovski. Sala was practically a member of the Petrovski family, decorating the Christmas tree and walking to school with the six children. One evening a few years earlier, she came home from school to find the Petrovski rooms being decorated as a dance hall. Later that night she heard shouts from downstairs: "Down with the Jews!" The next day when Sala and her mother went to Petrovski to ask about the previous night's events, he told them not to worry, because "You're good people—you're our Jews. We were just having a little rally to form a new party. Want to join? We need members right now." Evidently the landlord was forming a unit of the Andecia, the national party. The Kaminskas did not join, and the Petrovskis continued to be kind to them. Soon the Andecia unit grew so large that it had to be moved to another building. Petrovski's house was really in the Jewish section of town anyway.

Listening to the radio near the end of August 1939, Sala wondered what would happen if war came. Her Aunt Mina, who lived with them, comforted her by saying, "There was a war before, my love, and your mother and I lived through it. And there will probably be other wars, which we shall also live through."

In Danzig, Sybil Bannister, an Englishwoman married to a German doctor, felt at the center of the storm. It was calm now, but if anything moved they would all be blown away. Beyond the political crisis was Sybil's personal one—she was expecting her first child at any moment. Her British family had been begging her to come home and have the baby there. Sybil understood their fears, but to go now would mean the ruin of her marriage. If she fled to England and the war broke out, she and Kurt would be separated for years, and after the war there might be no way for them to understand one another. She decided to stay.

Danzig was a garrison ready for siege. In June, a thousand SS men from East Prussia had come for gymnastics contests and had remained. Houses were requisitioned for ammunition storage; approaches to high points throughout the city were cordoned off. Still, Danzigers had not believed Germany would go to war over their city. There seemed some chance that the military preparations would result in a political solution; Danzigers hoped so, for they were not in a position seriously to defend the city from the Polish attack they were sure would come if Germany crossed the border into Poland. Danzig, well within Polish territory, was an obvious target for Polish retaliation, and Sybil had nightmares about how the Poles might take vengeance:

> I imagined myself as a refugee, being trundled off in a cart, having to beg for bread and shelter, or having my baby by the wayside with no proper attention. At night I would have the most terrible nightmares and wake up

in a bath of perspiration. I dreamed that my baby would be taken from me and left to starve, or that ruffians would mutilate his little body, scorch out his eyes with red-hot pokers, while I was powerless to stop them. In broad daylight I would tell myself that these were the aberrations of an over-wrought mind and that such brutalities could never be inflicted in our civilized age.

It was some comfort when Kurt came home on leave. A gynecologist, he had been called up by the Luftwaffe to serve as a general practitioner at an airfield in East Prussia. While he was in Danzig they took walks, talked about the baby. The time went too quickly, and she was alone again. She stayed glued to the radio, even though she felt like smashing it to pieces. The waiting was unbearable. All you could do was guess and worry. She went to the movies. At least that would kill a few hours.

It was ten-thirty in the evening of August 28 when Ambassador Henderson, newly returned from London and fortified by a glass of champagne, drove the four hundred yards from the British embassy to the Reichschancellery in total darkness because of the trial blackout. Earlier in the day, rationing had been introduced for some foods, soap, and coal.

Hitler received Henderson with some warmth, which quickly faded when he learned the ambassador was not bringing him what he wanted. Hitler had postponed the invasion another twenty-four hours to see what England would say; he hoped for some dickering about the proposed Anglo-German alliance. Instead Henderson told Hitler that the British had persuaded the Poles to agree to negotiate face to face with Germany. Surprised, Hitler said he would study the proposal and give Henderson an answer in the morning. Henderson left.

When Göring, Hess, Himmler, Ribbentrop, and others joined Hitler, he mimicked Henderson's German accent and then (according to Himmler's diary)

> indicated that we now have to aim a document at the British (or Poles) that is little less than a masterpiece of diplomacy. He wants to spend tonight thinking it over, because he always gets most of his best ideas in the hour between 5 and 6 AM ... He often dozes from 3 to 4 to find the problems arrayed in pristine clarity before his eyes. Then he jumps up and jots down a few key words in pencil. He himself doesn't know how it happens—all he does know is that in the wee small hours of the morning everything that might confuse or distract disappears.

In the wee small hours that night Göring phoned Dahlerus with the news that the British reply was satisfactory and there were hopes that the threat of war was past.

When Dahlerus finally met Henderson the next morning and told him what Göring had said, the ambassador replied that Göring probably lied as much as Hitler did. Throughout the day the German papers reported the murder of six German nationals in Poland, together with news of a Polish general mobilization. And Henderson still had no answer to his proposals.

He was called to the Chancellery in the early evening. There he got the cold treatment. Hitler demanded an international guarantee of Poland's borders subject to Moscow's approval—an approval Poland might never accept—and insisted that a Polish emissary with full powers to negotiate show up the very next day, August 30. "My soldiers are asking me," Hitler said testily, "'Yes or No?'"

It was a smoke screen. General Halder noted in his diary Hitler's real timetable and intentions:

> Führer wants them to come tomorrow. Basic principles: Raise a barrage of demographic demands. . . .
> August 30th. Poles in Berlin.
> August 31st. *Zerplatzen* [blow-up of negotiations].
> Sept. 1st. Use of force.

Hitler had used the pressure-cooker technique before. He would demand a meeting with a man empowered to negotiate (Kurt von Schussnigg of Austria, Emil Hacha of Czechoslovakia), get that man into a room crowded with German military men, and then scream, promise, and above all threaten to invade unless his demands were met. The plenipotentiary, fearing a bloodbath, would give in. If the technique didn't work this time as it had in 1938, Hitler would go to war anyway. He had nothing to lose in trying the pressure cooker once more.

Two tired ambassadors sat down at the British embassy that evening, Henderson and Lipski. Józef Lipski had been in Berlin five years and was one of the chief architects of the supposed amity between Germany and Poland. A man sympathetic to the Nazis, an anti-Semite, and a friend of Göring's, he clung to the belief that if Hitler went to war the German people would overthrow him. Betrayed by his own sympathies, unable to reconcile his love for Germany with the clear indications that the Germans were about to invade his country, Lipski was on the verge of a nervous breakdown. Henderson was tough with him: the prospects for armed resistance were not good, and therefore Poland must negotiate. However, Poland should not give in to Hitler's schedule; the emissary should arrive soon, but not the next day. Lipski disagreed: he didn't want a Munich-style solution that wouldn't really help Poland but would get England off the hook.

In London, Chamberlain and Halifax received a minute of the Henderson-Lipski meeting. They no longer believed Hitler was in earnest in wanting to negotiate and did not even bother to transmit formally to Warsaw the request for an emissary. In the morning the ubiquitous Birger Dahlerus arrived bearing a strange missive, a page torn from an atlas and colored in red and green by Hermann Göring. This outlined, said the Swede, the extent of German demands on Poland. The missive was ignored.

Instead, the cabinet sent Hitler another note. In the convoluted logic of the moment, the reasoning went as follows: Hitler must be told to set forth his terms; once that was done he would be forced to stick with them, and then there would be negotiations. In these negotiations Hitler would lose because the British had at last determined not to give in. If he decided not to negotiate and went to war when it was plain to all the world that negotiations were possible and had been asked for, then his government would fall. This chain of reasoning was based in part on the cabinet's information from opposition sources in Germany which reported that Hitler's grip was slipping. These sources had previously provided the date of the proposed invasion, the date of the postponement, and now the second date, as well as the type of incident which would for propaganda purposes precede the invasion. Opposition leader Carl Goerdeler sent a telegram to Chamberlain from Stockholm: "Chief Manager's attitude weakening. Remain completely firm. No compromise. Take initiative only for general settlement under strong conditions."

The cabinet mistook as evidence of further erosion a report that a special council had been set up to pass laws without reference to Hitler, and an instance of Nazi posters being ripped down in Düsseldorf was seen as symptomatic of a general trend to revolution. London, in short, believed that war might bring Hitler down.

Henderson was told to hold firm, to demand precise proposals, and to tell the Germans that an emissary would come, but not that day. At midnight August 30–31, Henderson went to the Chancellery to see Hitler. Alerted by wiretaps as to Henderson's business, Hitler left the interview to Ribbentrop. Interpreter Paul Schmidt observed that "the atmosphere was highly charged, the nerves of the two men worn by protracted negotiations." Henderson read out the British proposals: negotiations would start "with all urgency," but "it would be impractical to establish a contact so early as today." In the meantime there should be a military standstill and a temporary *modus vivendi* arranged for Danzig. Ribbentrop received these proposals (Henderson wrote) with "intense hostility which increased in violence as I made each communication in turn. He kept jumping to his feet in a state of great excitement, folding his arms across his chest and asking if I had anything more to say." Henderson, to his own satisfaction, matched the German in vehemence and asked for the German proposals. Ribbentrop began to read them out in such rapid-fire German that Henderson couldn't get much of what was said; in the tenseness of the moment he did not ask Schmidt to interpret, either. Of sixteen points, he got the gist of a half-dozen. He asked for a written copy. Ribbentrop said that since the Polish emissary had not arrived the proposals were out of date—and refused to give him a copy. Moments later, when Henderson left and Ribbentrop had reported, Hitler issued the go-ahead for "Case White" to begin the morning of September 1, and he went to bed.

Henderson did not. He continued a frantic marathon to stave off the inevitable. He met with Lipski at two in the morning, beseeched him to phone Beck and get permission to receive the sixteen points. Lipski agreed. By eight, Henderson was phoning the Polish embassy to ask if Lipski had heard from Warsaw; Lipski, packing his bags, wouldn't even take the call. Henderson breakfasted with Attolico, who urged more pressure on the Poles and hinted at a forthcoming mediation offer from Mussolini. At nine, Henderson met with Coulondre, who also suggested the Polish squeeze and the Mussolini end run. At ten, Dahlerus turned up. He had wormed out of Göring a rough digest of the sixteen points. Many sounded reasonable: Danzig would return to the Reich, there would be a plebiscite in the Corridor, there would be an exchange of minority populations, Poland would retain an outlet to the sea at Gdynia. Dahlerus was detailed to take these proposals to Lipski. At the Polish embassy, Lipski was tearing up bits of paper and rolling them into little balls; nonetheless he promised to send Dahlerus's message along to Warsaw.

In the afternoon, Dahlerus, Henderson, and Göring had tea. Perhaps Göring could meet Polish marshal Edward Smigly-Rydz in Holland and, military man to military man, iron things out. If not, Göring declared, it would be most imprudent for Britain to side with the Poles, whom Germany would crush "like lice." While they were talking, Lipski was handed a telegram from Colonel Beck: "Please do not engage in any concrete discussions, and if the Germans put forward any concrete demands, say you are not authorized to accept or discuss them and will have to ask your government for further instructions."

That did it. Intercepted by the German wiretapping agency and brought to the Chancellery's attention, this telegram resulted in Hitler's confirming that the invasion would start at dawn. At six that evening, Lipski came to the Chancellery to have a meeting with Ribbentrop, his first since March. Ribbentrop, who had seen the Beck telegram, was cold and formal; he asked if the Pole was empowered to negotiate. Lipski said he was not and returned to his embassy, to find that his telephone lines had already been cut.

At seven, Ribbentrop and Hitler received Attolico. He brought a special plea from Mussolini. In exchange for his support, which, the Duce said, had never wavered, he wanted to be allowed to negotiate between Poland and Germany; he guaranteed that the result would be that Germany would gain both Danzig and the Corridor. France and even England were inclined to go along with this mediation plan, and would force Poland to accept. As he delivered his message, Attolico thought Hitler seemed in a dream, listening only to inner voices. He waved Attolico away, saying, "Too late, too late!"

"Am I to understand that everything is at an end?" the ambassador asked, anguished.

Hitler nodded.

That day the first sixteen thousand Parisian children left the city for the countryside, as did rare animals from the zoo at Vincennes. At noon, the Paris air-raid system was tested, sending thousands scurrying to the metro entrances. Gas masks were being carried. Though mobilization was not yet "full," streams of men continued to leave the Gare de l'Est for garrisons near the Maginot. Theaters canceled performances because many of the actors had been mobilized. The most valuable contents of the Louvre were stored in bank vaults. Cathedrals in Rouen, Chartres, and other cities were battening down, removing their stained-glass windows to safety.

Trainloads of bank employees and clerical workers left London, the men and women carrying files to temporary offices in the countryside. East End prostitutes swung their gas masks. Trenches were being dug in the parks; shelters were being prepared by Air Raid Precaution wardens. Only one bobby guarded the residence of the prime minister, however, and few servicemen's uniforms were to be seen. Theaters were full. The biggest hit was a revival of *The Importance of Being Earnest* with John Gielgud, Jack Hawkins, Edith Evans, Margaret Rutherford, and Peggy Ashcroft. Dance enthusiasts flocked to the Rachmaninoff-Fokine ballet about Paganini making a compact with the devil. Some stay-at-homes read H. G. Wells's *The Fate of Homo Sapiens*, which argued that we had reached the point where humanity could provide for itself totally, or destroy itself totally.

In Gleiwitz, a sleepy German town near the border with Poland, at eight in the evening, SS man Alfred Naujocks and a hand-picked team dressed in Polish uniforms attacked and took over the town's radio transmitter. They broadcast in Polish for several minutes, saying that Gleiwitz was in Polish hands and that the time had come for all good Poles to attack Germany. Ending with shouts of "Long live Poland," and revolver shots for sound effects, they left the station. Outside, they executed a man who had been in a group of prisoners taken from a concentration camp a week earlier; that afternoon he had been drugged with a fatal injection and dressed in a Polish uniform. Then they propped up his body to make him seem a casualty left behind after the station was stormed.

While Naujocks was at work, in a forest near Hohenspitzen some miles away, Heinrich Müller and other SS men placed against some trees and fallen logs the drugged bodies of a dozen other concentration camp inmates, also in Polish uniforms. Then they machine-gunned them to make it look as if they had died trying to invade Germany.

Police cars arrived at Gleiwitz within minutes after Naujocks left.

They had been alerted by an anonymous phone call. A group of foreign newsman "happened" to turn up too.

At nine, Berlin radio read out Hitler's sixteen-point proposal to Warsaw, and added that Poland had not seen fit to negotiate. Without knowing that Hitler had insisted on the pressure-cooker approach, and that he had no intention of negotiating, and that his demands would put a great deal of Polish territory and many Poles under German control, the Germans at home could only conclude that Poland wanted war. At ten-thirty, Berlin radio heightened this impression with reports of the attempt at infiltration at Gleiwitz. Hitler's promise to the generals had been fulfilled; he had provided reasons for starting the war.

Near midnight, ambassadors Henderson and Coulondre debated over the phone—duly wiretapped, of course—whether or not the Poles could formally accept delivery of the sixteen points by a roundabout route, since they had no direct official knowledge of them. The argument intensified until both men slammed down their phones in anger. Henderson wired Halifax, asking him to insist that Warsaw send a plenipotentiary to Berlin immediately. At one in the morning, Halifax agreed. At that hour CBS correspondents William Shirer in Berlin and Edward R. Murrow in London were still talking to each other and to a large radio audience via a link-up in New York. After his broadcast, at three-thirty in the morning of September 1, a weary Shirer wrote in his diary that the city was "normal in appearance this evening," that there had been no evacuations or excessive precautions, and concluded that no precipitate action would take place in Germany that night. Near dawn, he went to bed. An hour later the first waves of German soldiers crashed across the border into Poland.

4

The Silesian War

When his troops began to pour into Poland, Hitler was asleep in his living quarters in the Chancellery. Adjutant Nicholas von Vormann, his liaison with the army, had been instructed by his superiors that his most important task was to keep the Führer from interfering with the progress of the campaign.

This was the German military's show. Preparations had been worked out in meticulous and copious detail on a scale seldom before undertaken in the history of warfare. The invaders knew the country better than the inhabitants. Each division had intricate maps of terrain and the roads along which they were to advance; SS detachments with the troops had black books which listed prominent citizens of each town—nobility, clergy, intelligentsia, Jews—along with their addresses and, often, their descriptions. The armies had excellent radio communication; Luftwaffe squadrons, for instance, could be called into play at the request of a tank unit commander.

Bridges, tunnels, mountain passes, and other obstacles which might hinder the advance had been pinpointed, and plans laid to capture them intact or prevent defenders from blowing them. The Luftwaffe had flown practice raids in German territory over bridges similar to those they would be bombing in Poland; pilots for some missions had surreptitiously traversed their actual targets by train. A secret army had been raised and garrisoned in Danzig, supplied by night from an innocent-looking trawler. In Danzig harbor sat the ancient battleship *Schleswig-Holstein*, supposedly on a courtesy visit, just waiting to open fire. At border crossings, freight cars which usually contained ordinary cargo now held well-hidden troops who would disembark after locomotives had brought them into Poland. Nearly a million German soldiers waited on Poland's borders.

The pocket battleships *Deutschland* and *Graf Spee* had been ordered to stations in the North Atlantic, beyond the British Isles, three

48

weeks before. Twenty-one submarines—80 percent of Admiral Karl Doenitz's U-boat force—had been at sea with sealed orders for a week. The *Altmark*, whose crew thought she was an ordinary steamer carrying supplies from Norway to Mexico, was ordered to a rendezvous off South America under similarly sealed orders. On September 1, Germany was ready for the Silesian war, and more.

Poland was a heart-shaped target. Above the right cusp, in East Prussia, was the Third Army, poised just eighty miles north of Warsaw. On the left side, in German Pomerania, was the Fourth Army, which would strike east and cut the Polish Corridor from the main body of Poland. These armies were under the direction of Fedor von Bock, and were supported by part of the Luftwaffe; working with them were many panzers, the *Schleswig-Holstein*, and a sea-based force which would take Danzig.

Along the main German-Polish border were the bulk of the forces—about two-thirds of the German might—under Gerd von Rundstedt. In Central Silesia was Blaskowitz's Eighth Army (Hitler had doubts about this commander), and south of Blaskowitz was the Tenth Army, led by Walther von Reichenau (Hitler's pet general), with much of the motorized spearhead. South of Reichenau, hugging the corner of Czechoslovakia, was the large Fourteenth Army. It was to strike at Poland from underneath, going north and east to the important Galician oil fields just beyond the Carpathian Mountains at the conjunction of Poland, Czechoslovakia, and Hungary. These armies were also supported by air corps. The objective of Rundstedt's forces in the opening days of fighting was control of the industrial triangle of southern and western Poland bounded by the cities of Lodz, Cracow, and Czestochowa.

Poland was a dream target for the Germans, offering a border which extended 1,750 miles and which had three distinct vantage points for attack. The Polish countryside—flat and even—posed few natural obstacles for the invader; in the north were some forests, and on the Czech border were the Carpathian Mountains, but there were passages in both these sectors for tanks. That Poland was so vulnerable was well known to the commander of Poland's armies, Marshal Smigly-Rydz, another protégé of Pilsudski's. He had been given the appellation "smigly"—"speedy"—in 1920, and his military ideas had changed little since then. Rydz had been a cavalry officer, and Poland's armies still relied very heavily on horses. Germany had fifty-nine divisions; Poland—at full mobilization—thirty, but on September 1, mobilization was not complete, and some divisions had to be kept on the alert on the eastern border with Russia.

Rydz was fond of pointing out that Germany had spent, in the past six years, thirty times what Poland had spent for national defense, although Poland was putting half her annual budget into the military. Rydz knew that Poland could never withstand the invasion alone. His plan was to withdraw his forces from the borders quickly, give up a large part of western Poland, and retreat in orderly fashion to the only natural barrier, a group of rivers in the central area. Inside a diamond bounded by the Vistula, the San, the Narew, and the Bug were Warsaw and Modlin, the major cities of the central region. The rivers were broad, and in an ordinary autumn the rains would make them difficult to pass. Rydz would withdraw behind them, blow bridges, and wait for Britain and France to destroy Germany from behind.

At about four-thirty in the morning of September 1, Wolfram von Richthofen, brother of the famed "Red Baron," was groping toward the border of Poland from East Prussia when he heard the far-off rumble of artillery and rifles:

> The firing of these first shots made a stark impression on me. Now the war was surely on in earnest. . . . Am thinking about France and England, and believe no longer in the possibility of a political settlement after what is being done now. . . . From now on it is the practical business of making war, as ordered.

Despite the extensive preparations, all did not go well for the Germans during the first two days of the war. Lieutenant Bruno Dilley, commander of a Stuka squadron, took off from East Prussia on the first air raid of the war at 4:26 A M His target was the detonator wires alongside the Dirschau Bridge over the Vistula—he had been one of the pilots who had crossed this bridge by train incognito. From his cockpit, Dilley could see virtually nothing; total fog enshrouded the area. Under other circumstances he would have turned back, but a trainful of sappers was waiting to cross the bridge, so Dilley decided to make the raid. His bombs missed their targets, and the bridge was blown up by the Poles.

At the Jablunka tunnels, the premature attacks of August 26 had made the defenders wary, and they blew up the tunnels before the Germans could use them; at Graudenz, sabotage plans backfired as Germans in Polish uniforms were arrested by regular German troops—and another bridge was blown up before the mix-up was corrected. In Danzig, the garrison of the Westerplatte didn't surrender immediately, despite shelling from the *Schleswig-Holstein*, and there were many other instances of fierce Polish resistance. Nor did the Luftwaffe deliver a knockout blow. At 5:50 A M, Göring radioed that "Operation Seaside," an all-out bomber attack on Warsaw, would not take place that day because of low cloud cover.

But Germany was poised to invade at twenty different points, and through sheer weight of numbers some of the attempts succeeded. In Cracow, the ancient alarm bells had rung centuries before to warn of the approaching Tatars; on September 1, 1939, they rang as forty-eight tons of bombs fell on the old city. In smaller border towns, bombs woke the sleeping citizens. In some, field-gray infantry and motorized units streaked toward the east through the rubble created by the bombs, even before the flames had died away. In one Silesian town, where the Versailles-drawn border went through the middle of a sidewalk, the Germans just walked over it.

The panzers and the Stukas were most effective. Contrary to legend, there were not very many tanks, but they were concentrated in substantial packs, and a mass of tanks rolling on a town was terrifying. In the open countryside, Stukas, screaming as they dove, struck fear into people along the roads. Nobody knew the Stukas could not scream and fire their machine guns at the same time.

By evening, more than twenty Polish towns were aflame, and the population near the borders was becoming demoralized—but the Polish armies were intact. Where armor was evenly matched, as in the south, the Poles proved as good or better soldiers than the Germans. In the north the Poles were more easily overwhelmed, but even there instances of gallant defense abounded. Along the eastern border what von Rundstedt described as "phantom hosts" of Polish cavalry used the darkness of night to overwhelm German machine-gun units. In East Prussia, where the Poles invaded a slice of German territory, the inhabitants fled in terror.

But on balance, the night began to tip the scales toward Germany. In the darkness, in the clear air, the Luftwaffe was active and bombed towns large and small; the next morning, they took off after the elusive Polish air force. Göring was convinced it must be hiding, and he could not allow Polish planes to harass tanks, transports, and troops moving through the countryside in strength. Göring was right; the Polish planes had been hiding. Not many were destroyed on the ground, but the Luftwaffe's bombing of their airfields the second morning meant that many which had outfought the Germans in dogfights had nowhere to escape to when they were hurt or when equipment replacements were needed. And when a Polish plane went down in flames, there were none to replace it: Poland had only 160 fighters and 86 bombers; the Germans had five times as many of each.

The greatest damage inflicted by the Luftwaffe was to Polish communications. By the second day, telephone and teleprinter systems had broken down. Reports and orders from the Polish high command became confused, or reached the recipients too late. Effective military coordination was shattered. As a result, the Polish high command lost touch with the field commanders, and the individual Polish armies began operating independently of one another. This vitiated their acts of bravery: a single cavalry brigade with antitank guns held up an entire panzer battalion for a whole day, but was overwhelmed when no support materialized. The fact that the Polish armies were still essentially intact began to mean little.

Austrian infantryman Wilhelm Prüller noted the reaction in one village on the second day of the war:

> We drive through the first village. They hand flowers into our truck. In delight they stretch their hands toward us.... The blown-up bridges and the torn-up streets slow our advance. But all the Poles' efforts are shown to be of no avail. The German Wehrmacht is marching!... A family sits in front of their door. All of them crying. But we aren't harming anyone! Why didn't the Polish government give in? We haven't got anything against the people themselves. But where are our rights?

In other towns the reception was not so kind. Polish snipers killed German soldiers and those local sympathizers who welcomed them.

General Heinz Guderian, architect of Germany's tank forces and commander of a tank group attempting to cross the Polish Corridor, noted that in the first days of the war the officer corps took heavy casualties: two generals and State Secretary von Weizsäcker each lost a son who was an officer. Guderian's son, also serving, was still alive, but the commander himself was having difficulties. When the onslaught began, he rode an armored car into the Corridor, and was almost immediately bracketed by his own artillery fire. The first shell hit fifty yards ahead of him, the second fifty yards behind, and

> I reckoned that the next one was bound to be a direct hit and ordered my driver to turn about and drive off. The unaccustomed noises had made him nervous, however, and he drove straight into a ditch at full speed.... This marked the end of my drive. I made my way to my corps command post, procured a fresh vehicle and had a word with the overeager artilleryman.

Later that day Guderian found a regimental commander who had ordered his troops to rest rather than to cross a crucial river. Guderian took the troops across himself and found nothing on the other side but a Polish company on bicycles. At another sticking point he was amazed to see German soldiers setting up an antitank gun when there were no enemy tanks in sight. During the night, he managed to stop the withdrawal of an entire motorized division which had been frightened by the idea of a Polish cavalry attack. If Guderian was gallant, perhaps it was because he had a personal objective: he wanted to see Gross–Kolonia, an estate which had once belonged to his family, where his grandfather was buried and where his father had been born. He had never seen it in his life.

At ten in the morning of September 1, Hitler spoke to the Reichstag at the Kroll Opera House. Earlier in the day, Berlin radio had announced that German military units had "returned the fire" of Polish invaders. Ration cards had been distributed—conservation now, to ensure supplies later. The weather was hot and humid. The opera house was majestic, with its maroon walls and carpets, and a great eagle rising on a silver backdrop. Beneath the eagle, Göring sat presiding while diplomats and guests filled the boxes and balconies. A hundred deputies' seats were empty, their occupants mobilized or, like industrialist Fritz Thyssen, fleeing the country. Hitler had discarded his brown party tunic and wore a field-gray army uniform, which he swore never to take off "until victory is ours," or "not as long as I am alive." In case he did die, he nominated Göring to succeed him.

Hitler's purpose was to convince the Germans of the rightness, necessity, and inevitability of the war. He blamed its onset on the Polish raid at Gleiwitz. He thanked Mussolini for offering his support but added that Italy's assistance was not required. He assured his listeners the war would be fought "in such a manner that women and children are neither the target nor the victim." He also insisted that the Siegfried Line was the limit of Germany's westward ambitions.

This last was an attempt to keep Britain and France out of the war. For as Adjutant Vormann noted in his diary that evening, "Naturally everything is not yet clear. The big question—will Britain really stand by Poland?—is still open." The Allies' treaties called for them to go to the aid of Poland immediately, but that wasn't happening.

When the British cabinet met on September 1, information about Poland was incomplete and contradictory. The British ambassador in Warsaw had telephoned to say Polish cities were being bombed and Poland invaded, but German diplomats in London, when queried, denied it. Later the German press reported troops twenty miles inside Poland at a half-dozen points.

Chamberlain had already ordered mobilization, summoned Parliament, sent the fleet to stations, and ordered preliminary measures for the seizure of German property if war was declared. The big question was whether war would be declared. Several ministers were for immediately honoring the pledges and going to war; others were for exploring alternatives to war—a proposal for a Göring-Ironside-Rydz meeting, a proposal for a Mussolini-led mediation conference. This latter was backed by the French foreign minister, Georges Bonnet, who insisted the possibility had to be explored before France committed herself to war. General Gamelin was also insistent that forty-eight hours must elapse before war could be declared, so that he could complete mobilization without fear of being bombed.

All the cabinet could do was send a stiff note to Germany. The British couldn't act without the French, and as the Chamber of Deputies could not sit until the next day, they would have to wait. In the evening, in Berlin, Henderson and Coulondre separately handed notes to Ribbentrop which were, they admitted, "in the nature of a warning." Next morning in London news of the weak British note produced an uproar. Why wasn't England helping the Poles?

There was a reason for it, but it wasn't for public consumption. The cabinet believed that once war was declared, Hitler would bomb London and other large cities, causing an estimated half-million casualties inside of a month. A government report on the subject envisioned mass burials in cardboard coffins that would then be dissolved in quicklime pits. This horror to end all horrors haunted the leaders of the government.

On the morning of September 2, Chamberlain, a deliberate man, did not want to be stampeded into Armageddon. Nevertheless, France and Italy were told that England would agree to a Mussolini-led conference only if German troops were first withdrawn from Poland. Mussolini refused even to suggest this to Hitler, but it took most of the day for the cabinet to find out the idea was dead. When at last the ministers got up from their chairs in the cabinet room, it was with the impression that an ultimatum expiring at midnight would be given Germany. The French ultimatum might not coincide, but it would come shortly. Honor would be saved, war would be declared.

Members of Parliament had hung about the Commons all day, smoking, drinking, watching the lowering skies. They were twice put off when they expected a statement, but at 7:45 P.M Chamberlain appeared. He spoke for four minutes, telling them agreement had not yet been reached on coordination with the French, that the Italian proposal had caused delay, and that as a consequence no ultimatum had yet been issued. His statement provoked cries of outrage and anger. Arthur Greenwood, temporary leader of the Labour stalwarts, was urged to "speak for England." He did. It was time, Greenwood told the Commons, for honor. England must take a stand; he hoped that by tomorrow morning "there shall be no more devices for dragging out what has been dragged out too long." He was greatly applauded. Chamberlain feared for his government's stability.

Assault on the government also came from within. A group of cabinet ministers led by Sir John Simon began a sit-down strike and refused to leave Simon's office until war was declared. Simon threatened Chamberlain with a revolt that would topple the government unless the prime minister announced next morning that an ultimatum had been delivered, had expired, and England was fulfilling her guarantee and was at war with Germany.

At his residence at 10 Downing Street, the prime minister was sick at heart. Hundreds of thousands had already been evacuated from the large cities. He spoke to an aide about the French children who would be killed if war came, as if afraid to mention what might happen to those in England. In the Great War, both London and Paris had been bombed; the bombing had been relatively minor, but it was in the minds of all the leaders. Chamberlain could imagine the trains and the stations bombed, the children lying dead.

Chamberlain summoned Lord Halifax to dinner. The foreign secretary had been planning to dine out with his wife, and went to 10 Downing in his evening clothes. During the evening, Chamberlain sent for others of his inner circle, and they began to arrive—Britain's leaders during the appeasement years: Sir Alexander Cadogan, permanent secretary of the Foreign Office; Sir Horace Wilson, the industrial adviser who thought so highly of Hitler. Chamberlain told them that the government would fall in the morning if war was not declared. In the presence of French Ambassador Charles Courbin, Chamberlain telephoned Daladier directly and told him that England must present an ultimatum the next morning. Daladier said France could not do the same, citing Gamelin's mobilization and Bonnet's hopes for Mussolini. The French would present a note with no expiration time, said Daladier, and added that "unless British bombers are ready to act at once [to cover the French mobilization] it would be better for France to delay."

Chamberlain summoned the rebellious sit-in group. They came hazardously through blacked-out streets and a thunderstorm so heavy as to cause flooding. Scruffy, smelly, and unfed, they greeted their colleagues, some of whom were in evening clothes; then all went into the cabinet room. After a discussion lasting past midnight, it was agreed that Henderson should present an ultimatum to Hitler at nine; if there was no satisfactory reply by eleven, England would be at war. Chamberlain, now icy cold in manner, said, "Right, gentlemen, this means war." There was an immediate echo from the heavens, a thunderclap that shook the building and nearly deafened the ministers. After a few moments they went out into the night, determined, chastened, and thoughtful.

On September 3, the fate of Poland was decided. In a dozen places German units broke through. After a night approach of fifty miles through thick woods and mountainous terrain in the Carpathians, General Wilhelm von Thoma's tanks came over a ridge and descended into a valley: "I arrived in a village to find the people all going to church. How astonished they were to see my tanks approaching! I had turned the enemy's defenses without losing a single tank."

Far to the north, in wooded country west of Graudenz, Guderian's tanks, together with a motorized and an infantry division, caught a large Polish force; by the day's end Guderian had virtually severed the Corridor from the body of Poland. He watched a Pomorska cavalry brigade charge his tanks with lances. Men and horses were cut to shreds by machine-gun fire. As the surviving Poles were led away, some of them tapped the sides of the tanks in surprise—they had been told by their superiors that the tanks were made out of cardboard.

In Silesia, at the center of the attacking front, the big breakthrough was made not by tanks but by infantry and artillery. This was an old-style attack. The Poles in this area, instead of retreating on Smigly-Rydz's plan, had stood their ground for two days. Now they were broken and the Germans encircled large groups and forced them to surrender. On September 3, the Germans took Katowice in the south, Czestochowa in the midsection, Bydgoszcz in the north, and Graudenz. The line Smigly-Rydz envisioned holding for ten days was crossed in less than three.

Beilitz, sometimes called "Little Vienna" because it had once been part of the Austro-Hungarian Empire, lay close to the Czech border. Its inhabitants were a polyglot mix of ex-Germans, ex-Czechs, and Poles. During the still-dark hours of the morning, the Luftwaffe bombed Beilitz, frightening everyone and leaving scores dead. At first light, Polish troops hastily entered the town and withdrew through it toward Cracow. Two hours later, German motorcyclists yelling "Heil Hitler!" raced down the streets, followed by swarms of trucks, half-tracks, and other vehicles full of soldiers; the stench of gasoline was everywhere. Resistance was impossible.

Some Beilitzers welcomed the Germans with swastika flags and gave the soldiers wine and cheese; others hid or fled. In the early afternoon, the Germans herded a clutch of Jewish men into one of the town's temples. The building was set aflame and the Jews were burned to death. Leaving only a hundred men to guard the town, the main bulk of the German forces were on their way by late afternoon toward a larger objective, Cracow. But Beilitz had been radically transformed.

Meanwhile the Silesian war became a world war. In Berlin, at nine in the morning of September 3, Ambassador Henderson mounted the massive steps of the Chancellery to do his duty. He saw neither Hitler nor Ribbentrop, but handed the ultimatum, which would expire at eleven, to interpreter Paul Schmidt. Despite the objections of Gamelin and Bonnet, a French ultimatum was also handed in. It would expire at five in the afternoon. Receiving them, Hitler glared fiercely at Ribbentrop; Göring was nearly sick; other high German officials were taken aback: their worst fears were being realized.

Above London silver barrage balloons glinted in the sun. At eleven, Halifax and Cadogan walked through streets jammed with people aware that a historic moment was at hand. They joined Chamberlain at 10 Downing Street, and moments later Henderson called to say there had been no answer to the ultimatum. Chamberlain went to a BBC microphone and told the country that England was at war with Germany. At noon he reported to the Commons: "Everything that I have worked for, everything that I have hoped for, everything that I have believed in during my public life, has crashed into ruins." To former cabinet member Anthony Eden the speech seemed "rather the lament of a man deploring his own failure than the call of a nation to arms."

As air-raid sirens began to wail, all London hurried to shelter. In one cubicle were Winston Churchill and his wife. Churchill had at last been called by Chamberlain to take a post in the new war cabinet. Mrs. Churchill commented favorably on German promptness and precision in scheduling a raid just as war was declared. Churchill wondered if this raid was the beginning of a holocaust, the projected German "knockout blow" which might cause hundreds of thousands of casualties. He did not know that the government had overestimated the strength of the Luftwaffe and its ability to reach across the Channel. The siren was a false alarm. French air attaché de Brantes, returning in a small plane from Paris, had fouled up the radar defenses. It would have been comic except that two British fighters which scrambled to meet the "enemy" collided over the city and one pilot was killed.

In Paris, as in London, there was no cheering. The French wanted to get the dirty job done, to stop Hitler once and for all. Only in Warsaw was there delirious joy in reaction to the French and British declarations. Large crowds waving British and French flags marched through the streets to applaud and serenade ambassadors and any other citizens of the democracies they could find. The Poles expected British Blenheim bombers to do to Berlin what the Germans had been doing to Warsaw for three days.

In Berlin, Hitler believed that the British and French would wage only a sham war against Germany and would abandon Poland. After the first moment of chagrin, his resolve did not waver. He knew enough about the French mobilization to understand that the French army could not attack before another ten days, and he knew the British were reluctant to bomb Germany, because they did not want retaliation bombing by the Luftwaffe. So he gave two orders. In Poland, troops were to seize as much ground as possible, to make a fait accompli of German control. And the troops facing France, Belgium, Luxembourg, and the Netherlands were not to attack or even to fire on the enemy unless the enemy fired first. There were to be no provocations of the Allies or of the neutrals that might provide them with an excuse for waging war.

Although a similar "no provocations" order had long since been transmitted to the submarine fleet, one submarine disobeyed it. At dusk, U-30 fired a torpedo into the zigzagging British liner *Athenia*, two hundred miles off the Scottish coast. The big ship sank rapidly in a horrific whirlpool of blazing oil and shattered steel splinters. Rescue craft in the dark waters became so confused that they contributed to the drowning of some who had initially survived. Most of the 1,400 passengers were rescued, but 112, including 28 Americans, died. Berlin refused to admit the *Athenia* had been torpedoed, and suggested that Winston Churchill had planted a bomb aboard the ship or had a British submarine torpedo her in order to push the United States into the war.

The sinking of the *Athenia* did recall the sinking of the *Lusitania* in 1915, when an angry cry had arisen for President Woodrow Wilson to take the United States into the Great War. Wilson had refused to be provoked, and two more years had elapsed before America entered the war. Now the president was the man who had been Wilson's assistant secretary of the navy and was still a fervent believer in Wilson's pacific doctrines, and he had no intention of taking the United States into a new world war.

On the evening of September 3, Franklin Roosevelt spoke to the nation in a Fireside Chat. He said flatly that the United States was going to stay out of the war. Wilson, in 1914, had asked Americans to be neutral in word, deed, and thought; Roosevelt didn't think that attitude was possible in 1939; "This nation will remain a neutral nation, but I cannot ask that every American remain neutral in thought as well. Even a neutral cannot be asked to close his mind to conscience." Roosevelt himself thought, as did the majority of Americans queried in a recent poll, that Germany was the aggressor. Americans wanted Poland and her allies to win the war, but even more passionately they wanted to stay clear of it. In his "chat," the president warned Americans that they might eventually have to become more involved: "You must master at the outset a simple but unalterable fact in modern foreign relations between nations. When peace has been broken anywhere, the peace of all countries everywhere is in danger." Nonetheless, as long as it was in his power to prevent, there would be no "blackout of peace" in America.

In Berlin, Hitler told aides he would wind up the Silesian war before the American Congress reconvened and took up the question of revision of the neutrality laws. In his armored train *Amerika* he left Berlin for the front. There were no crowds to see him off and no cheers. Air-raid sirens sounded; they were for a false alarm. The city's mood was as dark as its blacked-out streets. War with the Allies—still unacknowledged by state radio but understood by Berliners from foreign broadcasts—was unexpected and very bad news. As Adjutant Vormann noted in his diary that night: "I'm not a grouser or defeatist, but the future looks very grim to me. This is just what we didn't want."

All through the military and high government circles, the leading men of the regime gave way to despair. Admiral Erich Raeder, chief of the navy, noted in his diary after a conference with Brauchitsch, Halder, Ribbentrop, and Hitler:

Today there began a war ... with which—to judge from all the Führer's utterances hitherto—we should not have had to reckon before about 1944; and a war which he considered until very recently he must avoid at all costs, even if it meant postponing a thoroughgoing solution of the Polish problem until later.

At the Foreign Office, Erich Kordt commiserated with Ernst von Weizsäcker (who did not yet know his son had died in Poland). Kordt said, "The majority of the German people abhor war; in the Reichschancellery few want it; really only a single man. Is there no way to prevent this war?"

Weizsäcker answered, "Do you have a man with a pistol? I regret that there has been nothing in my upbringing that would fit me to kill a man."

In private homes people were sad, afraid, and confused. Huddled with her friends, Ruth Andreas-Friedrich could not understand why destruction was not raining down on Berlin. "Wave assaults" of bombers were hitting Polish towns. France and England were at war with Germany—"yet neither Frenchmen nor Englishmen are marching across our frontiers. Why don't they, too, cross some river or other, and put an end to the madness of war before the best blood of all nations has been drained?"

5

The Death of Poland

The first morning of World War II, Adolf Hitler awoke on the way to the front in his armored train. From this headquarters train he ventured by car, airplane, and on foot to visit forward battlefields. He was eager, several times coming so close to enemy fire that aides were concerned for his safety. His presence inspired the troops.

With Guderian, Hitler retraced the route the tanks had taken to sever the Corridor. Passing the wreckage of Polish artillery, he asked, "Our dive bombers did that?"

"No," Guderian responded, "our panzers." Hitler was delighted that the panzer corps had lost only 150 dead and 700 wounded in crossing the Corridor. During the Great War his own regiment had lost thousands in a single day during which they had not gained an inch of territory. Guderian proudly showed Hitler his ancestral seat; people there showered the Führer with flowers.

Information reaching Hitler showed major resistance crumbling. In the north, several divisions had been captured during the battles for the Corridor. In the center, Blaskowitz had broken through the Polish lines. In the south, Polish Silesia had been engulfed. Now the German forces from Pomerania and from East Prussia converged and aimed at the Polish heartland. By the evening of September 5, advance units were racing behind the Polish armies toward Warsaw and Modlin. Halder wrote in his diary: "Enemy as good as beaten."

In the wake of the German armies' advance, particularly in the Corridor and along the western border, Polish civilians mounted a fierce resistance. For years the Polish government had incited the Poles against Germany, just as the *Volkdeutsche* had been incited by the Nazis against Poland. In towns along the western frontier Poles killed about five thousand of the *Volkdeutsche* who had aided the advancing troops.

In reprisal the SS began a ruthless campaign. In Bydgoszcz, where the Poles murdered several hundred ethnic Germans on the first two days of the war, the Germans pushed nearly a thousand people into a barracks that had once housed a cavalry regiment and machine-gunned them. That was the opening burst of the campaign of revenge: it has been estimated that fifty thousand Poles were similarly killed in the first weeks of the German occupation. Small villages were razed. In middle-sized towns entire populations were called into the main square, and dozens of people chosen at random were killed. In larger cities, such as Czestochowa, a center of Polish Catholic culture, hundreds were herded into venerable cathedrals and kept prisoner for several days without food or water, after which many were shot. Poland was to be terrorized into subservience.

On Hitler's authority, and with the aim of "radical suppression of the incipient Polish insurrection," Heydrich ordered his men to "put out of harm's way as far as possible" the Polish ruling class, the intelligentsia, and the Jews. The SS carried out this "political" mission with such mendacity and brutality that the regular military began to protest, but Hitler's planning chief, Wilhelm Keitel, brushed off any complaints by suggesting that if the army wasn't going to do the dirty work, it should not be indignant when others did it for them.

A large Polish army had pulled out of Cracow very nearly at the last moment before the Germans arrived. In the north, near Poznan, eight of General Kutrzeba's division were cut off and had to surrender because they did not pull out in time.

General Wladyslaw Anders, who had led a Polish division in the Corridor, received an order he found difficult to comprehend. Despite the danger of disorganization near the corridor, he was to leave his division and go to a small town some distance away. Not wishing to disobey orders, he started on his journey. It took two days to reach his destination, and in the process he was wounded in the back and nearly crippled. He found a new division in disorderly flight and stabilized them by his presence. Looking for a place to fight, he moved his men to a town on the northern Vistula, where he prepared to cross a bridge and make a stand on the far side. Suddenly he received orders not to cross the bridge but to blow it up and go to Modlin. He complied, and spent more days en route and not fighting. At Modlin he got ready to fight but was again ordered southwest, to the defense of Warsaw. This time Anders was so disgusted that he rejected the orders; his division would act on its own, as a wolf pack to harry the Germans.

General Kutrzeba, commander of the Polish Army of Poznan, had lost eight of his divisions because the high command had not responded early enough to his request to withdraw and regroup. Kutrzeba thought the high command had not been willfully wrong but had been lacking in information. With his still large and still well-equipped force, he too became crafty. He went into the deep forests, hid his men beneath the foliage during the day, and moved them slowly southeast by night, looking for the opportunity to make a significant counterattack.

In blazing indifference to the Polish need for rain, "Hitler weather" continued. Mud had halted Napoleon and had mired the Russians in 1920, but there was no rain—and no mud—in 1939. German Stukas and Junkers, with clear skies, strafed and bombed virtually at will. Fourteen German planes appeared at dawn and in a few minutes obliterated one small village, then machine-gunned survivors as they fled. "First," wrote a survivor of such an attack, there was "the shrill whine of the falling bombs, then sheets of flame, jagged at the edges. We hugged the smoking earth, listening to the debris ricocheting off branches and tree trunks."

Another survivor wrote that the bombs came with "an unforgettable sound which makes one think some gigantic knife is being sharpened." This man thought there were three stages of human panic. The first was the panic of screams, the second was the panic of flight, and the third was the panic of silence—an actual paralysis of the nervous system. Reaching for ways to describe the chaos, another survivor recalled the planes as swollen queen bees that disgorged obscene and monstrous eggs.

In the turmoil, Poles left their dead unburied, killed their household pets so they wouldn't have to suffer, and took to the roads by the hundreds of thousands. Refugees clogged the country's arteries, impeding any hope of swift movement by the Polish troops and thereby contributing to their country's fate.

Twenty percent of Poland's troops were never mobilized at all. The English novelist's husband was among them: he looked in vain for his post, asked everywhere, and was told nothing. They decided to leave Warsaw and try to get her over into Rumania. Many people were aiming for the narrow hundred-mile-long funnel of land at the southeast corner where Poland abutted Rumania. The novelist thought there were many questions they and the thousands of others who were traveling had not thought to ask:

> Where are you going to get petrol? ... Don't forget that the raiders are bombing every viaduct, every junction, every level crossing, every train carrying refugees. Don't forget that the Lublin Road is choked with army transport and that the raiders will bomb you there, too, every inch of the way.

Nevertheless the pair set out in a car. Plenty of gas was available and they had money to buy it. But the car foundered on dirt roads and couldn't cut across fields to get out of the way of diving airplanes. They left the car and rented a horse and cart. One day, they told each other, they would return to Warsaw; even as they said it they knew it was a fantasy. Her questions poured relentlessly on:

> How are [the evacuees] going to get food and water? Where are they to lie down and sleep? Even the peasants dare not boil potatoes or light a fire on their hearths for fear of showing smoke. What kind of money have you got? In a day or two, nobody will take coin from you any longer. Have you got salt to pay with? ... Is it any use running out of Warsaw to die, like a nameless dog, in a farther ditch?

Many in London were irate that British bombers were not going to the aid of the Poles. Sir Edward Spears wanted to raise the question in Commons, but he was persuaded not to because national security was involved. Like-minded MP Leo Amery asked Secretary for Air Kingsley-Wood why the government could not direct bombers to drop incendiaries on the tinder-dry Black Forest, where great stores of ammunition were kept. "Are you aware that it is private property?" Kingsley-Wood retorted. "Why, you will be asking me to bomb Essen next!" Essen was the home of the Krupp armaments factories. The policy of not bombing civilian targets had been established in March, and the government was reluctant to change it. Stark evidence that Germany was bombing civilian targets was presented to the government by news reports, by witnesses who came directly to tell high officials about it, and by the government's own attachés in Poland. All such evidence was ignored.

Sir Edmund Ironside, Chief of the Imperial General Staff, reported to the war cabinet that the Polish armies were doing all right in their unequal fight. Some of this information was transmitted by the misinformed Polish high command, but it was augmented by Ironside's hyperbole. Ironside looked like his name—six feet five, a military ramrod, curt of voice and inflection, an overbearing presence—but was known as "Tiny." For years he had been inspector general of the overseas forces. He had counted on being named to head the British expeditionary force as the war began, but the French didn't like him and requested someone else. Lord Gort was appointed to lead the BEF, and Ironside became the CIGS. Having been to Poland during the summer and been impressed by seeing Poles kill one another with live ammunition, Ironside echoed Gamelin's prediction that the Poles would hold out until spring. His misplaced optimism bolstered the cabinet's wish to limit England's involvement in the war.

On September 4, Kingsley-Wood suggested to his colleagues that England would be in a better position to refuse German peace proposals when they came "if on the one hand we still possessed our air force intact, and on the other hand had not used it in such a manner as to expose us to criticism." The idea that the RAF could bomb Germany at will had already been demonstrated by the previous evening's raids, which had dropped millions of leaflets over Germany urging the Germans to end the war and to throw off their corrupt leaders. Where leaflets had been dropped, it was clear that bombs could also be dropped. The air force should be conserved, even if that meant leaving Poland to fend for itself. However, such a policy would seem defeatist to the public, and some bombing would have to be done. If cities, land-locked military installations, and armaments factories were not accept-able targets, what were? Only enemy warships, it was decided.

That afternoon fifteen Blenheims and fourteen Wellingtons took off to attack the harbor at Wilhelmshaven, the major concentration point of the German surface fleet. Aerial reconnaissance had revealed that many ships were still at the naval base. It was expected they would soon steam out to harass British shipping, and therefore they were an important target. To underscore that the might of the whole empire would be striking at Germany moments after the declaration of war, crews for the bombers were made up of men from England, South Afri-ca, Canada, and Australia. The pilots were young, and inexperienced.

The cloud cover was so dense that the bombs the planes were to carry were changed four times—from semi-armor-piercing to eleven-second-delay—before the planes went aloft. On the perilous journey, some planes traveled as low as three hundred feet above the water.

Five of the Blenheims got lost and did not find the target. The ten others in the first wave achieved surprise. The Germans thought they were Luftwaffe planes gone astray. The RAF squad leader saw "the matelots' washing hanging out around the stern and the crew standing about on deck" as he dove and hit the *Admiral Scheer* with two bombs. Both were duds or did not explode on contact because the eleven-sec-ond-delay fuses did not work. Two more planes dropped bombs which missed. Another two veered off and one of these was shot down. Now on the alert, the Germans managed to shoot down four of the next five approaching British planes. The last Blenheim crash-landed into the bow of the cruiser *Emden*, killing many sailors.

By the time the wave of Wellingtons arrived, the Germans were entirely ready. The *Gneisenau* and the *Scharnhorst*, the two largest ships in the entire German navy, turned their flak guns on the planes and downed one. Another was shot down by a Messerschmitt.

That was the end of the raid. Of the twenty-nine British planes, seven were shot down and five never found the target. None of the bombs dropped managed to put an important ship out of action, and the worst damage was wrought by the crashing plane. Nevertheless the raid was celebrated in the British press as a daring exploit which had possi-bly crippled the best ships of the German navy. There were speeches about bravery, and decorations were liberally awarded. High govern-ment officials knew this was all balderdash, but they also knew the British public needed a victory, however fuzzy. No inquiries were made about the eleven-second-delay fuses.

The British expeditionary force began to cross to France. Lord Gort, who commanded, had no field experience, but the secretary for war, Leslie Hore-Belisha, had wanted to have him out from underfoot. Commanding the two corps were John Dill and Alan Brooke. Brooke had more field experience and seniority than either of the others. He swallowed his dismay at the chain of command but couldn't hide his anger at how badly the forces were provisioned. They had trained with flags instead of artillery, and delivery trucks instead of tanks. Since much of their heavy equipment was not considered ready to travel, they left for France without it. The equipment they did have was unsatisfactory: some bore the legend "Not to be used in action. Mild steel only. Not armour plate." They had virtually no antiaircraft guns and no wireless sets. Their rifles did not fit together properly because the parts had been made by several companies. Few air squadrons supported the forces. Brooke drew the obvious conclusion: the politicians had not sent the BEF to fight but to show Poland that England was doing something.

In Paris, Ambassador Lukasciewicz issued a call to 800,000 Polish expatriates to enlist in special legions which would fight for France under the Polish flag. Three recruiting stations were opened to sign up the Poles, but no one seemed eager to recruit Nazi-hating exiles from Germany or Austria, such as Leo Lania. Lania knew novelist and playwright Jean Giraudoux, France's minister of information, and made an appointment to see him. The meeting was canceled without explanation, and Lania received a note ordering him to report to a sports arena on the outskirts of Paris. He said good-bye to his wife and son, took sandwiches and a blanket, and went to the Stade de Colombes, where he joined several thousand men, some of whom he knew from exile and émigré groups. The gates locked behind them and they were prisoners. No one, not even the courteous guards, had any idea how long the detainment would last. No one seemed interested in looking at documents that proved how anti-Nazi one was, nor in listening to how eager one was to fight and die in the French army.

Major Denis Barlone stood at the head of his horse-drawn transport unit on a rainy night. Near the Maginot Line, they were under orders to move only in the dark because of the threat of enemy airplanes. They left Mother Maquin's village behind. The columns were unwieldy, sluggish, and plagued by minor accidents. The interminable "hurry up and wait" on the roads was a time warp which made Barlone feel he had never been at peace, but rather on leave for twenty years:

> Are those dumb shadows emerging from the night for a few seconds the men I knew in the last war, the dead rising to stride to the front to wreak their vengeance on the Hun, to finish the work we didn't end? Are they

the new generation, marked by destiny as the victims of this war? Are they not rather fleeting shadows, wraiths whom the night robs of being and substance?

There was a muffled noise up ahead and the column began once more to shuffle along. Soon they hoped to engage the Germans.

The Maginot and Siegfried lines faced each other for 250 miles; in between was a long no man's land of evacuated villages. General Gamelin commanded ninety-three divisions, some of which were on the Italian, Swiss, and Belgian frontiers, but the bulk of them faced Germany and did so with superior numbers, supplies, tanks, and ammunition. There was so much French equipment that some of it had not yet been scheduled to come out of warehouses. By his May 19 military protocol with Poland, Gamelin was committed to begin a major offensive within two weeks of mobilization, an attack intended to draw pressure away from the Poles.

On the night of September 7–8, well within the deadline set by the agreement, Gamelin began an offensive on the Franco-German border. But instead of a multidivision effort to smash through the Siegfried Line, Gamelin sent only a few divisions into a confined fifteen-mile-long sector opposite Saarbrücken, which happened to be the best-fortified, most defensible point of the German line. Gamelin's men were initially amazed as the Germans quickly retreated, then were doubly amazed when the evacuated towns turned out to be booby-trapped. Casualties slowed them. In one town, a single German machine gun held up the entire French advance for nearly a day. Rather than send his men in at another point, Gamelin had them drive pigs through a minefield on the theory that after the pigs had been blown up the soldiers would know where to tread. But the sight of disemboweled animals hardly encouraged *poilus* to bravery.

Veterans of the Great War could hardly believe such stories, for the hordes of men thrown against enemy emplacements in that sanguinary conflict would never have been held back by a single gun or by a minefield, no matter what the cost. But the "blood tax," as Churchill would later describe it, was the key: Gamelin wanted to conserve men more than he wanted to advance.

Perhaps this was because he had begun to fear that a large and ever-increasing German force waited to oppose him if he came through the Siegfried Line in strength. In fact, the force which was behind that line was skeletal—thirty-three divisions, of which eleven were untrained reserves. The Germans were without air support, without tanks, and had only three days' ammunition. Moreover, the Siegfried Line, or Westwall, was nothing like the Maginot Line. As Colonel General von Rundstedt said upon seeing it:

The second-class troops holding the Wall were badly equipped and inadequately trained, and the defenses were far from being the impregnable fortifications pictured by our propaganda. Concrete protection of more than three feet was rare, and as a whole the positions were by no means proof against heavy-caliber shelling. Few of the strong points were sited to fire in enfilade and most of them could have been shot to pieces by direct fire, without the slightest risk to the attackers. The Westwall had been built in such a hurry that many of the positions were sited on forward slopes. The antitank obstacles were of trivial importance.

In some portions, the Westwall consisted merely of plywood silhouettes, and nowhere did it have the concentrated firepower of the Maginot fortresses. But French intelligence did not reveal the flimsiness of the defenses, and the Allies did not take advantage of their superiority to attack in strength.

No one in authority questioned Gamelin's actions. On September 4, he told Ironside that the push toward the Siegfried Line was to be an opening move in a chess game, in the nature of a probe, not an assault. The CIGS did not object. Daladier also had doubts about such timidity, but considered it unseemly to question the military establishment so early in the war.

The French glorified the offensive. One bulletin announced the conquest of 100,000 acres of German territory—a figure which sounded good but meant only that France had gone forward on a fifteen-mile front to a depth of one and a half miles. Communiqué No. 11 said, "A brilliant attack by one of our divisions has won for us an important piece of territory," but did not say that territory was the mined and booby-trapped Warndt forest. Just as quickly came Communiqué No. 12, "the enemy is resisting along the whole front," and No. 13, "German forces have counterattacked at numerous points along our front." These bulletins were enough to make readers and radio listeners chary of government pronouncements from then on.

At the headquarters of the German army in Poland, Keitel, Halder, and Brauchitsch were amazed that there was no real attack on the Siegfried Line—they believed a strong attack would easily have pushed to Berlin unopposed, for on Hitler's command the Westwall had been seriously stripped of forces. Because the Führer had gambled that the West would not mount a meaningful offensive and had won, the commanders' respect for his hunches increased.

The field commanders wanted Guderian to use his tanks to support the Third Army, which was marching south toward Warsaw. Guderian argued rather for a full-speed dash along uncontested terrain east of Warsaw toward Brest-Litovsk, where the retreating Poles hoped to establish new defensive positions. As his logic was strong, and as he was one of Hitler's favorites, the commanders let him go. There were larger considerations: German intelligence had completely lost track of several of the main Polish armies. Were they still west of Warsaw, or already east and southeast of the capital? Inclining to the latter hypothesis, the high command wanted von Rundstedt, who was in midcountry, to cross the Vistula and advance south toward Lublin. Deciding the high command was wrong, Rundstedt boldly wheeled Blaskowitz's Eighth and Reichenau's Tenth armies sharply north to surround the capital.

On September 8, advance German units reached the outskirts of Warsaw but could go no further. So they tried a propaganda maneuver. After saboteurs put the Warsaw radio station out of commission, a German transmitter began to broadcast on the same wavelength the message that Warsaw was falling. To give foreign listeners the impression Warsaw had been captured, the Germans enacted a deadly drama in English, with voices interrupted by screeching bombs and gunfire, and then by Chopin's funeral march.

But Warsaw had not fallen. The true Warsaw radio came back on the air within hours and broadcast Mayor Stefan Starzynski's appeal to citizens to take up arms against the invaders. South of Warsaw, General Anders surprised some isolated German units and annihilated them. On the Gdynia peninsula, Polish forces held a small strip of land against hopeless odds. And the Westerplatte garrison at Danzig resisted an onslaught by land, sea, and air for seven days before its surrender.

The most important Polish strike now came from the combined forces of General Kutrzeba and General Bortnowski. The Poznan and Pomeranian armies had infiltrated a large area west of Warsaw and north of the upper arm of the Vistula. On the night of September 8–9, when German intelligence believed they were hundreds of miles away, Kutrzeba and Bortnowski fell on the rear of Reichenau's Tenth Army. Fighting was fierce. At dawn, Reichenau called for Luftwaffe air strikes to rescue his men.

Meanwhile the advance on Warsaw was stopped by partisans who overturned streetcars to block roads, by men who sniped from windows, by women who approached tanks with baskets of hand grenades and did not seem to care if they themselves died in the explosion so long as they halted a tank. General Reinhardt had to pull back his XIV Corps, and he wrote headquarters:

> After heavy losses my attack on the city has had to be discontinued. Unexpectedly sharp resistance by the enemy with all weapons has rendered a single armored division supported by only four infantry battalions a quite insufficient force to obtain a decisive outcome.

The Luftwaffe could not help Reinhardt because it now had to rescue Blaskowitz's Eighth Army as well as Reichenau's Tenth.

Bortnowski and Kutrzeba cut down the extended and vulnerable lines of the German force. Without reinforcements this was a battle the Poles must eventually lose, but in the meantime they were inflicting great damage. Hitler's answer was more Luftwaffe pounding. For several days the action around Warsaw halted as the German air force lit into the Polish armies along the Bzura River. Hitler worried because every day that passed without total victory meant the danger of mud and the possibility of stepped-up Allied action.

When the war began in England, there was no singing, no will to victory, no overwhelming hatred of the enemy, as there had been at the onset of the Great War. Novelist Margery Allingham noted that this time

> everything moved with a sort of slow, irrevocable violence. All disasters must come like that, I fancy, but in the normal way one is so excited that one does not notice it. This time everything had been thought over so much that there was not the muddle of ideas which is excitement's staple ingredient, and you could see your section of civilization, the bit you had helped to build for better or for worse, cracking and splitting and crumbling as the shell hit it.

But there were no shells hitting England; no Luftwaffe planes screamed out of the skies to dive on English towns. As a consequence the British didn't quite know what to believe about the war. The government said the Polish situation was not yet out of hand, but if that was true and honor and commitments were to be kept, then why wasn't England really fighting?

Mass Observation, a government polling organization, reported in the first weeks of the war that people said it was useless to buy newspapers, because all the front pages were identical and therefore could not be believed. People chafed at the restrictions on information when there were no German air raids and no indication that Hitler was interested in doing anything whatever about the British Isles.

On September 11, Ironside told the war cabinet three half-truths. The first was the the the Poles "were putting up a good fight and were defending Warsaw vigorously. Their main army was still intact." This was technically correct, but wide of the mark. Ironside submitted a report that the Germans were conducting themselves "probably not in violation of the generally accepted principles of war . . . [and] were making an honest effort to restrict their bombing to military objectives." The report implied that the cabinet should continue to believe that the Germans were not bombing Polish civilians. Ironside also told the ministers that Gamelin's attack in the west was about to be launched with renewed vigor.

Next day Chamberlain met Gamelin and Daladier at Abbeville, France, and got a completely different picture of the war. Gamelin told the two governments' leaders: "It was evident that Poland could no longer resist, threatened in the rear by the Russians, and that the Germans were going to be in a position to turn their forces rapidly against us."

In making this judgment, Gamelin disregarded reports that the Polish armies were holding out in the country's center, and that German tanks were running out of fuel and were being blasted by the few remaining Polish fighter planes. For Gamelin, Poland was lost. He would, he said, encourage the Poles to fight on only so that he could have more time to build up France's defenses in the west. Poland was to be only a delaying action on behalf of the Allies, for "he had no intention of throwing his [French] army against the German main defenses. He had in fact issued strict instructions forbidding anything of the kind." The Allied Supreme War Council approved Gamelin's decision to stop the offensive in the west, and by implication accepted his reasoning for doing so. Thus on September 12, while the fate of Poland still hung in the balance, Allied intervention, which might still have altered that fate, ceased.

General von Briesen had just lost an arm as well as fifteen hundred men in the engagement on the Bzura. Nevertheless when Hitler arrived, Briesen briefed him on the fighting at the exact spot where Briesen's own father had fallen in battle in the Great War. German thrusts had reduced Kutrzeba's and Bortnowski's forces to one-third their former size, but the Poles still refused to surrender and were battering their way east to join the Warsaw garrison. Warsaw, Brest, Lublin, and Lwow had been ordered by the Polish high command to fight to the death so that other Polish army units could retreat to the Hungarian and Rumanian frontiers. From wireless intercepts, Hitler knew of that order. After von Briesen's briefing, Hitler said exuberantly, "That is just what I always imagined Prussian generals looked like when I was a child." He thought he would make Briesen head of the SS.

One of Hitler's adjutants noted in his diary, "It is the Führer's and Göring's intention to destroy and exterminate the Polish nation. More than that cannot even be hinted at in writing." Orders pertaining to the "intention" were deliberately kept verbal, so there would be no written records. Many high German officials tried not to know about Poland's agony—but nearly all knew the thrust, if not the details, of SS activities.

For example, when red-haired, green-eyed teenager Sala Kaminska came out of the forests near the Grabia River and returned to Lask, she talked with a German soldier who had taken over the family's rooms. The soldier thanked the family for the use of the rooms, and said, "You must not be afraid of us. We are only the Wehrmacht. You're a very sweet Polish family and we will not harm you. But soon the Gestapo, the Secret Police, will come, and those men you must fear. I hope you are not Jewish."

Next day the soldiers left, and the following day the SS arrived. Soon Jewish houses and stores were marked with the Star of David, and an order was posted on each door to deliver to the town hall by noon the following day all money, jewelry, and bedding except for one blanket per person. As people turned in their goods, some were beaten. Sala, being young and pretty, escaped this punishment. That night three Jewish men were shot to death.

Wilhelm Prüller, who was with a German unit marching toward Lublin, appears from his diary to have been one of the more pleasant and courteous soldiers. He paid for milk and cigarettes in one town, eggs and chocolate in another. In a third town he learned that the Jewish shops had all been plundered by the townspeople. Since his unit usually received only coffee for breakfast and soup for dinner, they foraged during the marches. One night they slaughtered and roasted a pig, made plum sauce for it, and ate it with gusto. The meal made them all long to be home. They were young and lonely, and yet for them, Prüller wrote in his diary, the first days of war had been "full of danger and wonderful experiences." Passing through the midsection of Poland, he described what he saw:

> Imagine a town of 30,000 inhabitants without even granite or stone-laid streets, much less an asphalt street. Dust. Nothing but dust. You just have to look at the houses the Polish peasant is forced to live in, you just have to consider the hundreds of thousands of illiterates here in Poland. It is quite natural that "social progress" proceeds at exactly this pace.

Prüller believed the ruling clique of Poland had withheld any sort of culture from the peasantry. "So it is now our job to free the Polish people from all this wretchedness, and, under our leadership, to make Poland into one of the happiest nations on earth."

As she fled from the Germans toward Rumania in a horse-drawn cart on a quiet back road, the English novelist contemplated the fate of Poland and the Poles, as exemplified by her husband. He spoke a half-dozen languages, knew intimately a thousand years of his country's history and culture, and was an engineer and a soldier. Now he was fleeing for his life, and the cities he had loved were being destroyed by the "barbarians." They moved slowly, the late afternoon lit by flares. The dull roar of bombers filled their ears, and they had the sense of the Germans continually at their heels. They waited for "something apocalyptic." One instant the novelist saw her husband frantically flogging the spent horse, and then experienced

> a red and searing agony, a mouthful of blood, eyes blind and warm with it, screams from the dying horse, the cart smashed to matchwood, myself knowing I must not lose the handbag with my papers and tearing my nails as I clawed for it on the road . . . the traffic perfectly unconscious of us in its path . . . blood streaming down my neck inside my dress.

She had five shrapnel wounds in her head, but felt lucky because both she and her husband were alive. For a time she could not see; when she could, her clothes had great sticky patches on them and dried blood fell out of her hair like powder. They continued to flee. Twenty-five people lay in a ditch, disemboweled by a bomb. In a town in which they took refuge, she saw children who had gone mad, roaming about, stopping to watch houses as they burned. She observed bitterly that war had taught her many new things:

> One of them is that the human animal is not, as a matter of fact, either sensitive or vulnerable. On the contrary, the creature has been given the most horrible powers of endurance. Almost nothing will finish it off. Shock after shock produces some further form of adaptation. Even starvation, provided it does get something about every sixteenth day or so, is not fatal to it. Bombed and shelled out of its home, it simply transfers its instinct for shelter to the four walls of a filthy railway truck, where the sun and the Heinkels find it. Bombed and machine-gunned out of the truck, it lies on its face on the ground and after an hour or two transfers its instincts to the hole it has clawed or to a doorway or a couple of planks.

In the chaos, she lost track of her husband, but kept on heading toward Rumania, hoping she could escape and one day be reunited with him. She made do with what she could; life was perilous and she took it a step at a time. Exhausted, she slept one night in a doorway, her body crowded on top of someone else. During the night she realized that instead of growing warmer, her neighbor was growing colder: he was dead.

One hundred fifty thousand Poles were captured near the Bzura, but Kutrzeba's army managed nevertheless to enter Warsaw, where a million people were now bottled up. General Blaskowitz angrily wrote, "What shocked even the most hardened soldier was how at the instigation of their military leaders a misguided population, completely ignorant of the effect of modern weapons, could contribute to the destruction of their own capital."

Warsaw held out. It was September 16. Hitler came to the edge of the city. His staff favored starving Warsaw into submission, but if he chose to starve the Poles, it might take some time. On the other hand, less blood might be shed than in an attack. Militarily the campaign was over, but Warsaw had not yet fallen. It was important to Hitler that Warsaw capitulate shortly, because the Russians would soon come into Poland, and he would be in a better position to bargain with them if he held Warsaw. Hitler ordered the Luftwaffe to drop leaflets giving the Poles twelve hours in which to leave before a saturation bombing would begin.

Because of an oversight or by nefarious design, the two designated exit roads were kept under heavy German artillery fire, and the Poles were unable to leave Warsaw. At midnight September 16–17, when the ultimatum ran out, Hitler stayed the bombers and tried once more to persuade the Poles to abandon the capital. They refused. He hesitated again, and as he waited, in the early dawn hours of September 17, across the whole thousand-mile front ranging from Latvia in the north to Rumania in the south, the Russian armies began to roll into Poland.

Moscow had been preparing the Russian people for this moment for about ten days. *Pravda* repeatedly cited the deteriorating situation in Poland and the necessity to "protect" Ukrainian and Byelorussian minorities there from "anarchy" resulting from the rapid German advance. Poland, *Pravda* said, had been following a scorched-earth policy against the Slavic brethren. The Red Army must do its "sacred duty." The propaganda machine built its case on three great fears. The first was that Germany, tacitly encouraged by Great Britain and France, would roll right through Poland and attack the U.S.S.R. The second was that Britain and France might threaten to bomb Russia from bases in Poland to force the U.S.S.R. to enter the war on the side of the Allies. The third was that Japan would reach agreement with Great Britain to attack Russia from the rear.

On September 16, a favorable and well-publicized peace treaty had been signed with Japan, ending the conflict in Mongolia. That eliminated the most realistic fear, and the next morning the Russians rolled into Poland.

In many cases the Russians had meager equipment. Horses and carts carried most of their million men. Some carts bore white flags. Russian propaganda troops shouted at Polish frontier guards not to shoot, saying they had come to assist them against the Germans. Echoing the slogans of 1917, they distributed leaflets which said the Russians had come to liberate the Polish workers. Soviet troops advanced forty miles the first day, virtually unopposed.

With a sigh and the knowledge that the game was up, Marshal Smigly-Rydz ordered his armies to oppose the Russians only if they became violent. In a few days the Russians encompassed thousands of square miles and millions of people at a cost of about five hundred Russian dead. Smigly-Rydz believed that what was left of Polish national honor would not be burnished by senseless fighting, which could only result in more casualties. He ordered his soldiers to cross into Rumania at a small bridge over a river. In order to avoid leaving their weapons for their enemies, the Poles carried their rifles with them; but to avoid giving the rifles to their friends, the Rumanians, they threw them in the river as they crossed. It seemed a paradigm of what had happened to the country. France had mounted a parody of an offensive on Poland's behalf; England had sent no bombers; Germany had refused to negotiate and had invaded; Russia had come in to pick up the spoils; and the Poles themselves had been stubborn when they might have yielded. The water flowing under the small bridge became clogged with guns and the bridge itself became jammed with diplomats, civilians, and soldiers trying to squeeze through the bottleneck to safety. Colonel Beck was among the stragglers. At one time, he had negotiated a mutual defense treaty with Rumania; he could therefore have asked Rumania to honor the treaty and declare war on Russia, but he decided that would only add to the confusion and make life more difficult at the border for those still trying to cross.

As Poland lay dying on September 17, the old British aircraft carrier *Courageous* steamed off Davenport, hunting U-boats. In fourteen days of war, twenty-one British ships had been sunk by submarines. To spot the undersea killers the *Courageous* sent her airplanes up, but they found nothing. In the late afternoon, as the cruiser-converted-to-carrier turned into the wind to receive the planes, two German torpedoes rammed the ship below the waterline.

The explosions immediately caused the carrier to begin to sink. Within five minutes, Captain W. T. Makeig-Jones gave the order to abandon ship. More than 500 men managed to swim to the escorting destroyers, but 687 died with the *Courageous*. Among the dead was Makeig-Jones, who was last seen on the bridge saluting the white ensign and exclaiming, "What a damned fine shot!" After the survivors had been rescued, the destroyers hunted the submarine which had fired the torpedoes, and believed by evening that they had sunk her. In English newspaper headlines the death of the *Courageous* nearly outweighed the final agony of Poland.

On September 19, CBS correspondent William Shirer, a close observer of Germany since the early 1930s, stood on a hill in the midst of Gdynia watching a battle between Poland and German troops that could not have been better planned if it had been personally arranged by Goebbels. A pocket of Polish resistance at Kepa Oksywska was hemmed in on three sides by German firepower and on the fourth by the sea. The *Schleswig-Holstein* fired shells at the Poles. Tanks, artillery, and dive-bombers attacked the enclave. The outnumbered and outgunned Poles fought on. Below in the streets of Gdynia, Shirer saw bitter-faced, silent women and children who watched the battle as they stood in line to obtain free food from the German conquerors. The pocket of resistance was soon annihilated, and Shirer could not help but be impressed by the efficiency of the Germans.

In the afternoon all the correspondents were escorted to the Danzig Guild Hall for a speech by the Führer. Hitler had wanted to deliver this speech in Warsaw, but that city still held out despite round-the-clock bomber raids. Shirer observed that the speech was not one of Hitler's better efforts. It was full of vilification of England and of the Poles, who had acted "in the most bestial fashion" and with "perverse instincts." But Hitler was proud that his armies had vanquished Poland in two and a half weeks.

The invasion and conquest of Poland was labelled a blitzkrieg by the Nazi propaganda machine. It was not a lightning blow with tanks and air cover; most of the victory was won by conventional arms. But in its speed, thoroughness, and guile the German assault changed many rules of warfare which had stood for centuries. There had been no time allowed to redress the grievances before the invasion, no declaration of war by the aggressor, no will to honor commitments on the part of the Allies, no time for the ponderous machinery of the democracies' military might, no refusal to hurt civilians, and no courteous treatment of a vanquished enemy. Poland was done, and a strange passage of the war was about to begin—a war that was not war.

Danzigers cheered lustily as the Führer rode through the crowded streets toward a seaside resort hotel. He planned a week of rest. That night at the hotel, as his aides drank champagne toasts, he joined the celebration, though his glass held only sparkling water. His mood was irrepressible.

part two

THE PHONY WAR

⟞‑◦◦◦‑⟝

September 1939
to May 1940

6

Beginnings

After the death of Poland, it seemed to many as if the war was over, even if there was no peace treaty. There began a cold, curious, and unsettled time which Senator William E. Borah almost immediately dubbed "the phony war." In this time, many of the great themes of the war to come had their origin; most began to be sounded quietly, behind the scenes, where the public did not know of them.

President Roosevelt believed the war would soon continue, and he needed information on its future course. His ambassadors in the Allied capitals did not provide it. During the shooting war he had received a cable from Ambassador Joseph P. Kennedy in London that said the war was nearly over and that Roosevelt should jump in as a peacemaker. The president characterized the cable to Postmaster General Jim Farley as "the silliest message . . . I have ever received," and told Henry Morgenthau, Jr., that his old supporter and campaign contributor Joe Kennedy was a pain in the neck and an appeaser: "If Germany and Italy made a good peace offer tomorrow, Joe would start working on the King and his friend the Queen and from there on down to get everybody to accept it."

It seemed as if Kennedy had neither principles nor fighting spirit in him. Ambassador to France William Bullitt was not much better. Bullitt was an anti-Nazi, an anti-Communist, and an ardent Francophile. He and Roosevelt had been young men together at the Versailles Peace Conference in 1919. Roosevelt told friends he would receive a morning cable from Paris saying the political situation was calm; then Bullitt would go to lunch with a high official and Roosevelt would receive an afternoon cable saying precisely the opposite. Bullitt's September dispatches contended that France might fall instanter if enormous American supplies did not reach her armies. The acute phase of the war ended, and France still stood. Roosevelt told friends he had begun to discount by half everything in a Bullitt-in.

Believing that the war would continue, Roosevelt set out to change America's neutrality laws. He called Congress into special session and brought to the task of revision all the qualities of political generalship that had characterized the early fervor of the New Deal. He mended fences. He made peace with Jim Farley, who had become disenchanted, placated Vice-President John Garner and mollified Representative Sam Rayburn, who had begun to ally himself with a 1940 Garner presidential bid. These men he then sent to do battle in the halls of Congress. He also went after more avowed political opponents. He asked Al Smith for help. Ever since Roosevelt had beaten Smith for the 1932 Democratic presidential nomination, Smith had opposed much of Roosevelt's social legislation. But the threat of war meant more to Al Smith than his ideological differences with Roosevelt. The country's leading lay Catholic, Smith agreed to speak out to counter the rhetorical fog of the isolationist and anti-Semitic "radio priest," Father Charles Coughlin. Roosevelt further persuaded his 1936 election opponent, Alf Landon, along with former cabinet officer Henry Stimson and newspaper publisher Frank Knox—Republicans all—to make radio broadcasts in favor of the proposed changes.

As the controversy grew, the main challenge to Roosevelt came from the elusive hero Charles A. Lindbergh. In the years since his solo flight over the Atlantic, Lindbergh had become the foremost advocate of air travel and one of the world's most recognized men. A private person, he had not made a radio speech in eight years, not even when his son had been kidnapped and the airwaves had been offered to him so that he might appeal for help. Neutrality revision was anathema to him. His father, a congressman, had openly opposed United States entry into the Great War, and Lindbergh felt that to repeal or to alter the strict existing statutes would be to start again on the road to war. On a Sunday evening he told an immense American radio audience that should we ever go into the war,

> we must throw the entire resources of our entire nation into the conflict. Munitions alone will not be enough. We cannot count upon victory merely by shipping abroad several thousand airplanes and cannon. We are likely to lose a million men, possibly several million—the best of American youth. We will be staggering under the burden of recovery during the rest of our lives.

Lindbergh had seen the Luftwaffe and did not think that it could reach our shores. He said we should retreat to safety behind our oceans— quite a statement from one who had himself bridged an ocean in a small plane—and stay completely out of "the internal struggles of Europe."

Lindbergh was a serious man, and his ideas demanded serious consideration. That they echoed the thoughts of many was reflected in the fact that his speech generated a million pieces of mail to Congress supporting his views. Polls showed that 80 to 90 percent of the people queried wanted no part of "Europe's war." These polls also suggested that if Roosevelt pushed too hard he risked arousing the electorate to anger and his efforts might boomerang.

Roosevelt reacted savagely to Lindbergh. He privately let it be known that Lindbergh's aura had been considerably dented because he had accepted a medal from Göring and implied that Lindbergh was a Nazi admirer. According to Lindbergh's most recent biographer, Walter S. Ross, Roosevelt forced the aviator onto the inactive list of the army reserve and also ordered his tax returns audited. Taking another tack, Roosevelt let Lindbergh know through intermediaries that if he behaved himself and made no more speeches, he might be offered the cabinet secretaryship of a new American air force. Neither threats nor blandishments deterred Lindbergh. He continued to speak out.

Publicly Roosevelt ignored Lindbergh and took the stance that the issue was above petty squabbling. The reason for changing the neutrality statutes, he told Congress, was to keep us out of war, and "regardless of party or section, the mantle of peace and of patriotism is wide enough to cover us all. Let no group assume the exclusive label of the 'peace bloc.' We all belong to it." Part of his reform package called for new regulations to keep American ships out of European waters: if such regulations had been in force in 1917, Roosevelt said, the United States might never have entered the Great War.

There were some things the executive branch could do without waiting for congressional action. Roosevelt ordered forty destroyers out of mothballs and sent Secretary of State Cordell Hull to confer in Panama with the other countries of the western hemisphere. At the conference, Hull proposed an inter-American patrol which would protect all the Americas (excluding Canada, already at war). The patrol would be made up of American coast guard and navy vessels, but would serve all the countries. The security zone would be off limits to ships of belligerent countries, and for the duration of the war, inter-American commerce would replace trade with Europe. Having nothing to lose, the other nations quickly agreed to the plan. Wags dubbed the new zone "the pan-American chastity belt," but Roosevelt saw it as a thinly disguised pro-Allied Atlantic patrol. He personally ordered United States ships and planes to report in plain English and not in code the sighting of suspicious submarines or surface ships and to "remain in contact as long as possible" with such vessels. This would obviously alert nearby British ships, which could then move in for the kill.

When on the afternoon of September 3 Winston Churchill came to the Admiralty, it was to take up a post he "had quitted in pain and sorrow almost exactly a quarter-century before." The signal went out to the far-flung fleets, "Winston is back," and the reaction was joyous, for

Churchill's return to office meant an end to shilly-shallying. The first lord of the Admiralty marveled that his old chair, desk, and map case still awaited him. Moreover:

> Once again the defense of the rights of a weak state, outraged and invaded by unprovoked aggression, forced us to draw the sword. Once again we must fight for life and honour against all the might and fury of the valiant, disciplined, and ruthless German race. Once again! So be it.

The Admiralty's famous board room was a place encrusted with tradition. Between portraits of Nelson and William IV was an intricate wind dial which was connected to a weather vane on the roof. The dial's face was faintly mapped with Britain's bordering seas, ornamented with whales and other allegorical figures; heraldic symbols represented the neighboring countries. Adjacent to the dial were hand-carved pearwood medleys of fruit, flowers, nautical instruments, and the royal insignia. In this room Churchill and the ranking admirals made their decisions. One of the first was to order submarine-hunting ships to sail separately from convoys. Naval historian Stephen W. Roskill contends this resulted in the sinking of the *Courageous*, as there was no reason to send such a large ship on the mission which brought her to grief:

> Although the disaster caused the immediate withdrawal of fleet carriers from U-boat hunting, this was by no means the last occasion on which the old fallacy regarding the alleged superiority of seeking for enemies in the ocean spaces instead of convoying shipping with the greatest possible strength, and so forcing the enemy to reveal his presence within range of immediate counter-attack, reared its hoary head in British circles. Half a century previously Mahan had condemned it, and after World War I both Admiral Beatty (R.N.), and Admiral Sims (U.S.N.) went on record with similar opinions based on their recent experience; yet in 1939 the whole massive weight of historical evidence was ignored.

Soon after the *Courageous* went down, orders were issued for sub hunters to travel only with convoys.

Some 2,500 ships daily sailed to and from and around the British Isles and supplied the nation with food and raw materials. Maintaining this lifeline became the first priority for the Royal Navy. Churchill quickly decided to stop construction of large destroyers, which took too long to build, and to order the rapid completion of small corvettes, which would serve just as well for antisubmarine hunting. Nearly a dozen corvettes could be constructed in the time it took to finish one destroyer.

Some things that affected the navy were out of Churchill's control. In the early weeks of the war the bomber command of the RAF decided not to "waste ammunition" on submarines, even though three air squadrons had been specifically established to hunt U-boats. Such edicts made it evident to Churchill that no one understood the gravity of the war except himself, and so he set to work with great personal force to make everyone aware of the urgency of the struggle. With his memos, many beginning "Pray inform me," or demanding "action this day," he inspired his Admiralty staff. Admiral Godfrey wrote that his bag of tricks also included "persuasion, real or simulated anger, mockery, vituperation, tantrums, ridicule, derision, abuse and tears, which he would aim at anyone who opposed him or expressed a view contrary to the one he had already formed, sometimes on quite trivial questions."

Daily Churchill sent memoranda to Chamberlain, for he simply could not and would not restrict himself to naval matters. He wrote missives on civilian blackout precautions, air force bombing policy, the age of ministers in the new war cabinet, the utility of telegrams to the Foreign Office, the need for a ministry of shipping. As the shooting phase of the war came to a close, an already exhausted Chamberlain replied, "All your letters are carefully read and considered by me, and if I have not replied to them it is only because I am seeing you every day, and moreover, because as far as I have been able to observe your views and mine have very closely coincided." Churchill ignored the hint to stop, and sent more letters on the problems of the exchequer, an antiwaste campaign, the peace offensive, relations with Russia, and the fact that he would be away for the weekend.

At about this time a letter came to Churchill from a most unusual source, the president of the United States. Roosevelt chattily suggested that, as men who had occupied similar positions in the Great War and who were interested in naval matters, they keep in close personal touch and use the diplomatic pouches to convey informal letters. As a good subordinate should, Churchill showed the letter to Chamberlain and asked the prime minister's permission to answer it, promising that whatever he might write to Roosevelt would be shown to Chamberlain before it went out. Chamberlain gave permission, and a famous correspondence was born.

The relationship between Chamberlain and Churchill was a delicate one. They were far from friends, yet Churchill, grateful for the chance to serve, was consistently proper with Chamberlain, and on his side the prime minister was deferential. Though in peacetime Churchill could not muster enough power to become prime minister, so long as England was at war his reputation gave him the power to bring down Chamberlain's government if he so chose. He did not use this power.

During the interwar years, unofficial groups had formed. One, the December group, included Churchill, Leo Amery, Edward Spears, and such younger MPs as Harold Macmillan, Harold Nicolson, and Duncan Sandys. A second group formed around Anthony Eden, who had resigned in 1938 as foreign secretary as a protest against appeasement. The membership of both groups overlapped. Opponents called them "the glamour boys," and feared and despised their collective power. They were among the more brilliant of the politicians, and from the outset of the war they became a political nucleus that bypassed party affiliations to support Churchill. Chamberlain's cabinet contained none of these men except Churchill, and no ministers from the Labour party—and was therefore considered somewhat unstable for a wartime cabinet. A hard push might topple it.

Chamberlain knew Churchill was a powerful speaker and knew the government could use that power, so he let Churchill speak out. The first lord's speeches in Commons were as fully reported as Chamberlain's. One, *The New York Times* said, "covered many fields beyond the scope of the Admiralty, not excluding foreign relations, and it was an address such as one might expect the head of the government to deliver." Through such speeches Churchill began to build a position as leader of an "alternate government" waiting in the wings.

As for Churchill's military ideas, they were sometimes brilliant and sometimes harebrained. Some sparks generated by his overheated mind caught fire, others fizzled out. He was the champion if not always the originator of ideas for carrying the war to Germany without an actual invasion. Three early ideas were significant. Operation Catherine was a plan to cut off Germany's oil supply; Operation Royal Marine would disrupt Rhine River traffic by means of fluvial mines which would explode barges, ships, and floating bridges; Operation Wilfred would cut off Germany's access to Swedish iron ore by mining the Norwegian coastal waters.

In London the *Daily Telegraph* reported that the entertainment trade unions had petitioned for the reopening of theaters and movie houses; the *Daily Mail* noted that football leagues had reformed out of town now that their London grounds were off limits; according to the *Daily Herald,* authorities in three towns had applied for the relaxation of blackout restrictions because of serious automobile accidents. For England, the war seemed to have come and gone.

But the social catastrophe was just beginning. Over a million and a half children, mothers, and teachers from London and twenty-six other cities had been evacuated to the countryside. Not many country women wanted to take more than a couple of children, and very few of them enjoyed having the mothers and teachers sharing their hearths. Some of the children had head lice or wet their beds. Some of the mothers and teachers were much too attractive to the local men. The government had made no attempt to house middle-class children with middle-class families, or lower with lower. Upper-class children presented no such problems, for they went where money could send them—frequently abroad.

Exiled Londoner Ursula Bloom had taken in some children and

observed others in her neighbors' houses. She concluded:

> The Cockney child very soon becomes homesick for its lamp standards
> and pavements. It pines for cinemas and fried fish shops. It finds the wide
> open spaces bleak and unsatisfactory, is afraid of the country's animals,
> and cannot understand a form of life where it is not able to spend its spare
> time . . . playing hopscotch on convenient payment squares.

Letters-to-the editor columns were filled with complaints about the
personal habits of evacuees, the inadequate money paid to harbor
them, and the fact that they tended to drift off toward home after a few
weeks and were not particularly grateful to their former hosts for their
hospitality. The cabinet was obliged to spend considerable time on such
problems.

Believing the war was far from over, and that a blitzkrieg aimed at
the West was imminent after Poland's fall, one day in late September
Belgium and the Netherlands opened their dikes. The sea inundated
many hundreds of square miles around Utrecht, Liège, and Antwerp.
These "experimental floodings," the first since 1672 (when Britain and
France had invaded Holland), were described as a warning to Germany
that the Low Countries could halt an invasion. Access to the entire
western portion of Holland, which included Amsterdam, Haarlem, Rotterdam, and The Hague, could be denied by flooding. The Dutch also
let it be known that they had mobilized 600,000 troops (far more than
England had) and would keep them at full readiness despite the enormous cost to their economy.

As September wore on, the neutrals' fear of war was exacerbated
by the hardships caused by the joint German and Allied blockades. In
Holland, glucose mills closed because there was no imported grain;
without imported iron the steel mills let their fires die, and without
imported Australian wool the clothing factories shut down. Thousands
were thrown out of work. Lest the Belgians transship food to Germany,
grain ships bound for Belgium from her own African colonies were
diverted to France. Belgium, Holland, Denmark, and Sweden all began
rationing.

Other small countries felt the jaws of war in an even more serious
way. Worried by the inordinate speed of the German advance, and by
the fear that his partner might next turn on him, Joseph Stalin quickly
began to rake in the chips owed him under the secret protocol of the
nonaggression pact: "In the event of a territorial and political transformation in the territories belonging to the Baltic States, the northern
frontier of Lithuania shall represent the frontier of the spheres of interest both of Germany and of the U.S.S.R."

Translated into practical terms, this meant that the Soviet Union
was to have a free hand in the Baltic. The team of Vyacheslav Molotov

(hammer) and Stalin (steel) worked out a standard procedure to effect control of the region. A plenipotentiary would be summoned to the Kremlin from, say, Estonia. Molotov would be tough with him. The official would be asked to sign a mutual defense treaty with the Soviet Union, and would be told that 100,000 Red Army troops would shortly arrive on his borders to guarantee the peace of the region and that these troops would be billeted in his country at his country's expense. The visitor would blanch at the idea and beg a little forbearance. Molotov would take him to see Stalin; the dictator would benevolently suggest to Molotov in the official's presence that perhaps only 50,000 troops would be required and that the official and his friends might be relied on to stay in power and help administer the peace. Inordinately grateful for the lessening of the burden and the sparing of his neck, the plenipotentiary would forthwith sign on the dotted line.

Estonia became a Soviet protectorate within weeks of Poland's death. Before Estonia was completely in the fold, Molotov began the same playlet with Lithuania and Latvia. These countries also entered the protective sphere and disappeared. Few in the world community raised more than an eyebrow over these victims of the twilight war, and those who did objected on humanitarian grounds.

Winston Churchill, who had consistently argued against letting the strong take over the weak, did not rail against Russia's expansion, even though he had been a vociferous opponent of Communism for more than twenty years. Russia, Churchill said in a much-quoted line in the fall of 1939, might be "a riddle wrapped in a mystery inside an enigma," but the explanation of Russian expansion was straightforward and simple:

> Russian national interest. It cannot be in accordance with the interest or safety of Russia that Germany should plant herself upon the shores of the Black Sea, or that it should overrun the Balkan States and subjugate the Slavonic peoples of southeastern Europe.

Churchill concluded that Stalin had moved so that Russia would have a clear eastern front against the Nazis, and that Russia's move was good for the democracies. He wanted to send a new emissary to Moscow. Chamberlain, who still hated the Russians, did not; he was unable to forgive Stalin's rapid turn toward Germany.

Mikhail Soloviev had been a deskman on *Izvestia* when Stalin had tired of editor Nikolai Bukharin's advice. Bukharin died, but Soloviev's punishment was slighter: he had been forbidden to reside within a hundred kilometers of any of Russia's six largest cities or to do any newspaper work. For several years Soloviev had lived in a dreary factory town one hundred kilometers outside Moscow and had taught literature and journalism to young men and women when they were not at work at the Proletarka and Vagzhanovka factories. In September, his courses were closed, and students who showed real interest were sent to the Moscow Institute for Journalism, where, Soloviev was sure, their zest for newspaper work would be effectively eliminated.

On a rainy fall day, Soloviev was summoned to the regional office of the secret police. He observed that for some reason Cheka men were fond of the old seigneurial estates, perhaps because they had high walls and hidden rooms which could be used for torture. With fifteen other men he stood in a garden near the guardhouse, afraid to lean against the newly whitewashed walls or talk. One by one the men were called into an office. None returned. Finally the orderly shouted Soloviev's name, and as he walked down a long corridor Soloviev had no idea whether he was to be imprisoned, or worse. He was thrust into an office occupied by a minor official. The man had indifferent eyes and an outsized uniform; with a bored look he told Soloviev that his period of "minus six" was now over and that he was to report within the hour to military headquarters for induction.

All summer long, twenty-one-year-old Vyaschlev Oreshin had been "hanging about between heaven and earth" and trying to get a job as an editor of extracts from Komsomol documents. Meanwhile he had practiced throwing hand grenades with his training unit. As he told his diary, "Everything that is dangerous attracts me. For instance, I am very fond of catching snakes with my hands. I wonder why this is? Perhaps I want to learn to know myself (a man only knows himself in a moment of danger)?" Oreshin wrote letters to his fiancée, Shura, who was away on a collective farm, and tried to keep his thoughts about her pure. He hoped for the day when his application for membership in the Communist party would be approved, for then he could become a full-fledged *politruk*, an officer in a propaganda unit charged with the political instruction of the soldiers. After Poland, he was mobilized. He learned that his unit would be moving into Estonia, although possibly Estonia might not be its final destination.

One afternoon after the war was officially over in Poland, Wilhelm Prüller was captured by a band of Polish soldiers in a swamp near Lwow. One moment the place was peaceful, but the next moment he found himself caught in a cross fire between his own unit and the Poles. He clutched his diary and believed it and his talisman would keep him alive. When the shooting stopped, he was amazed to find himself captured by the Poles, who were kind and correct to him and who gave him food. "Many of them are actually human beings!" he noted in the diary. He had faith that the German army would soon rescue him. For nearly a week he and twenty-two other prisoners moved with the Poles. Prüller grew faint with hunger and weary from lack of sleep, and took small comfort from the fact that his guards suffered exactly the same conditions. One afternoon when the Poles drove their wagons into a wood, Prüller crawled behind a tree, and anticipated nothing more than another night without food. He heard shots in the woods and saw the Poles emerging with their hands raised. He wondered:

> Are the Germans coming? The Ukrainians? It's a foreign command, anyhow! As I get out of the woods I recognize them: they are our Russian allies! I can't describe this moment, the emotion inside of me. I felt no joy. I didn't laugh. Or cry. Or weep. I wasn't touched at all. Only someone who rises from the dead can know this feeling.

Almost at once the Russians gave the twenty-three Germans rifles, and then, Prüller noted in the diary, they were soldiers again.

The defense of Warsaw had been magnificent. Every thirty seconds the city's radio had broadcast the opening notes of Chopin's "Polonaise" to announce to the world that Warsaw still lived. By September 25, Luftwaffe raids had left the city without food, gas, water, or electricity for a week. Twenty-five thousand lay dead in the rubble; starving people cut pieces of flesh from dying horses. The war was over, but out of some ancient conception of honor and resistance 800,000 civilians and 100,000 troops in Warsaw defied the Nazis. On Hitler's direct orders the bombing escalated. After two more terrible days of round-the-clock bombing, resistance ended. On September 28, the Warsaw radio played a funeral dirge, and the city surrendered. Many of the dead lay undiscovered in the rubble until the following spring.

Joachim von Ribbentrop arrived in Moscow for toasts, bear hugs, a banquet, and to arrange the "final partition" of Poland. In the negotiations, Poland ceased to exist. Germany got full control of Warsaw, and the Reich's frontier was once more moved eastward from the Vistula to the Bug River. This delighted Ribbentrop, but Stalin was more delighted because in exchange for that worthless territory he obtained important concessions from the gullible foreign minister, taking over a section of Polish territory which abutted Rumania and included the oil fields near Lwow. Germany was left with no common border with Rumania. This meant that the Third Reich could obtain oil from Lwow or from the Ploesti oil fields in Rumania only if that oil was shipped over Soviet-controlled lines. Such shipments were assured so long as Germany and Russia remained partners, but should Russia ever wish to shut off Germany's oil supply, it could be easily done.

"Housecleaning" was the euphemism for the executions and other repressive measures the SS took against the Poles. Halder noted that housecleaning was to be deferred until after the military had ceded power in Poland to a civilian government, but soldiers were only slowly being transferred to the Westwall when Heydrich deported a first group of Jews to German labor camps and presented a report to Hitler which suggested setting up ghettos in Poland. Such enclosed areas would assist the SS in keeping track of three million Jews; in his report Heydrich used for the first time the chilling phrase "final solution." Its meaning was as yet obscure. Hitler appointed his former lawyer Hans Frank to head the civilian government in Poland. Artur Seyss-Inquart, an Austrian cabinet minister who had betrayed his country from within and then helped to govern it, was appointed second in command. Together with the SS, these men set out almost immediately to complete the destruction of all that was Polish.

General Johannes Blaskowitz had earned Hitler's displeasure by allowing his troops to be caught near the Bzura, and perhaps as a punishment he was made military governor of Poland and chief of the army's peacekeeping force. Blaskowitz wanted only to be left alone. There was no joy in being military governor of this conquered province. He knew at least in outline what the SS was doing, as did all the upper-echelon officers, and he didn't want to know the particulars. He set up headquarters in a forest, put roadblocks on the access routes, had a private landing field installed, and told his troops, "The Eastern Army must concern itself with purely soldierly assignments and is freed from all that has to do with administration and internal politics."

Nevertheless soldiers from all ranks made their way to Blaskowitz and complained of SS atrocities. From Cracow General Ulex blasted "the multiplication of deeds of violence on the part of police forces which show an absolutely incredible lack of human and moral feeling, so that one can actually speak of men becoming animals." This situation, Ulex said, was "staining the honor of the German nation." Blaskowitz slowly began to agree, and to amass evidence against the SS. People had been shot as examples in many small towns, and they had also been unjustly rounded up and put in prison. Five thousand people had been crammed into the old citadel at Poznan, which had been built to handle perhaps two thousand at most. When Blaskowitz had accumulated enough specific evidence, he sent it to Berlin. It was ignored.

There were more and uglier things going on in Poland than ever reached Blaskowitz's eyes or ears. The prison at Poznan had actually become a Gestapo training school in torture methods. As the coldest winter in forty-six years began, guard trainees played vicious games with the prisoners. In "dog," prisoners had to go about on all fours and bark, after which they were whipped into unconsciousness; in "rabbit," prisoners were shot for sport as they ran along interior passageways. In the country as a whole there were constant executions. Gallows were set up in Lodz. People were burned alive in Lublin. In other cities men and women were beheaded. There are no accurate documentary records, but the best educated guess is that in the latter months of 1939 between fifty and a hundred thousand people in what had been Poland were executed or died of neglect at German hands.

In Lask, Sala Kaminska was assigned to clean the washrooms in the police barracks. All Jews were given similar work. Their German masters seemed split down the middle: one moment the band would play marches and waltzes; the next moment the musicians would throw Jewish sacred scrolls in the mud, kick Catholic crucifixes out of windows, and rob passersby. Every few days gray execution lists plastered the walls. Many tried to escape. Sala and her family stayed. One day in the back room of the barracks some SS men grabbed her and forced her to strip. When she didn't remove her clothes quickly enough they ripped them from her. Afraid for her life, she heard one of the Germans shout, "I can't have you, scum, because you're Jewish, and filthy. Here's what you can have instead for being a dirty Jew!" And he whipped her until she fainted. Much later her mother came to fetch her. At least, Sala said, she was alive.

The Jewish community in Munich often sent packages to Poland to aid the unhappy Jews. Elspeth Rosenfeld, whose husband had succeeded in emigrating just before the war had begun, was active in such work. As one who could pass for an Aryan and who was only half Jewish, Elspeth went often to mail the small parcels at the post office. One day a colleague very precisely defined the plight of the Jews who were still left inside the Reich:

> Let us keep in mind that, whatever happens to us, there is nothing we can undertake to save ourselves from the fate the Nazis decide for us. We have hoped for a long time that the other nations might come to our help. . . . Nothing has happened. On the contrary, most other countries have made it more difficult for us to go there. During the last year every Jew in the whole Reich has tried to leave Germany. They have collected the dozens of necessary papers and their passports with the large "J" on the cover. This has given the Nazis all the documents and records about every one of us, and it is all efficiently and neatly filed. Even passive resistance would be utterly hopeless. It could only make it easier for them to destroy us. That's our situation. Let us try to go on from day to day, do what we can to help our people when they are penniless. That is all we can do.

Journalist Charlotte Beradt might have applied such a description to all Germans who were not avid Nazis. For years Beradt had roamed the country to collect people's dreams. She transcribed them, hid the transcripts in her books, and sent some to "safe" addresses out of the country whence she would eventually recover them. In one dream, a factory owner participated in a tension-filled version of an ordinary scene:

> Propaganda Minister Goebbels was visiting my factory. He had all the workers line up in two rows facing each other. I had to stand in the middle and raise my arm in the Nazi salute. It took me half an hour to get my arm up, inch by inch. Goebbels showed neither approval nor disapproval as he watched my struggle, as if it were a play. When I finally managed to get my arm up, he said just five words—"I don't want your salute"—then turned and went to the door. There I stood in my own fac-

tory, arm raised, pilloried right in the midst of my own people. I was only able to keep from collapsing by staring at his clubfoot as he limped out. And so I stood until I woke up.

Beradt found that people struggled in their dreams with the implacable forces of the regime. An elderly gentleman dreamed that:

> In place of the street signs, which had been abolished, posters had been set up on every corner, proclaiming in white letters on a black background the twenty words which people were not allowed to say. The first was "Lord"—to be on the safe side I must have dreamt it in English. I don't recall the following words and possibly didn't even dream them, but the last one was "I."

Even in dreams it was difficult to resist:

> It was in a motion picture theater.... Newsreel. Göring appeared in a brown leather jerkin, shooting a crossbow, which made me laugh out loud.... All of a sudden, I was standing there next to him, wearing the same kind of jerkin and carrying the same kind of crossbow—how I got there I don't know—and he made me his personal archer.

Sybil Bannister and her husband, Kurt, who was on leave from the Luftwaffe, went house hunting in a newly German town. Bromberg had been Bydgoszcz, where ten thousand Poles had been executed in retaliation for assaults on the *Volkdeutsche.* Sybil and Kurt knew about the killings, but felt they could do little about them. They had their own problems. Kurt, the only gynecologist in town, was exhausted from his work. Sybil wanted to find a home and proper food for the baby. Their marriage was often under a strain. Kurt went to parties without Sybil, as if he believed that his career would be hurt if too many people knew he was married to an Englishwoman.

Sybil hoped that a house of their own would bring them closer together. They were sent to look at a large and comfortable one. The German woman who lived there could not understand why they had come. She and her Polish husband had owned the house for many years; a few days before, her husband had been taken away without warning. She asked Kurt to help find him. Presented with the problem in such personal terms, Kurt agreed. He made inquiries and found out that the husband had been shot that very morning—which was, of course, the reason he and Sybil had been sent to look at the house in the first place; the wife was to be evicted at any moment. When Kurt protested, he was told to mind his own business. He and Sybil expressed their dismay by not taking the house. They would not add to the distress of the woman they had met. But they soon moved into another equally large and comfortable house and did not ask questions about how it happened to be available.

Hitler planned an invasion of the West, code name Fall Gelb, or

Plan Yellow. Within a month, German armies would sweep into Belgium and France. As the invasion was charted he simultaneously pursued peace in an attempt to get the Allies out of the war. He had information that factions in England and France might find a peace proposal appealing.

Despite the success of his Luftwaffe in Poland, Göring still worried about Allied numerical superiority in planes. He proposed that Dahlerus go to London and ask Chamberlain to arrange a meeting at which Göring and Ironside would set up a Polish state in which to resettle all of Europe's Jews. Hitler agreed to the scheme.

Dahlerus did meet with Chamberlain, but what happened to the proposal is unclear. British files on the subject are closed to the public until 1990, and other British files on negotiations with Germany during this period are closed until 2015. German evidence suggests that the proposal was not rejected out of hand, and that there were other peace feelers: someone in the British Air Ministry made an approach through Switzerland, and someone else revived Sir Horace Wilson's divide-the-world proposal. A possible conclusion is that while some in England favored negotiations with Germany in late September and early October of 1939, others—perhaps Churchill—argued that to negotiate away Poland would vitiate the British reason for having gone to war in the first place, and would be unacceptable at home. Further feelers came through Italy. Tacitly encouraged by the British and the French, Mussolini continued to press for a revival of his own peace initiative. He was ignored by Berlin.

An odd episode involved the United States. William Rhodes Davis, a man with extensive Berlin contacts and Mexican oil holdings, asked John L. Lewis, head of the powerful United Mine Workers union, to set up a meeting for him with President Roosevelt. At that meeting, Davis said that his sources in Berlin told him that Göring wanted peace, and that the air marshal might manage to force Hitler from power in order to achieve peace. Davis proposed that he go to Berlin and get Göring to tip his hand. Roosevelt did not encourage such a move but did agree that Davis might go to Berlin as an unofficial emissary to find out whether Hitler would initiate negotiations and to suggest that the United States could act as an intermediary—but only if officially asked to do so.

In Berlin, Davis met with Göring, an old acquaintance. According to German reports, he told Göring that Roosevelt wanted peace and would pressure the Allies to negotiate, and that Roosevelt had said America's main concern was to break England's trade monopoly. He outlined a peace settlement in which Germany would keep Danzig and the former German provinces in Poland, would regain her former African colonies, and would get financial assistance from the United States to help achieve a higher standard of living. Should England and France not go along with the program, the United States would supply arms to Germany and not to the Allies. (Davis represented these ideas as Roosevelt's, but no American evidence supports his contention.) Göring reported to Hitler, who determined to make some use of the information. He sent a special ambassador back to Washington with Davis and Davis was directed to obtain Roosevelt's reply to the "initial proposals"—in other words, an official recapitulation of the above arrangements—by October 5. Hitler could then incorporate them into a speech scheduled for October 6. Roosevelt did not see Davis until October 12, and no more was heard about the affair.

On October 5, Hitler took a planeload of international newsmen with him to Warsaw. Seventy-five percent of the city lay in ruins and was uninhabitable. In the least damaged section, which had been embassy row, Hitler reviewed fifteen thousand German troops. Before his arrival, all the Poles had been forced away from the parade route and reviewing platform, and newsmen reported that it was doubtful if even a single Pole saw Hitler during the visit. German communiqués boasted that a half-million Polish troops had been captured and one hundred thousand Poles had been killed. Twenty-five thousand of the dead lay in the Warsaw rubble. "Take a look around Warsaw," Hitler told the newsmen. "That is how I can deal with any European city."

Next morning for two hours in the Kroll Opera House, Hitler painted a glorious picture of the Polish campaign before turning to the subject of peace. He had no quarrel with France and would like to come to an understanding with England. An international conference should settle the fate of Europe and encourage disarmament, but the fate of Poland had already been decided by Germany and Russia. There must be peace on his terms, or war. The true roadblocks to peace were such men as Winston Churchill, a representative of international Jewry.

That evening General Wilhelm von Leeb, commander of Hitler's forces in the West, noted in his diary that Hitler's speech was not a real peace offer because "all arrangements . . . point to the intention of making this insane attack in violation of the neutrality of Holland, Belgium, and Luxembourg. So Hitler's speech was nothing more than the deception of the German people."

7

Winds of Change

After his October 6, speech, Hitler spent two days dictating a fifty-eight-page memorandum which was designed to quash any possible objections to the invasion of the West. On October 10, he assembled Brauchitsch, Halder, Keitel, and a few other senior officers for an important meeting.

Hitler said the German struggle for Europe had begun in 1648. His current military aim was "the final military dispatch of the West," so that the democracies could never again block German expansion. The Reich must strike "this autumn," before England rearmed, before British troops (who must not be underestimated) bolstered the lackadaisical French, before raw materials became scarce. "Time is to be viewed as working against Germany." The Allies might make a pre-emptive invasion of Holland and Belgium to obtain bases from which to strike at the vulnerable Ruhr. Therefore Germany must strike first, in order to protect the Ruhr, and to gain bases from which to reach England. Fall Gelb must thrust through Belgium and to the Channel while avoiding the big cities; the Polish campaign had taught them that tanks must not be tied to slow-moving troops but must have the opportunity to break free and cover territory. In the West the objective would be the destruction of the British and French armies. In a few days he would give the date on which this campaign would commence.

Though many of the military chiefs had military, political, and ethical objections to this scheme, none spoke out. Admiral Erich Raeder advised Hitler to think also about invading Norway to assure supplies of iron ore. "The earlier we begin, and the more brutally," Raeder urged, "the earlier we shall see results; the shorter will be the war." All present agreed that under no circumstances must the war last long enough to involve the industrial capabilities of the United States.

Chamberlain and Daladier replied separately to Hitler's peace speech, saying that their countries had taken up arms against aggression and would not put them down again until Poland was restored. There would also have to be safeguards against peace being shattered every six months. Hitler's word, they said, was not an acceptable guarantee. The British cabinet announced that England was preparing for a war that might last three years, although originally the public had been led to believe the dirty job of ousting Hitler would be accomplished in a matter of weeks.

In Paris, Daladier outlawed the Communist party; seventy-four members of the Chamber of Deputies were unseated and many were arrested. The Communist party in France had very nearly disintegrated under the twin shocks of the Nazi-Soviet alliance and the Russian invasion of Poland. Daladier's decree, which disfranchised a half-million voters, was widely interpreted to mean that the government officially refused to recognize the patriotism of those who believed in France yet were committed to radical economic doctrines. The decree drove the Communists underground, where, instead of dying, the party flourished.

France also set up internment camps for Communists, aliens, and refugees. Leo Lania was incarcerated at Meslay, a town a hundred miles west of Paris, which was better than being shut up in the Stade de Colombes. Meslay was a large meadow surrounded by a wall and barbed wire; in the distance Lania could see the spire of a château and cows grazing peacefully: the landscape reminded him of a Corot painting. But there was a ditch for a latrine and close-quartered drafty tents which slept 250 men, and for quite some time there was only cold food.

The French had first used internment camps after Franco's victory in the Spanish Civil War in order to house tens of thousands who fled Spain. Those camps in the south of France were once again filled. Meslay was new. Lania could not understand why the same treatment was being given those who were openly pro-Nazi (and who goose-stepped as they came to the mess) and the exiles who had been the Nazis' victims. To keep boredom at bay and to take their minds off internment, Lania and other inmates organized a university without buildings which gave courses in languages, history, economics, and even films. Everyone enjoyed the courses. One exile who had also been at Dachau said things at that concentration camp had been "clearer and simpler. The Nazis were our enemies. We were on one side, they were on the other. We couldn't show our weakness in their presence, and that gave a man courage and strength. Here our friends and allies are—our jailers."

At a charming Lorraine village slightly forward of the Maginot Line, Denis Barlone and his men, waiting to make the definitive attack on the *boches*, used "gangster methods" to obtain provisions:

> Throughout the day the squeals of the doomed pigs and poultry can be heard, while the men go off to thrash the walnut trees, shake down the

mirabelles and quetsches, unearth the spuds, uproot the salads. My men
feed sumptuously, pastry cooks make flans with the flour, found in abundance, and butter made in the dairy. This is the land of milk and honey.

The men also worked diligently at a less frivolous task: they fortified
the territory taken from the Germans and awaited the signal to attack.
"We are all burning with desire and jumping for joy at the idea of
entering the fray," Barlone noted. But the signal never came.

On September 30, convinced that the Germans were behind the
Siegfried Line in force and that France must remain on the defensive
until spring, Gamelin ordered a strategic retreat. French troops scurried
back behind the Maginot Line and abandoned the territory they had so
cautiously won. This angered Daladier, since the public had been
cheered by the troops' advance, but he again acquiesced in the order.
After having backed the military without question for twenty years, he
could not afford politically to criticize it now.

A General Armengaud had been in Poland during the fighting and
had observed the Wehrmacht in action. In his report, Armengaud
warned the French military establishment of Germany's ability to
"break through a defensive front inadequately manned" and gave a
detailed and exact disquisition on the workings of the new German
system of mobile warfare that could not have been bettered by Guderian. The report clearly sounded the alarm and in the strongest terms
called for France to shift tactics to meet the new kind of warfare.
Knowing that what he had to say was important and problematical, Armengaud personally told Gamelin of his conclusions. Gamelin's response was that Armengaud's observations were irrelevant because in
France the army was stronger, the air force was stronger, the defenses
were stronger, and intelligence would provide adequate warning of an
attack. He shunted the general to the relatively minor post of commander of the Paris air region.

While disregarding Armengaud's warning, Gamelin made a mountain out of a molehill. In mid-October he received information of an
imminent German counterattack. Even though he had postulated that
the big German push would not come until spring, he conceived of the
coming attack as the battle that would decide the fate of France. His
order of the day was expressed in hyperbolic terms: the troops must
stand or die, the empire depended on them. When the attack came, it
was small and only in the sectors where frontier villages had been
abandoned. With a bare minimum of effort, the Germans in two days
recaptured what it had taken the French a month to occupy. At the end,
the frontiers were almost precisely where they had been at the outset of
the war on September 3.

Near midnight on October 13–14, U-47 commander Gunther Prien
worked his submarine at periscope depth past the almost completed

defenses of the British naval stronghold at Scapa Flow. In the dark waters below he could barely make out the rotting hulks of German ships scuttled after the Great War. On the surface the British battleship *Royal Oak* was a sitting duck. Prien fired his aft torpedoes, but they did not detonate. Still undetected, he turned his ship about and then fired his forward torpedoes: more duds. After managing the cumbersome twenty-minute-long task of reloading the empty tubes, he fired again. The last two torpedoes hit the *Royal Oak*, and she sank like a stone, causing the death of 833 British seamen. By this blow, one-twelfth of the Royal Navy's battleship strength was obliterated.

Churchill recognized that the sinking of the *Royal Oak* "might well have been politically fatal to any Minister who had been responsible for the pre-war precautions. Being a newcomer I was immune from such reproaches in the early months." He immediately ordered the other ships away from Scapa Flow, and from all major fleet bases. The decision was made just in time. Next day the Luftwaffe attacked the naval base at the Firth of Forth in Scotland. German intelligence had reported no air protection there; the information was in error, but through a stroke of German luck, at noon when the Ju-88 bombers approached the base, the British radar station's power was out. It was not until the bombers had been visually spotted that the squadron of Hurricanes and Spitfires took to the air. German orders were to sink the battle cruiser *Hood* if it was not docked. Hitler's direct command was that civilians must not be killed. The *Hood* was docked, and so the dozen bombers loosed their payloads and hit two medium-sized ships and one small one, none of which was completely destroyed. The Spitfires downed three of the bombers. Pressing the advantage, next day more German bombers attacked Scapa Flow, but all they found and bombed at anchorage was the ancient supply ship *Iron Duke*, a small prize at best.

Yet these German penetrations convinced Churchill and his admirals to remove the home fleet from within striking distance of German aircraft and place it west of Scotland. Now if the Royal Navy wished to reach Norway, the fleet would have to steam an extra day to reach the target. As the official British naval history suggests, "By two or three boldly executed strokes, at a total cost of four aircraft, the German Air Force and the U-boat service between them scored a resounding strategic success."

A funeral solemnized at the Tomb of the Unknown Soldier on Unter den Linden in Berlin drew every high dignitary of the German armed forces except Hitler. While he was with his artillery regiment in front of Warsaw, Colonel-General Werner von Fritsch had been killed by a stray bullet. Rumor said it was a bullet in the back, perhaps aimed by the SS. No one knew for certain. But the old army's finest soldier was dead, and for many at the funeral his death signified the passing of an era. Tradition was gone, independent military thought was done, and the army was at the service of a dictator who distrusted its genius yet who was all too keen to use its strength.

Army headquarters were at Zossen, eighteen miles outside Berlin. There, soon after Fritsch's funeral, Franz Halder entered the office of his superior, Walther von Brauchitsch. Hitler had told these two officers that the invasion of the West might mean a million dead on each side, but that victory would be worth such a price. Halder could not countenance Hitler's arithmetic. He was in some ways a sensitive man, though with many blind spots. That day he offered Brauchitsch his resignation. He did not like the projected invasion, and as an older man not used to doing things as the younger Brauchitsch did them, he would get out of the way.

Brauchitsch had been with Hitler since the day the Führer assumed power—indeed, his decision to support Hitler at that time had been crucial to the Nazi takeover—but his opinion of Hitler had changed. "I cannot do without you," Brauchitsch said to Halder. "How am I to contend with this man without your help?" For a while the two officers wrung their hands in despair, and then they worked out a deal. Halder would become supreme quartermaster general in charge of supply, a separate but equal command which had been held in the Great War by the legendary Erich Ludendorff. It would remove Halder fron the army's decision-making process but would use his extensive talents for organization. Halder would retain his prestige, his prosperous life style, and his honor, and he would have the satisfaction of believing he had not in any way sanctioned the invasion. In exchange, Halder would help Brauchitsch face Hitler. Tearfully the two men clasped hands and agreed they would at least try to oppose the dictator's plans.

They had much ammunition to bring to bear. Field reports from the Polish campaign indicated the sorry quality of the Wehrmacht troops, some of whom had often refused to advance under fire, many led by officers who then sustained "excessive" casualties. Economics expert Georg Thomas gave the generals a detailed analysis which showed that the raw material demands of the Wehrmacht were even then far beyond what could actually be obtained. Each month the army was short 600,000 tons of steel, and there was currently only a fourteen-day supply of powder for one-third of the divisions. General von Leeb wrote the chiefs that the men of the reserves could be counted on to hold their positions along the Westwall only if the enemy made no major attack.

Halder noted in his diary three alternatives open to the chiefs: "Attack. Await events. Basic transformation." Translated from his cryptic shorthand, that meant the chiefs could let Hitler launch the attack on the West, or they could wait and see if events would alter the plans for the attack, or they could engender a basic transformation in the society—that is, undertake a coup. Brauchitsch was neutral on the last alternative. Halder was the man who would have to do it. He thought about assassinating Hitler himself, and carried a pistol in his pocket even when he visited the Reichschancellery—where, as a high-ranking officer, he was not questioned about it.

But Halder was not a man of iron. He was terribly troubled, and he pleaded for "younger, energetic" men to take over the planning of the coup. All he could do, he felt, was to prevent the transfer of several army divisions and keep them near Berlin so they could support a coup. An opposition stalwart noted in his diary:

> Canaris visits Halder. Returns shaken. Complete nervous collapse. Brauchitsch also helpless. Führer demands attack. Closes his ears to arguments. [It is claimed that] nothing can be done [in the way of revolt] as we would be smashed by the English. . . . A Chief of the General Staff *has no business* breaking down.

Many of the other top military men in the country believed an invasion of the West would bring military and political disaster to Germany. Von Rundstedt and von Reichenau—the latter a particular Hitler favorite—both publicly and privately agreed with that estimate. Von Leeb let Halder know that he would go along with whatever the chiefs wanted to do. On October 22, Hitler ordered the invasion to begin on November 12. Halder had twenty days, and plenty of military backing, in which to stage the coup.

On October 24, 1939, newspaper headlines reported that the *City of Flint*, an American freighter, had been seized by Germany in the mid-Atlantic and was now in the Russian port of Murmansk. Thereby hung a tale which over the next few days was told in juicy installments. In early September the *Flint* had been a bystander at the opening tragedy of the war. She was near the Irish Sea when the *Athenia* was torpedoed, and picked up many of the survivors and took them to New York.

Returning to her regular service, on October 3 the *Flint* left New York bound for Liverpool and Glasgow with a hold full of tractors, grain, fruit, leather, and wax—some of which were considered contraband materials. On October 9, a boarding party from the pocket battleship *Deutschland* came on board to investigate. "If any of you makes the slightest move," a German boarder said to the *Flint*'s crew, "he'll get one of these." The raider tossed a grenade overboard into the sea, where it exploded. No one made a fuss.

A prize crew ran the *Flint* while her crew of forty-one Americans was detained on board, along with the British crew of a ship which the *Deutschland* had sunk earlier near Jamaica. Having painted out the American name and placed a time bomb in the engine room, the nervous German crew took the *Flint* northward under a Danish flag. On

October 20, the *Flint* raised a German flag and picked up a Norwegian harbor pilot to navigate the coastal waters into Tromsö. In the port the Norwegian authorities deduced the American identity of the ship and refused to allow her to sail until American flags had been repainted on her sides. The British crew was taken off, but before the *Flint* could be turned over to her original crew the Germans managed to escape with the ship (and the forty-one Americans) and make for Murmansk. There the Russians interned the Germans, but rather than turn the ship loose, as international law dictated, the Russians held it.

In Washington, the Roosevelt administration, while publicly dismayed, was privately elated. The *City of Flint's* plight was a marvelous argument for the passage of the revised neutrality legislation, which contained key provisions that would have prohibited the American vessel's sailing blithely into the waters where it had been seized. While Secretary of State Hull cabled Ambassador Steinhardt in Moscow to try to obtain the release of the American crew and the ship, administration stalwarts in Washington worked to get wavering senators to vote for revision. The idea that the Communists at the behest of the Nazis were holding Americans in violation of international law made even the most isolationist senator think twice about the existing neutrality statutes.

Steinhardt was denied access to the American crew. Negotiations for territory in the Baltic between Russia and Finland were at a delicate stage, and if Stalin let the Americans go he might slight Hitler, who might then back Finland against Russia. Stalin ordered Murmansk to release the German prize crew, and to put them back in charge of the *Flint*, instructing them to take the ship posthaste out of Russian waters. On October 26, with the forty-one Americans again held captive, the freighter left Murmansk for ports unknown. The next day the American Senate passed the revised neutrality bill. The *City of Flint's* odyssey came to a satisfying close as the Norwegians forced the ship into the port of Haugesund, threw the Germans into prison for violating Norway's neutral waters, and returned the ship to the American crew. By the time President Roosevelt signed a compromise version of the bill, the *Flint* was on its way home.

While the *Flint* made headlines, an incident of potentially equal importance made none. In the waters west of the Orkneys, Winston Churchill, First Sea Lord Sir Dudley Pound, and the commander in chief of the home fleet, Sir Charles Forbes, conferred aboard HMS *Nelson*. The *Nelson* was protected by the *Rodney* and the *Hood*, but German submarine U-56 managed to maneuver inside their protective screen and fire three torpedoes at the *Nelson*. In the submarine's radio room the German sailors listened for explosions. They heard only faint clangs as the torpedoes hit the *Nelson* but did not explode. So dejected was the captain of the U-boat that he did not send a message about the torpedo failure until several hours later, and none of the other submarines in the area were then able to find the *Nelson*. Churchill and the admirals never found out how close to death they had come.

At the end of October, at a ceremony in the marbled and gilded Reichschancellery, front commanders of the Polish campaign gathered to receive decorations for their valor. Halder and Brauchitsch waited until after the festivities to corner Hitler and importune him to delay the invasion. They argued that the army would not be ready until November 26. Privately they hoped that if this delay was granted, bad weather would set in and cause a postponement throughout the winter. Hitler was adamant that the date would be November 12.

Halder told his diary he was "worn out and depressed." Under increased pressure from Hans Oster, from his own deputy Karl Stülpnagel, and from other opposition members, he agreed to begin a coup on November 5, if on that date Hitler should definitely order the attack to take place on the twelfth. Hoping to obtain more evidence which would argue for a postponement, the chiefs toured the western commands on November 2 and 3. Although some generals privately told Halder that a coup was questionable, because they could not guarantee what their men would do, there was solid unanimity against a coming invasion. When the chiefs went back to Zossen they were in a position to state that none of the commanders of the five western armies believed the invasion "to have any prospect of success," while all the commanders agreed that "an attack with a far-reaching objective cannot be made at this time."

Despite this unanimity, the chiefs did not know exactly how to present their findings to Hitler. And Halder was frozen by two fears—the first, that the invasion would take place and would result in a military catastrophe; the second, that he would actually have to attempt a coup to prevent the invasion. He worried that Hitler might have found out about the impending revolt. There were too many men involved for a leak not to have occurred somewhere. The hours crept closer to November 5. On that day Brauchitsch, as senior officer, would go in alone and see the Führer and hand him the conclusions from the western tour.

A hesitant Halder sent Stülpnagel and Oster to alert Beck, Goerdeler, and the others to be ready to perform their tasks in the government's overthrow. But his resolve was strengthened when he received from Georg Thomas, the economist, a document which argued convincingly that the invasion would ruin all chances for the peace which Hitler's opponents were actively pursuing with the British. Thomas told Halder that if Germany drove westward she would lose Swedish iron ore, Yugoslavian copper, and Rumanian oil, and that the United States would either enter the war or bring its economic might to bear. Looking to the far future, if the invasion should succeed, Germany would eventually be forced to defend at enormous cost the Flanders coast and whatever other territory she might hold. In the end, Germany could not rule all of Europe with impunity. Halder was completely convinced. Should Brauchitsch's meeting with Hitler not result in an immediate postponement of the invasion, Halder would launch the coup.

The two chiefs drove the eighteen miles from Zossen to the Reichs-chancellery in the late morning of November 5. At noon Halder left his younger colleague in the anteroom to Hitler's office and went back to the car to wait. Alone, Brauchitsch entered Hitler's office bearing the memorandum which stated the conclusions of the western generals.

After handing it over, Brauchitsch did not bother to summarize the contents, but instead started talking about the possibilities of bad weather. "It rains on the enemy too," Hitler retorted. Brauchitsch chose this moment to chide Hitler for his interference in the Polish campaign, and asked the Führer to limit such intrusions in future campaigns. He spoke of the sorry performance of the German troops under Polish fire, of the breakdown of discipline, and of parallels with troop failures during the Great War.

Hitler erupted. How could Brauchitsch talk of minor grievances when the armies had just won a magnificent victory in Poland? This was defeatism! He wanted the details of the alleged infractions—who and what units had acted badly, how many death sentences had been handed down for dereliction of duty, what exactly was being done about the allegations. He was near the end of his patience with "the spirit of Zossen" and would take steps to stamp out the defeatism and anti-Hitlerism he knew existed in the army's higher circles. As Hitler went on with his tirade, Brauchitsch's face twisted into a grimace and became chalk white; he choked and could not give specific answers to Hitler's questions. The Führer continued to probe, added demand to demand and insult to insult—and then abruptly turned and slammed the door as he went out of the room.

When Halder saw a completely cowed and white-faced Brau-chitsch come down the stairs and get silently into the car, he was aghast. His chagrin deepened as they drove back to Zossen; his brain raced as he pried the story, word by word, out of the commander in chief of the Wehrmacht. What struck Halder most was Hitler's reference to knowing all about the spirit of Zossen; that could only mean that Hitler must know about the coup. When they reached headquarters Halder panicked. He still carried the pistol with which he had planned to kill Hitler, but he had been defeated by an outburst of fury in which he had not even been personally involved. Halder sent for his fellow conspirators. All evidence of the intended coup must be burned; at any moment the SS might come and take him away, and along with him the whole of the upper echelon of the army's staff; all arguments of the military for refusing to go ahead with the invasion had been exhausted, and "therefore the forces which reckoned on us are no longer bound."

At Zossen, at Abwehr headquarters, at private homes in Berlin and the suburbs, papers were burned in ashtrays and in wastebaskets. Plans for the takeover of the Chancellery, plans for the movement of troops, and plans for the official proclamations of the new government were all destroyed. The coup was aborted, and the invasion, confirmed to begin November 12, was still on.

8

The War of Words

Gijsbertus Sas, the Dutch military attaché in Berlin, was an army veteran, a man of charm and insight, a Dutch patriot, and a close friend of Hans Oster's. Throughout September and October of 1939, Oster had quietly warned Sas that a German invasion of Holland and Belgium was a distinct possibility. Sas reported this information to The Hague, and was chagrined to learn that the Dutch military discounted it because he, for reasons of honor, refused to name his German informant. As November began, Oster's warnings became dire, frantic, and precise: fifty German divisions were scheduled to enter the Low Countries on November 12. Sas sent a most urgent message to The Hague and followed it himself. At the same time, Oster alerted the Vatican, and the Holy See warned the ambassadors of Belgium and Holland as well as Belgian princess Marie-José, the wife of the Italian crown prince.

These alarums sent Leopold III, king of the Belgians, with his military aide van Overstraeten and the Belgian foreign minister, Paul Henri Spaak, racing from Brussels through the gathering dark on the evening of November 6 to confer with Queen Wilhelmina of the Netherlands at the royal palace in The Hague. The sovereigns talked through the night.

Leopold was thirty-eight and had been on the throne only five years, during which time an automobile accident had taken the life of his young wife. The chief cross he had to bear was being the son of King Albert the *roi-chevalier*, a national hero of the Great War who had personally led his troops into battle, ate and slept with them, and had been such a perfect monarch that it was nearly impossible for a mortal man to follow in his footsteps. Albert had allied his country with the victorious Allies and pushed Germany off Belgian soil. Leopold was a cousin of George VI and had been educated at Eton. Nevertheless, when he watched Hitler march into the Rhineland in 1936 while England and France stood passively by, he decided it was time for a change. He broke with the Allies and declared Belgium's neutrality, reasoning that strong ties to Britain and France would only invite a German invasion that might once again turn Belgium into a battlefield for other nations.

Queen Wilhelmina was older, a widow who had been on her country's throne for many years. In the matter of ties with the Allies, she felt as strongly as Leopold. Lest it seem that the two small countries were conspiring against Germany, the Dutch had even refused to hold joint staff talks with the Belgians. Both countries were neutral but both took strenuous defensive measures against a possible German attack. They had larger armies per capita than Great Britain, and spent lavishly on defense. Earlier in 1939, Gamelin had suggested that Belgium and Holland join the Allies in staff talks, but he had been rebuffed. As the Dutch foreign minister explained in a letter to the editor of the London *Times*: "What possible advantage could there be in military talks at a time when England is not ready for war, France is in chaos, and the Germans are rearmed?"

Holland was on continual semi-alert. At the push of a button, most of the countryside could be flooded and the Dutch would retreat inside "Fortress Holland," which included the heavily populated industrial sector Amsterdam-Rotterdam-Utrecht-The Hague.

Belgium had a larger area to defend, but had Holland as a partial buffer against Germany. The Belgian defenses were concentrated along the long eastern border with Holland, most of which was the Albert Canal. The many bridges over the canal were continuously manned by guards ready to blow the bridges into the water before any Germans could cross into the country. At the south end of the Albert Canal where it met the Meuse River near Maastricht not far from the German border, the Belgians had built Fort Eben Emael, the most modern fortification in the world. With three miles of underground tunnels and a garrison of a thousand men, it outshone the concrete battlements of the Maginot Line. It bristled with gun turrets and steel defenses; while one side dropped sheer into the canal, others were difficult of access. Eben Emael dominated the gentle landscape, the two waterways, and the nexus of roads which led west into southern Belgium. It was considered impregnable. The enemy would have to pass it to conquer Belgium, and they would be stopped there. With Eben Emael at the southern corner, and with Holland buttressing the eastern border, the Belgians considered their country safe from a German attack.

In September, after war had been declared, Gamelin had at last persuaded the Belgians to hold secret staff talks with the French. As neither Holland nor Belgium could long hold out against Germany in the event of an invasion, sooner or later the French and British would have to come to their aid. As everyone else had for years, Gamelin now formally proposed that the Allies be allowed into Belgium sooner rather than later, for instance at the first hint that an invasion might take place. The line along the Albert Canal would be better held if rein-forced by more troops. Leopold rejected this argument on the grounds that the presence of Allied troops on Belgian soil might provide Germany with an excuse to invade.

Gamelin proposed a rather drastic alternative. The Allies would enter Belgium after an invasion had taken place—but only if between now and then (whenever "then" might prove to be) Belgian troops were kept on continual alert, and would agree, when the invasion came, to hold the Albert Canal line while the Allies maneuvered into position many miles to the west along the Dyle River. Gamelin did not expect the Allies to go all the way to the Albert Canal, nor was he willing to have the Belgians fall back to the Dyle. Without much choice in the matter, Leopold accepted Gamelin's plan.

On November 6, after a long night of conferences, Leopold and Wilhelmina decided to send Berlin a message which offered their services as peace negotiators between Germany and the Allies. They believed such an offer would make it more difficult for Hitler to justify an invasion of their countries. The message was sent, and both countries were put on full military alert, with towns near the border in Holland placed under martial law.

On the morning of November 7, the sovereigns' message arrived at the German Foreign Office. The only person of suitable rank present to receive it was Erich Kordt, a committed anti-Nazi. At the outset of the war Kordt had asked Weizsäcker why no one was prepared to assassinate Hitler. After the aborted coup of November 5, and against his personal scruples, Kordt had decided he must do the job himself. Hans Oster would procure explosives from the Abwehr's laboratory, and Kordt would make a bomb to blow up both Hitler and himself. As yet Oster had not obtained the explosives, and Kordt had to go to Hitler empty-handed but for the message from Leopold and Wilhelmina.

He found Hitler preparing to leave the Chancellery to deliver a speech in Munich. "Tell the Dutch and Belgians that I am on a journey and cannot be reached. There is no need for responding to this overture right away," Hitler told Kordt. Then, before leaving and out of Kordt's hearing, he postponed the invasion to November 15 because of inclement flying weather.

Hitler's speech was to be the feature of the annual gathering of the Nazi "Old Guard" on the anniversary of the Beer Hall Putsch of 1923. Hundreds of party members, dignitaries, and relatives of those killed in the putsch celebrated the occasion in the cellar of the Munich Bürgerbräu. Because he had to hurry back to Berlin to make further decisions about the invasion, at the last moment Hitler advanced the time of his speech and cut it from ninety minutes to sixty. It was rousing and vehemently anti-British, and at nine-twelve Hitler left the hall to make his train. At nine-twenty a bomb exploded in the pillar in front of which

Hitler had been speaking minutes earlier. It killed many and injured scores of others.

Erwin Rommel, chief of Hitler's security staff, viewed the damage and wrote: "Six feet of rubble cover the spot where the Führer spoke. . . . One dare not think what would have happened if the assassination had succeeded." Hitler described his own escape as a miracle, and thereafter agreed to ride in a bulletproof limousine and to take other precautions. All laboratories having access to explosives were carefully monitored; as a result, even the high-ranking Hans Oster could not get into the Abwehr laboratory to obtain explosives for Erich Kordt, and Kordt's suicide bomb plan came to naught.

In the summer of 1939, S. Payne Best, one of England's leading secret service agents on the Continent, made contact with a German refugee in Holland. The German said he knew men high up in anti-Nazi circles, and through the opening weeks of the war Best held a series of clandestine meetings on the Dutch side of the border with German "opposition" officials. It was touch and go at every turn because the Germans were skittish. During one rendezvous at a café near Dinxperloo, Best and his fellow agent R. H. Stevens were talking with several Germans when Dutch border guards came over to ask questions. The Germans nearly jumped out the sealed windows of the café before a Dutch policeman named Klops, who worked with the British agents, managed to reassure the border guards. Best gave the Germans a secret radio transmitter with which to stay in touch. The Germans carried out their instructions faithfully. Best met with a German major named Schaemmel, who convinced him that the army was willing to stage a coup but reported that his superiors first wanted assurances that the British would negotiate honorably with a new German government. Citing orders, Best said he could not give such assurances, but personally pledged himself to that goal.

On November 8, after the bomb blast, firm in his belief that the British had set the device which nearly killed him, Hitler ordered SS chief Heydrich to wind up the cat-and-mouse game the SS had been playing with Best and Stevens. He wanted to find out what the British agents knew. He also needed a propaganda reason for invading Holland, and if he captured a Dutch agent acting in collusion with the British secret service, that would certainly give the lie to Dutch neutrality. The supposed Major Schaemmel, who was in fact Walter Schellenberg, an up-and-coming SS man, sent Best a radio message that he could meet the high-up anti-Nazi general he had been told about at the border village of Venlo in the late afternoon of November 6.

As Best, Stevens, and Klops sped toward the border, they noticed the Dutch forces were on full alert. Their car was held up at every barrier and roadblock, and they worried about being late. They were stopped twice between Venlo and the border café. But Klops, summoned to the telephone at the guardhouse, was assured by his headquarters that everything was all right. They went on, and moments later saw "Schaemmel" standing on the veranda of the red-brick café, with swings and seesaws in the garden beyond.

As the three men pulled up to the café, automobiles cut off their car, and Germans from the automobiles started to fire submachine guns over the agents' heads. Alfred Naujocks, who had earlier taken over the transmitter at Gleiwitz, shouted at the agents to raise their hands. Best and Stevens complied, but Klops fired at the raiders and single-handedly stood off seven Germans for a minute before he was killed. The astonished border guards did not know what had happened, and the Germans quickly drove the cars and their captives into Germany.

After having kidnapped the two top British agents in Europe, the SS brazenly continued to send false messages over the radio transmitter Best had given them, and soon received information which compromised British methods of operation, informants, spies, routes of travel, and contacts in Germany and in neutral countries. Klops was dead, however, and the grilling of Best and Stevens revealed that they had nothing to do with the Munich bomb plot, so the two prime purposes of the raid were foiled. A parallel investigation turned up a lone disgruntled German watchmaker who confessed to having set the bomb in Munich. Hitler was disappointed. Schellenberg sent off his last wireless transmission to the British: "Negotiations for any length of time with conceited and silly people are tedious. You will understand, therefore, that we are giving them up. You are hereby bidden a hearty farewell by your affectionate German opposition. (signed) The Gestapo."

Apart from such incidents, there was hardly a feeling of war; there was no sense of battle, and nothing like the terrible stillness that had characterized the Great War in the long winter months, when opposing armies had been locked in frozen trenches, unable to dislodge one another. In 1915, 1916, 1917, reporters could feel the power of rock against rock. Now all they could report was lethargy. In November 1939, though the threat of invasion was still present—and on the German side was a drumbeat that could not be ignored—to the vast majority of people the war seemed primarily one of words.

The democracies were not good at this kind of war. The English Ministry of Information was torpid, without a genius or a brilliant spokesman. Churchill had not yet become the voice of democracy. The chief French propagandist was novelist and playwright Jean Giraudoux, a gentle and reflective artist whose works were marked by their literacy, charm, and poignancy—none of which qualities were well suited to a propaganda effort.

In Germany, however, there was Dr. Joseph Goebbels. An early and fervent convert to Hitler, Goebbels had become a national figure in the early 1930s as the Nazis' chief propagandist. Since 1933, he had steadily increased his power over all the instruments of public information in Germany. Whereas in the democracies the government could control the media through censorship, in Germany Goebbels controlled everything that was printed, everything that went out over the airwaves, everything that was seen in movie houses and theaters. The press was government owned or controlled by government stooges; deviation resulted in confiscation. By 1939, such control was nearly absolute, and to find out what they should disseminate, all the disseminators came to a daily conference with Goebbels and his staff.

Goebbels's main effort was directed at the German people. During the Great War and in its aftermath they had suffered dreadfully, and were believed to be opposed to war. If they knew the true nature of Hitler's plans or had a clear understanding of the outside world and the forces it might bring to bear, the German people might not support this war. It was Goebbels's job to make them accept the war and the privations that were bound to accompany it.

His techniques could be seen in his handling of the many crises of the fall of 1939. It was growing cold in Germany, and there were many shortages, even though the economy was not yet on a true war footing. In the satellite regions of the Reich, in Prague and Vienna, there were riots. There were also the Munich bombing and the Venlo incident.

The propaganda machine continued to link the Munich bomb to the British agents captured at Venlo, even after the SS had disproved the connection between them. Goebbels saw no reason to burden people with the truth if that truth ran counter to the Nazi version of the events. The disturbances in Prague and Vienna he first downplayed as the work of juveniles; later, when nine Prague students were lined up against a wall and shot, he preached that the highest virtue in a state was obedience to authority. Throwing spitballs at blackboards in a German university was condemned in the same terms as the uprising in Prague, with the clear implication that if German students did not shape up, they might suffer the same fate as the Prague students.

A more ticklish job was to prepare the public for rationing at a time when the war did not seem real. An adult's weekly ration provided less than a quarter-pound of butter, less than a half-pound of meat, and only powdered milk. Ration cards had even been issued for farm animals. People hoarded food and spent many of their waking hours scrounging for coal, which was in especially short supply. As the winter grew colder, Goebbels had to tell the public that clothing would also be rationed, but when he announced that regulation, there were runs on clothing stores, and all of them had to be closed for two months. People made wooden clogs at home.

Goebbels's major task was to prepare the nation for the invasion of the West. In November, the press was ordered to stop portraying Chamberlain as a foolish old man with an umbrella, and to start painting Germany's enemies as vicious and Jewish controlled. Churchill in particular was to be denounced. As for the countries soon to be invaded, one typical ploy was Goebbels's use of a prophecy of the sixteenth-century French seer Nostradamus, whose description of the "33rd Century" read:

> Brabant, Flanders, Ghent, Bruges, and Boulogne
> Are temporarily united with the Great Germany.
> But when the passage of arms is finished
> The great Prince of Armenia will declare war.
> Now begins an era of humanity of divine origin.
> The age of peace is founded by unity.
> War, now captive, sits on half the world,
> And peace will be preserved for a long time.

Goebbels forbade the publishing of all prophecies, including those of Nostradamus, but suggested at his daily conference that the above lines

> be disseminated only by handbills, handwritten, or at most typed, secretly, and in the manner of snowball letters. The thing must have the air of being forbidden. The following points are to be added by word of mouth: The magic agreement between the 33rd Century and the year 33, our Seizure of Power. Interpretation: Introduction of the new order in Europe by Greater Germany, occupation of France only temporary. Greater Germany ushers in the thousand years' Reich and a thousand years' peace. Naturally all this silly rubbish must also go out to France over the transmitters. As for the great Prince of Armenia, we'll put him on ice until Herr Stalin from Georgia declares war on us—or we on him.

The secret transmitters which broadcast Goebbels's efforts to Western Europe made it seem as if the propaganda were homegrown. A station that appeared to be Belgian incited the Walloons against the Flemish; a similar station emphasized the Teutonic roots of the Dutch. These were subtle efforts. Others were more direct. German state radio made slanted broadcasts in English and French. The French acknowledged that German radio broadcast better music than their own. To induce apathy and antipathy to the war in French soldiers stationed along the borders, leaflets were sent over by balloon, predicting that the poilus would fall "like the leaves of autumn," while the British stood back and reaped the spoils of war. Other propaganda suggested that officers readily obtained leave to go home to their wives while common soldiers stayed in the lines and worried about being cuckolded. German bands stood on riverbanks and played French popular songs for the poilus, and everywhere in no man's land the Germans erected signs which said they were not barbarians and would not fire on the French unless the French fired first on them.

In response, the Allies' direct broadcasts to Germany did not sway the closely controlled German soldiers, but had some effect on the German populace. A measure of their success was a German decree which forbade listening to foreign broadcasts.

Else Wendel never listened to the foreign radio. Listening was proscribed, and as a loyal German, a secretary in the Strength through Joy Office, she would not think of doing anything illegal. Since it was unusual enough to be a working woman, she must in other areas of life maintain the correct attitude. After a day at work, when she came home to her apartment she kept her coat on and did not light the stove. That was part of her attempt to conserve her ration of coal so that at Christmastime the stove could warm a household complete with children. Else's husband had gladly taken the bonuses awarded for having children, but had divorced her and abandoned them to her care. With two at home she could not work, and if she worked to earn money to stay alive she could not care for the children properly. So she had temporarily farmed them out. One was with a married cousin, the other was with a nonrelated family.

During November, Else began to feel that the foster families were shutting her out of the children's lives. She could do little about it. Her weekend visits became strained. The children began to forget her. The families wanted them in part, Else believed, because they entitled the families to extra food coupons and more clothing points. One weekend Else's cousin refused to let her take her son for a walk, and Else realized with a start that the children would not be allowed to come home for Christmas. She began to feel numb, not only with the cold.

In the air-raid safety course that Ruth Andreas-Friedrich took, citizens were reminded that owners of buildings need not permit "persons of alien race" in their basement shelters. Ruth and her friends were ashamed before their Jewish acquaintances and therefore went to see them more often. But their conversations with Jews began with "Remember when?" and ended with "Do you still recall?" It was very depressing. Ruth read a pamphlet which contained a holiday gloss on "Silent Night":

> Silent night, holy night;
> All is calm, all is bright.
> Only the Chancellor stays on guard,
> Germany's future to watch and to ward,
> Guiding our nation aright.

Ruth's flesh crawled. This treacle was celebrated while Stefan Zweig and Franz Werfel had been forced to flee Germany, and for six years Heinrich Heine's poetry and the writings of Hermann Hesse had been proscribed and burned. Ruth poured her anger into her diary:

> The intellectual disaster has been worse than the material one can ever be.

The mischief, the falsification of history, distortion of truth, and slanders upon art that have been pounded into people's heads through years cannot be effaced from these heads so easily. Each of us bears the stamp of the Third Reich somewhere. Even the downfall of the government will not conjure democrats out of Nazis, personalities out of Mass Man. Hitler has accustomed the people to ecstasies. There's got to be a "bang" somewhere all the time. People are constantly going to excess. The upsetting of all values has spread to everyday speech. We don't call anything simply "beautiful" because it is beautiful any more, simply "great" because it is great. Anything that doesn't strike us as "tremendously great," "divinely beautiful," or "uniquely wonderful" has as little savor in our mouths as unseasoned food. Germany has lost its ear for gentle notes.

In the early days of the war Hermann Göring had spoken on the radio like a fond Dutch uncle who, despite his three hundred pounds, could still make jokes about rationing: "Of meat it can be said that we eat far too much of it in any case. With less meat we shall get thinner and so need less material for a suit." Else Wendel thought Göring had a knack for admitting weaknesses and then explaining them away. While he forbade the reading of British leaflets, he deprecated the idea that British bombers could ever really reach into Germany. (One British leaflet asserted that Göring's own overseas stash, which he would pick up after the war, amounted to five million dollars.) In the midst of the peace offensive Göring had said:

> All we want is peace. Peace with honor, Mr. Chamberlain. We do not want to fight the English people. Nor do we want one inch of France. It is the English who are inciting the war. Remember, you Frenchmen, what England has said in the past: "We will fight to the last Frenchman!" Not to the last Englishman, mark you!

For all this bluster, Göring still retained his love of England and was the advocate of peace within the Nazi hierarchy. But after his peace overtures had been rejected, his attitude changed. Hitler thought of invading Holland; Göring advised taking all of Holland, rather than just a slice of it, in order to obtain bases from which to bomb England. Hitler was not that interested in bombing England; Göring was no longer afraid of the RAF and wanted vengeance. The raids on Scapa Flow and the Firth of Forth, and air battles over Heligoland Bight proved to him that his Luftwaffe was the equal of the English air force. War with Poland had broadened his art collection and had sharpened his appetite for the riches of the Low Countries and the countless treasures of Paris.

The Munich bomb attempt gave Göring a moment's pause. After it he told his wife, Emily, that had Hitler died he would immediately have called for a cease-fire, withdrawn German troops from all non-German territory, and would have begun peace talks with the Allies. Hitler had not died, and a week after the attempt Göring told him that the Luftwaffe ought to be shifted to the west to begin attacks on England as soon as the invasion began.

Secret training and preparation for that invasion continued. At Hildesheim, a select group of sequestered volunteers were allowed no leave while they practiced techniques for assaulting a superfort whose name and location they did not know. Day after day they placed explosive charges, climbed up sheer walls, and rehearsed glider landings. When their technique had improved, they were taken inside Czechoslovakia to perfect their assault. Czech Sudetenland fortress bunkers were patterned after those of the Maginot Line. The soldiers did not know each other's names, though every man knew the others' missions. Two of the men were given suspended death sentences for trifling security lapses.

All German conscripts who spoke foreign languages had their files tagged for future reference. Abwehr agents procured Dutch police uniforms. Parachutists blossomed near German bridges to secure them before charges could be exploded. Army units crossed rivers in canoelike rubber boats. "Joy riding on the Moselle is forbidden," Guderian said to some overeager participants. Engineers erected pontoon bridges, Pioneer battalions competed for prizes in the disarming of tank traps and the dismantling of roadblocks. Pictures of such activities were released to the world press, but they were ignored as just more German scare tactics.

Few people in the democracies believed an invasion of France would come before spring, and most believed it might never happen, for Hitler would be economically strangled before then. This was not the Great War with its chaos and horrors; it was "the phony war," it was "the bore war," or "*la drôle de guerre*," or the new German word "*Sitzkrieg*." It was a twilight war, a time when all that people could do was wait, a time of nothingness, a time of boredom born of the need not to think, a time of mordant expectancy that stifled enjoyment and excitement and the wish for life. The phony war was a still and ugly calm at the center of a storm, a vacuum into which seeped the fears and frustrations of societies which knew and did not want to know that disaster was imminent.

In England, the government, invoking the emergency, suspended habeas corpus, and the rights of free assembly and to demonstrate and to public dissent. Such curtailments had long been viewed as the worst aspect of the Nazi state. It was forbidden to publish weather forecasts, which might give information to the enemy. Aliens were detained for indefinite periods on suspicion alone. They were confined in jails where room had been made by an amnesty for prisoners with less than three months of their terms to serve. Patents, houses, hotels, vehicles, and whole factories were commandeered, even though most were not immediately put to use. The myriad regulations hurriedly enacted as the war began resulted in curious contradictions. Lighthouse keepers were to be drafted at age eighteen, physicists at age twenty-one, trade union officials at thirty, and shorthand writers at thirty-five; people had hardly finished contemplating the incongruities of such a list when it became known that recruiting stations were to be shut down because of a lack of training camps and military units to which to assign the draftees. Vacant lots went untouched while forty-foot craters were dug in Hyde Park to obtain dirt with which to fill sandbags.

Under the threat of German bombs, people who went into the countryside to live, or who had to be away from home for some time, killed many of their household pets. They did not want the animals to suffer when bombs began to rain down. Piles of dead cats and dogs appeared in veterinarians' garbage receptacles. Letters to the editors argued for and against such practices. Other letters, from dachshund owners, urged that vengeance not be taken against these dogs of German origin as it had been in the last war.

A national poll, Mass Observation, with reporters in nearly every community, found that people complained most about blackout precautions and forced evacuations. The inconvenience of the blackouts got on their nerves. Windows were covered by heavy curtains. Pubs were forbidden to have doors opening directly onto the street, for they might spill light. Instructions were issued for painting white stripes on cows so that cars wouldn't hit them at night. Reportedly, sexual activity went on in doorways and bushes only a few yards from blacked-out lighted interiors. It was important to know the dates of the waxing and waning of the moon.

The Germans were expected to drop poison gas. Hence everyone, including infants, had to have and carry a gas mask at all times. Infants' masks came in pastel colors with Walt Disney characters painted on them. The minister of home security (known to wags as the minister of some obscurity) announced in early November that

> The attention of women is drawn to the fact that the temperature conditions inside the face-piece of the mask cause eye-black to run, leading to smarting of the eyes, profuse tears and spasms of the eyelids. This produces an urgent desire to remove the mask, with dangerous results if gas is present.

An advertising campaign was begun for waterproof makeup which would not cause such problems. Additional war-related tie-ins were common: one should not be caught in a shelter with a hacking cough; one might purchase a piece of rural property well out of range of German bombers.

After the first crop of problems with evacuees, the second crop arose. The evacuated children became financial burdens on the local districts in which they had been placed when the central government proved lax in paying local governments and local householders for their upkeep. The cities suffered too. Schools had been shut, and when parents brought their children back from the hinterlands they discovered there was nowhere to send them during the day. Bands of unruly children roamed the streets. Mass Observation learned that by Christmas of 1939, 43 percent of those who had been evacuated had returned, and that there were no schools, no free milk, no hospital beds, and no social services to care for them.

More money was being paid to air-raid wardens, who seemed to have nothing constructive to do, than to those in the military services. The budget for the Air Raid Precaution program was higher than that of the most prosperous service, the navy. Yet 38 percent of the people questioned by Mass Observation at the onset of the war knew nothing about air-raid precautions; and in November, 33 percent still knew nothing about them. The poll further showed that 90 percent of the people questioned still mistook a car changing gears for an air-raid siren. In the London working-class sample, half the people queried—especially those who had been evacuated and who had returned to London—didn't think there ever would be any air raids, and the other half wished Germany would get on with the war, because they couldn't stand much more empty waiting.

In short, it seemed that while the government claimed to have prepared for war, the war that had come was not being run very well. Historian A. J. P. Taylor commented:

> The war machine resembled an expensive motor car—beautifully polished, complete in every detail, except that there was no petrol in the tank. In 1936 a government advisor had pointed out that there could be no adequate manpower policy (nor, indeed, war policy of any kind) without a "general recognition of the issue before the country, popular support of the Government, and a Government strong enough and decisive enough to make use of this popular support."

In November 1939, popular support of the government was low. Chamberlain still refused to take representatives of either the Liberal or the Labour party into his cabinet, and the fact that the military was disorganized, conscription lumbered along aimlessly, the laws were vexatious and confusing, and the war could not be seen helped put distance between the people and the government. The cabinet, not wanting to alarm people unduly, at first refused to consider such precautionary measures as food rationing, and made no attempt to dictate what civilian industry was manufacturing. Pleasure cars were being turned out while the BEF did not have enough tanks. Because Labour was not in the government, the cabinet was unable to ask labor unions to reduce their demands for the duration of the emergency. At the other end of the scale, little was done to prevent the rich from moving their money out of the country to Switzerland or to the United States to avoid paying the new, still low, taxes. Typical of the government's difficulties was a propaganda poster which asked people to save money and proclaimed "YOUR resolution will bring US victory." Many believed this meant "resolve on the part of the lower classes will bring victory to the privileged few." Eventually the poster was withdrawn and another substituted.

The real problem was that, as far as the war was concerned, the country was running smoothly even without public support. There were no air raids. There were no casualties. Chamberlain's government was content in the belief that the navy's blockade of Germany would produce starvation and economic ruin and would win the war. No solid information pushed the government to this erroneous conclusion. In fact, all evidence pointed to the contrary, for Germany had stockpiled a great many essential items before the war and Russia was currently supplying the Reich with huge quantities of food and raw materials. "The main weapon," as Chamberlain called the blockade, was in truth hurting only neutral Belgium and Holland, sapping their economic strength and causing great resentment against England.

Rather it was the German blockade which was hurting the British Isles. In the late months of 1939, a combination of U-boats, surface raiders, and lethal devices nearly crippled British commerce. There were heavy losses in September and October, but these quadrupled in November. The entrance to the Thames was shut, the English Channel itself was closed to shipping, and London was left with only a few weeks' food supply.

Mines accomplished most of this. Laid by German ships and low-flying planes, they could not be detected by minesweepers, yet when a ship passed over them they exploded and all but blew the ship out of the water. The explosions were so severe and so sudden that there was little time to launch lifeboats or to signal for help, and the sinkings were terrifying and accompanied by great loss of life. Both neutral and British vessels were being blown up indiscriminately. After many attempts, a mine was captured intact, but it blew up and killed its investigators. On November 23, a grueling search turned up another mine. This one didn't blow up.

One day in November a document turned up in the hands of the British attaché in Oslo. Someone, obviously a scientist or a technician who enjoyed access to advanced German technological reports, packed an enormous amount of information into a few detailed pages that became known as the Oslo Report. It described the development of the long-range bomber, remote-controlled gliders, pilotless aircraft, rocket-propelled artillery shells, electric fuses for bombs and shells, new kinds of magnetic torpedoes, aircraft range finders, new methods of attack on concrete bunkers with flamethrowers and smoke grenades, and the location of secret Luftwaffe testing laboratories, including the most important one, at Peenemünde. The information was so astounding that the British for some time discounted it as too fantastic to be true.

On December 2, Thomas "Digger" Foley had the lookout watch in the crow's nest of the freighter *Doric Star*, which was carrying meat, butter, canned goods, and wool from Australia around the Horn of Africa to England. They were midway between Capetown and Freetown. Foley had spent the last sixteen years away from home as an Australian sheep shearer, hotel maintenance man, boxer, and stevedore; Captain Stubbs had promised they'd be home by Christmas, and that had sounded good to Foley. At 1:20 P.M, Foley heard an explosion and a half minute later saw a shell splash a hundred yards to port. Before the captain could get the gun unlimbered, another explosion sent a shell fifty yards astern. Now they could see their attacker. It was a pocket battleship, and it was closing quickly. Captain Stubbs had just ordered "Sparks" Comber to send out an SOS when the raider's boarding party pulled up and a sign on board the battleship came into view: STOP WIRELESS OR WE FIRE The captain canceled his order to "Sparks." After the crew was taken off the ship, the *Doric Star* was sunk by the battleship, the *Graf Spee*. Four days later Foley and the other seamen were transferred from the *Spee* to the supply ship *Altmark* while it pumped oil to the battleship; Stubbs and the officers remained on board the *Spee*. All were prisoners.

Neither the prisoners nor their German captors knew that the *Doric Star*'s SOS had been heard and that word of it had gone out to the Royal Navy.

Launched in 1936 as the most advanced design in compact battleships, the *Graf Spee* bristled with armament and was sheathed in heavy armor plate. In command was Hans Langsdorff, a veteran of the Imperial Navy who had fought at Jutland, the largest naval battle of the Great War. Since September 30, when Berlin had signaled the raiders to begin operations, Langsdorff and the *Graf Spee* had been capturing British freighters and sinking them. Langsdorff was proud that not a single sailor from any of the nine ships he captured had lost his life. A gentleman warrior, Langsdorff could also be cunning: he transmitted false radio messages to throw off pursuit, and rigged dummy funnels and turrets to make his ship look in silhouette like the British *Repulse*. The *Doric Star* was the *Graf Spee*'s largest prize.

On December 2, after receiving the report of the *Doric Star*'s SOS in his cabin aboard the *Ajax*, Commodore Henry Harwood guessed that the German raider that had captured her would next strike either at Rio de Janeiro, at the River Plate, or near the Falkland Islands—the three targets each separated by a thousand miles. Forced to make a choice,

Harwood gambled that the raider, whose name he did not yet know, would choose the Plate estuary near the Uruguayan capital of Montevideo and the Argentinian capital of Buenos Aires. Harwood ordered the *Ajax*, the *Achilles*, and the larger *Exeter* to converge off the Plate. For a day the British practiced concentrating their fire, sending signals, and executing flanking maneuvers. On the night of December 12, they were in position, and at four minutes after dawn the next morning it became apparent that Harwood's guess of ten days before had been spectacularly right. Out of the darkness on the horizon loomed the *Graf Spee*.

An unequal battle was joined. The *Graf Spee's* eleven-inch guns, which delivered payloads of 4,140 pounds each, dwarfed the eight-inchers of the *Exeter* (1,600 pounds) and the six-inchers of the *Ajax* and *Achilles* (900 pounds). But the British ships could move faster, and Harwood had split his forces so that Langsdorff could not fire on all three at once. The combatants were eleven miles from one another, and were firing artillery shells which ascended three and a half miles into the air at velocities of up to 2,000 mph. Each shell stayed aloft nearly a minute before crashing down. The near-misses which splattered the decks with steel splinters were almost as damaging as the direct hits. During a furious ninety-minute battle, the *Graf Spee* wrecked the *Exeter*, put her gun turrets out of action, and caused more than fifty deaths. But Langsdorff did not know he had won, and with thirty-seven dead and forty--seven wounded of his own, he headed for port, harassed by the diligent *Ajax* and *Achilles*.

The *Graf Spee* docked at Montevideo near midnight December 13–14. Next morning, newspapermen, newsreel cameramen, radio commentators, and other reporters descended in droves on the Uruguayan capital. Standing by in the *Ajax* just off the mouth of the estuary, Harwood received a cable promoting him to admiral and notifying him that he had been elected knight commander of the Order of the Bath. That was fine, but what he really needed was reinforcements. No British fighting ships of size were within thousands of miles. Should the *Graf Spee* try to make a run for the open sea, she could probably blast the *Ajax*, the *Achilles*, and the approaching *Cumberland* to smithereens. Somehow the *Graf Spee* had to be persuaded to stay in port four or five days, until the arrival of the *Ark Royal* and the *Renown*.

The BBC cooperated by broadcasting a report that the two large ships were just over the horizon and already in position. The Foreign Service provided a feint as the British ambassador asked Uruguay to deny the *Graf Spee* permission to stay in harbor for more than twenty-four hours. The British knew the Uruguayans would not honor the request for fear of alienating Germany. Instead, Uruguay obligingly told Langsdorff that the *Graf Spee* would have to leave within seventy-two hours, or by late in the day on December 17.

On a hillside above Montevideo, Langsdorff sprinkled earth over the coffins of the thirty-seven dead German sailors, while five English ship captains, representatives of the sixty-one Britons he had freed when the *Graf Spee* had docked, placed beside the coffins a wreath inscribed "To the memory of brave men of the sea from their comrades of the British Merchant Service." It all seemed proper, correct, and out of an older world. The reporters had a field day.

Langsdorff wired for instructions. He told Berlin that he believed the *Ark Royal* and the *Renown* stood off the estuary. He could perhaps fight his way to Buenos Aires, which was across the wide river, but that was full of risk. If he could not get across the river, should his ship be interned or should he scuttle her in the shallow waters of the estuary? Hitler first insisted that Langsdorff get pictures of the *Ark Royal*, which a Luftwaffe pilot claimed to have sunk on September 28. His second instruction was that Langsdorff must fight his way out, and if he could not escape, he must at least take a few British ships down with him. Internment was not permitted, and scuttling was not encouraged. Langsdorff faithfully attempted to get pictures of the *Ark Royal*, but there were no planes available for charter. On his own, he took note of his low ammunition and the damaged state of his ship, and decided that a suicidal battle to get the *Graf Spee* to Buenos Aires would accomplish nothing. So, regretfully but humanely, he decided to scuttle the raider. Believing that he had already told headquarters what his alternatives were and that he had received adequate guidance, he did not inform Berlin of his plans.

Sunday afternoon December 17 was glorious in Montevideo. The sun shone brightly on the 750,000 people who had come to watch the *Graf Spee*. Radio commentators broadcast the scene to a waiting world. Along with tens of millions of people, President Roosevelt stayed glued to his set all afternoon. In the fading light, the *Graf Spee* with a small scuttling party aboard slipped her moorings and steamed toward the estuary mouth. Several miles away from the big cities, where there was no danger of hurting anyone, Langsdorff nosed the ship onto a mudbank. After setting charges, he and the crew transferred to tugboats and headed for Buenos Aires. At 8:54 PM. the moment of sunset, when the *Spee* was silhouetted most beautifully against the horizon, the charges went off. Flames and black smoke spiraled to the sky as the battleship sank into the mudbank.

Hitler had expected the *Graf Spee* to fight to the death, and he was incensed. Goebbels tried to salvage the event by releasing a bulletin that the scuttling had been ordered by the Führer because he would not allow his ship to surrender. But the ignominious end of the *Graf Spee* was a great British propaganda victory. It gave Britain and France hope and for a time stopped surface commerce raiding in the Atlantic. One day after the scuttling, Langsdorff assembled his crew for a farewell, left letters for his wife, his parents, and for the German ambassador to

Buenos Aires, and shot himself with his revolver. He chose to spill his blood on an old Imperial German Navy ensign, rather than honor with his death the swastika flag.

As the *Graf Spee* held the world's attention, one of the eighty-five German ships which had been interned in Latin American ports since the onset of the war tried to make a dash for home. The *Columbus*, a luxury liner which was larger than the old *Lusitania*, left Veracruz and soon encountered American naval patrols. The American ships were polite and kept their distance. The captain of the *Columbus* regarded them as his protectors and did not suspect that they were broadcasting the *Columbus's* position in plain English on a frequency known to be monitored by the Royal Navy. When the *Columbus* turned, she would signal her followers; at night she hung out a safety light; when one of the American ships left the pack, she semaphored, "God speed, a safe return." The charade ended about 350 miles off the New Jersey coast. The American ships stood off as the British destroyer *Hyperion* came up and fired two blanks at the *Columbus*, preparatory to searching her. In a panic, the captain of the *Columbus* scuttled the ship, and American boats rescued five hundred survivors and took them to New York. The German ambassador to the United States was so grateful for the rescue that he profusely thanked the State Department and never suspected that it had been the American neutrality patrol that had handed over the *Columbus*, lock, stock, and barrel, to the Royal Navy.

9

Christmas in Finland

Soviet-German cooperation continued unabated through the fall and winter. Russia and Germany exchanged large unwanted groups of people in the various portions of what had once been Poland, while the Gestapo and the NKVD met to discuss the suppression of dissidents in the area. Stalin also sent over 200,000 Polish prisoners of war and an equal number of Polish civilians to Russian camps.

Under the provisions of the Nazi-Soviet pact, Stalin had undermined the independence of Estonia, Latvia, and Lithuania. Now he looked forward to taking Bessarabia and thereby getting closer to the Rumanian oil fields—but he decided he must first have dominion over the entire Baltic, and had begun negotiations with Finland to gain it. He wanted Russia to have some breathing space on the Karelian Isthmus above Leningrad, and some Baltic bases, but he didn't want the whole of Finland. He had spent a lot of time there before the Revolution, and he liked the people; he was even willing to make some trades, such as giving Finland territory to broaden her narrow waist—but he was not willing to wait. All through October the Finnish negotiators had dragged their feet.

In early November, Stalin called the Finns to his office, stabbed his stubby finger at a map, and said with brutal casualness, "Do you need these islands?" Three small dots near Hanko were circled in red; along with a small sector north of Leningrad, these were Stalin's "moderate" demands. The negotiators, one a former prime minister of Finland, had never even heard of the islands, and they wanted either to cede them or to make a counteroffer. But Helsinki wanted to stand firm: the Finnish cabinet believed that giving Stalin the inconsequential islands would not end the issue; once those demands were met, there would be larger and larger ones until full Soviet domination of Finland would be achieved. Stalin broke off the talks on November 8.

In Finland a period of relaxation set in. The negotiators had held firm, and Stalin had backed away. Reservists went home, householders took antishatter strips off windows, and schools resumed classes. In Moscow, O. W. Kuusinen, the head of the exiled Finnish Communist party, Stalin's ghostwriter and secretary general of the Comintern, told Stalin that capitalist Finland was ripe for revolution. Andrei Zhdanov, Stalin's heir apparent and the ruler of Leningrad, said a few hundred thousand soldiers could topple Finland. Helsinki and Moscow thus perfectly misunderstood one another: Finland believed Russia would not attack, and Russia believed Finland would immediately cave in. In vain a German military attaché warned a Finnish general to settle with Russia without war "Otherwise nothing might remain of Finland but a tale of heroism."

On November 26, the Finnish ambassador in Moscow was handed a note which said Finnish artillery had killed Russian troops near Mainila, the far northern suburb of Leningrad. There was a border commission to mediate all such incidents, but Molotov wasn't looking for satisfaction: in the tradition of the faked raid on Gleiwitz, Mainila was to be a *casus belli*.

On November 28, the nonaggression treaty between the two countries was canceled by Molotov, and just after midnight on November 30 the Finnish ambassador was informed that relations between his government and Russia were now severed.

In the morning, Soviet bombers flew over Helsinki, dropped leaflets which said Finland wanted war, and loosed bombs which killed 65 and left 120 wounded. On the Karelian Isthmus, at two points in Finland's waist, and at the Arctic port of Petsamo, Russian troops attacked in strength. The Russian navy shelled the base at Hanko. With an air, land, and sea assault reminiscent of the German attack on Poland, the Russians had begun a war with Finland.

The assault on Finland outraged the world, more perhaps than the assault on Poland, because there had been no preceding period of acrimony between the aggressor and the smaller country. CBS correspondent William Shirer noted in his diary:

> The whole moral foundation which the Soviets have built up for themselves in international relations in the last ten years has collapsed like a house of cards. . . . Stalin reveals himself of the same stamp as Hitler, Mussolini, and the Japs. Soviet foreign policy turns out to be as "imperialist" as that of the czars. The Kremlin has betrayed the revolution.

In near-panic, 200,000 people fled Helsinki. The government was forced to resign, and a new one was formed in which banker Risto Ryti became premier and Väinö Tanner foreign minister. Tanner had long been a stalwart of the labor movement and had recently been finance minister and one of the negotiators who had failed in Moscow. Immediately after the shooting began, Tanner tried to re-establish contact with the Russians. He and most of the new ministers did not want a war, and were more than ever willing to negotiate. Their efforts were to no avail. Stalin established Kuusinen, a former friend of Tanner's, as head of a puppet government which was set up by the Red Army across the Finnish border in the abandoned beach resort of Terijoki. Thereafter Stalin refused to talk about Finland's future with anyone but Kuusinen and the "Democratic Republic of Finland."

The Russians pushed into four areas. From Leningrad they drove north up the Karelian Isthmus. In the narrow midsection of Finland, they pushed west toward Sweden at two points a hundred miles apart. Two other divisions headed for the warm-weather port of Petsamo.

Making many thrusts at different places at the same time was the blitzkrieg pattern, but the Russians were not adept at it. To accomplish the task, Meretskov, the military commander of Leningrad, had 700,000 men in four armies. Over Meretskov was Semën Timoshenko. Both promised Stalin that fighting in Finland would be completed in three weeks, in time to celebrate the dictator's sixtieth birthday on December 21. Because the conflict was not expected to last, the troops had had little training and wore lightweight uniforms. The best of the troops were held back while peasants from rural areas were put in the front lines with the expectation that they would roll over their objectives by sheer weight of numbers.

Vyaschlev Oreshin was attached to a propaganda brigade of the Red Army. As the young soldier went into Finland, he believed that army to be the organ of glorious revolution:

> Stern and relentless as the punishing hand of Nemesis it will call such [Finnish] warmongers to account. It will drive them forth from their cafés and restaurants, it will drag them from their concert halls and compel them to the majestic symphony of war!

However, a few days after he entered Finland, Oreshin complained of the Finnish tactics—snipers, booby-trapped bicycles, night attacks by skiers—and wrote:

> For four days now we have tried in vain to take Loimola Station. The men have lain in snow for three days and didn't dare lift their heads. Several of them are frostbitten. We are compelled to sleep with our clothes on, and can't even take our felt boots off.... Our casualties are heavy ... more from frostbite than from enemy fire. The butchers are accustomed to fire carefully at our troops from the side of the road. We can't even put our noses out of the trenches. Our men have launched several attacks but have always been beaten back. The barbed wire is man-high. Tank obstacles are everywhere. The marshes and splendidly camouflaged posts around us make the Finns invulnerable.

He wrote a letter to be delivered in the event of his death, and hoped the war would go better; he was soon to be made a full-fledged *politruk*.

Finland was honeycombed with thousands of lakes and waterways, which made it difficult for the Russians to advance along broad fronts or to join up their armies. As they had in Poland, men in tanks confronted men on bicycles, but this time the weather was on the side of the underdogs. Rune XXXII of the *Kalevala*, the Finnish national epic written in medieval times, expressed the wish, "Let our contests be in the winter,/Let our wars be on the snowfields." So it was with this war. The winter brought temperatures of thirty to forty degrees below zero. The Finns were used to such cold: along the frozen waterways they carved roads of ice; on these roads they dragged equipment atop hollowed-out log sledges and soft-tired bicycles, and sent raiding parties dressed in white capes and on silent skis to attack Russians huddled about cook fires. The Finns slept in weatherproof tents, wore thick boots and gloves of fur (not felt) which were carefully made with slits for trigger fingers. They ate reindeer meat or farm produce or went hungry.

Equipment came from all over. There was artillery from Sweden and England, parts of planes from France, and grenades from seven different nations. The Finnish State Liquor Board provided seventy thousand empty bottles, which became "Molotov cocktails" and were thrown against the Russian tanks. Although the casualty rate for those who threw the explosives was 60 to 70 percent, the Finns threw them anyway. "Death boxes," the Finns called the Russian tanks; "moving zoo," they called the numberless attackers. For every Finn and Finnish airplane that perished, the Finns killed ten Russians and downed ten Russian planes.

Field Marshal Baron Carl Gustav Emil von Mannerheim commanded Finland's army. Fit and mentally sharp at age seventy-two, he was considered a great tactician. Born of a Swedish family in Russian-controlled Finland, he rose to general in the czar's army before the Revolution. In 1918, he led Finnish anti-Bolshevik forces and threw off Russian domination of Finland. In 1919, though nearly a dictator, he ran in the country's presidential election, and when he lost he retired. In the early 1930s, he was again called on to create Finland's defenses and to lead the army.

The Mannerheim Line, Finland's only extended fortification, was as primitive in its own way as the Molotov cocktail. It was no more than sixty-six concrete nests with some tank traps in between, spread across the eighty-eight-mile-wide Karelian isthmus. None of the bunkers had anything like the design or the armaments of the Maginot Line. The strength of the line, Marshal Mannerheim wrote, was "in the tenacity and courage of the soldiers" who manned it.

After the first week of shock, the Finns began to halt the Russian invaders. On the Karelian isthmus, the Mannerheim Line held. In the waist, the Finns blocked numerically superior forces. And in the north, two regiments of Finns stood off two divisions of Russians.

Newspapers and broadcasting companies fell all over themselves to get reporters to Finland. The Russo-Finnish conflict was so remote, and so seemingly simple—red versus white—that it beguiled the world. However, Mannerheim maintained that this was war, not Hollywood, and would not allow reporters near the front. As a result, the reporters knew only the Finnish side of the campaign and precious little about that. They sent home reports of the Finns laughing at the antics of Kuu- sinen, whose followers had been photographed in traditional Finnish costumes which no one had worn for a hundred years. Kussinen's wife was a *lotti*, a member of the women's assistance corps in Finland, and his sons were in the Finnish army. Reporters wrote in detail about Finns on skis and in their *lummi pukkus*, white snow capes, swooping down on the Russians to deliver *belaya smert*, the white death.

All this was true, but wide of the mark. The newsmen failed to point out that Finnish counterthrusts in December did not push the at- tackers back into Russia. Nor did they note, as the Finnish military did, that for every Russian who died, three came to replace him. They praised the help given Finland by other countries—even though Italian planes were refused through-shipment to Finland at the German bor- der, British and French supplies were sent in quantities too small to be decisive, and the volunteers from Scandinavian countries and from the rest of the world amounted to only ten thousand men. In mid-Decem- ber, newspapers devoted an inordinate amount of space to reporting that the all-but-moribund League of Nations had expelled the Soviet Union from membership because it had invaded Finland.

What perhaps gave everyone hope was the idea that, in December, the Finns seemed to be winning the unequal battle. They had cut off a large unit of the Russian army, and surrounded it near Suomussalmi. This surrounded area they called a *motti*, the word for a cord of wood that was stacked up to be chopped. For some days the Finns could not get inside the Russian ring of tanks, but neither could the Russians get out, nor could supplies reach them. When starvation set in, they tried to break out and advance in a thin five-mile-long column toward their nearest compatriots. The Finns annihilated them. On Christmas Day, James Aldridge of the North American Newspaper Alliance sent home a report from the scene of the battle:

> It was the most horrible sight I had ever seen. As if the men had suddenly turned to wax. There were two or three thousand Russians and a few Finns all frozen in fighting attitudes. Some were locked together, their bayonets within each other's bodies, some were frozen with their arms crooked holding the hand grenades they were throwing. . . . Their fear was registered in their frozen faces. Their bodies were like statues of men throwing all of their muscles and strength into some work, but their faces recorded something between bewilderment and horror.

This moment of war haunted all who saw it, especially those who reached for words and photographs compelling enough to describe it for the newspaper readers of the world.

Deep in their war, the Finns that Christmas experienced a religious revival the likes of which had not been seen for a generation. Soldiers in the snow-covered fields said they had seen an angel in the sky guarding them.

In the United States, parties were given for Finnish relief. The chairman of the relief fund was former president Herbert Hoover, who had aided Finland after the Great War. Americans contributed over two million dollars: in this war their sympathies were clear, and they were not plagued by the questions raised by the Allies' conduct in the larger conflict.

Though President Roosevelt expressed great concern for Finland, he did not commit his administration to doing much for it. At Christmas he reached out for peace in the larger war. For the first time in American history, a United States ambassador was sent to the Holy See to ask the pope to join the president in an appeal to end the war. Roosevelt was photographed among the many stockings which were hung on the White House mantelpiece, and he told reporters that he would read Dickens aloud to his grandchildren. He also lit the national Christmas Tree. But later, out of sight of the reporters, Roosevelt composed his thoughts for a New Year's speech, and they were dark: "It becomes clearer and clearer that the future world will be a shabby and dangerous place to live in—yes, even for Americans to live in—if it is ruled by force in the hands of a few."

In Moscow, the focus of attention was the stalemate in Finland. At the Kremlin, Nikita Khrushchev, a minor party functionary, went to a private dinner shortly after Stalin's birthday celebration. Russian troops had been ordered not to attack unless the way had first been prepared by artillery and they possessed overwhelming superiority in numbers; with such orders, few Russian commanders saw any need to take the offensive. At dinner, Khrushchev listened to an enraged Stalin shout at Commissar of Defense Voroshilov, who had overall charge of the military effort in Finland. Voroshilov, the man who had negotiated with France and England the previous summer, was equally angry at Stalin. The commissar, Khrushchev wrote,

> leaped up, turned red and hurled Stalin's accusations back into his face. "You have yourself to blame for all this! You're the one who had our best generals killed." Stalin rebuffed him, and Voroshilov picked up a platter with a roast suckling pig on it and smashed it on the table.

In Rome, for the first time in a hundred years, the king of Italy and the pope exchanged visits. Since the pope was known to be anti-Nazi, the visit was interpreted as the expression of the king's displeasure with Italy's Axis partner. Mussolini expressed his own displeasure in a letter to Hitler that marked the high-water point of his resistance to Berlin's policies. The Duce sided with Finland against Russia. Hitler must stop backing Russia and get on with the real business of the Axis, which was to destroy Communism and the Western democracies:

> You cannot abandon the anti-Semitic and anti-Bolshevist banners which you have flown for twenty years. . . . You cannot abjure your gospel, which the German people have blindly believed. . . . The solution for your *lebensraum* is in Russia and nowhere else. Russia has 21 million square kilometers and 9 inhabitants per square kilometer.

Mussolini recommended that Germany set up a separate Polish state, and stop its horrifying treatment of the recently subjugated Poles.

In Poland, during the worst winter in forty-six years, the Germans were moving a half-million people from various regions into an area near Lublin. Most were Jews; Catholics and others were taken to other destinations. All through November and December they had been transported in boxcars, in open trucks, and by forced marches. Thousands died en route, and their bodies were thrown onto the wayside, where they lay unburied. By Christmas the city of Lublin had become a vast concentration camp for a quarter-million Jews. A survivor wrote a few weeks later in a New York Yiddish newspaper:

> The congestion, the stench, the poverty, the disease and chaos which reign in Lublin cannot be paralleled anywhere else on earth. Men live in the streets, in cattle stalls, in cellars, in carts and in the debris of devastated houses. You see their clothes hanging on trees along the main streets. Men die like flies in the thoroughfares, their bodies strewn on the roadway like burned-out cinders. Shrouds are no longer used for the dead because they cannot be bought. At night everything is pitch black. The electric cables were smashed in the bombardment, and when they were repaired later, there was no coal to keep the power stations going. . . . Foodstuffs are unobtainable. The whole city is girt with barbed-wire fences, and the Nazis allow no traffic to pass through. The water has turned foul and cannot be drunk. All the wells have become polluted. Cholera and typhus are already rampant. . . . Men die like flies faster than one can bury them. Hundreds and thousands of bodies are thrown together into mass graves.

An estimated fifty thousand people died en route and in Lublin at this time, twice as many as had been killed in the bombardments of Warsaw.

Adolf Hitler spent Christmas with his troops at the front. He crossed the French border at Spichern, a small town which the Germans had taken; it was the first time he had set foot on French soil since the Great War. He then went to the Berghof, where he spooned molten lead into ice water and tried to read his future in the contorted shapes that emerged as the metal solidified again. The lead made no clear prophecies. It was the weather which made him postpone for two more weeks the date of the invasion. Currently there was too much fog for the planes.

American journalist A. J. Liebling visited French soldiers on the Maginot Line at Christmas and tried to get a handle on the inexplicable phony war. He was a guest at a small fort; a tea cart which held twenty bottles of various alcoholic beverages was wheeled out:

> The Colonel took an obvious pride in his gamut of alcohols; it proved he could "defend himself." The verb *se defendre* has acquired a very broad meaning in the French army; it signifies "getting along." An officer pulls a pair of old socks over his shoes so that he will not slip on the ice; a private meets a stray hen and wrings her neck because otherwise she might fly into Germany. . . . It follows logically that a colonel must defend himself on a grander scale than that of a subordinate, lest he lose face in this most reasonable of armies.

After dinner, coffee, Armagnac, and a theatrical show in a dungeon, the party broke up at dawn. The only unhappy man was a regular army officer who said to the colonel:

> "This is all very well, my Colonel, but it isn't really war." The Colonel, whose chest was covered with campaign ribbons and decorations from 1914–1918, stopped chuckling and looked at the captain steadily. "Sometime you may look back on this evening," he said, "and you will say, 'The days at the fort were the good ones.' What the devil! A fellow has to defend himself."

French soldiers on leave found the spirit of Paris darkened by blackout restrictions. Churches were crowded for midnight mass, and at the last minute the shops were full of the usual delicacies. People gladly bought them regardless of price, but a reporter noted that Parisians were filled with foreboding, that they celebrated because they did not know what the new year would bring and were not sure if there would ever be another such celebration.

Behind the scenes in London, the cabinet received a holiday present as Churchill announced that the German puzzle had been solved: the mines were magnetic, and a way had been found to "degauss" British ships to protect them from the mines. London would not starve.

A cartoon in one of the city's papers showed Santa's sleigh as a flying object fired upon by antiaircraft guns. The blackout and the evacuation put crimps in the traditional holiday; many children were away from home and church bells could not be rung, because they might be confused with air-raid sirens. As if the idea would help, it was pointed out that the Holy Family's evacuation before the birth of Christ had come about as the consequence of an early dictator's power politics.

On Christmas Day, King George VI braved his stutter to deliver a short radio address to the nation. It was an exhortation to courage—in dark times all had to do their best—and closed with some lines the king had been sent by a friend:

> I said to the man who stood at the Gate of the Year, "Give me a light that I may tread safely into the unknown." And he replied, "Go out into the darkness and put your hand into the Hand of God. That shall be to you better than light, and safer than a known way."

It took reporters a whole frantic day before they were able to track down the authorship of those lines. Minnie Louise Haskins, a retired lecturer in economics, had penned them in 1908. *The Desert*, her obscure volume containing them, was immediately reprinted and became a best-seller.

10

A Plane Crashes

On January 10, 1940, two million German soldiers poised on the borders of Belgium, Holland, and France made ready to invade those countries on January 17. Once more the imminence of the invasion had been leaked to the West through Oster, Sas, and the Vatican; and this time preparations to resist the German thrust were in high gear.

At ten that morning, Major Helmut Reinberger, who was late for a meeting in Cologne, hitched a ride in Major Erich Hönmanns's Messerschmitt-108. Since the subject of the meeting was the relief of German paratroops who would land in Belgium when the invasion began, Reinberger had in his yellow briefcase the Luftwaffe's orders for the invasion. It was contrary to regulations for an officer to fly with such secret papers, but Reinberger was late and felt that he must cut a few corners.

Almost immediately after takeoff the plane flew into heavy fog and mist. Hönmanns, who had never taken the controls of an Me-108 before, guided the plane down to six hundred feet in order to follow the Rhine River from Westphalia to Cologne. But the river he saw was too narrow to be the Rhine. He panicked, and in fumbling with the instrument panel he cut off the plane's fuel supply. The plane dived; the wings sheared off between two trees; and the fuselage, the majors, and the yellow briefcase all spilled onto a high ridge. An old peasant came up to the men. He spoke no German, and Hönmanns deduced that they were in trouble. In bad French, the major asked where they were. In Mechelen-sur-Meuse, near the Dutch border of Belgium, the peasant responded.

Reinberger begged a box of matches from the old man and began to burn the papers; if higher-ups discovered that he had traveled with them, he would be shot; the first batch of papers was alight when soldiers on bicycles captured Reinberger and Hönmanns, and stamped out the fire. Men and papers were taken to a control point. Inside the office, Reinberger threw his papers into a stove; a Belgian officer reached into the fire and took them out, severely burning his hand. Reinberger tried to seize the officer's pistol and commit suicide, but that attempt was also frustrated. Next morning Belgian army commander van Overstraeten read the partially charred papers and noted in his log: "The veil has been torn away"; the German intent to invade was not only crystal clear but documented.

On hearing the news, Hitler flew into a rage. He shouted, "It is things like this that can lose us the war!" He demanded a list of what had been in the yellow briefcase and had the majors' wives thrown into prison. Then he issued an order that henceforth no one was to see secret papers who had no real need to know the contents. But he did not cancel the invasion.

Göring, Reinberger's ultimate superior, fired the western sector's chief of air operations and the chief's deputy, though neither man had had anything to do with the incident. Emily Göring consulted her soothsayer. Without any knowledge of what had happened, Dr. Augustus Heerman concocted a surprisingly accurate version of the occurrences in Belgium. He also said that the legible matter that survived after the papers had been burned was only so much as could be covered by a normal hand placed in the center of a page. Apprised of this, Göring telephoned Hitler, and the Führer came to the Göring apartment to listen to Emily's tale. A copy of the original batch of papers was brought to them, and the two leaders of the Reich placed their hands over the papers to see what could be read. That test proved inconclusive, so the two went down to a boiler room and threw equivalent batches of papers into the fire and afterward studied the charred remains. Only then were they satisfied that Reinberger had probably destroyed enough of the papers so that no harm had been done to the invasion plan.

That notion was contradicted by intelligence reports that showed an increase in Dutch and Belgian mobilizations. Further information, which came from French and Belgian transmissions in codes previously broken by German intelligence, related that the Belgian army had been ordered to offer no resistance to British and French troops who were about to cross into Belgium, but should dismantle frontier barriers to assist the Allies' passage. To all this information Hitler added that of his weather bureau, which predicted steady fog for the near future, and he postponed Fall Gelb indefinitely.

The invasion was off, but it was not forgotten. One additional reason for the postponement may have been Hitler's wish to have the plan itself revised. As far back as September of 1939, he had begun to worry about the efficacy of Fall Gelb. Halder had taken the old Schlieffen Plan, which had been used in the Great War, and had fancied it up a bit—but it was still the old plan. Troops were to invade the northern part of Belgium through Holland, and were to push the defenders across to the Channel, after which they were to wheel south and drive down on Paris. In late September, Hitler suggested to Brauchitsch and Halder that they consider an invasion that might strike farther south, through the supposedly impenetrable Ardennes forest at Belgium's southeastern corner; such an attack would skirt the Maginot Line and would be unexpected. The chiefs did not find the suggestion compelling.

The same idea of a punch through the south had been brewing in the mind of Erich von Manstein, a brilliant and abrasive lieutenant general whom Guderian called "our finest operational brain." Manstein had served in the battle of Verdun, in which a half-million men had been killed before the carnage was stopped. Like Guderian, who considered tanks to be a life-saving weapon because they allowed an army to conquer territory without vast attendant slaughter, Manstein was an advocate of the new mobile warfare. Guderian was the tactician, the brilliant on-the-spot innovator. Manstein was the grand strategist. When Ludwig Beck had resigned before Munich, Manstein, who was his chief of staff, was put out to pasture. In early 1939, Karl von Rundstedt rescued him for his own planning staff. In October 1939, Manstein examined Fall Gelb and did not like it. In his view, the plan was a prescription for half-measures rather than for full victory; if Germany was to invade, she must do so decisively. Manstein wrote a memorandum that suggested that the focus of the attack be shifted to the south, and that a feint be made in the north. It was well known in German army circles that the Allies would move up and into Belgium at the moment of invasion. In the plan Manstein was evolving, if the Allies moved up, attracted by the northern feint, then the major German punch through the south would come up behind them and cut them off; the Allied armies would thus be encircled, and the war would be over. Manstein's was a simple yet daring plan. Von Rundstedt backed it, but Halder and Brauchitsch squelched Manstein's memo and it did not reach Hitler.

The idea of a punch through the Ardennes nagged at Hitler, but in unfinished form. Perhaps Guderian's panzer corps might take a jab at the area of Sedan, on the Meuse; Guderian liked the idea, but said two panzer corps were insufficient to do such a large job. In late November, Hitler delivered to 180 of his top military men a scathing lecture on cowardice, lack of imagination, and obstructionism. The tirade had the effect of softening the opposition of Brauchitsch and Halder, both to Hitler and to the emergence of new ideas. Manstein tried to advance his idea several times more, and each time he rewrote his memorandum the plan took on more subtlety and daring. When Reinberger's plane crashed, Manstein saw his big chance. On January 25, he took his sixth memorandum in hand, confronted Brauchitsch, and accused him of defeatism. Two days later Manstein was posted to a remote area.

But before Manstein was scheduled to depart for his new posting, the army held war games. In these top-secret exercises Manstein's guesses were verified: a northern thrust might meet stiff Allied opposition, while a southern punch coupled with a northern feint might result in a smashing victory. Colonel Rudolph Schmundt, Hitler's chief adjutant, talked with Manstein at the games and returned to Berlin bubbling with enthusiasm over Manstein's plan for the invasion. He conveyed his thoughts to Hitler, who immediately summoned Manstein. In the Führer's presence the strategist became a great salesman. The day after seeing Manstein, Hitler presented Manstein's plan as his own to Brauchitsch and Halder, and told them to implement it.

Having already been convinced by the war games of the new plan's logic, the chiefs for the first time were eager to agree with Hitler. The feeling that he should be assassinated faded. With a viable strategy in hand, with thoughts of battlefield success in their heads, the generals forgot certain principles they had professed to admire only a few months before, and became wholly converted to Hitler's long-held tenet that victory was the only measure of rightness.

Even as the chiefs moved toward him, Hitler was moving away from them. The Manstein plan was a first sign. Another was Hitler's decision to promote Erwin Rommel.

In the Great War, Rommel had distinguished himself by acts both brave and foolhardy. He led small infantry groups on dangerous missions behind enemy lines. Such actions earned him medals, but did not result in his being taken seriously as a commander. During the interwar years, without proper background or an older champion, he languished. In 1939, he was given the backwater task of guarding Hitler's headquarters, and he slavishly devoted himself to the Führer. After Poland, he begged a combat command, and Hitler gave him a tank corps. He had never before worked inside a tank, knew nothing about tank tactics or the mechanics of tank operation, and he had only a short period before the invasion in which to familiarize himself with tank warfare. In the war games and practice drills, Rommel, not being a longtime commander, insisted on staying at the front rather than remaining in the rear, where one could see the big picture.

A third affront to the chiefs was Hitler's plan for an invasion about which they were not even consulted initially. In October, Admiral Raeder had first suggested an invasion of Norway to assure Germany's supply of Swedish iron ore, which during the winter months was shipped through Norwegian waters. Hitler preferred Norway to remain neutral. In mid-December, Vidkun Quisling came to Berlin to see Nazi philosopher Alfred Rosenberg. A military man, Quisling hated Communists and feared that the Russo-Finnish war would spread to Norway. He had some credentials as a leader, having been Norwegian defense minister from 1931 to 1933, and currently led an anti-Semitic fascist party, the Nasjonal Samling. Quisling wanted Germany to back a coup by his party, after which he would ally Norway with the Reich. The coup must come soon, he told Raeder in December, because "a British landing is planned in the vicinity of Stavanger, and Kristiansand is proposed as a possible British [air] base. The present Norwegian government as well as Parliament and the whole foreign policy are controlled by the well-known Jew Hambro."

Against Ribbentrop's advice, Hitler met Quisling, but was only partly convinced by what he had to say. Quisling claimed 200,000 followers; Hitler's reports showed that he had 30,000. So, while he ordered Quisling briefed on ways to disrupt Norwegian shipping, foreign trade, and fisheries, and had him given the money to achieve such disruptions, behind Quisling's back and without his knowledge Hitler made plans to invade Norway. In mid-January the work on that invasion, code named Weserübung, was being done entirely under Hitler's personal tutelage.

In September, Hitler had signed an order which created a secret euthanasia program. The initial purpose was to obtain hospital beds for use by wounded German soldiers. One-third of all hospital beds were then occupied by the aged, the disabled, or the insane—and it was their beds Hitler wanted. In October, doctors were asked to fill out seemingly innocuous forms listing patients under their care who were senile, debilitated, criminally insane, or of non-German blood. The doctors did not know how the information was to be used, but soon after, the killings began, and by early 1940 several thousand hospital patients had been given lethal injections.

A family would be informed by letter that their aged or incurably insane relative had been transferred to a new hospital and had died there; because of the danger of contagion, the body had been cremated. People began to compare these letters and found a pattern to them. Clusters of letters had been sent from hospitals at Grafeneck, Hartheim, and from the ill-named Medical and Nursing Institute near Pirna. Knowledge of the deaths spread mostly through religious circulars, which had not yet been fully suppressed, and protests began to be heard. Among the best-known protesters were imprisoned clergyman Martin Niemöller and Dr. Friedrich von Bodelschwingh, another pastor and the head of the Bethe! Asylum for mental retardates. As the clamor rose, the government backed down on the euthanasia campaign; there were not many wounded soldiers as yet, and the hospital beds were not urgently required.

No similar public clamor arose about the fate of the Poles, whom many Germans considered subhuman creatures. The argument is often advanced that the German people did not know what was going on in Poland. Many did know. Letters home from soldiers told them:

> The wildest fantasy of atrocity propaganda is feeble in comparison to what an organized murderer, robber, and plunderer gang is doing there [Po-

land], with the supposed tolerance of highest quarters. I am ashamed to be a German! This minority, which by murder, plunder, and arson is besmirching the German name, will be the disaster of the German nation if we do not soon put a spoke in their wheel.

Some commanders—both in Poland and near the Siegfried Line—gathered their staffs and gave them lectures on SS atrocities in Poland. Although these were put-downs of the SS rather than a stimulus to effective action, the knowledge of SS sadism did filter home and to high military authorities.

Military Governor Johannes Blaskowitz's first report to Berlin on SS excesses had produced no visible result, so, possibly with the aid of Admiral Canaris, he made his second report even stronger. In early 1940, he listed thirty-three separate indictments of the SS—mass executions, unwarranted torture, unnecessary seizure of property—all of which had been witnessed and attested to by army officers. In a commentary, Blaskowitz reasoned that such SS behavior would not intimidate the Poles or help to subjugate them, but rather would provide the enemies of the Reich with ammunition for denouncing Germany. "Every soldier," he concluded, "feels disgusted and repelled by these crimes.... He cannot understand how things of this nature can go unpunished, especially as they occur, one might say, under his protection." Blaskowitz personally handed a copy of his memo to Brauchitsch, but the commander in chief had just heard the siren call of the Manstein plan and was in no mood to listen to complaints. Yet the memo did reach Hitler, and the Führer ordered an investigation into the practices. It was to be conducted by Himmler and Hans Frank, under whose guidance the atrocities had been perpetrated in the first place.

It is also often claimed that the outside world knew nothing of what was going on in Poland; this, too, is false. Eyewitness reports from Poland contemporaneous with the events reached the corners of the globe. Cardinal Hlond's February 11, 1940, report to the pope stated in a preamble:

> At this moment hundreds of thousands of persons are being banished in a barbarous manner from Poznania, Polish Pomerania, Lodz, Wlocawek, Kalisz and the countryside. Young men and girls are being deported to Germany. The leading classes will soon be exterminated in prisons, concentration camps and forced labor camps. Many persons have been shot. The Germans rob, sack and carry away everything they like, without giving any receipt. If this goes on, we shall perish miserably. It is not astonishing that a profound and terrible hate is being born in every heart.... With few exceptions [the Germans] are only executioners and sadists, without any human feeling. Terrible indeed is the trial which God is imposing on us. But, despite everything, the people is strong and enduring. It does not complain, but suffers heroically.

Hlond's report cited names, dates, and places of the atrocities, and was reprinted in truncated but understandable form in the Belgian, Dutch,

French, and British press. Other reports recounted, for one small example, the murder of a hundred Jews in a temple in Lask, where Sala Kaminska lived. The tale of Poland's agony was told but was not acted upon. No one believed it was possible to do anything to alleviate it.

In January 1940, in Poland near the border of East Prussia, the SS established the first *Todesborn,* or death camp. Several thousand Poles were sent there—Cardinal Hlond refers to the camp—and were slated for execution as soon as the western invasion should provide a diversion. Construction of a new concentration camp at Oswiecim was also begun in January 1940; I. G. Farben, the German industrial combine that moved into Poland along with the conquerors as it had moved earlier into Austria and Czechoslovakia, agreed to build the new camp to house workers for its own new synthetic-rubber plant next door. Several thousand Jews were rounded up for the construction at Oswiecim, which the Germans preferred to call by its German name, Auschwitz.

As the SS was concerned with death, so was it concerned with life. It sponsored the *Lebensborns,* maternity homes for unwed mothers of Aryan heritage. Originally, SS men gave part of their salaries for upkeep of the homes, but when Austria was annexed the financing of *Lebensborns* began to shift to money and property expropriated from Jews. Also, the *Lebensborns* slowly became places where the SS could couple with young women and hide the results from society. A young woman would enter a *Lebensborn* and have sexual relations with an SS man; if she became pregnant she would spend her confinement at the home. The child might be adopted by a family, or the mother might retain it and raise it with a state subsidy; she might repeat the process several times, all under the guidance of the *Lebensborn.* In January 1940, the scandal of the maternity homes that had become part brothels reached public consciousness. A Christmas "Open Letter to an Unmarried Mother" became the focal point for criticism. It urged that girls submit to soldiers who were about to go on active duty, since the children of such unions would be cared for by the state. People saw this as an open invitation to promiscuity, an extension of Himmler's edict issued in the early days of the shooting war:

> Every war involves a tremendous letting of the best blood. . . . Beyond the boundaries of bourgeois laws and customs . . . it will be a high duty of German women and girls of good blood to become the mothers, outside the boundaries of marriage, and not irresponsibly but in the spirit of deep moral seriousness, of children of soldiers going on active service of whom fate alone knows whether they will come back again or die for Germany.

Eighty percent of birth announcements had begun to read, "Girl with child seeks comrade for life with view to marriage." More than three-quarters of the girls in the *Lebensborns* came from the ranks of the BDM, the distaff arm of the Hitler Youth—girls fourteen and fifteen who had been thoroughly indoctrinated with the notion of serving the national interest. Mothers complained that their underage daughters had been effectively removed from their care, from society, and from the possibility of living normal lives. The homes were soon over-crowded, and there was a rash of new applications for places in them. Some people cynically suggested that, confronting a hard winter, the girls were becoming pregnant in order to assure themselves of food and warmth.

Rather than admit embarrassment at all this, the SS characteristically put on a positive publicity barrage. Himmler personally visited a *Lebensborn* to congratulate Frau Annie O—all mothers, wed or not, were allowed to use the title "Frau" in the homes—on her unusually large production of mother's milk. Public clamor soon subsided. There didn't seem to be much the German people could do about the excesses of the SS.

Himmler had dreams beyond the *Todesborns* and *Lebensborns*. He wished totally to restructure society, to return the German people to the feudal era of noble Teuton warriors closely tied to the soil, with humble and docile serfs at their command. In the winter of 1940, it occurred to Himmler that this ancient state of affairs could now be reproduced in the East (formerly known as Poland), where the SS held sway. The SS would be the warriors; they could rule what used to be Poland; and the myriad despised people of that region would become their serfs and work the land for them—or for less perfect German settlers who would come to the East for their lebensraum. He would cull the best of the polyglot peoples of Poland, deem them to be of Teutonic stock, and send them to *Lebensborns* to be Germanized; the rest he would turn into serfs or into factory workers forced to subsist on bread and water. If they died out, that would be no great loss. In a moment of passion Himmler confided this scheme to his masseur, including the comment that the East would become "the everlasting fountain of youth replenishing the lifeblood of Germany."

The plane crash on January 10 provoked a crisis in Allied relations with Belgium. Everyone thought the invasion would happen at any moment, even in such terrible weather. There was feverish activity on the part of Belgian, Dutch, French, and British troops and commands. Lord Gort and Alan Brooke of the British Expeditionary Force were summoned to a meeting with the Belgians.

John Standish Surtees Prendergast Vereker, Sixth Viscount Gort, was what the Germans would have called *nur-Soldat*, nothing but a soldier. To the Germans, that was a term of honor; to the British, it connoted competence but not brilliance. Gort was a man of acknowledged personal bravery, loyalty, and ease in the heat of battle, but he was not considered a great commander. He had been given leadership of the BEF to get him out of London's hair; he wouldn't have to do much in the field, because he would be under Gamelin's orders. Brooke liked Gort personally but thought he didn't really understand the big picture.

At the meeting, the two men met a man dressed in "most disreputable clothes" who had the air of cloak-and-dagger about him. He was Sir Roger Keyes, long a personal friend of both Leopold III and Winston Churchill. Keyes told them he was on a secret mission that might result in the British being allowed to take up positions inside Belgium before the invasion. Gort and Brooke agreed that nothing could be of more importance. Even though the British had fortified many positions on the Belgian border and would be loath to move from them in case of attack, if they were allowed to go into Belgium now and fortify new forward positions, that would be even better. Gamelin also was most eager to get into Belgium before an invasion. Leopold sent a message, via Keyes and Churchill, to Chamberlain. It was not a request for aid; rather it was a query as to whether such a request ought to be formally made.

Two days later, replies came back from both Chamberlain and Gamelin. The British were willing to give the Belgians far-reaching guarantees of military and financial aid not only on the Continent but in their colonies, and to give that aid not only in the present but in the future should Belgium be forced out of the war—but only if "the invitation [to take up positions inside Belgium] is given in sufficient time to enable British and French forces to secure a strategical advantage of position before any German attack begins." Gamelin's note was even more obvious, and said that the Allies must be allowed to bring major forces into Belgium before an invasion, or there would be no guarantees of aid at all.

The notes seemed to Leopold more in the nature of threats than offers of assistance. They clearly implied that should he refuse the Allies' help now, there would be no equivalent guarantees given him in the future. Leopold was appalled. He had given the Allies an inch, and they wished to take the whole arm. Should he encourage the Allies to enter his country as they proposed, Belgium's neutrality would cease to exist, and the Germans would have a perfect excuse for invading. The memoranda of Chamberlain and Gamelin left no room for any compromise or bargain. Earlier plans had envisaged Allied observers investigating the Belgian defenses and helping to build fortifications, while Allied troops stayed out of Belgium until the invasion: these were no longer considered. The choice given Leopold was all or nothing. He declined the gambit and did not request Allied aid in January.

The Allies were incensed at his refusal. Churchill, enraged, spoke in public about the potential victims of a crocodile who, in the hope of being eaten last, grovel shamelessly before the monster. Gamelin was vindictive. He complained to Daladier that Belgian intransigence had caused the French army to move needlessly up and back, and had worn out his soldiers. He was now less inclined to send his forces to the defense of the Belgians. At the same time he wanted to do battle on Belgian territory so that the war could be kept away from what he had earlier referred to as "our rich northern provinces."

Gamelin confronted the problem of the yellow briefcase. Was it a real find? Was it a German plant? If the plans found in it were the actual invasion plans, should he change his strategy?

After remarkably little soul-searching, he decided that the briefcase was indeed a real find and not a plant, but that he would disregard its contents except as they sustained his thesis that the Germans meant to launch their major attack into northern Belgium. With this decision, Gamelin dismissed out of hand any possibility that the Germans, who knew the briefcase had been captured, might take the occasion to alter their strategy. For a student of logic, this was folly—but then Gamelin was not so much a student of logic as the victim of it.

His plans to counter the invasion had begun to set themselves in his mind before the war began. French forces augmented by British units would move into Belgium to take up positions along the Escaut (or Scheldt) River from Antwerp to Ghent. This "low-risk" advance would enable the Allies to defend a small but tenable portion of Belgium—but it would mean that Brussels and the bulk of Belgium might be left to the invader and would not be contested. However, after Poland had fallen the Escaut move seemed politically unacceptable, since it would mean throwing both Holland and Belgium to the wolves.

Gamelin began to rethink his strategy. He had a somewhat new idea, but it ran into strong objection from his principal subordinate, General Alphonse Georges. In 1934, Georges had suffered severe injuries in the course of the plot which assassinated King Alexander of Yugoslavia. Many considered him France's best soldier, and said he would have been in Gamelin's place had it not been for the infirmities caused by his wounds. Georges and Gamelin disagreed on everything—the disposition of forces, the necessity of attack, the chain of command, even the location of headquarters. Georges's headquarters were in a resort city forty-five miles away from Gamelin's headquarters at Vincennes (which was itself some distance from Paris). Only telephones connected the two men, and as these were seldom used, communications between the commander in chief and his second often took days.

Gamelin's idea in November was that after an invasion French forces should go into Belgium beyond the Escaut to the Dyle, which stretched from Antwerp to the Meuse River at France's northeastern corner. Brussels and most of Belgium would thus be within the sphere protected by the Allied armies. In the wake of the January plane crash, Gamelin now proposed that the Allied forces should go even farther north, to the Breda area of Holland. Georges exploded at this:

There is no doubt that our offensive maneuver in Belgium and Holland should be conducted with the caution of not allowing ourselves to commit the major part of our reserves in this part of the theater, in face of a German action which could be nothing more than a diversion. For example, in the event of an attack in force breaking out in the center, on our front between the Meuse and Moselle, we could be deprived of the necessary means for a counterattack.

If the Armengaud report could almost have been written by Guderian, Georges's memorandum anticipated with remarkable insight the Manstein plan. Georges was concerned that the Dyle—and Breda—lines might be difficult to defend, and that the area left lightly defended when French forces went up into Belgium might prove to be the focal point of the German attack.

In the summer of 1938, French maneuvers under the direction of General André-Gaston Pretelat had already proved Georges's contention. Out of the "impenetrable" Ardennes forest area came seven French divisions who were masquerading as German units. Four of the divisions were motorized, and two had tank brigades with them. The "Germans" swept down on the Meuse River and with ease smashed the French defenses there. The results of Pretelat's maneuvers were so startling that one headquarters-bound general begged Gamelin not to publish them because they would upset the troops. Gamelin agreed, and they were not published. Georges appears to have remembered these important maneuvers, but when he raised his voice in warning, Gamelin did not want to hear what he had to say.

In January, Gamelin reorganized the chain of command and gave Georges complete responsibility for the northeast theater. If something went wrong in that sector, it would be Georges's responsibility. Georges had no objection to being responsible so long as he was able to shape the strategy for the defenses—but the strategy had been determined from above, by Gamelin. After the plane crash, Gamelin beefed up his commitments to Plan D. Instead of ten French divisions, thirty would move up after an invasion, and these would include two out of three of the new armored divisions, the bulk of the motorized forces, and all of the British units; moreover, General Henri Giraud's well-equipped Seventh Army would race from the border through Belgium and up into Holland to man the Breda Line. Georges hated the plan. Giraud's forces had formed the main bulk of his reserves, and now Georges would have no reserves. In case of an invasion, thirty divisions as directed by his superior would try to accomplish a maneuver which he was sure would end in disaster—and those thirty divisions would be under his command and his responsibility. Should they succeed, Gamelin would reap the glory; should they fail, Gamelin would heap the blame on Georges.

In the Dyle-Breda plan, one sector of the French forces would not move at all; rather they would wheel on the point of Sedan and take up positions along a fifty-mile stretch of the Meuse River in the Ardennes. This sector was partly defended by General Corap's Ninth Army and partly by General Huntziger's Second Army. These were by anyone's standards second-rate outfits. They were largely horse-drawn rather than motorized, had only half-complements of artillery, and were composed of the oldest reservists and of men from as far away as Indochina, North Africa, and Madagascar. The Ninth's officers had largely been called out of retirement. Corap's troops had made an indelible impression on Alan Brooke in November:

> Seldom have I seen anything more slovenly and badly turned out. Men unshaven, horses ungroomed, clothes and saddlery that did not fit, vehicles dirty, and complete lack of pride in themselves or their units. What shook me most, however, was the look in the men's faces, disgruntled and insubordinate looks, and, although ordered to give "Eyes left," hardly a man bothered to do so.

In late January, in the depths of a frigid winter, nothing much moved along the "front." An occasional sortie was made by the Germans, but it seemed to the French that such actions were made more out of a need to keep moving and keep warm than for any bellicose reason. In the Maginot Line, in the small towns which had been taken over for the soldiers' use, and along the Belgian border, the French armies fell into a routine that led to boredom and inefficiency. French officers busied themselves with ingenious and luxurious preparations for meals. On guard, the *poilus* listened to the insidious broadcasts of Ferdonnet, "the traitor of Stuttgart," who was employed by Goebbels. Ferdonnet told the soldiers that their leaders neglected them and there was no reason to go out and die for the English, who in any event got better pay than they did.

To counter boredom, and to seem magnanimous, the army gave out free wine. Many cases of drunkenness were then discovered, and the army set up *salles de desethylation*—drunk tanks—to take care of them. Many soldiers suspected that the free wine contained bromides. François Fonvieille-Alquier, who studied the boredom in the French lines, told of the soldiers' worries:

> Was it not this bromide which explained certain strange weaknesses which happened during a leave and thoroughly spoiled the long-awaited return of this or that conscript with his wife? Though a common subject for jokes, this was no minor problem. The soldier to whom this weakness happened felt his male dignity diminished, and he was secretly, though deeply, wounded. The frustrated wife imagined that her husband had been having far too good a time and wasting his forces in guilty love affairs.

The wives knew about those villages near the frontiers where brothels were numerous, leaves were frequent, and bored soldiers looked for a good time.

At home the wives had their own problems. An anonymous letter to *Marie-Claire's* advice column wondered: "My husband is mobilized. Every day, at the bus stop, I meet a young man with whom I have a chat. But when I leave him I find myself thinking of him and scarcely any more of my husband. What ought I to do?"

Amounts paid to dependents of servicemen were so low that women had to change the way they lived just to make do. In blocks where large percentages of the men had been mobilized, landlords tried to shut off heat to all the apartments, claiming they had no money to pay for fuel since tenants who had gone to the front were exempt from paying rent even if their wives remained in the apartments.

Aircraft production, which had been at sixty planes a month in September, did not increase through the winter. Not a single tank came off an assembly line in France. Artillery still gathered dust in warehouses while some units at the frontier sent endless memos which decried their lack of adequate firepower. Only 200,000 1936-model rifles were available for the army; over a million soldiers had rifles that dated back to the Great War; others had rifles that were even older. Some machine guns and grenades were of equally ancient stamp.

In January 1940, Edouard Daladier, while riding a horse in the forest of Rambouillet accompanied by Jeanne de Crussol, fell and broke his ankle. The forceful treatment used by his doctor at his request— infrared and mechanotherapy—caused him considerable pain. His broken ankle added to his hundred other worries, and he muttered that politicians were not allowed to have accidents.

Countess Hélène de Portes saw Daladier's misfortune as Reynaud's opportunity. In her salon she murmured that Daladier was failing mentally as well as physically. One could not expect such an ill man to fill the posts of premier, war minister, and foreign minister simultaneously; since the war was not being prosecuted with vigor, it was time that Paul Reynaud had a chance to show what he could do. The gossip was duly transmitted to Jeanne de Crussol, and thence to Daladier, who for weeks did not speak to Reynaud. In the meanwhile, Reynaud consolidated an alliance with Léon Blum; the rightist and the socialist, despite their political differences, had for years been personal friends. Blum had become disenchanted with Daladier, his natural ally on the left, because the premier seemed more authoritarian and dictatorial than circumstances warranted.

Daladier's hold on his office was admittedly fragile; he could neither sack Reynaud nor openly break with those who sided with Blum, lest he fall. He now needed the continual support of Pierre Laval, Georges Bonnet, and Anatole de Monzie, who were at best soft-liners on the war.

The battle between Daladier and Reynaud, or between Daladier's survival in office and political oblivion, blended with the continuing debate over what to do about Finland. Many in France wanted to strike out at the Communist bear. To the French, the Finns were heroic, Mannerheim was an obvious figure of awe, and Finland was upholding the light of democracy while all the rest of the world was filled with bystanders. Finnish fashions and parties for Finnish relief became the rage in Paris. Since many agreed that France had not done its duty in the case of Poland, here was a chance to redeem the cause of civilization. Rising to the bait, Daladier diverted some of France's new airplanes to Finland, and also sent new rifles and other supplies. French field commanders, who desperately needed the new rifles and could have used the new airplanes as well, grumbled that the politicians were throwing France to the dogs in order to save their own skins.

The Allied Supreme War Council met in Paris on February 4–5 and made three crucial decisions. Those in attendance included Daladier, Gamelin, Chamberlain, and, for the first time, Churchill. Those not in attendance included Leslie Hore-Belisha, who had been secretary of war, and Paul Reynaud. Hore-Belisha had been popular with the troops but unpopular with the officers; in December Lord Gort had some conversation about H-B with George VI when the king visited the troops in France, and the monarch's hand was partly responsible for the minister's fall. (Goebbels's radio crowed that when the British wanted to get down to brass tacks, they, too, got rid of Jews like Hore-Belisha.) Reynaud was so out of favor with Daladier that the premier did not even invite the second most important man in his government to a dinner he gave for the council.

Decision One was to back Gamelin's Dyle-Breda plan. For several months Gort and the British had offered serious military objections to this plan, as they preferred to defend the Franco-Belgian border where they were already dug in. But if the British were to be the chief strategists of the air war and the sea war because of numerical superiority, they must concede leadership on land to the immensely larger French army. So, over the protests of every other available military opinion including those of Georges, Gort, and Ironside, Gamelin's plan was approved.

Decision Two was that there would be no bombing of Germany now. Despite the avowed British policy of not taking chances and of conserving the air force, the British had come to the meeting with the suggestion that the Allies bomb synthetic-fuel depots within Germany in order to cripple the Nazi war machine's ability to move. To this bold idea, both Gamelin and Daladier were opposed; they feared German bombers would retaliate by bombing French targets, which were, of course, closer to Germany than British ones. Not wishing to act alone, the British agreed to leave the bombers at home.

Decision Three was to do something about Scandinavia. On this all the participants were agreed. Churchill had long advocated a pre-emptive strike into Norway to deprive Germany of the iron ore shipped from Sweden through Norwegian coastal waters. No less an authority than the exiled Fritz Thyssen, who six months before had been the leading steel manufacturer in Germany, said that if Germany was denied iron ore the war would be shortened or ended. Daladier was not opposed to Norway, but he was determined to go to the aid of Finland. The Supreme War Council saw an opportunity to kill two birds with a single stone. The Allies would send a force for transshipment through Norway to aid the Finns. While crossing Norway, this force would secure the iron-ore route for the Allies, and when it got to Finland, would relieve Mannerheim and start to knock back the Russians. To prevent the loss of the iron ore and to aid Russia, Germany would attack both Norway and Finland, the whole battleground would shift away from France and England to the frozen north, and there would never be an invasion of the West. With a secondary Allied force based in the Middle East driving north to seize the Caucasus oil fields, and with the main Allied force thrusting south through Scandinavia, a decisive victory could be won over both Germany and Russia. The godly and the democratic would triumph over the godless and the totalitarian, and the Second World War would be over.

11

Residue of Fortune

On February 5, Chamberlain, Churchill, and the rest of the British delegation left Paris to go back to England. There were a few technical problems to be solved, but in a month, perhaps sooner, a force to aid the Finns would go to Norway. As they crossed the Channel, the two leaders were observed by Captain J. S. Litchfield:

> When we embarked at Boulogne Churchill ordered the Admiralty Flag to be hoisted and clearly regarded himself as Chamberlain's host afloat. Mr. Chamberlain looked decidedly put out, no doubt regarding himself as Number One ashore or afloat. They both put on tin hats; somehow Mr. Chamberlain looked most incongruous in a steel helmet and a naval duffle coat whereas Churchill, of course smoking a cigar and grinning, looked everything that any cartoonist had ever made him out to appear. During the crossing a floating mine was sighted. Instantly Winston personally ordered it to be destroyed, and it was duly potted by a rifle and exploded with a huge bang. Winston was overjoyed, and no doubt felt he was really in the war.

Once home, the indefatigable Churchill goaded those around him with his own precision and excitement. When the repair work on Scapa Flow was not going at top speed, he fired off a memo:

> Two and a half months have passed since the *Royal Oak* was torpedoed. What, in fact, has been done since? How many blockships sunk? How many nets made? How many men have been in work how many days? What buildings have been erected? What gun sites have been concreted and prepared? What progress has been made with the run-ways of the aerodrome? I thought we settled two months ago to have a weekly report.

One night Churchill took Chamberlain, Ironside, and other guests down into the basement of the Admiralty to demonstrate what he called his "White Rabbit." It was to be a trench-cutting tank, its military designation "Cultivator #6." What the gentlemen saw was a three-foot-long working model constructed by engineering wizard Stanley Goodall, but the actual machine was to be eight feet high, nearly eighty feet long, and would weigh a hundred and thirty tons. It would be capable of digging out a trench six feet deep by three feet wide at the rate of one mile an hour. Let loose among the deadlocked trenches which had characterized the Great War, this monster would burrow ten miles forward under cover of darkness, so that by morning a phalanx of troops which followed behind it would be able to emerge behind the enemy's lines. Though mobile warfare had already rendered it obsolete, soon after this demonstration the cabinet approved construction of 240 of the Cultivator #6 machines.

Churchill's most important step toward power in these early months of 1940 was to become the mainspring of the Military Coordination Council. Though a chairman still ran its meetings, this council became Churchill's bailiwick. He urged on the suppliers, established ties with important contractors, developed relationships with the career officers in all the services, and came to understand every aspect of England's war effort. Yet he was continually frustrated by the "immense walls of prevention" which faced him. In order to get approval for the move into Norway, he had to overcome the objections of the economic department, the supply department, the Board of Trade, and had to run the gamut of criticism from the Joint Planning Committee, the chiefs of staff, and the cabinet, as well as take into account the attitude of France and the "military, moral, and juridical" objections of the neutrals. These "many angles of criticism" made him feel that "under the present arrangements we shall be reduced to waiting upon the terrible attacks of the enemy, against which it is impossible to prepare in every quarter simultaneously without fatal dissipation of strength."

Churchill argued strongly for going into Norway, but the argument against doing so was equally strong. Alan Brooke wrote that plans for the Norway invasion "fill me with gloom," based as they seemed to be on the assumption that Germany would not then be able to attack in the West. In his bones, Brooke knew there would be an attack in the West. He told Dill, "There is only one Front that matters in this War during 1940, and that is this Front [in the West]. It is the only front during the present year on which the war can be won or lost, and it is quite shattering to see its security endangered." For Brooke, as for many other secondary players in the drama of the phony war, actions seemed now to turn on mere whim or fancy, strokes of luck, the residue left in the wake of fortune.

In February, the Royal Navy captured from German submarine U-33 some very precious small machined parts—three wheels for the Enigma code-setting device. By way of Poland and France, the British had earlier obtained enough parts to build a version of such a machine, and had been working on perfecting a device which they called the Bombe. By a laborious process of hand computation, some settings of the Enigma—primarily those used by the German navy—had already been solved. But it did little good to know three weeks after the event that a particular German submarine had been directed to a particular location off the Irish coast. The Bombe would interpret the settings by a mechanical process, and thereby enable German code traffic to be read and understood immediately. The recovery of three more wheels from another U-boat brought the British Cypher School a jot closer to solving the codes. To the military chiefs it still seemed that British intelligence was slow as molasses, but with each passing week the code-breakers actually came closer to a major-penetration of German security.

Mired in the phony war, the British public was fed official pablum. André Maurois, the French biographer and novelist, who had invented the very British Colonel Bramble in the Great War, wrote charming pieces about typical British eccentricities cropping up as the BEF made itself cozy in northern France. Somerset Maugham wrote of the great efforts being made by the determined French people in the Continental redoubt. The London *Times* printed a gushing account of French industry "transformed into a gigantic war machine . . . in full blast for victory."

At the same time, many in Britain were listening to a mysterious English-speaking newscaster and commentator on a radio channel which was beamed at England from Germany. The press dubbed the mystery man "Lord Haw-Haw," because of his half-aristocratic accent, his voluptuous and sometimes incongruous turns of phrase, his acerbity, and his wit. He sometimes commanded as large an audience as Churchill. Haw-Haw was William Joyce, who had been born in America but brought up in Ireland. For six years before the war, Joyce had been propaganda director of the British fascist organization; just before the war broke out, fearing internment, he fled to Germany. In Berlin, he applied for a job, and Goebbels set him to reading handouts into a radio microphone. Joyce convinced Goebbels that his own scripts would be far more effective than those written by non-Englishmen. They were.

Haw-Haw seemed to listeners to have information on everything in England—stalled trains, village meetings, troop movements and leaves, blackout accidents. His scripts implied that because he knew so much, he was able to predict that England would lose the war. During the nights when Britons were forced indoors and to their radios for entertainment, when the BBC news was censored as well as bland and uninformative, when the winter was at its most depressing, and when many people in England were themselves questioning British participation in the war—Haw-Haw was an effective propagandist.

The British government wondered whether it should deny Haw-

Haw's contentions or ignore them. If the government answered, that might only increase his audience. In January, a Mass Observation survey showed that 26.5 percent of the people queried said they had listened to Haw-Haw within the previous twenty-four hours. The British government ignored Haw-Haw and hoped he would go away.

Haw-Haw did not go away, though his audience did slightly diminish; and the opportunity for a British propaganda victory to counter his popularity knocked in mid-February.

After the *Graf Spee* had been scuttled in December, Captain Heinrich Dau had taken his attending supply ship *Altmark* north. Thoroughly disguised, the *Altmark* evaded an extensive British search and steamed through the waters of Iceland, past the Faroe Islands, and then into neutral Norwegian waters.

The 299 British prisoners aboard the *Altmark* considered the ship a floating concentration camp. Crowded together belowdecks in large holds, they slept on the deck, had very bad food, and were allowed outside only once every other day for a half-hour of exercise. They smoked tea leaves wrapped in toilet paper. "We would have bartered away our salvation for a smoke, a real smoke," "Digger" Foley wrote. In the Great War, Dau had been a British prisoner of war; he spoke English but hated all that smacked of England. For infractions of his rules prisoners spent three days in a narrow oil barrel that was completely dark and intensely cold. This chamber was never empty.

On reaching Norwegian waters on February 14, Dau for the first time in two months radioed Berlin to announce his position. He then dismantled his guns and continued the voyage as a merchant ship; the prisoners were forbidden all exercise and were locked belowdecks. However, the *Altmark* was immediately spotted as suspicious, and a Norwegian torpedo boat went out to meet her.

A tangle of diplomacy, subterfuge, and military shenanigans followed. Dau insisted that, as a warship, the *Altmark* was immune from search, and also that she was on a peaceful trip home. Without inspecting the ship, three different Norwegian boarding parties accepted this reasoning and were ready to let the *Altmark* go. A fourth boarding party arrived, insisted on making a thorough search, but did not go belowdecks. When the prisoners set up a tremendous clamor by banging on the ship's sides and shouting at the top of their lungs, Dau ordered the winches started to drown out their noise. Aboard, the searchers were politely deaf, but when they returned to shore they told their superiors that there probably were prisoners on board. Upset by this news because it might force them to take some action which would anger Germany, government officials in Oslo first tried to ignore it, and then to let the *Altmark* go, on the grounds that none of the inspectors had actually seen any prisoners.

But the British had learned of the *Altmark*'s presence, and a destroyer force under the command of Captain Philip Vian had already raced for Norway. On February 16, a spotter plane located the *Altmark*, and the *Intrepid* began to give chase. For many hours a Norwegian gunboat planted itself between the two ships, and prevented the British ship from capturing its prey, on the legal grounds that the *Altmark* was in Norwegian waters and the British had no rights there. Then Dau made a mistake. He drove the *Altmark* into a layer of ice in the small Jossing fjord, and was trapped. As Vian's main force came up, the Norwegians again interposed themselves and announced they would resist any effort by the British to board the *Altmark*.

From the Admiralty, Churchill sent Vian an explicit order: "Unless Norwegian torpedo boat undertakes to convoy *Altmark* to Bergen with a joint Anglo-Norwegian guard on board, and a joint escort, you should board *Altmark*, liberate the prisoners and take possession of the ship pending further instructions." Vian should "suggest to Norwegian destroyer that honour is served by submitting to superior force." He did. The Norwegians did not agree, but made no move to stop him.

Vian came up the fjord in the *Cossack*. The *Altmark* was bright in the night lights against the snow-covered mountains. Attempting to ram the British ship, she only ran farther aground. As a British boarding party fired across at her, some of the German crew fled over the ice toward shore; a half-dozen of them were killed.

Once aboard the *Altmark*, a British seaman opened the hatch and shouted belowdecks, "Any British down there?" There were answering hoots of relief, to which he replied, "The navy's here." When "Digger" Foley got topside he tried to borrow a rifle to shoot one of the fleeing Germans who had particularly tormented the prisoners; he was brusquely told that the rifle was not to be used for private business. Vian did not disable or attempt to hold the *Altmark*, because he felt that enough violence had already been done to Norwegian neutrality. By midnight it was all over and the ex-prisoners were headed home. A few days later, Churchill celebrated the rescue in a speech that painted Vian as a hero and elevated the event into British naval legend: "To Nelson's immortal signal of 135 years ago, 'England expects that every man will do his duty,' there may now be added last week's not less proud reply, 'The Navy is here.'"

Daladier pointed out that the *Altmark* was bad publicity for Germany and that the rescue was good publicity for the Allies, and that the combination now gave the Allies a wonderful excuse for immediately going into Norway. However, Chamberlain still demurred, and the plans for the force to aid Finland proceeded only at a slow and methodical pace. *The New York Times* drew an important conclusion from the affair: "This is the first time since the war began that the Allies have deliberately violated neutral territory."

Hitler agreed with that estimate, and drew the further conclusion that Great Britain would not hesitate again to violate Norwegian neutrality. He grumbled that the *Altmark's* crew had offered no resistance and that there had been no British losses. Two days after the *Altmark*, he ordered ships equipped and army units made ready to invade Norway and Denmark.

Evidence of the hastiness of his decision was Hitler's choice of Lieutenant General Nikolaus von Falkenhorst to command the Norwegian invasion because he had fought in Finland in 1918 and knew icy environments. Falkenhorst was summoned to the Chancellery at noon on February 21 and given four hours in which to come up with ideas for the invasion. The astounded Falkenhorst bought a Baedeker travel guide: "In order to find out what Norway was like. I didn't have any idea." In a hotel room he outlined the most logical invasion plan he could dream up on the spur of the moment: one division each would go to Norway's main ports of Oslo, Stavanger, Bergen, Trondheim, and Narvik. Hitler loved Falkenhorst's proposals.

There were some who cautioned Hitler that an invasion of Norway could spill over into Finland and involve Germany with Russia. Though Hitler had disparaging staff reports as to the quality of the Russian army—"fighting qualities of the troops in heavy fighting, dubious"—he had no wish now to tangle with Russia on the battlefield. That would come, he told advisers, much later, after he had conquered Norway and the West.

At the moment Stalin, too, had no wish to clash with Hitler. He himself was currently involved in German trade negotiations in Moscow, which had been going on for some time. He had even spent New Year's Eve in the negotiating room. According to an agreement that would be monetarily four times as large as the trade pact signed before the war, Russia would obtain a new cruiser, the plans of Germany's newest and largest ship (the *Bismarck*), heavy naval guns, thirty Me-109 fighters and Ju-88 bombers, locomotives, generators, machine tools, artillery, tanks, explosives, and other industrial items—in exchange for sending to Germany a million tons of cereals, a half-million tons of wheat, 900,000 tons of oil, 100,000 tons of cotton, 50,000 tons of phosphates, and other raw materials. The German negotiators reported to Hitler that Stalin drove hard bargains and seemed to know the real prices and details of every item. Hitler told his negotiators to conclude the agreement as soon as possible.

Sometime in January, Stalin made a decision. He heard that it was being rumored in Berlin and the Western capitals that he was being made a fool of by the Finns, and that he had lost control of the war. At home, the war was becoming unpopular as the hospitals filled with frostbitten soldiers who told terrifying tales of combat in Finland. Stalin shook up the army. He ordered new rifles, tanks, and planes sent to the front, and supplied troops to the commanders in virtually endless numbers. He had decided that the winter war would be won, regardless of the cost. Little Finland must no longer resist the Soviet colossus.

Behind the Russian lines in Finland, Mikhail Soloviev was told to report to an old acquaintance, a man who was among the most feared in all of Russia, Stalin's chief propagandist, Meklis, who had been put in charge of cleaning up the Finnish campaign. Meklis circulated stories that the Finns shot prisoners; he meted out severe punishments—including executions—for dereliction of duty, and he sent Soloviev to snoop among the troops and report their problems to him.

Soloviev went forward and sat with men who used the frozen bodies of their dead comrades as benches. "They can't feel you, and it makes no difference to them," he was told. As soldiers they had become used to the thought of dying in battle, but the idea of freezing to death was frightening. It was fears such as these which engendered what Soloviev reported as cases of mass epilepsy among the troops.

Near the end of December, Vyaschlev Oreshin had volunteered for front-line duty. "I don't feel the nervousness which they write about in books," he told his diary. On New Year's Eve, in his baptism of fire, he was thrilled as he captured a Finnish civic guard. Now he was a real soldier. He sent off to his fiancée, Shura, the letter that was only to be opened in case of his death, and he continued to fight. In late January, he had another great experience and fulfilled a lifetime dream: he became a *politruk*, a political officer, on the occasion of his aceptance into the Communist party. The evening after this great moment, he wrote in his diary: "All is ready for the attack which is due to start in the morning. The men are resting. All believe in victory. Today I enter the battle as a party member. I don't think I shall lose my courage, even tomorrow." The next day he died in battle. The Finns found his diary in the snow.

Hella Wuolijoki was Finland's leading woman playwright, a leftist whose plays were full of strong-willed women who outwitted their male opponents. Her sister was the wife of the British Communist party leader, and among her oldest friends was Soviet ambassador to Sweden Alexandra Kollontay, a legendary beauty who had fought on the barricades in the Revolution and had been romantically linked with many Soviet leaders. In January of 1940, Hella Wuolijoki told Foreign Minister Väinö Tanner that she would like to go to Stockholm and talk to Alexandra, and perhaps the two women could end the war. Willing to try anything, Tanner agreed. Wuolijoki flew to Stockholm and secretly met Kollontay at the Grand Hotel. Historian Max Jakobson writes that the women's method of conducting negotiations was

> by the standards of professional diplomacy, horrifyingly unconventional and haphazard; they kept no proper records; they freely spiced their reports with personal comments; they drew upon their vivid imaginations to

embellish, and improve upon, their official instructions; in short, they acted like two matchmakers determined to lead, or, if need be, mislead a
reluctant and suspicious couple into matrimony.

But the two ladies made progress. By the end of January, Moscow had
in effect agreed to give up the pretense of recognizing Kuusinen, and to
substitute the reality of negotiating with Tanner. The Finnish foreign
minister rushed to Stockholm in disguise, went up the back stairs at the
Grand Hotel, and talked clandestinely with Kollontay.

But on February 1, along the whole breadth of the Karelian Isthmus north of Leningrad, a great barrage began. The Russians lobbed
300,000 shells in a single day in the most massive artillery attack since
the hell of Verdun. Timoshenko had been told to win the war before
the late spring thaw could envelop both sides in mud. Stalin wanted
victory; at the very least, that would force concessions. As with Hitler in
Poland, he seemed not truly interested in a negotiated settlement.

The barrage could be heard a hundred miles away, and lasted until
February 6, when the Russian offensive against the Mannerheim Line
commenced. With three divisions, 150 heavy tanks, and 200 airplanes
on this front, the Russians had a vast numerical advantage over the
Finnish forces.

A week later Finnish pilot Eino Luukanen, one of his country's top
aces, reported that he was in the air as many hours a day as there was
daylight. The Russians were breaking through the Mannerheim Line
and simultaneously pushing north and west on both sides of Lake Ladoga. On a sortie, Luukanen's heart sank as he saw below him fires
burning in nearly a dozen cities within his field of vision. It did not
seem to matter any longer that the Finns were shooting the Russians out
of the sky at a ten-to-one ratio. More planes came at them. Similarly
Luukanen would strafe a column of men and horses and artillery as it
marched across a frozen lake—black targets against a white background—and he would kill half the column. The rest of the men and
horses would go back to their own lines. In an hour or two an equally
long column would attempt the crossing, and the pattern would be followed again and again until eventually the Russians got to their objective. Luukanen was exhausted:

> We had virtually forgotten what it was like to be at peace; to enjoy regular
> meals undisturbed; to have eight hours continuous sleep. . . . We had
> ceased to wonder when or how it would end, or what the future held. We
> were living from one hour to the next, and now that the war was entering
> its fourth month we all felt as though we had aged at least ten years. . . .
> We had learned the true meanings of comradeship, fear, and sorrow, but
> most important, we now knew ourselves, our capabilities and our limita-
> tions.

As February drew to a close, Mannerheim and the Ryti-Tanner

cabinet had to make a decision of overwhelming importance. Finns were dying at the rate of a thousand a day, and there were no more reserves with which to replace the dead. Negotiations with Moscow were agonizingly slow, yet Stalin had still not demanded a complete takeover of Finland but only some painful and difficult territorial concessions. The question was, Should Finland continue the fight or sue for peace? Mannerheim had earlier requested Allied help; he now said that if sufficient Allied troops came to Finland's aid, the war could at least be pushed to a stalemate. If he knew that the Allies would arrive in the latter part of March, say in three weeks, he could hold on. His troops had been fighting so valiantly that perhaps he believed they could continue to do so for the next several weeks, but the evidence of Finnish exhaustion and Russian numerical superiority was almost incontrovertible. Yet, Ryti, Tanner, and the Finnish cabinet believed Mannerheim and compounded his error. They refused to accede to the Russian demands, and passed on to the Allies Mannerheim's appeal for troops, while at the same time they kept from the Allies the knowledge that they were pursuing secret negotiations.

In late February, Allied plans for transshipment of "volunteers" through Norway and Sweden to Finland were not yet complete. Gamelin said that the earliest Allied troops could arrive in Finland would be April 1, and that he could spare only 20,000 to 25,000 men for Finland's defense. The British agreed with these numbers. The question narrowed: Could Allied troops in sufficient strength arrive in Finland in time to make a difference? This military decision, as with so many others, slid over into the political arena.

In France, Daladier had just managed to beat back another challenge by Reynaud. The finance minister wanted to become the economic czar of the country in order to accelerate France's preparations for war; he had threatened to withdraw support from Daladier if the premier did not agree. They had compromised, but it was clear that Reynaud's next challenge might topple the government. Newspapers and public opinion clamored for France to go to the aid of Finland. As Helsinki awaited word from the Allies, the decision that affected the continuation of the Russo-Finnish war merged into the question of what would be politically helpful to the Daladier government.

Without consulting the military experts or the British, Daladier unilaterally upped the ante. He cabled Helsinki that fifty thousand troops, along with planes and other military equipment, would leave shortly and arrive in Finland by the beginning of April.

Helsinki had many reasons to disregard Daladier's cable. There were grave doubts as to whether the Allies could deliver troops so early, or in such large numbers. There were also grave doubts as to the Allies' sincerity. As Tanner later wrote: "Finland was regarded as an important piece in the strategy of the Western powers. To be sure, we ourselves had never imagined that their aid was offered to us for the sake of our fine blue eyes."

It was February 29, 1940 in Helsinki. On the one hand there was Daladier's offer, which was perhaps unreal; on the other hand, the massive Russian thrust. Three-quarters of a million men and endless supplies of tanks, artillery, and ammunition pushed north toward Viipuri, the second-largest city in Finland. Of the volunteers promised from foreign countries, only ten thousand had arrived; of the foreign supplies that were to help win the war, the Italian planes had never arrived, American planes were still in Sweden, and French planes were yet to come. Ammunition was low, and Finnish soldiers were dying at an ever increasing rate.

The Helsinki government chose to believe Daladier's offer. Within a month the cavalry would ride out of the west 50,000 strong, and would hold off 750,000 men. Rather than seek an immediate cease-fire, Finland decided to continue the war.

In the next two weeks Finland's Karelian Isthmus and its surrounding waters became a charnel house. In waves thousands strong, the Russians came across the frozen bay near Viipuri and would not stop coming despite immense carnage in their ranks. Tens of thousands of men died, most of them Russian. Finnish soldiers went literally mad from the endless strain of firing machine guns into hordes of approaching Russians. Finnish guns were used so much that they required reboring. And of course, Finns were dying along with the Russians.

In Allied ports, troops waited to board ships and sail to Norway. British submarines and planes moved into position to guard their passage. All forces were on alert—and then the Allies found out about the secret negotiations. It was incomprehensible to Daladier and to Chamberlain that Finland could ask for help and at the same time negotiate for peace. The Allies demanded that Finland drop the negotiations with Moscow or there would be no aid to Finland, not even economic assistance to help her recovery after the war. As Max Jakobson comments:

> Overnight the Allied promise of aid became a threat of aid, and Finland was being blackmailed. . . . It would be hard to find in history another case of a small nation fighting for its life being bullied and cajoled by two Great Powers insisting on helping it against its will.

A welter of possibilities loomed. If Finland dropped the negotiations and called in the Allies, that in itself might force Hitler into the war, since he would not want to lose Sweden and Norway to the onrushing Allies. If the Allies came in, Stalin might be forced to ally himself still more closely with Hitler, which would be disastrous for him, since his aim in going into Finland was to secure the Baltic against Germany. His negotiators moved slightly toward accommodation with the Finns, even as the number of corpses piling up in the frozen Gulf of

Viipuri reached macabre proportions. It seemed almost a question of whose nerve would break first.

Väinö Tanner finally understood that Allied troops would not be able to rescue Finland, and he convinced the last wavering cabinet members that Finland had lost the war and must sue for peace. But Stalin refused to agree to a cease-fire during the negotiations, and the slaughter continued. Premier Ryti went to Moscow. Viipuri was still unconquered, but about thirty thousand men had died in the past ten days, and even though most were Russian, Finland could take no more. On March 11, as Allied commanders received a briefing on the through-transit to Finland, Ryti in Moscow was authorized to sign a drastic treaty giving Stalin the same territory Peter the Great had ruled in 1721. Russia took slices of territory in Finland's waist, bases in the far north, and the whole Karelian Isthmus and Lake Ladoga region. Shortly before midnight on March 12, Ryti signed. Next morning, the cease-fire took effect. Finland's president, Kyosti Kallio, had said on authorizing the treaty's acceptance, "Let the hand wither that is forced to sign such a paper!" In a few months, a stroke paralyzed Kallio's right arm and hand.

Because of the illusions and intransigence of the politicians and the generals—on all sides, from Moscow to Helsinki to Paris—some tens of thousands of men had perished in the period between February 29 and March 11, without altering the outcome of the conflict one iota.

After having successfully held out for 105 days, the Finnish defenders of Viipuri laid down their arms and began their retreat to the western part of the country. It became the greatest mass movement in Finland's history. To avoid becoming Russian citizens, the 200,000 remaining inhabitants of the isthmus (200,000 had been evacuated earlier) closed their homes, abandoned their livelihoods, and traveled in carts, in sleighs, and in caravans of cars and trucks which came to help from as far away as Sweden. (Months before, an equivalent number of Poles had fled the Germans and into Russian hands to avoid becoming Nazi vassals.)

The Russians had lost somewhere between 200,000 (Mannerheim's estimate) and 1,000,000 dead (Khrushchev's later revelation). There were 25,000 Finnish casualties. When prisoners were exchanged, there were only a few Finns though there were hordes of Russians. The Finnish POW's went home, but the returned Russian soldiers were shot by the Red Army on orders that seem to have emanated directly from Stalin. Such was the ordinary soldier's lot for having the misfortune of being captured. It was a gesture wholly emblematic of the worst aspect of the phony war.

12

Mission to Nowhere

As 1940 began, Roosevelt was besieged with appeals to help Finland. Columnist Walter Lippmann and Under Secretary of State Sumner Welles urged the United States at the very least to break off relations with the Soviet Union.

Roosevelt found such suggestions naive. He would not do anything to push Russia further into the arms of Germany. Nonetheless he had to respond to the pressure. In speeches which linked Russia's aggression with Hitler's and condemned them both, he asked for a "moral embargo" of the Soviet Union and refused to apply the newly revised neutrality statutes to the Russo-Finnish war, with the excuse that to do so would hurt Finland more than it would hurt Russia. Finland had consistently been the only country to repay its Great War debt to the United States, and Roosevelt offered to suspend the schedule for repayments—until it turned out that Finland had already prepaid the next installment. Also, three hundred businesses in fifteen states had contracts with Russia which totalled thirty million dollars, and only one small firm bothered to comply with the "moral embargo." Red Army troops ate American bacon and ran their vehicles partly on American oil as they crossed the Mannerheim Line.

In January, Senator Prentiss Brown introduced a bill to permit the Export-Import Bank to grant Finland sixty million dollars in aid. Three months before, at Roosevelt's behest, Secretary of State Hull had turned down a direct Finnish request for fifty million dollars, but the climate had changed, at least in the Congress. Roosevelt would not say publicly whether he supported the Brown bill, but his men quietly helped push for its approval. Though few drew the conclusion, the Brown bill was a step along the road to involvement in a foreign war, even if it restricted purchases to, as one congressman put it, "powder puffs, silken scanty pants, and creampuffs when we know the Finns need shrapnel, buckshot, barbed wire, and all the fiercest implements of hell because they are fighting to stop the antichrist and the hosts of hell."

Many of the isolationists who had opposed other moves toward involvement came from Midwest states, which had heavy Scandinavian constituencies, and in an election year they found it prudent to mute their opposition to aid to Finland. The Brown bill eventually passed, though it was too late to aid Finland materially. However, as historian Robert Sobel points out, the bill marked the halfway house between intervention and nonintervention, the first time since 1918 that a United States government agency had been mandated to do anything in support of a belligerent:

> Interventionists could applaud its passage as a sign of American willingness to participate in a limited way in the European conflict; the noninterventionists could justifiably observe that it also signified a determination to remain aloof militarily.

In early 1940, what Henry Morgenthau called "the battle of Washington" heated up. It had begun before the war had started.

In mid-1939 France had placed orders for a thousand American planes. Daladier thought France needed ten thousand planes, and since engines were the bottleneck to greater plane production, France had agreed to finance a doubling of airplane engine production capacities at Pratt and Whitney and at Curtiss-Wright. By early 1941, French orders for planes were to total $305 million, and British orders would add another $96.5 million.

Then the war had begun. After revision of the neutrality statutes, Roosevelt insisted that the Allies form a joint purchasing commission to obtain supplies. This ran into the continuing skirmishing between Reynaud and Daladier. The finance minister argued that he should personally have the major say in the purchases, since France was the major buyer. Daladier, upset at delays, petulantly threatened Reynaud, England, and the United States in one fell swoop. He said if he couldn't get enough planes from America he would resign and turn the government over to Bonnet or Flandin, either of whom would make a quick peace with Germany. Conversely, he offered to resettle France's war debts by allowing the United States to buy whatever French real estate it wanted, be it Devil's Island or Versailles.

In November 1939, in an air battle over the Maginot Line, nine American P-36s flown by French pilots tangled with twenty-seven Me-109s, and shot nine Germans down without the loss of a single P-36. The P-39s and P-40s were supposed to be even better than the P-36s, and Daladier wanted every single one of them that was scheduled to come off the assembly lines. But the American Air Corps chief of staff, Hap Arnold, refused point-blank to sell France planes that were more advanced in design than those he himself had ordered for the American Air Corps. If the French bought everything, Arnold's dream of an expanded Air Corps would be dealt a serious blow. Arnold's superiors, Secretary of War Henry Woodring and Assistant Secretary Louis Johnson, were both isolationists. Woodring told Congress:

> I continue, as for several years, to absolutely disapprove of the sale of any surplus U.S. Army property. I insist, regardless of any higher authority directions, that if any Army surplus is to be sold, it only be sold by this government to another neutral government.

Similar statements forced Roosevelt to take the supervision of arms sales to foreign countries away from the military and give it to a liaison committee which included Morgenthau and reported directly to the White House. He also took other steps to handle the monumental tangle. In a series of late-winter meetings, he suggested to Hap Arnold that recalcitrant officers who did not go along with their commander-in-chief's wishes might find themselves posted to Guam; he told Woodring to get in line with administration policy or resign; he forbade Louis Johnson to make any more statements to the press; and he told the Allies to nominate one man to deal with him and generally to get their house in order. Roosevelt also pointed out to Arnold, Woodring, and Johnson that if the French bought all the planes currently under construction, United States airplane production capacity would be so greatly enhanced that expansion of the Air Corps would be facilitated; moreover, defects in the American planes which had shown up in battle could more easily be corrected in the next generation of planes, and so the American Air Corps would reap the benefit of obtaining battle-tested models. To cap his argument, Roosevelt claimed (according to Morgenthau's diary) that "These foreign orders mean prosperity in this country, and we can't elect a Democratic Party unless we get prosperity." That broke the logjam, and the "battle of Washington" was over for the moment, but the Allies still required a gift of time in which to take delivery of the planes.

On February 9, 1940, the State Department announced that Sumner Welles would visit Rome, Berlin, Paris, and London on a fact-finding tour and to see if any common ground existed on which these governments could begin the peace process. It was widely assumed that Welles, as a longtime Roosevelt friend, might carry a Roosevelt peace proposal to Europe. There was no such proposal. Roosevelt had long since shown that he was not interested in facilitating negotiations with Hitler—but he was deeply interested in separating Mussolini from Hitler's side. That was the first hidden purpose of the trip. The second was to buy time for the Allies, since it was unlikely that Hitler would invade the West while Sumner Welles was in Europe seeking peace. Thus the Welles trip was Roosevelt's venture to try to influence the coming course of the war.

When Welles crossed to Naples on the Italian luxury liner *Rex*,

European anxiety mounted. His trip evoked unpleasant memories of the busybody meddling of Colonel Edward M. House, President Wilson's emissary when the United States had been neutral during the Great War. Neville Chamberlain felt the Welles trip was a Roosevelt re-election ploy which would unwittingly support Hitler if it led to approaching him on the possibilities for peace and thus acknowledging him as a rational head of state. French statesmen thought Welles's presence in Europe would strengthen the neutrals and make it more difficult for the Allies to move into Scandinavia. On the German side, official reaction was cold, and behind the scenes Halder spoke for most in his cryptic diary entry: "Elections! Angel of peace!"

In Rome on February 26, Welles met with Ciano and was impressed with Mussolini's son-in-law and his evident anger at Hitler and Ribbentrop. "No country would want to have Germany as a neighbor. . . . We must do the best we can to get on with her," Ciano said. Welles suggested that the two neutrals, Italy and the United States, might work together to maintain some stability in the world.

Next day, as Welles and Ambassador Phillips walked down the vast and dark Mappamundo Hall, Mussolini came forward to greet them. Welles was shocked by the dictator's appearance. Mussolini was grossly fat, and with his white hair close-cropped he seemed seventy rather than fifty-six, "ponderous and static rather than being vital. He moved with an elephantine motion; every step seemed an effort," Welles later wrote. Most of the time Mussolini talked with his eyes shut, and only opened them into their famous wide stare to emphasize a point. He seemed to Welles to be under a great strain. (The source of Mussolini's anxiety was that for nearly two months his Christmas letter to Hitler had gone unanswered, and he was afraid they had fallen out just when Hitler was about to march to glory.) Welles tried hard with Mussolini, because

> Only in Italy was it remotely conceivable that the policy of this government might have some concrete effect. If by some means the United States could prevent Italy from actually taking part in the war against France and Great Britain, if Hitler could not obtain the active participation of his southern partner in an attack upon France, the outcome of the war might be less certain than it seemed.

The under secretary handed Mussolini a chatty letter from Roosevelt which suggested that the two leaders could meet, perhaps on an Atlantic island, and between them settle the fate of the world. Mussolini flirted with the idea. Coming to the heart of the matter, Welles asked directly, "Do you consider it possible at this moment for any successful negotiations to be undertaken between Germany and the Allies for a lasting peace?" Mussolini pondered for a moment and then uttered a resounding "yes." Welles was elated. He told a friend later that he was

absolutely convinced that Mussolini had "opened the door of concilia-
tion a little." If Mussolini was helping to instigate peace talks, he could
not simultaneously be marching at Hitler's side. After promising to return when he had visited the belligerents, Welles left Italy and entrained for Berlin.

Before Welles arrived, Hitler issued the go-ahead for the invasions
of Norway and Denmark to proceed on schedule, and forbade anyone
to even hint to Welles at the possibility of peace.

What Welles saw on the way to Berlin deeply affected him. "My
feeling of oppression was almost physical." As one who had spent some
time in Germany between the wars, he noticed all the changes wrought
by the Nazi regime. The absence of real news in the controlled papers,
the inevitable swastikas and ubiquitous uniforms, and the dead looks
on people's faces all bothered him. The sight of Polish prisoners of war
shoveling snow in the Berlin streets was another shock.

From Ribbentrop, Welles received as icy a welcome as he had ever
experienced. Refusing to speak English, with his eyes closed and his
hands gripping the arms of his chair, for two hours Ribbentrop angrily
denounced the English craft and guile that had for two decades prevented Germany from achieving her rightful place in the sun. Welles
sat with his face immobile—"a pencil between two ears," interpreter
Paul Schmidt said of him—and noted that Ribbentrop in his diatribe
had not once mentioned Italy. Later in the day, Welles spoke with his
old friend Weizsäcker, who suggested that if Mussolini were to approach Hitler directly and secretly about peace there might be a slight
chance for success, but that if Ribbentrop found out about such a maneuver he would block it.

Welles noted with amazement that the attendants in the entrance
hall of the Reichschancellery wore liveries of light blue satin and had
powder in their hair. He saw Hitler on March 2, and found the Führer
trim and fit, a man who spoke a German Welles could understand, pronounced with "clarity and precision." Hitler repeated the version of
history Welles had heard from Ribbentrop, but with one new note added. He cited Sir John Simon's speech of the night before, which had
outlined as a British war aim the complete destruction of Hitler and
National Socialism. Hitler called this the key to the situation:

> I can see no hope for the establishment of any lasting peace until the will
> of England and France to destroy Germany is itself destroyed. . . . I believe
> that German might is such as to make the triumph of Germany inevitable,
> but, if not, we will all go down together, whether it be for better or for
> worse. . . . I did not want this war. It has been forced upon me against my
> will. It is a waste of my time. My life should have been spent in construct-
> ing and not in destroying.

Welles paid a few courtesy calls—one to Hjalmar Schacht, one to
Rudolf Hess, and the last to Hermann Göring. The air marshal, whose

hands seemed "like the digging paws of a badger" encrusted with diamonds and an emerald an inch square, told Welles his mission was
hopeless, because Hitler's position on England had hardened. Welles
spoke of Germany's inhuman treatment of the Jews; Göring countered
with remarks about America's inhuman treatment of Negroes. Riding
back from Karinhall, Welles concluded, "There was only one power on
earth which could give Hitler and his associates pause. That would be
their conviction that, in a war of devastation forced upon Europe by
Germany, the United States, in its own interest, would come to the support of the Western democracies." Welles could not promise that to anyone, at the moment.

The Russo-Finnish war was coming to its shattering conclusion as
Welles arrived in Paris. He had spent summers in France since child-
hood, and was at home there. He found Paris full of pessimism. Daladier, still in pain from his accident, was "lucid, vigorous, and realistic,"
able to give Welles the best analysis of the war and of Hitler's policies
that he had heard from any European statesman. Old friend Paul Reynaud, lunching with Welles at the Louvre, boasted that he was known
as "the hardest man in the government" against Germany, and contended that France should have declared war in 1938 when Czechoslovakia
was invaded. Welles visited another old friend at his modest apartment:
Léon Blum had none of the trappings of power, but he was full of humanity and he believed the hours of his country were numbered.

In London, Welles learned from the king and queen that they had
closed down much of Buckingham Palace. Chamberlain grew hot-faced
and angry as he spoke about Nazi policy and the hopeless task of trying
to make the German people understand what Hitler's dictatorial rule
was doing to them. For all that, Welles found the British more optimistic
than the French.

The day after the Russo-Finnish peace treaty took effect, March 14,
Welles returned to Paris. He found there three thousand letters from all
over France which protested his visit to the Jew Léon Blum "in the most
violent and insulting terms. . . . For the first time I realized how widely
the poison engendered by the Nazis had already seeped into Western
Europe." Welles immediately left for Rome.

The French Parliament convened in secret. Food restrictions had
just spread to restaurants and cafés; Finland had fallen; the war with
Germany and the war effort seemed wholly inert. On the floor of the
chamber, old phantoms rose to castigate Edouard Daladier. Chief
among the attackers was former premier Pierre Laval, who had uttered
scarcely a word in Parliament in the fifty months since he had been
given a vote of no confidence as a result of his disastrous foreign policies and steady appeasement of Mussolini in Ethiopia. Laval, who had
voted against expenditures for the war, now accused Daladier of having

gone to war "lightheartedly in a formidable adventure" against an adversary who could not be beaten—Germany—and of not going to war against the correct adversary, the Soviet Union. Another deputy asserted, "You had in Finland an almost miraculous opportunity to vanquish the Soviet Union. You let it slip by. France weeps over it! Her heart bleeds!"

Then Blum raised his considerable voice. He asked pointed questions about France's aid to Finland and pounced on the figures that Daladier produced as unreliable. Later, when a colleague protested that Blum was being too harsh with Daladier, the Socialist leader replied, "Let's say that he is paying today for the many occasions on which we let him off too easily."

Daladier seemed unwilling to help himself. He would not reshuffle his cabinet, would not give up the post of foreign minister, and he grumbled to a friend, "The worst thing in time of war is the intrigue in the corridors of Parliament substituting for responsibility." Six weeks before, his government had won a vote of confidence 534 to 0. At three in the morning on March 20, there was a similar motion of confidence, and the vote was 239 in favor of the government, one opposed, with 300 abstentions. Those who were all-out for war—Mandel, Reynaud, Blum—combined their votes with those who were "soft" on the war—Laval and his ilk—and assembled a majority that, by their abstentions, opposed the government's policy. Daladier drew the obvious conclusion that he no longer had a consensus to rule, and in the still-dark hours he rode to the Elysée Palace and tendered his resignation to President Lebrun. At dawn, Lebrun offered the premiership to Paul Reynaud.

Reynaud had waited for this opportunity all his life, but it came at a perilous time, for with one parliamentary misstep his mandate could disappear. An outsider and a loner, he had difficulty forming a cabinet. Hélène de Portes, though out of town, considerably influenced his choices. The right would not agree to Léon Blum's presence in the cabinet, and the left would not agree to join the extreme right. Daladier, as the chieftain of the centrist party which controlled the most votes in the Parliament, had to be propitiated. Reynaud offered him the Foreign Ministry, but he wanted to be war minister or stay out. But if Daladier retained the War Ministry, it would mean that Gamelin and the whole military hierarchy against whom Reynaud had long railed would remain in place. Nevertheless Reynaud had to pay that price. On hearing the news that Daladier would be war minister, Charles de Gaulle, the friend Reynaud had wanted as secretary of the war cabinet, decided to refuse the honor of joining the government.

In the interwar years, de Gaulle had written books about tanks and mobile warfare and ways in which the army should be reorganized. He, too, was a loner. His powers of persuasion were considerable. (Hitler said to Speer, "I have again and again read Colonel de Gaulle's book on methods of modern warfare employing fully motorized units, and I have learned a great deal from it.") Over the years, de Gaulle had provided Reynaud with ammunition for criticism of the military, and he contributed bold phrases and a sense of backbone and resolve to Reynaud's first speeches as a premier.

Reynaud submitted his cabinet list to the Chamber of Deputies for ratification. The vote in the chamber was 268 for the cabinet, 156 against, with 111 abstentions. Ten out of his thirty-five choices for the cabinet had voted against him, and with the abstentions added to the nays, the vote stood at 268 for and 267 against—a margin of exquisite slimness. Reynaud was nervous and shaken. De Gaulle wrote that in the press, the trade unions, and even inside the government,

> very influential groups were openly supporting the idea of ending the war. Well-informed circles affirmed that this was the view of Marshal Pétain, Ambassador in Madrid, who was supposed to know through the Spaniards that the Germans were quite willing to come to terms. "If Reynaud falls," it was said on all sides, "Laval will take power with Pétain at his side. The Marshal, in effect, is in a position to make the High Command accept an armistice."

To quell this drift toward peace, and to prove he was capable of governing and of winning the war, Reynaud needed a bold stroke. As yet he did not know the direction of that stroke, but he knew it would have to be spectacular.

When Sumner Welles arrived in Rome on March 16, winter was gone, spring was in the air, and everything else had also changed. Ciano confided that a German source had told him the invasion of the West was imminent, and that there would be no solution other than one imposed by a German military victory. Peace was not in the cards. To Welles, Mussolini looked far better physically and was not "laboring under the physical or mental oppression. . . . He seemed to have thrown off some great weight."

The cause of Mussolini's transformation was a visit from Ribbentrop while Welles was in Paris and London. The idea that Welles might lure Mussolini away had galvanized Hitler into answering the Duce's months-old letter. On March 8, he wrote Mussolini that Welles was "really only gaining time for the Allies, that is, to paralyze possible German intentions for an offensive." Ribbentrop brought this letter to Mussolini along with a bribe. Since the British navy in the Mediterranean had been stopping coal shipments bound for Italy, Germany promised to send by truck over the Alps all the coal Italy would ever need, so that Italy's economy would not collapse. Grateful, Mussolini agreed to sign a new trade agreement which would give the Reich what he deemed "essential vitamin-C foods" as well as copper. (In August of 1939, Mussolini had told Hitler he had to obtain an immense amount of copper from

Germany in order for Italy to go to war.) Mussolini also promised Ribbentrop that Italy would enter the fray as Germany's ally when an appropriate moment arrived, and agreed to meet Hitler at the Brenner
Pass in ten days.

A rumor floated through Rome: Mussolini, bolstered by guarantees
from the United States, would, at the Brenner Pass meeting, force Hitler to make peace. Welles, who had been asked to delay his departure
for home until after Mussolini's return, told the Duce that the Allies
were not, in principle, opposed to negotiations with Hitler, but that they
were insistent on practical and trustworthy guarantees which would ensure that any peace treaty signed with Hitler would give them future
security. Mussolini called Welles's bluff. He asked if he could tell Hitler that Welles had gained the impression during talks with the Allies
that territorial and political questions were not insurmountable barriers
to peace. Welles, who had exaggerated the Allies' willingness in order
to stimulate some action, said he would have to check with Roosevelt.
On the telephone, the president said no. He would not risk creating the
impression that the United States was even faintly willing to participate
in a deal with Hitler. Shamefacedly, Welles had to tell Mussolini that
he could not repeat to Hitler what the Allies had said in confidence to a
representative of the United States, even though he, Welles, had already violated that confidence in his talks with the Duce.

Mussolini's train arrived early at the Brenner Pass and waited on
the Italian side of the mountain frontier. There was heavy snow outside; the peaks and the fir trees were blanketed in white. The night
before, Mussolini had had a dream which "tore away the veil from the
future," and he wanted to tell Hitler about it, perhaps to emphasize that
he was still the far-seeing Fascist, the man of important dreams.

He never got to reveal the dream. Hitler climbed into the train, was
deferential and respectful, and talked for several hours in what
amounted to a monologue. With the help of charts that inflated the
strength of his forces, he declared that Germany's might was overwhelming, and that the Allies would have no chance against the coming
western offensive. (He did not mention Norway or specify the western
invasion plan because Italy leaked information like a sieve.) Nearly
drowned in the flood of words, statistics, and charts, Mussolini asserted
himself only far enough to plead that Italy could not stand a long war.
Hitler said the war would be short, and that Italy could enter after
Germany had the situation well in hand, but nevertheless in time to
participate in some good battles and to have a share in the spoils.
Thrilled, Mussolini agreed to everything and in a few hours the meeting was over.

Ciano may have hated Ribbentrop and Hitler, but he did not want
to be shot for treason, and so, when Mussolini returned from the Brenner Pass, Ciano told Welles that nothing of substance had been said

there. In his diary, Ciano wrote that if Welles had come several months earlier, in December or January (when Welles had first wanted to come but had fallen ill), he might possibly have detached the Duce from the Führer. Welles boarded a ship to cross the Atlantic.

In Germany, after the Brenner Pass conference, Goebbels instructed his daily propaganda conference to begin to prepare the German people for the long-awaited struggle with the West: "In these days even more than before, the word 'peace' must really disappear from the German press. For the Reich there will be no compromise whatsoever."

Over the Easter weekend, as Welles cruised home, as Reynaud hurriedly formed his government, as the last of the Viipuri refugees straggled into Helsinki, Hitler made up his mind about Norway. The Scandinavian press was already speculating about a possible Allied move; to beat the Allies to the punch he would have to invade Norway and Denmark on April 8 or 9, and begin the invasion of the West about five days later.

The Brenner Pass meeting sent the Balkan states of Rumania, Yugoslavia, and Hungary into panic. They believed Hitler and Mussolini had made a deal to let Italy absorb part or all of the Balkans. In fact, at the meeting Mussolini had asked Hitler to arrange Russia's noninterference in the Balkans, and Hitler had agreed. Later Hitler was to brush his agreement aside as impractical.

After the Brenner meeting, Molotov informed the Supreme Soviet, "Of the neighboring states to the south, Rumania is one with which we have no pact of non-aggression. This is due to the existence of an unsettled dispute, the question of Bessarabia, whose seizure by Rumania the Soviet Union has never recognized." It was a clear indication that Russia was not going to sit by idly while Hitler went foraging in the West or Mussolini tried to strong-arm the Balkans. Although the nonaggression pact between Germany and Russia did allow the Soviets to take Bessarabia, Hitler had thought that if Stalin was going to take it, he would have done so in the fall. In fact, Stalin had wanted to do just that, but Finland had upset his timetable. Now the Finnish war was over.

Fearing both Russia and Italy, Rumania began to swing back toward Germany, and King Carol foiled a British attempt to float dynamite barges along his rivers which would have blocked oil shipments to Germany. Yugoslavia on the other hand, after learning that the Hungarian foreign minister had made a clandestine visit to Italy, possibly to arrange a joint Italo-Hungarian attack, started closed negotiations with Moscow. Pro-German citizens in Belgrade were arrested, and articles in the Yugoslav papers praised the Russians for their courteous dealings in trade negotiations. In the end, it was Stalin who reaped the largest benefits of the Brenner Pass meeting.

Paul Reynaud hastily called for the Allied Supreme War Council to meet in London on March 28. At the meeting, he was united with his longtime friend Churchill, who was joyous at Reynaud's takeover. Chamberlain, however, was not happy to see Reynaud. He had long told Daladier (who did not attend because of his injured foot) that if Daladier yielded to Reynaud, he, Chamberlain, would surely have to yield to Churchill.

In council, Reynaud insisted on two actions. First, that France and Britain sign a treaty guaranteeing that the two countries would fight together or die together: there was to be no separate peace. This was more than a question of honor. It intimated a concept that might eventually unite France and England into one country with one philosophy of foreign affairs and government, and possibly even one prime minister. The first step along this road was the unity of military command, for which the treaty also provided. Knowing this treaty would help Reynaud at home, the British approved it.

Reynaud's second demand was for approval of Churchill's plan to shorten the war by mining the Norwegian coast and then invading Norway to cut off Germany's iron-ore supply. Reynaud suggested that since preparations had already been made for this venture, and merely interrupted by the debacle of the Russo-Finish war and its untimely end, they could be quickly reactivated. Chamberlain and Churchill heartily agreed, provided—a bone to a friendly bulldog—that Churchill's cherished fluvial mines would be dropped into the Rhine to disrupt river traffic at the same time as the Norwegian channels were mined. The Allied invasion of Norway was scheduled for ten days later. Pleased and giddy with success, and with the prospect of a show of force in the offing, Reynaud returned to Paris a happy man, ready to save France and win the war with his bold stroke.

Sumner Welles, just home, gave the press a dour statement that there was not "the slightest chance of any successful negotiation at this time for a durable peace." Welles had no sooner got back to his office when, on March 30, Germany released to newspapers around the world the "Polish documents."

These documents, which the German army purportedly found when they took Warsaw, indicated that in August 1939 American ambassador Anthony Biddle had encouraged the Poles to take a strong stand against Germany by implying (though never directly stating) that in case of war the United States would ultimately intervene on the side of the Allies. Aside from some rabble-rousing memos from Bullitt, the most incriminating of the Polish documents was one which reported that Roosevelt had said he regarded the French Army as "the first line of American defense." Hitler and Goebbels maintained that these documents showed that the United States had never been neutral and had in fact encouraged the small nation to war against Germany. Goebbels informed his propaganda people that the documents

> prove the degree of America's responsibility for the outbreak of the present war. . . . [We publish them now] to strengthen American isolationists and to place Roosevelt in an untenable position, especially in view of the fact that he is standing for re-election. It is however not at all necessary for us to point out Roosevelt's responsibility; his enemies in America will take care of that.

The controversy stirred by the documents—which proved only a faint embarrassment when completely examined—diverted the world press, and made a fitting end to Welles's mission. By the time the furor died down, German ships were racing England's to Norway.

13

Norwegian Adventure

Daily, sometimes hourly, during the last days of March and the first days of April, Hitler would walk down the corridor of the Reichschancellery to visit the new war room and the people of OKW. Wilhelm Keitel (administration) and Alfred Jodl (chief strategist) were in charge of plans for the Norwegian adventure. Both by location and temperament the OKW people were closer to Hitler than the OKH chiefs Brauchitsch and Halder, whose headquarters were eighteen miles away. Keitel and Jodl, in addition to being right next door, responded to Hitler's advice on the invasion with far more willingness and good grace than did the regular army chiefs.

The OKW plans were daring. Norway would be invaded by a skeleton force of six divisions, paratroops, and planes. In its crucial opening moments, the invasion would depend on the German navy, which would ferry the troops to the Norwegian ports. During the transit, the ships would be seriously at risk and at the mercy of the far stronger British navy. Hitler had told Admiral Raeder there was no other way to accomplish the invasion, and Raeder acquiesced. Göring at first complained angrily because he had not been consulted about the invasion, but later he too caved in.

The Germans were optimistic about the invasion because they had good intelligence about the Allied plans for Norway. In February, Churchill had said some incautious things at a press briefing held for foreign attachés. In March, many newspapers speculated about an Allied invasion. Word of the Allied Supreme War Council's March 28 decision to mine Norwegian waters also got back to Hitler, as did Reynaud's March 30 boast to a diplomat that the Allies would within days make an important move. When on April 1 Hitler scheduled the invasion to begin on April 9, he knew it would be a race.

In the next few days he sent forty-two U-boats into Norwegian waters and started supply ships disguised as coal transports on the 1,250-

mile journey to Narvik. He also ordered troops trained in mountain warfare to travel in secret to embarkation points. On April 6, when his troops were already embarked, new intelligence alerted him to expect a British operation in Norway within fifty to a hundred hours. That meant there was still a danger that the British might annihilate the German ships as they went to sea.

At two in the morning of April 7 fifteen German destroyers, two battleships, and a heavy cruiser passed Lighthouse F at the mouth of the Weser River and headed north. They ran into gale-force winds and heavy seas; on some vessels there were engine failures; ten men were washed overboard, but no attempts were made to rescue them because the ships had to keep to their timetable. The heavy seas forced the destroyers to slow down so as not to capsize. At 1430 hours on April 7, a dozen British bombers appeared in the sky over the German fleet, and many thought the whole Norwegian adventure was doomed.

The British were expecting the Germans to invade Norway. They imagined the sequence of events as follows: The British would mine the Norwegian Leads; this would draw a German response, which in turn would trigger an Allied strike into northern Norway that would seize control of the area from Narvik to the Swedish Gällivare ore fields.

The plan was Churchill's, and although it sounded good there were some objections to it. For one thing, the fjords were now melting and Sweden would soon be able to ship ore to Germany over routes other than the Norwegian coastal waters. In addition, Gamelin raised the question that the British might not be able to deliver enough troops in a quick enough time to be effective in Norway. Privately, Ironside agreed with Gamelin, but told him there was no use in pursuing this objection because "with us the Admiralty is all-powerful. It likes to organize everything methodically. It is convinced that it can prevent any German landing on the west coast of Norway." Also, Churchill was now head of the Military Coordination Council and thus even more powerful.

Another stumbling block was Daladier. When Reynaud told him of the plans that had been agreed to, Daladier erupted. The object of his anger was not the idea of mining the Leads, but rather Churchill's pet notion of the fluvial mines. After some delay, the British agreed not to drop the fluvial mines simultaneously with the Norwegian operation, but as a consequence of Daladier's protests, the date for the mining of the Norwegian Leads was put back from April 5 to April 8.

The British had no lack of information on Germany's plans for Norway. Dozens of separate intelligence reports poured in from Germany, Danzig, Norway, Denmark, Sweden, Holland, and Rumania. The warnings mounted daily; they reported the presence of ships; the locations of troop units, parachutists, and aircraft in the jump-off area; they cited such ominous signs as communications blackouts and suspension of traffic on the Weser River. Oster told his Dutch friend Sas the date, place, time, and objectives of the coming invasion. All the warnings were ignored. Both Chamberlain and Churchill believed that an amphibious landing in Norway was beyond the capabilities of Hitler's forces. On April 4, in a show of cockiness during a speech to union leaders, Chamberlain said:

> When war did break out, German war preparations were far ahead of our own, and it was natural then to expect that the enemy would take advantage of his natural superiority to make an endeavor to overwhelm us and France before we had time to make good our deficiencies. Is it not a very extraordinary thing that no such attempt was made? Whatever might be the reason—whether it was that Hitler thought he might get away with what he had got without fighting for it, or whether it was that, after all, the preparations were not sufficiently completed—however, one thing is certain: he missed the bus.

The last phrase was to haunt him the rest of his life.

On the morning of April 7, the German ships were spotted, as they assembled and headed out to sea. British bombers were sent aloft, and the fleet at Scapa Flow was alerted to sail in an hour's time. But then very little happened.

The bombers appeared over the ships and loosed their bombs. Not a single bomb hit one of the German ships, and the bombers returned to base without having called for additional strikes. Then it was the turn of the Royal Navy, but because of a variety of mix-ups, it was not able to get under way before a dozen hours had elapsed. And it went in the wrong direction. Believing as they did that an amphibious landing was beyond the capabilities of the German navy, Churchill and the admirals had come to the conclusion that the objective of the German ships must be to "break out" of the North Sea into the Atlantic in order to damage British shipping. Consequently, the fleet sailed from Scapa Flow not to intercept the German ships in mid-passage, but to go northeast and prevent them from breaking out into the Atlantic at the far edge of the North Sea.

On the morning of April 8, British ships laid down three series of mines near Narvik. After the mining, rather than lingering in Narvik harbor or near the other Norwegian coastal towns, the minelayers and their escorting destroyers started for home. One of the destroyers, the *Glowworm*, left the pack to look for a man who had washed overboard, and at nine in the morning unexpectedly came on five German warships bound for Trondheim. The *Glowworm* fired on the nearest of the five, but was soon under fire herself from the much larger German cruiser *Hipper*. In moments, the *Glowworm* was mortally wounded; she got off a message home, then rammed the *Hipper* before she herself exploded and sank. British ships and planes went to look for the *Glowworm*, but the unfortunate ship and the German vessels as well had all vanished in the fog. Farther to the south, the Polish submarine *Orzel*, which was attached to the British navy, sighted and sank the German transport *Rio de Janeiro*—and the crew were amazed when Wehrmacht troops in full battle dress jumped off the decks into the icy waters. Some of these troops, who straggled ashore or were rescued, said they were on their way to fight in Norway. No one paid them much attention, and so another opportunity to head off or counter the German invasion was lost.

All during the dark night of April 8–9, German and British warships roved up and down the Norwegian coast, each fleet in ignorance of the other's strength, direction, and intentions.

German planning for the takeover of Denmark was so meticulous that when General Kurt Himer, chief of staff for the operation, sauntered into Copenhagen in civilian clothes on April 7, he had little to do but report home that the harbor was ice-free and that Danish troops had not been put on alert. Himer called the German attaché and instructed him to tell the Danish government to surrender at precisely 4:15 A M on the ninth. At 4:10 the invasion of Denmark began. From the south, panzers rolled into the country along roads that were unmined, across bridges that had not been blown, and against troops unwilling or too shocked to fight.

The northern Denmark airfields were quickly overpowered, in some instances without the defenders having fired a shot. The Germans needed these airfields as a jump-off point for Norway. Before dawn, having passed all the coastal defenses unchallenged, a troopship carrying a German assault battalion moved into Copenhagen harbor. Before five in the morning, the assault troops disembarked and soon captured the Citadel. As the elderly King Christian conferred with his hastily wakened cabinet about the German ultimatum, rifle fire could be heard from the Germans approaching the palace. German planes flew so low over Copenhagen that windowpanes shook; they did not drop their bombs, because the noise of their approach was enough to panic the government. A few minutes before 6 A M, King Christian surrendered his country. Danes woke to their morning breakfast and learned from their radios that they were vassals of the Third Reich.

The invasion of Norway went off almost as smoothly and, because of the ease with which it was accomplished, gave rise to a number of myths.

There was a Trojan Horse myth that said for days German troops had lain in wait concealed in coal boats until the moment came to strike. Actually, swift destroyers had carried the Wehrmacht toward

Bergen, Stavanger, Kristiansand, Trondheim, Oslo, and Narvik; the colliers which had been sent to the ports earlier held only military hardware beneath their thin layers of coal.

An invasion-from-the-sky myth postulated that German parachutists in enormous numbers had dropped on the major cities and taken the country by surprise. A small parachute company did secure Stavanger's Sola airport for the Luftwaffe, which then delivered columns of soldiers who marched into the city and took over; but the attacks on Bergen, Trondheim, Kristiansand, and Narvik were made without parachutists. And the attack on Oslo, which was supposed to be made by airborne troops, nearly became a German disaster.

In the early morning of April 9, two German capital ships crept up the long Oslo Fjord. One was the brand-new cruiser *Blücher*, the other was the pocket battleship *Lützow*, which had been named the *Deutschland* until Hitler decided not to risk having a ship with that name sunk. Halfway up the fjord, a little Norwegian armed whaler spotted the German ships and sent a warning to Oslo before the Germans blew her out of the water. At the main defenses of the Drøbak Narrows, the ancient batteries of Oscarborg (built by Krupp in 1905) opened fire in the darkness and sank the *Blücher*. Among the thousand men who perished were army leaders who were supposed to go into Oslo and induce King Haakon VII to surrender and agree to govern his country under German control—as his brother King Christian X of Denmark had already done. When the *Blücher* sank, the *Lützow* turned and ran back down the fjord.

The German air attaché waited at the Oslo airfield for parachutists to land, but they never came. Thus, for several hours there were no German soldiers anywhere near Oslo, and the German invasion timetable was in jeopardy. Had the Norwegians defended the capital then and held the airport open for British planes, Norway might have been preserved. But it didn't happen that way. Reports from many areas other than Oslo convinced the Norwegian king and government that a massive invasion was in progress and that it could not be resisted at that moment. By 7:30 A M, after having decided to send out mobilization orders by mail, King Haakon, his cabinet and members of the Norwegian Parliament, plus twenty-three trucks full of gold and important papers fled seventy miles inland to Hamar, and the chance to hold central Norway was lost. A lone Messerschmitt flew boldly down and landed at Oslo airport; after it, several fighters touched down and ringed the field so that the Luftwaffe transports could come in without fear of being attacked. By noon, eight infantry companies had landed.

These troops formed into ranks behind a military band and marched into and through Oslo in a faked victory parade whose purpose was to convince the citizens that the battle for Oslo was already over. The Norwegian troops that held the capital melted into the hills, the civilians watched the parade in awe, and Oslo and 250,000 Norwegians passed into German control.

A third myth was that a fifth column, consisting of Vidkun Quisling and his men, insidiously took over Norway from within. Berlin had not even alerted Quisling that there was to be an invasion. Nevertheless, he moved quickly to take advantage of the events of April 9. He bullied his way into the Oslo radio station and announced to the nation that the government had fled and that he was now the prime minister; moreover, he would help the friendly Germans repulse the British attackers. Ribbentrop recommended to Hitler that he disavow Quisling, but Hitler, who was in a magnanimous mood because of his victories, let Quisling remain as prime minister.

Quisling's speech enraged the Norwegians, as became obvious the next morning when Brauer, the German attaché in Oslo, went to see King Haakon. The king refused to accept his fate. He would not yield the country to German control and become a figurehead, nor would he appoint Quisling as prime minister. Haakon's refusal to give in spurred his ministers, and the country as a whole, to resistance.

Haakon counted on the Allies to come to his rescue. But that was not so simple a matter as it once had seemed.

British troubles with Norway, which had begun even before the Leads had been mined, continued to worsen. In the hurry to get ships under way, the Admiralty disembarked some troops and left them on the piers while destroyers steamed with their equipment for Norwegian waters.

There were other mix-ups. At 3:30 A M, April 9, near the north end of the North Sea, the British *Renown* engaged in a firefight with the larger German ships *Scharnhorst* and *Gneisenau*. The *Renown*'s salvoes hurt one of the German ships, but the Germans lured her far north into mist and snow squalls, and away from the coastal landing areas.

Admiral Sir Charles Forbes, commander of the vessels off Norway, convinced that the real threat was the invasion and not the two large German ships, dispatched four of his own cruisers and seven of his destroyers in the direction of Bergen. But First Sea Lord Dudley Pound called them back because the Admiralty feared the Germans were already in control of Bergen. At that point, the German hold on Bergen was tenuous, and had the destroyers gone in they might have blasted the few German destroyers, landed British troops, and taken control of central Norway.

Yet the British did score some important victories that day. Naval aviators sank the cruiser *Königsberg*, and submarines sank seven other medium-sized ships and shot off the propeller and part of the stern of the *Lützow*. Thus four out of five of the large German capital ships were damaged or sunk.

The most important battle of the first phase was for Narvik, the Norwegian northern port that was the gateway to the Swedish iron-ore fields. On the eighth, British ships had mined the waters below Narvik.

On the morning of the ninth, Commodore Friedrich Bonte with three German destroyers and five troopships entered Narvik waters. They had no trouble with the mines, but a Norwegian coast guard vessel which loomed up out of the dark and swirling snow fired a shot across Bonte's bow. Raeder had issued instructions to be ruthless. Bonte was devious as well as ruthless. He sent an officer to demand the surrender of the Norwegian captain. The Norwegian refused to comply and ordered away the German in his small boat. Bonte had arranged that when he saw a red flare he would fire. As the small boat pulled away, it sent a flare into the sky, and moments later Bonte sent two torpedoes into the Norwegian cutter. It broke apart and sank in seconds; a few minutes later another cutter met the same fate. Several hundred Norwegian sailors and two ships died within minutes, even though neither vessel had been any danger to the overwhelming German might. Bonte's ships then landed a division under the command of General Eduard Dietl at key points around Narvik harbor.

To the first officer he met on shore, Dietl said, "I greet the Royal Norwegian Army. The German army has come to protect Norway and her neutrality." Dietl requested the bewildered officer to take him to the garrison commander. A Quisling supporter, the commander surrendered the town to Dietl. (Later a Norweigian inquiry decided the man had been more incompetent than traitorous.) By 6:15 A M, German forces were in command of Narvik, and Dietl told the young mayor, Theodor Broch, that he wanted to make it clear that the Germans were there to protect the Norwegians from any further British interference with their neutrality. Broch protested the unnecessary killings in the harbor. Dietl answered, "Sad, isn't it? ... I can assure you, gentlemen, that we do not wish any bloodshed. I am happy to inform you that Norway is now occupied peacefully in the name of the Führer."

Under heavy pressure from the Germans, Broch supervised the printing and distribution of ration cards. There was some flour, some canned goods, and an abundance of freshly caught fish, which had been destined for sale to Germany but which now were salted and kept for local consumption. Broch hoped against hope that the British would come to the rescue. After all, Dietl had only two thousand men and was inordinately far from Germany.

That very afternoon British captain B. A. W. Warburton-Lee steamed near Narvik with five destroyers and learned from a harbor pilot that ten German destroyers were inside Narvik's waters. Despite the fact that his force was outnumbered two to one, Warburton-Lee cabled the Admiralty that he would attack at "dawn high water," and at four in the morning of April 10 he did just that.

Aboard the *Hardy*, he forced his way inside the harbor and aimed his firepower at the German ships within easy range. With a torpedo he blew away the stern of the *Wilhelm Heidekamp*, which sank and ended the life of Commodore Bonte. (All the German destroyers were named for sailors who had died at Jutland.) British shellfire sank the *Anton Schmitt*, damaged the *Roeder* and the *Lüdemann*, and sank six other German merchant ships. However, as Warburton-Lee was withdrawing from the harbor, five German destroyers that had been in a side fjord came up, and a running fight developed. The British won, and managed to get outside again, but in the battle the Germans sank two of the British destroyers and damaged a third—and killed Warburton-Lee.

Dietl began to sweat: the British had sunk his ammunition ship, his equipment was thin, and his destroyer protection was bottled up in the harbor. He believed the British would soon arrive in strength, blow up the remaining destroyers, and land troops in force to oust him from Narvik. The civilian population was melting away from the town to hide in the snow and the rocky hills; many of them had become *franctireurs* who sniped at his men. Broch, the young mayor, was openly showing pro-British sympathies. Dietl wired Berlin for supplies. Eleven German transport planes came, but when they landed on the improvised landing field of frozen Lake Hartvig, the ice melted under them and they all sank. A desperately needed mountain battery disappeared into the murky waters. Now Dietl would be unable to oppose any sizable British force, so he sent his men into the hills, where they would be more difficult for the British to find.

At noon on April 13, the 30,000-ton *Warspite* and nine British destroyers gathered off Narvik. In a daring feat of seamanship, the huge *Warspite* maneuvered inside the confined harbor area, where its fifteen-inch guns gave it complete command. One German destroyer tried to escape, and bore down on the *Warspite* as if to ram; the big ship's guns sank the destroyer before it could approach. Then the British destroyers fired into the German ships and turned the harbor into a shambles of wrecks, with fires, smoke, and drowning men. Every German destroyer in the area was either sunk or so badly damaged that it had to beach. The British ships even managed to sink a German submarine, and after the battle nothing German moved in Narvik waters.

"Narvik can be taken by direct assault without fear of meeting serious opposition on landing," the *Warspite* signaled the Admiralty as it steamed back outside the harbor. The destroyers followed.

Dietl was astounded when the British left the harbor, for the battleship and the destroyers could easily have used their guns to blast his men from the hills, and could have landed a small force which would have finished him off. He ordered his men to pick up 2,600 surviving sailors from the useless German ships, and prepared to defend Narvik from the British assault whenever it might begin.

In Berlin, the news of the British strike at Narvik threw many into panic. Karl Doenitz, chief of the submarine force, recalled his submarines to their bases. Over and over again, the submarines had had chances to blow British ships out of the water, but every single torpedo of the hundreds they had fired had been duds. The submarines were removed from service, and several months' work was undertaken to determine why the torpedoes had failed. Raeder was gloomy. He had lost four out of five capital ships and half his destroyer force; his navy was shattered. For the next six months, the German navy would be virtually helpless. Raeder had warned Hitler that this might be a consequence of the invasion plan, but Hitler had been willing to take the risk. Later, in the summer, when he had to consider whether he could invade England with an inadequate naval force, Hitler was not so sanguine about the loss.

Hitler, too, was frantic. The news of the naval disaster was bad, but the idea that the British might shortly take Narvik was anathema. When news came that some British troops had landed north of the city and had joined hands with Norwegian troops there, he decided that Dietl should abandon Narvik immediately and fight his way down the coast to Trondheim. "The hysteria is frightful," Jodl noted in his diary, and he tried to bring some semblance of reason to the headquarters. "Mein Führer," Jodl said, "I have been there. An expedition there is like a Polar expedition." For Dietl to fight down to Trondheim would be an impossible task, Jodl said. Hitler listened, but nevertheless insisted on sending Dietl an order to abandon Narvik—the point of access to Swedish ore and thus the objective of the whole Norwegian campaign.

Keitel wrote out Hitler's order, but for transmission it was given to Colonel Bernhard von Lossberg, a junior officer. Lossberg, an enormous man with a game leg, told his superior officer (Jodl) that he would not send it. Quietly Jodl told him that the order was Hitler's and must be sent, but Lossberg got permission to speak directly to Brauchitsch. The commander-in-chief of the army refused to intercede: "I have nothing whatever to do with the Norwegian campaign. Falkenhorst and Dietl are answerable to Hitler alone, and I have not the least intention of going on my own free will to that clip joint [the Reichschancellery]."

However, Brauchitsch suggested that Lossberg send Dietl a message congratulating him on his promotion and assuming that Dietl would defend Narvik to the last man. In front of Jodl's eyes, Lossberg tore up Hitler's order and sent the message Brauchitsch had suggested. His action stiffened Jodl, who then calmly reminded the Führer, "You should not give up anything until it is really *lost.* . . . In every war there are times when the Supreme Commander must keep his nerve!" Hitler contritely asked Jodl what he would do in this instance, and Jodl produced the draft of an order directing Dietl to hold on as long as possible. Hitler signed it forthwith.

14

Preparations

The day after Norway was invaded, Molotov called the German envoy into his office and told him that under no circumstances should Sweden be drawn into the conflict. Germans in Sweden would be next door to Finland, and Stalin wanted no Germans in close contact with the still-troublesome Finns. Berlin agreed to Stalin's strictures.

The Soviet press blamed England and France for the spread of the war to Norway, but behind the scenes in London Ambassador Ivan Maisky again got in touch with Lord Halifax about trade negotiations. It was the first time that representatives of the two countries had discussed anything of real importance since the previous August. The Soviet press also appealed to Sweden, Yugoslavia, Hungary, Bulgaria, and Rumania "to make common cause with the larger states in order to assure their status of neutrality." In other words, they ought to turn to Russia as a bulwark against Germany and Italy. In December, on his birthday, Stalin had received profuse congratulations from Hitler; now Hitler's birthday had arrived, and Stalin did not send any congratulations. He did continue to live up scrupulously to the letter of the trade agreement with Germany, but his eye was already on the time when he would no longer be able to do so.

For instance, he bluntly ordered his military commanders to study modern warfare, for in the light of the blitzkriegs and the debacle in Finland, the traditions and experience of the Revolutionary era were no longer relevant. He introduced a sweeping reform of the Red Army, increasing the authority of officers and recalling many officers who had been banished during the purges. Voroshilov, who had dared to suggest that Stalin had gutted the army in those purges, was demoted and replaced by Semën Timoshenko, who had finally won the Russo-Finnish war. Georgi Zhukov, who had shown great ability in the war with Japan (and who had managed to avoid the slippery ice of Finland) was also promoted. Later Zhukov called 1940 "the year of the great transformation" of the Soviet armed forces.

In the democracies, newspaper readers and radio listeners could hardly believe that the Allies would once again let Hitler take over a small country without a fight. But British troops northwest of Narvik languished and did not attack. The naval commander, Lord Cork and Orrery, wanted an immediate attack, but P. J. Mackesy, the army commander, insisted that he needed more men to take the city. He awaited several British units supposedly on their way to Narvik. Unfortunately, these units had been diverted.

Earlier, Churchill's instructions and counterinstructions (some of which had come at the request of higher authorities) had delayed the transit of several divisions to Narvik. The Joint Planning Committee ("that machinery of negation," Churchill fumed) added to the delay by insisting that the troops might be better used at Trondheim. Their reasons were political. Narvik was the key to control of the iron ore, but since Norway was now formally an ally, and since King Haakon was in central Norway, Trondheim had become more important. The Norwegian military believed that if Trondheim could be retaken, all of central Norway could be returned to Norwegian control and Oslo could also be retaken. Churchill and the Military Coordination Council at first objected to sending men to Trondheim, but gave in under heavy political pressure. However, instead of rerouting *all* the troops to Trondheim, Churchill divided the troopships in mid-passage and sent half to Trondheim and the other half to Narvik. By this stroke, which he later was at pains to deny, Churchill dispatched inadequate forces to each city. As a result, neither objective could be achieved.

Major General Adrian Carton de Wiart had lost an eye and a hand in the Great War. When the War Office called him in the middle of the night, he assumed that since Norway was one of the few countries in the world where he had not lost some portion of his anatomy, he would be sent there. He was correct. He was put in charge of "Mauriceforce," the northern pincer of a planned pincers movement north and south of Trondheim. His men landed north of the city at the small port of Namsos.

Namsos was a mess. De Wiart's antiaircraft guns had gone to Narvik, and his men had reindeer saddles but no skis. The French Chasseurs Alpins had skis but did not have proper straps for their boots, and the French supply ship was too large to enter the harbor.

The southern pincer, "Sickelforce," landed south of Trondheim at an equally small town, Andalsnes, and encountered similar problems. Officers had wound up at one destination while their men had been landed at the second; field telephones had gone to Trondheim, but their cables were on the way to Narvik. Ammunition for the mortars and carriages for the Bren guns had been left in England.

Sickelforce had additional difficulties. They had no maps of the Trondheim area. And when they landed they found that their orders had been countermanded, and that they were now to proceed south to link up with the Norwegian army. The attempt to carry out the new order was a continual nightmare. Except at close range the British were unable to distinguish Norwegian from German uniforms and were machine-gunned by what they first took to be friendly soldiers. They had no transport except for commandeered Norwegian cars and trucks whose drivers spoke little English. Furthermore, their antitank guns could not penetrate the German tanks. Whole Sickelforce battalions were wiped out, and hundreds of Britons were taken prisoner.

Some of the Britons were flown to Berlin, where they were greeted by Hitler and were shown off to the public. One of the captured units had the plans of the proposed February occupation of Stavanger, which had never taken place. The plans for Stavanger were displayed in Berlin as evidence that the British had long plotted to compromise Norwegian neutrality.

As for Mauriceforce, though it outnumbered the Wehrmacht in the area by a ratio of two to one, it was nearly blasted out of existence by the Luftwaffe. De Wiart signaled the War Office, "I see little chance of carrying out decisive, or, indeed, any operations unless enemy air activity is considerably reduced." But the Luftwaffe reduced Namsos to a rubble heap and left Mauriceforce without a base or a port through which to receive help. And the Royal Navy learned at Namsos what it had been reluctant for twenty years to admit: that air power could completely negate sea power. British battleship and destroyer guns could only be raised to an elevation of forty degrees which meant that attacking aircraft that flew directly overhead were out of range. On the open sea this might not have mattered, but in the close quarters of a harbor the ships could not train their guns on the attacking planes. With carriers busy in the Mediterranean and with home air bases too far away for bombers to be effective, the British navy and air force could not send enough planes to defend Namsos. De Wiart cabled London that his forces were being cut to shreds in the air raids and would soon have to be withdrawn.

Back in London, Sir Roger Keyes's wife had come up with an idea and Keyes was red-hot to act on it. He suggested to Churchill that since the Royal Navy apparently had no fighting spirit left, he personally would lead a frontal attack on Trondheim, in out-of-date ships if necessary. Churchill considered the idea for a time—it was appealing to think that the navy could save the day by a bold stroke—but others pointed out that Trondheim was at the end of a narrow, thirty-nine-mile-long fjord, and that in such confines the ships would be helpless under the enemy's air superiority. Dudley Pound indirectly let Churchill know that he would resign if Keyes were allowed to proceed with his suicidal attack. In 1915, it had been the resignation of a first sea lord because of Churchill's blunders at Gallipoli that had led to his downfall; if Dudley Pound were to quit now, Churchill might again suffer the same fate. He told Keyes he was sorry, but that the attack could not be made. The irate Keyes swore to bring down the government over that veto.

Churchill had made the right decision. By April 23, four days after de Wiart had landed, the MCC and everyone in the war cabinet understood that for the Allied forces central Norway was an unmitigated disaster. Thousands of men had already been killed and wounded. On April 26, London, without consulting either the French or the Norwegians, ordered de Wiart to begin an evacuation. When the Norwegian commander learned from a British officer that Allied troops north and south of Trondheim were to be evacuated, he was bitter. "So Norway must go the way of Czechoslovakia and Poland. But why? Why withdraw when your troops are still unbeaten?" the Norwegian asked. The British officer could only shrug his shoulders.

On the night of April 29, King Haakon and members of the Storting, carrying a quantity of gold, waited at Andalsnes to board a British ship. The pier was in flames, and the cruiser *Glasgow* had to wet it down with firehoses before the royal party could be embarked. Haakon and his group were taken up the coast to Tromsö, a town near Narvik. Over the next several nights, and under the same hazardous conditions, British and French troops near Trondheim made their way aboard ships and out to sea. During the evacuation, two destroyers, one French and one British, were sunk by the Luftwaffe, but most of the troops returned safely to England. And then, except for the Narvik area, Norway belonged entirely to Germany.

On April 24, the *Warspite* had steamed into Narvik harbor for the second time and had led a bombardment which served as a cover for the attempt by four Norwegian battalions to take the city itself. Because of Mackesy's continuing timidity, the British, French, and Polish troops were not brought forward in time to assist the Norwegians, and half the Norwegians were killed, wounded, or taken captive. Churchill and Ironside were appalled at Mackesy's inaction.

Soon after, three battalions of Chasseurs Alpins, two battalions of Foreign Legionnaires, and four battalions of Polish exiles arrived, and Mackesy had nearly 25,000 troops under his command against only a few thousand under Dietl. Still he did not give the signal for an all-out attack. As April turned into May, the combined forces inched up on Narvik, and it seemed as if any day they might take the city. If they did, the objective of the British campaign might still be accomplished, though Norway itself had already been lost.

In the beginning of April 1940, before the invasion of Norway, the political future in the United States had still been cloudy. A whole smorgasbord of Democratic presidential candidates were in the field— Cordell Hull, John Garner, James Farley, and Paul McNutt were among the better-known. Roosevelt had refused to endorse any of them, and behind the scenes his men were busy in the effort to dominate state conventions so that the delegates sent to the July nominating convention would be committed to the president. Roosevelt could thus control the convention and make sure the Democratic nominee would be pledged to continue his policies.

Germany had a finger in the American political pie, spending perhaps as much as five million dollars to publish and publicize the "Polish documents" and to boost the chances of political candidates who might keep America neutral. William Rhodes Davis, who had visited Berlin during the fall as an emissary from Roosevelt, boasted to his German friends that he could assure them of Roosevelt's defeat in 1940 because John L. Lewis, the influential mine workers' leader, had broken with the president in January and was going to support isolationist senator Burton K. Wheeler's drive for the presidency.

In early April, Roosevelt was not considering another presidential term. He wrote friends that he looked forward to being out of office and issued provisional invitations to many people to come to his home in Hyde Park in a year's time. But the onset of the war in September 1939 had deeply troubled him; he was not sure that any of the proposed presidential candidates could lead the country if the war became more serious. And when Germany invaded Denmark and Norway, everything began to change. Roosevelt told a press conference that the invasions "will undoubtedly cause a great many more Americans to think about the potentialities of war." Greenland and Iceland were Danish territories; should Germany force Denmark to give them up, the Third Reich might be on the doorstep of the Americas. A week after the Nazis' northern invasion, the president announced that most people in the United States considered Greenland within the area covered by the Monroe Doctrine. In other words, Greenland was vital to United States security and the U.S. would fight for it if necessary. Polls indicated that with the rising tide of European hostilities, more people had begun to consider the possibility of a third term. The president told intimates he would await events before he made any final decision on the subject.

On a sunny, warm day in Berlin, Else Wendel sat in a garden with her sister, brother, and mother. The women persuaded Rudolf to talk about Norway. He had been aboard the *Blücher* when it was torpedoed; the ship had keeled over violently, and he had jumped into the icy waters. It was so cold that after a few strokes he could hardly feel his own legs and arms; by a miracle he escaped the ship's suction as it went down, and reached the stones and the shore where he lay more dead than alive:

> Some men did ... strip off their clothes and go back into the water to try and help their comrades. Often they failed, as the men in the water were too frozen to cling to anyone. Worst of all was the screaming from the men in the water who were burning in the oil patches. The oil had caught fire suddenly. Those in them had only two choices, to sink and drown, or go on swimming and be burned to death. The sounds and sights were ... absolutely terrible. When I was a little boy, I wanted to have an exact description of what hell was like. No one could give it to me. Today I can say I have seen hell.

Still shaken by the events, Rudolf went out for a walk. The family, stunned by the story, said they could never get away from the war, no matter how remote it currently seemed. Else's mother lifted her glass and proposed a toast: "To the end of all wars, and hope to all people."

For years, the Grossdeutschland regiment had been the pride of Berlin, an elite unit of the Wehrmacht that stood guard around official buildings and trooped the colors in parades and on ceremonial occasions. Each province sent its best men to be part of the GD, and every month it was each province's duty to supply its GD men with local sausages and local beer. Sometime in April, the GD stopped trooping the colors and began to practice crossing a river by swimming in full kit or in rubber boats while under heavy fire from the opposing bank. As they practiced every day, they got better at it. Even Heinz Guderian, who came to watch their exercises, said so.

En route from Kiel to Narvik on April 26, German patrol boat VP2623 ran into fire from the British navy and surrendered. A swarm of British sailors looted the small ship for souvenirs; later, officers carried out a thorough search and came up with some papers that seemed of interest. The papers were cipher settings for the German naval code machine Enigma, and when they reached the British Cypher School, along with the news that other papers had been lost to the looters, a howl was raised. The Admiralty immediately issued instructions that any captured vessel must be carefully searched by officers and looting was forbidden. In early May, the papers of VP2623 enabled the cryptanalysts to read the German naval code for six April days. The time interval between the capture of a clue and the reading of a setting was growing shorter. Soon the Bombe would be operational, and then British intelligence would know daily what the Germans were doing.

In a hospital near Douai, Alan Brooke visited his son Tom, who lay desperately ill with a burst appendix and peritonitis. Brooke also had professional worries. John Dill had been recalled to London to become vice chief of the Imperial General Staff and to reinforce Ironside, whose aura had been tarnished by the debacle in Norway. Dill's departure left Brooke "in the depths of gloom," for,

> I had an absolute conviction that the German offensive was coming soon. I now had no illusions as to the efficiency and fighting value of the French Army. I had little confidence in Gort's leadership in the event of attack, and now Dill was gone there was no one left in the BEF with whom I could discuss my misgivings freely. . . . Meanwhile we remained short of essential arms such as planes, tanks, anti-tank guns, anti-aircraft guns, wireless, and the dark clouds were gathering fast.

Brooke was proud that the BEF, which now included 250,000 fighting troops and 150,000 rear-based and lines-of-communications troops, had during the winter constructed forty miles of antitank obstacles, four hundred concrete pillboxes, fifty-nine airfields, and over a hundred miles of railroads. The way to beat the Germans, Brooke believed, was to stay in the well-dug British and French positions and wait for the Germans to come to them.

Yet according to Gamelin's Plan D, this was precisely what the British and French armies were *not* going to do. Brooke observed that the roads on which the British and French must advance into Belgium were inadequate, and that the plans for the move up to the Dyle Line had become an "inflexible organization which did not lend itself to many changes." When he tried to speak to Gort, Georges, and Gamelin, they refused to heed his objections, and instead concentrated on details and on training exercises.

Denis Barlone, who was with Blanchard's First Army, received a great shock near the end of April. As he was over forty, he was to be relieved of command and sent home to take charge of a labor battalion. Similar orders had been issued to remove many of the older officers from the front. By pulling strings, Barlone was able to remain in command, and with his Second North African Division, but hundreds of other experienced officers were sent home.

Barlone's men worked daily in the fields of the local farmers, while he and the officers picked the first radishes from their own recently planted gardens. Once in a while he visited higher officers, and played bridge after dinners which ranged from stuffed lobsters to truffled fowl. The men's letters home, opened by postal censorship, showed that they were fed up with "this life of dormant war in which they have the impression of being useless," Barlone noted in his diary. He was commanded to organize distractions. He conjured up an orchestra and held a dancing competition. Soccer matches between the English and French troops proved good for morale, especially when they ended in a tie. Gamelin did not expect a German offensive until July, and since the temperature had soared into the nineties and. everything was so beautiful, furloughs were granted. Thousands of officers and tens of thousands of *poilus* drifted south toward their homes and vacation spots.

Generals André Corap and Charles Huntziger commanded respectively the French Ninth and Second armies, assigned to defend the Meuse River at the edge of the Ardennes forest. Corap was a slovenly man, timid and plodding, who had spent most of his career in North Africa. Huntziger was trim and intelligent, and at just under sixty was one of the youngest army commanders and Gamelin's probable heir.

Both commanded mostly "B" troops, territorials from North Africa, Indochina, and Madagascar, and "crocodiles," older men with families. The high command did not expect much action in the Meuse sector. Huntziger told his superiors in March that no further reinforcement of his sector was necessary, which was, at best, a delusion on his part. Neither the Second nor the Ninth Army had had much training, and none at all in the use of the newer equipment or in combating dive-bomber attacks. The Africans had suffered greatly through the hard winter, and the older men, who like all *poilus* received only centimes a day, often applied for leave so that they could drive taxis or do extra work to supplement the miserly allowance given their dependents.

When central Norway fell and the British and French troops were evacuated, André Maurois was visiting the Ninth Army. A lieutenant who served as his escort observed:

> It's a bad business that our first enterprise in this war met with failure. A young horse must never be defeated in his trial runs. If he is, he gets the habit, loses his self-respect and comes to consider it perfectly natural that he should stay behind.

To Maurois, Corap's men seemed suffused with ennui and unable to believe any longer in the reality of the war. When in early May Huntziger set his men to tearing down antitank barriers at the edge of the Ardennes forest, they did not object. It seemed to them to be one more piece of busy-work. Later some saw it, darkly, as evidence of a conspiracy, but it was probably due to nothing more than Huntziger's need to clear the way for his troops, which were scheduled to advance into the forest as soon as the Germans appeared. No one remembered the lessons of Prételat's maneuvers in that area, or considered that a cleared road could be traversed in more than one direction.

Paul Reynaud's disenchantment with Gamelin grew by leaps and bounds. The premier had not liked finding out about the German invasion of Scandinavia from the Reuters news service, and he was incensed that after Finland Gamelin had dispersed the troops that might have immediately gone to Norway. His anger was momentarily deflected when Gamelin backed Admiral Darlan's plan to move Allied troops into Belgium and Holland while the Germans were busy in Norway. While Reynaud went to London to discuss this daring and interesting idea with the British, Gamelin gave a sumptuous luncheon for General Maxime Weygand, the seventy-two-year-old commander of France's forces in Syria. Weygand—who, rumor said, was the illegitimate son of Maximilian of Mexico, or the son of Belgium's Leopold II, or the offspring of a Jewish businessman in Brussels—had been a disciple of Foch. After the Great War, Foch said that if France got into trouble, the people should call for Weygand. In August of 1939, Gamelin had done just that. He had beseeched the old commander to come out of retirement and take up the command of France's armies in the Middle East.

Throughout the luncheon party (chicken *mascotte*, *foie gras* with truffles, Beaune '33 and Monbazillac '29), Gamelin talked philosophy and uttered not a word about current military problems. Near the end of the meal, he suddenly posed the question: "When will the Germans decide to attack so that I can begin my grand maneuver in the north?" Neither Weygand nor anyone else had an answer, and so the generals and their guests attacked the *profiteroles* with chocolate sauce.

London backed Darlan's plan, but it was quashed because Belgium would still not agree to admit Allied troops. Gamelin seemed relieved, and this reaction further irked Reynaud. As evidence mounted of the ineptitude of French planning and activity in Norway, he resolved to sack Gamelin and replace him with either Georges or Weygand. He introduced the issue at a cabinet meeting, but Gamelin had learned of his intentions and wrote out his resignation. Daladier threatened to resign and sink the government if Gamelin were allowed to resign, and once again Reynaud was forced to back off. Soon the great confrontation with Germany would occur, and France had a generalissimo who, in the premier's opinion, was at best marginally competent. Reynaud began to amass proof of Gamelin's ineptitude and resolved to force the issue at the next cabinet meeting regardless of what Daladier might do.

But before that meeting Reynaud got the flu and took to his bed. For a week, while he was ill, Hélène de Portes very nearly took over the reins of government. At one point, she sat behind Reynaud's desk surrounded by generals and high officials and chaired an important meeting. From time to time during the proceedings she stuck her head through the bedroom doorway and asked after Reynaud's health. "I'm doing my best to replace him," she told a journalist.

Earlier Reynaud had confided to Maurois, "You don't know what a man who has been hard at work all day will put up with to make sure of an evening's peace." One of Hélène's allies was Paul Baudouin, whom she had nominated as secretary of the war cabinet, even though he was an open admirer of Mussolini and in favor of allowing Nazi

Germany to find its place in the sun. Hélène also persuaded Reynaud to bring both Marshal Pétain and Pierre Laval into closer contact with the government.

The Deuxième Bureau learned that German military intelligence was studying the routes from Sedan to Abbeville; the French military attaché in Switzerland warned that the German attack would come between May 8 and May 10, with Sedan as "the center of gravity"; Oster told Sas to "burn the Meuse bridges for me"; and the German opposition alerted the Vatican, which briefed the Belgian, Dutch, and French ambassadors to the Holy See. There was so much evidence of the intent and direction of the coming German offensive that Ambassador Bullitt reported to Roosevelt in Washington, "French government convinced this information being put out by German government and it's considered probable that Hitler will turn his attention to Yugoslavia and Hungary before attacking the Netherlands." French air reconnaissance planes reported sighting a German armored column which stretched more than seventy-five miles back into Germany and which was headed for the Ardennes. None of this intelligence was believed.

The French had more tanks, more planes, more troops, more artillery, and more supplies than the Germans. But the planes and the tanks were so dispersed that each army had small numbers of them, and even though a half-million French troops were poised to move up into Belgium and Holland, the bulk of the French army was stationed in the Maginot Line or in clusters near Paris and even facing the Alps and Italy.

What was wrong, Charles de Gaulle argued to his friend Reynaud, was the strategy. De Gaulle had been promised a command within a fortnight, but he was more concerned about the over-all fate of the army. On May 3, he gave the bedridden Reynaud a scathing memo which argued in the strongest terms that the French battle plan must be revised to take into account the events of Poland and Norway and the great revolution in mobile armored warfare. France had more tanks than Germany, and tanks were essential to the new warfare; France must use the tanks in bunched formations as spearheads and must not dissipate them as adjuncts to foot soldiers. They must be used as offensive rather than defensive weapons. If this strategy was adopted, France would be saved. More broadly, de Gaulle insisted that Reynaud must reform the army from above, because its own generals could not and would not perform that task.

From this memo Reynaud gained a new perspective: there was nothing wrong with France's forces per se; the trouble was with their disposition and their administration. Over the next several days, he tried to discern the mood of the cabinet and of President Albert Lebrun. The president counseled Reynaud not to act hastily, but the premier's mind was at last made up.

In the cabinet meeting on the morning of May 9, still suffering from the effects of the flu, Reynaud read in a hoarse voice a two-hour indictment of Gamelin. The incompetence of the generalissimo in the matter of Norway was inexcusable, and he had to be replaced or "we are certain to lose the war." Most of the ministers agreed. Daladier defended Gamelin as "a great military chief" and again implied that he would resign if Gamelin were sacked. The moment had come. "In view of such grave opposition," Reynaud said in a voice reduced to a whisper, "I shall have to consider the government as having resigned." He begged the cabinet to stay on and not to say anything to the public until a successor could be found. Later in the day, on learning of Reynaud's action, Gamelin again wrote out his resignation, not wishing, he said, to be the cause of yet another government crisis. Thus France, on the eve of the invasion, had neither a premier nor a commander in chief.

The reckoning for the considerably larger British failure in Norway came also in early May. Although 25,000 Allied troops were still inching toward Narvik, the troops from Namsos and Andalsnes had returned home, and the dimensions of the British folly in Norway were becoming known.

On April 11, in the first blush of news from Norway, Winston Churchill had addressed the Commons with what Harold Nicolson called a "feeble, tired speech" that was simply "playing for time." He stressed the difficulties the Allies had experienced in going to the aid of formerly neutral countries only after they had been invaded. But, he said, Hitler had committed a strategic error by invading Norway, and he would soon pay dearly for it. On April 15, Churchill repeated that Hitler had made a strategic blunder.

It was Churchill himself who had blundered. The first lord of the Admiralty had planned the overall strategy of the British mine-laying and the riposte to the German invasion; he had been involved in the constant changes of plan which had deprived the troops of essential equipment and lost precious time; and he had subtly interfered in the day-to-day operations of the navy and army. He bore heavy responsibility for what Hitler called the Allies' "frivolous dilettantism" in Norway.

Yet Chamberlain refused to lay the blame at Churchill's door; the buck stopped at the prime minister's desk, and he was willing to accept it. As the troops returned from Namsos, pressure gathered from many quarters to depose Chamberlain. He could have thrown Churchill to the wolves, as Asquith had in 1915, but even though in danger himself, he did not do so; in the months of working together a bond had formed between them. Churchill had been intensely loyal and properly deferential, and Chamberlain had found Churchill to be the one cabinet minister who most consistently strove to win the war. A Gallup poll in March showed that 57 percent of the people queried supported Chamberlain and 36 percent were against him; in early May the percentages were reversed: 32 percent for Chamberlain, and 58 percent against.

On May 7, the debate on Norway began in the Commons. Leo Amery and other old supporters of Churchill agitated for a true government of national unity in which all the major parties would be represented. Chamberlain had rejected this demand in September and now rejected it again. But the times had changed. In full naval regalia, with six rows of medals and the Grand Cross of the Order of the Bath, Sir Roger Keyes rose to fulfill his vow. He said the government had been incompetent over Norway, and, worse, it had no attacking spirit. Keyes had spoken to de Wiart just prior to the debate, and he cited chapter and verse on the Norway fiasco. The House bristled with uniforms, many of them worn by MPs who had been in Norway. Other members represented districts that had raised units that had suffered extensive casualties in that campaign. Keyes said that his friend Churchill was constrained and hampered. "Today he cannot dare to do the things he would have dared in 1915"; the blame, Keyes said, belonged not to Churchill but to Dudley Pound and to Chamberlain.

Other speakers were not so kind to Churchill and pointed out his responsibility for the debacle in Norway. But since September, Churchill, by his speeches, his sagacity and bellicosity, and his detailed knowledge, had made himself indispensable to the war effort. Had the crisis come at any time before May, Churchill might have been dropped; now the majority of the Commons were lenient with the first lord. Leo Amery stood up. He had found a line of Cromwell's which decried "decayed serving men and tapsters and such kind of fellows." He said the members of Chamberlain's government were of that ilk, but the problem was Chamberlain rather than those around him. He went on:

> This is what Cromwell said to the Long Parliament when he thought it was no longer fit to conduct the affairs of the nation: "You have sat too long here for any good you have been doing. Depart, I say, and let us have done with you. In the name of God, go!"

The Loyal Opposition benches took up the cry. The next day Herbert Morrison, a leading Labour MP, cited evidence he had gathered from Martin Lindsay, de Wiart's second at Namsos. The government had misused the troops in Norway. MPs Quintinn Hogg and Roy Wise, both army captains who had been at Namsos, concurred with Morrison's judgment. The Labour benches also castigated Chamberlain for having kept them out of the government.

When Chamberlain recognized that he himself was the issue, he said, "No government can prosecute a war efficiently unless it has public and parliamentary support. I accept this challenge. I welcome it, indeed. At least I shall see who is with us and who is against us."

The old Welsh warrior Lloyd George answered this thrust with one of his own: "It is not a question of who are the Prime Minister's friends.

It is a far bigger issue. The Prime Minister must remember that he has met this formidable foe of ours in peace and in war, and he has always been bested."

There was the nub of the matter. As another old warrior—Léon Blum—had said of Daladier, "Let's say that he is paying today for the many occasions on which we let him off too easily." It was now Chamberlain's turn to pay.

The government traditionally had the last word in such debates, and the last speaker of the day was traditionally the best. Chamberlain chose Churchill rather than himself to defend the government's actions. It was Churchill's all but impossible task to defend the government and the prime minister without sounding ridiculous and without further damaging his own prestige. How well he performed this delicate task he did not know, for at the end of the evening when a vote on a motion to adjourn became a vote of confidence in the Chamberlain government, such members as Hore-Belisha, Macmillan, Amery, Duff Cooper, Spears, Hogg, Wise, Keyes, Lloyd George, and Lady Astor voted against the government. The final count showed a majority of eighty-one for the government, but this was considered too slim a margin for comfort. It was virtually certain that the government would fall on any new vote. Macmillan and a few others began to sing "Rule Britannia" in tuneless voices, and soon the MPs chanted, "Go, go, go, go." Decorum had already gone.

On the morning of May 9, Chamberlain invited Amery to join the government in the hope that by taking in a few former enemies he would satisfy the wolves. Amery said he would not serve unless Labour was also invited in. Chamberlain arranged to have tea at four o'clock with Halifax and Churchill, after which the Labour leaders would arrive to discuss the prospects of a coalition government.

In the garden of 10 Downing Street, it was a splendid sunny afternoon. The air was warm, the trees were in bud, a few birds chattered. The prime minister, the foreign secretary, and the first lord of the Admiralty toyed with their teacups. Chamberlain had made up his mind to resign. Churchill could fairly sense that the prize which he had chased for a quarter-century was near and yet was not quite his—for it might still go to Halifax. This prospect had given the foreign secretary a terrifying stomachache, which got worse as Chamberlain said he would serve under either man. Halifax had long wanted the job of prime minister, but to lead the government in the Commons he would (he thought) be forced to give up his peerage; more to the point, he would be constantly harassed by the ebullient and bellicose Churchill, who would militarily run the show until, Halifax believed, he himself would "speedily become a more-or-less honorary P.M. living in a kind of twilight just outside the things that really mattered." He urged that Churchill become the next prime minister.

The three were still having tea when the Labour delegation arrived. Chamberlain said not a word about the previous discussion, but asked for Labour's support. The visitors refused, point-blank, and informed him that at their party congress the following week they would decide whether they could support Halifax or Churchill or neither. When they left Downing Street, Britain was virtually leaderless.

Wilhelm Prüller had had a difficult winter. He was stationed first near the Franco-German border at Saarpfalz, and then near the Dutch border. He had been involved in a brawl and had spent some days in prison. After that, he was promoted and attached to regimental staff headquarters. When the Wehrmacht went into Norway, he wrote in his diary "Dear God in Heaven, we thank Thee that we are Germans, and still more that we are allowed to live in this gigantic epoch."

In early May, all the soldiers knew that the invasion was near, though none knew exactly when it would occur. Prüller wrote out his thoughts about the countries to be invaded:

> As far as I am informed about conditions in Holland—in Belgium it's much worse, I'm told, not to speak of France and England—it's quite clear to me that the Western powers are afraid of us. Perhaps not because of our National Socialist regime, and not only because we're Germans. No, they are afraid of our national orderliness, they are afraid of our sense of justice, of our proper economic efficiency, of our holidays. . . . They are afraid of our German gift for propaganda; afraid that their people will wake up by themselves and drive their rulers from the country with sticks, or drown them like dogs. That's what the gentlemen in London, Paris, Brussels, etc., are afraid of. But don't worry, gentlemen! Your hour is rapidly approaching, and any minute now you'll be in touching distance of us. Germany's coming, all right; her Wehrmacht, at the head of which will be our dearly beloved Adolf Hitler! We'll find you, sure enough.

On May 3, Hitler postponed the western invasion by a day; on May 4, he pushed it back another day. Fog was a problem. Then, because of leaks and warnings, he decreed that there would be no more postponements. Holland had canceled all military leaves; Belgium had arrested pro-Nazi leaders and had increased the guards on important bridges. On the morning of May 9, the whole of the German military machine went on alert for an attack at dawn on May 10. The code word was "Danzig."

With that word, Hitler linked the coming invasion of the West with the war he had sought to continue immediately after the death of Poland. In the interim between mid-September and early May, much had changed. Russia now controlled the Baltic and considerably more territory than Hitler might have liked, and its army had been hardened in battle. New leaders were coming to the fore in the democracies, especially England. The United States was moving toward more military readiness and toward more involvement with the Allies. Italy had proved spineless as an ally but useful as a neutral. Germany's own forces had been handsomely augmented; they had also become more battle-tested and were used to victory. And, what perhaps was most important, Hitler now had an excellent invasion plan. To go through the Ardennes with *Sichelschnitt* was the supreme gamble, but it was one to which he and his military subalterns were now firmly committed.

In the German "matador's cloak" gambit, the great bull of the Allied armies was to be pulled away from its prepared positions and up into the Low Countries. The cloak's motion must be subtle, yet definitive, and carried out with persuasive power; it must buy time for the mustering of the major force in the south; above all, it must echo the Schlieffen plan and seem to be the real offensive. For if the Allies ever realized in time that the northern theater was only a diversion, they might race back and, with their considerable power, destroy the thin file of German tanks trying to emerge from the Ardennes. That could mean disaster. But Hitler was convinced that the Allies would use Plan D and fall into his trap—and once the great bull had been lured far enough away and for a long enough time, nothing would be able to stop his thrust.

In the Eifel region of Germany, seven strong panzer divisions formed into columns and aimed at the Ardennes. Back and back they stretched, some seventy-five miles. When dusk fell, the tanks moved with their lights out. A tank rider described the scene: "We overtake marching, riding, and driving columns. The noise of the motors gets on one's nerves in this night of uncertainty.... It's pitch dark.... Now we realize why we so often came here to carry out peacetime maneuvers."

The seven panzer divisions aimed at the Ardennes included more and heavier tanks than had been available for use in Poland. Three additional panzer divisions were aimed at upper Belgium and Holland. Behind all of them were the foot soldiers, the reserves, the artillery, and the planes. A few divisions were stationed opposite the Maginot Line to give credibility to Goebbels's last propaganda maneuver, a supposed leak that the attack would be made near Switzerland.

Hitler and his secretaries boarded a train in midafternoon, ostensibly to celebrate the victory in Norway. The train did head north for a while, but then quietly turned west. In the dark early hours of the morning, it pulled into Euskirchen, a town that was thirty miles from the western border. As the Führer's entourage transferred into automobiles and started into the hills, Hitler was silent. The cars wound their way ever higher, and the sun began to fill the hills with color. At first light, the caravan reached headquarters, a modest concrete bunker, which was a converted antiaircraft emplacement. A whole nearby town had been evacuated to make room for the headquarters staff, but Hitler would stay here. Dawn broke. He and a few others stood and watched the far horizon. They could hear the gruff rumble of the convoys, then the muffled beats of the far-off artillery, and then, overhead, the grand thunder of the warplanes as they headed west.

part three

BLITZKRIEG

⋖⟨⟨⟨⟨⟩⟩⟩⟩⋗

May 1940 to
July 1940

15

The Invasion of the West

May 10, 1940, dawned misty in northern Europe, but the fog soon cleared. Quietly, Hitler ordered a suitable reward for the meteorologist who had predicted just that.

In accordance with the master plan, the Luftwaffe concentrated its fighter planes over the sword aimed at the Ardennes, and its bombers over the northern cloak. As the offensive began, the German planes attacked dozens of airfields in Holland, Belgium, and France, and knocked out half the Low Countries' air forces. In the north, on the ground, the armies of von Reichenau and von Küchler moved, respectively, into Belgium and Holland.

Speed and surprise were essential to the German offensive. Should either speed or surprise falter, the offensive might fail.

Forty-one gliders were to take Fort Eben Emael and nearby bridges over the Albert Canal, but only nine of the gliders managed to land atop the flat-roofed fort. Many went astray. Atop the fort, eighty-five men jumped from the gliders, threw grenades, and captured a few turrets; the other turrets were staunchly defended, but the thousand defenders within the fortress itself stayed inside. Had they come out, by sheer weight of numbers they might have overwhelmed the attackers. The Germans used flamethrowers at the gunports, hollow charges on the casements, and explosives in the ventilating system. The defenders were being asphyxiated, and no help came. Within an hour the giant fortress was neutralized from outside, though it did not surrender until the next day. Other German gliders took the nearby bridges over the Albert Canal so quickly that the defenders did not have time to ignite the detonators. Shortly after dawn on May 10, the Germans had a foothold on the Albert Canal, the most strongly defended point in Belgium.

They tried to enter Holland from several directions. At Maastricht, which was not far from Eben Emael, the Dutch saw through a ruse and blew up the bridges. Back of the ruined crossings, miles of panzers which had been waiting to vault the Maas jammed the roads. It was the same at Arnhem. But with so many possible crossings, and so many German attacks, a ruse was bound to work somewhere, and at Gennep it did.

The Gennep bridges sat in the morning sun, long and intricate leaps across the natural barrier. At the Dutch end of the bridge, the guards were at ease when they saw a handful of German soldiers with their hands up being marched toward them as the prisoners of two Dutch policemen. As it always did at that hour, a railroad train lazily crept over the tracked portion of the bridge. The border guards stopped to talk with the Dutch policemen, and were engaged in conversation just long enough for the disguised Germans to pull out weapons and fire at them, while at the same time armed men on the train machine-gunned the bridge's other defenders. In this way the Gennep crossings were captured intact. Over them poured the Austrian Ninth Army panzer divisions and some crack infantry, who then raced toward Breda to prevent a link-up of Allied and Dutch forces.

Despite the incident at Mechelen-sur-Meuse during which German plans for parachute landings had been captured, the Dutch and the Belgians had not seriously considered the airborne threat. German parachutists captured the vital mile-long bridges at Moerdijk, a town sixteen miles outside of Rotterdam and the one place where it was possible to approach "Fortress Holland" from land. The dikes had been flooded, but the Germans were coming anyway. Another detachment dropped on the bridges at Dordrecht, which were even closer to Rotterdam. The defenders at Moerdijk and at Dordrecht had time to blow up the bridges, but they were not blown. A third parachute team wafted down to Rotterdam's airport. Accompanying planes dropped bombs on some of the hangars; the flames incinerated Dutch troops sleeping inside. One Rotterdam airport defender described the invasion:

> As if by magic, white dots appeared over the airfield . . . like puffs of cotton wool. First there were twenty, then fifty, then over a hundred of them! And still they came popping out of the planes and began their low oscillating descent. . . . A hoarse command, then every machine-gun opened up . . . at the parachutists, at the planes. With so many targets, the men just did not know where to aim.

Most of the parachutists got through. The defenders called for artillery strikes from nearby batteries, but the Germans knew that the Dutch signal for the batteries to cease fire was a green Very flare, and fired one up. The artillery obligingly stopped, and the airport was soon taken.

Some German airmen were upset about the deaths of the parachutists. Gottfried Leske wrote, "It's a rotten, beastly business, shooting at defenseless parachutists. Typically Dutch. I think it isn't according to international law, anyway." But Leske had no qualms about bombing civilians in frequent raids on Brussels and Antwerp:

People were running out of houses. Trying to escape. We can swoop down low enough to watch them running. Some of them have bicycles. Some are pushing baby carriages. When we get low enough we strafe them. Then they throw themselves into the ditch on the side of the road. It doesn't help them.

Another flier said he "wasn't so keen about shooting the people who ran," but Leske argued, "They are our enemies, aren't they? One must kill his enemies, too! . . . Who are we to decide whether to do or not to do? The Führer decides."

The Führer had personally designed a seaplane and parachute attack on Rotterdam proper. It miscarried. Even with the help of the men who had landed at the airport, German detachments could not take the city. For several days fighting raged on the edges, and the invaders sustained high casualties and became more desperate with each passing hour.

Plans also backfired at the Hague. Oster's warnings to Sas were finally believed. The airfields were sown with obstacles, and the defenders were ready. At one field, eleven out of thirteen German transport planes were shot down; at the two others, the runway obstacles wrecked the planes as they landed, and Dutch machine guns massacred the Germans as they emerged. The German commander had brought along a dress suit and his horse in preparation for inducing Queen Wilhelmina to surrender her country; he crash-landed in a field and called headquarters. He was told the attack on The Hague was to be abandoned.

A million blossoms in the sky; nuns in hobnailed boots; sentries shot by traitors; poison gases hidden in endive caves; cryptic messages on chicory billboards; these were the rumors of German fiendishness that the people of Belgium and Holland invented to escape the realization that their countries had been unprepared for the German invasion. In fact there had only been four thousand parachutists spread out among dozens of objectives. Some invaders wore mufti, but none were disguised as nuns. The sentries at Gennep had been shot not by traitors but by Dutch-speaking Abwehr men. No gas was used at Eben Emael, nor were messages encoded on the "Pacha" chicory billboards. The fifth column—sum total of these myths—was mostly an exaggeration. Yet as rumor deepened into panic, it did what the German offensive by itself had not yet done: it produced demoralization and flight.

In the early morning of May 10 in Paris, Paul Reynaud retracted his resignation and sent a message to Gamelin: "The battle has begun. Only one thing counts: to win it." Gamelin crumpled up his own resignation and wrote back, "France alone counts."

Gamelin had already telephoned Georges, and with Belgian permission, they had started the "grand maneuver in the north." Giraud raced for Breda. The BEF and Blanchard's well-equipped First Army began to move to occupy the Dyle between Louvain and Namur, while below, Corap and Huntziger probed the Ardennes. According to a subordinate, Gamelin appeared confident, with "a martial and satisfied air" which became more pronounced as he learned that the German invasion was taking the direction of the old Schlieffen plan. Gamelin allocated heavy air cover for Giraud's race to the north, but ordered other units to "limit air activity to pursuit and reconnaissance." This meant no bombing, despite evidence that the Germans were already bombing Allied towns. After a furious protest from a French air force general, this edict was slightly amended to allow the bombing of enemy columns but not of Allied towns, even if German troops were in those towns.

Despite the months of intricate planning, the move up was somewhat chaotic. Units left without waiting for men who were still on leave. Trains full of Allied troops were held up for hours before they were connected with Belgian locomotives. In one instance a BEF unit had to crash through a frontier barrier when a Belgian sentry wouldn't let the British in without a note from his superiors. Nevertheless the BEF got a warm welcome from the townspeople. Tulips and narcissus were handed into a truck in which J. L. Hodson traveled:

> This is a day of great beauty, and if the occasion were not so grave, one could enjoy it thoroughly. Even so, it is difficult not to enjoy it. The sun is always the sun, and flowers are no less lovely because bombers zoom overhead. Indeed, war puts an edge on beauty—it is as though beauty said, "Take a long look at me, enjoy me while you may, who knows for how long it will be?"

When the British and French reached the Dyle, they got a great shock. Fortifications, tank traps, ditches, and even bunkers were at best half finished and at worst nonexistent. Because the Allies had not been allowed to see the fortifications during the phony war, they did not know how incomplete these were. The all-or-nothing position of the Allies toward Belgium in the phony war rebounded on all sides; now the Allies had virtually no time to dig in.

Bernard Law Montgomery's corps advanced so quickly that during the night the Belgians mistook them for German parachutists and fired on them. That mistake was corrected, but then the Belgians would not let them actually occupy front-line positions. Alan Brooke, Montgomery's superior, went to Belgian headquarters between Brussels and Antwerp to resolve the problem. There he came upon the peripatetic Sir Roger Keyes, who was back in Belgium at Churchill's request; even Keyes could not help Brooke get around van Overstraeten. The Dutch military aide not only blocked Brooke from talking with the king but flatly refused to coordinate any of the Belgian armed forces with the

Allies. The issue was later untangled at a conference between King Leopold and General Georges, but valuable hours had been lost.

At the end of the first day of the invasion, when word reached Hitler that the Allies had raced up to the Dyle-Breda line, he nearly "wept for joy," because "they'd fallen right into my trap." Hitler's room at the "Eagle's Nest" headquarters was a spartan cell which contained a cot and little else. Keitel, in a windowless air-conditioned room next door, could hear the Führer reading newspapers. Hitler was pleased at the success at Eben Emael, but was slightly annoyed that Reichenau was not going as swiftly as the schedule demanded. Several times during the night he got up to go into the operations room and pore over relief maps. Keitel's major victory that day was to get everyone to consent to a news release which reported that Hitler was at the front. Keitel argued it was too good a psychological point to pass up and could do no harm, because the Allies had not the slightest idea where the headquarters was located.

Despite minor setbacks, the invasion was proceeding triumphantly according to plan. No one on the Allied side guessed why the Luftwaffe had not attacked their troops as they moved into Belgium. But when Giraud tried to link up with the Dutch at Breda he was bombed. He did not draw any conclusions from the fact that the Luftwaffe had concentrated its power on him, nor did he use his large force to dislodge the Germans from the Moerdijk bridges ten miles from Breda, where he arrived well before the panzers. It was one among many incidents of lost Allied opportunities.

At many points the Belgians and the Dutch outfought the Germans man for man, but outnumbered, outflanked, and outgeneraled, they could achieve little. Once Eben Emael had collapsed, the Albert Line was gone. Next day the Belgians tried to bomb the Albert Canal bridges after some Germans had crossed them, but the Belgian planes had vulnerable undercarriages and were shot out of the air by German anti-aircraft fire. The bridges stayed intact, and more Germans poured over them.

In particular, German tanks under the direction of General Hoeppner came over and on May 12, in the "Gembloux Gap" between Huy and Tirlemont, engaged General Prioux's onrushing French First Cavalry Corps. It was the first large-scale tank battle on earth. The French heavy tanks were more than a match for their German counterparts. There were about equal forces in the field. It was a battle of distances. The tanks were hundreds of yards from one another. They roamed among hills and scattered buildings, and for much of the battle few human beings could be seen. By evening, the French First Army had gained time to consolidate the Dyle positions, and reports to headquarters that night praised Prioux for a great victory. The Paris newspapers were celebrating that victory the next morning when the tide changed. Stukas bombed the French, who were without air cover. German tanks concentrated in groups destroyed individual French tanks, and so did German soldiers with antitank guns. Over a hundred French machines were destroyed in two days.

Just as important, the tank battle diverted the Allies' attention from the German thrust through the Ardennes: the Gembloux Gap battle was the grand finale of the matador's cloak gambit.

At six in the morning of May 10, Winston Churchill ate fried eggs and bacon and smoked a cigar, having already seen the Dutch minister and the Belgian ambassador and having promised them aid. At eight, at the meeting of the war cabinet, he took a moment to show off his latest gadget, a homing antiaircraft fuse. During the day, Chamberlain made a last attempt to stay on, but that idea was quashed. A report that Canterbury had been bombed—it was an isolated raid by a single German plane—added urgency to the situation. In the early evening, Neville Chamberlain presented his resignation to the king and recommended Churchill as his successor. The king did not especially favor Churchill, since the first lord had been a champion of his brother, now the Duke of Windsor. He expressed a preference for Halifax, and was told Halifax had declined. That same evening, George VI summoned Churchill and invited him to form a government. With the knowledge that he had at last come to power, Churchill went to bed at three in the morning. "I took it all as it came," he wrote:

> I felt as if I were walking with Destiny, and that all my past life had been but a preparation for this hour and for this trial. . . . I thought I knew a good deal about it all, and I was sure I should not fail. Therefore, although impatient for the morning, I slept soundly and had no need for cheering dreams. Facts are better than dreams.

For the next several days Churchill was primarily occupied with the task of forming a government, and after satisfying himself that his cherished fluvial mines had been launched into the Rhine, he did not otherwise interfere in the grand strategy of the war. For the most part, he could have done nothing to prevent the ensuing debacle. In one instance only might a firm hand have helped. British air forces in France were scattered under several commands; during the first crucial days of the invasion they operated in piecemeal fashion and were never concentrated enough to achieve any of the objectives they might have gained if correctly used. When Churchill learned of this, it was too late to make a difference.

In order to allow the Chamberlains ample time in which to vacate Number 10, Churchill continued to live and work at the Admiralty. He proposed Chamberlain as leader of the Commons and as chancellor of the exchequer, but Labour objected and Chamberlain agreed to take the minor post of lord president of the council. Churchill did include him in the trimmed war cabinet, along with Halifax and Labour's Clement Attlee and Arthur Greenwood; but Leo Amery, who had done so much to sink Chamberlain, was not immediately included in the government. Anthony Eden became secretary of state for war (but was not in the war cabinet); and Kingsley-Wood and John Simon, who had drawn fire for their actions under Chamberlain, retained important posts.

In the evening of Monday May 13, after the Whitsun holiday, Churchill for the first time faced the House of Commons as prime minister. His Conservative fellow members sat on their hands as he entered, and he was mostly cheered by the Labour members. When he told the Parliament, "I have nothing to offer but blood, toil, tears, and sweat," General Spears noted that an electric current passed through the House, and as the new PM's speech went on, cheers began to punctuate every sentence, and exploded at the peroration:

> You ask, What is our policy? I will say: It is to wage war, by sea, land, and air, with all our might and with all the strength that God can give us: to wage war against a monstrous tyranny, never surpassed in the dark, lamentable catalogue of human crime. That is our policy. You ask, What is our aim? I can answer in one word: Victory—victory at all costs, victory in spite of all terror; victory, however long and hard the road may be; for without victory, there is no survival.

At the Admiralty, when his bodyguard congratulated Churchill on taking office, he answered, with tears in his eyes, "I only pray it is not too late."

In the *Schwerpunkt*, or power punch of the *Sichelschnitt* plan, the panzers for several days had to lead the way through and adjacent to the Ardennes forest, after which they would emerge and push across the Meuse River. Once across, they would easily traverse the flat and open terrain west to the sea.

Although important battles had taken place in the forests of the Ardennes since the time of Julius Caesar, Western intelligence and even tank theorists such as Basil Liddell Hart had considered the Ardennes impenetrable for tanks. Heinz Guderian had fought in the area in the Great War. He believed that the Ardennes contained high plateaus that would prove ideal for tank passage, that the leafy trees would provide shelter from enemy aircraft, and that the roads would prove more than adequate. German intelligence had thoroughly mapped the area and marked out routes for all the tanks.

There were three waves of panzers. In the far south of the German spearhead was Guderian's XIX Corps, which consisted of three panzer divisions. This was by far the strongest force, and it had the most difficult objective to achieve. In the center, there would be the XII Corps of two divisions under Reinhardt. Their passage was through the tangled section of the forest. To the north, the XV Corps under Hoth had two divisions; one of those divisions, the Seventh Panzer, was commanded by Erwin Rommel. Hoth's panzers would not go through the forest for the whole drive toward the Meuse, but would for some time skirt around it.

On the morning of May 10, the border crossings were phenomenally easy, but soon after Rommel crossed into Belgium north of Luxembourg, he encountered obstacles that slowed his advance—roads and forest tracks that were permanently barricaded, bridges that were so thoroughly demolished that the shards could not be used to make new ones. His pace slowed to two kilometers an hour, which would not put him on the Meuse at his appointed time. But the Belgian Chasseurs Ardennais had been ordered not to defend the obstacles. Rather they were to withdraw, and not to the south, where they could join with the advancing French, but to the north in the direction of Belgium's big cities.

Had the obstacles been aggressively manned, Rommel's advance would have been stymied and thrown completely off schedule—as evidenced by an encounter late in the afternoon with a group of Chasseurs who stopped, fought, and halted him a dozen miles from the River Ourthe, which was his objective for the first night. The next morning, Rommel broke out and by midday reached the Ourthe. As his first vehicle started across the bridge, men from the French 4th DLC (light tank division) blew it up. The French now had a real chance to defend the Ourthe, but like the Belgians, they obeyed orders and retreated five miles. They believed it would take the Germans two days to fashion a makeshift bridge. It took two hours, after which Rommel's tanks surprised and mauled the 4th DLC; at nightfall Rommel wrote his wife, "Everything wonderful so far. Am way ahead of my neighbors. I'm completely hoarse from orders and shouting. Had a bare three hours' sleep and an occasional meal. Otherwise I'm absolutely fine."

The French DLC's consisted of tanks, but also plenty of motorized vehicles and cavalry. French headquarters did not believe anything or anyone could get through the Ardennes before May 14, and so ordered the 2nd, 3rd, 4th, and 5th DLC's to engage only in skirmishes with the Germans. The plan was for massive French reinforcements to arrive at the Meuse on the fourteenth and strike at the panzers as they came out of the forest. But in the forest battles, such as the ones with Rommel, the DLC's were mauled. One French officer reported:

> Groups of unsaddled horses returned, followed on foot by several wounded cavalrymen who had been bandaged as well as possible; others held themselves in the saddle by a miracle for the honor of being cavalrymen. The saddles and the harnesses were all covered with blood. Most of the animals limped; others, badly wounded, just got as far as us in order to die, at the end of their strength.

By nightfall on May 12, Rommel's motorcycles, which ran ahead of his tanks, rammed down the narrow gorges which led to the Meuse crossings at Dinant, Yvoir, and Houx. The 4th DLC, whose resistance had lasted two and a half days instead of five, managed to blow up the crossings before Rommel could use them.

At Houx, Rommel's motorcycle corps explored at river level and found an old weir, or small dam; it was still intact and they clambered across it to a wooded island in midriver. There they came under fire from the French on the heights, but the Germans waited for dark and until one French company had been relieved by another, and then crept across the island to the far side of the Meuse. Climbing silently, they surprised the defenders.

The Meuse had been crossed, but only at one point. At three in the morning Rommel saw his tanks at Dinant destroyed by French artillery fire, while down at the river's edge riflemen who attempted to cross in rubber boats were being massacred, although Rommel ordered some houses to be set afire so that the smoke would conceal the attempted crossings. As he raced toward Houx, his aide was shot, and at Houx itself the situation was also bad. Summoned to a meeting with his superiors, he requested and received permission to move up his heavy tanks and use them as mobile batteries. Firing across the river at short range—120 yards—the heavy tanks began to destroy the French pillboxes, which had not received their full complement of armor plate.

Taking personal command of a rifle company, Rommel leaped onto a rubber boat and led his men across under heavy fire. They encountered a French tank unit on the heights and, even without antitank weapons, managed to scare the tanks away. Rommel's bridgehead was absurdly small, only a rifle company without heavy weapons or tanks that was holding on for dear life, but though the French had scores of tanks and thousands of men in the area, they took no advantage of the situation. During the next night, Rommel's engineers completed pontoon bridges and by the following morning had fifteen tanks across the Meuse.

In the southern part of the Ardennes, it was the same story, writ large. On May 9, an inordinate number of German tourists on bicycles and in cars had entered the Grand Duchy of Luxembourg; in the early hours of May 10 these men took over the frontier and the bridges. After that, Guderian's crossing became a mere matter of traffic control, and Luxembourgers watched endless tanks pour over their roads.

Just inside the Belgian border, one of Guderian's divisions encountered a minefield and a destroyed bridge and was held up an entire day. His two other divisions continued apace, passing villages and gaily waving their hats as they cruised west. An Allied air attack posed no real threat, after flak gunners and hovering Messerschmitts destroyed thirteen Allied bombers and damaged the other nineteen in the attacking squadron. Reinhardt's two divisions followed Guderian's the next day. During it his tanks got mixed up with Guderian's, with near disastrous results. Many overheated panzers stalled, but they were well camouflaged beneath the trees, and while the traffic jam was highly vulnerable, no bombers came over to exploit the Allied advantage. After this the panzers passed into the forest and were all but invisible to Allied planes.

By the eleventh, Guderian was at Bouillon, on the Semois. On the twelfth he was nearly killed. He was doing some paperwork in an office at the Hotel Panorama, surrounded by hunting trophies and with a view out a grand window onto the river. Suddenly

> There was a series of explosions in rapid succession; another air attack. As though that were not enough, an engineer supply column, carrying fuses, explosives, mines, and hand grenades, caught fire and there was one detonation after the other. A boar's head, attached to the wall immediately above my desk, broke loose and missed me by a hair's breadth; the other trophies came tumbling down and the fine window in front of which I was seated was smashed to smithereens and splinters of glass whistled about my ears.

He was bombed twice more before the day was over, but by the day's end his panzers—as well as Rommel's to the north—could see the heights across the Meuse. The battle of the Ardennes forest had already been won. In three days, the panzers had gotten through the Ardennes and were on the Meuse—a feat which only Guderian, Manstein, and Hitler had initially believed possible. But there was still the Meuse to cross, and the commanders from Hitler on down recognized that all would be for naught if that didn't happen quickly so that the tanks could break free in the open country beyond.

On the French side, the Meuse was badly held. Troops had been brought up slowly and in haphazard fashion; there were sectors of great risk where the edge of Corap's Ninth was fuzzily interlocked with the edge of Huntziger's Second Army. Each of their divisions was to hold ten miles of difficult riverfront, while on the Dyle the Allied divisions were to hold only three miles each. Many of the troops were exhausted by long marches. Some were drunk and had raided abandoned villages. Some disregarded orders—the most important of which was Corap's explicit instruction to defend the river at the very edge of the water, not on the more comfortable and less exposed heights above. That was one instance of what happened opposite Rommel.

On the night of May 12, at all levels from Gamelin down to the battalion commanders on the bastions of the Meuse, the French both knew and did not want to know what faced them. The panzer columns moved with their headlights on along the Ardennes forest roads. They had been spotted by French air reconnaissance, which reported concentrations that were headed for Dinant in the north, Monthermé in the center, and Sedan in the south (Rommel, Reinhardt, and Guderian, respectively, though the French did not know their names). But the high command that crucial night was full of talk of Prioux's "victory" in the Gembloux Gap. Gamelin debated if the DLC's that had retreated from the Ardennes should be sent to round up parachutists or to assist Prioux. Troops in the Maginot Line were not ordered out in large numbers to help Huntziger, nor were the guns of the last fort in the line, which was only a few miles from Sedan, trained on areas near that city. Georges's last report of the night informed Gamelin, "The defense now seems well assured on the whole front of the [Meuse] river."

At Sedan on the tumultuous day of May 13, there was the ultimate clash in this phase of the war. On the German side, there were the intense and detailed thought that had gone into the planning, the will to attack, the hand-picked top-grade soldiers with a sense of mission, there was the strong cooperation between the services, and there was plenty of air power. On the French side there were half-measures, the fuzzy thought patterns of the leaders, the complacency of the defense, the inadequacy of the weapons, the half-completed fortifications, the older soldiers with their sense of futility, the mix-up of commands, and the near-total absence of air power.

At a conference with Evald von Kleist the night before, Guderian had played the offensive; he took out of a briefcase February war-game orders and updated them. The Führer had promised 1,500 fighters and bombers, nearly the entire strength of the Luftwaffe. Kleist wanted that air power delivered in one grand punch; Guderian had arranged months before to have the planes come in waves. The Luftwaffe conveniently decided that Kleist's commands had not arrived in time and gave Guderian exactly what he had ordered.

First the regular bombers flew over. They started at seven in the morning and kept up their attack on the French positions for four hours, graduating to a crescendo that was topped about noon by the appearance of the Stukas. These planes were the most shocking, most disruptive, and the ultimately decisive weapon that day. For hours they came, wave on wave, cresting and dropping on the French fortifications, on the troops of the La Marfee heights above the Meuse, and everywhere else on the French at Sedan. As a panzer sergeant described their attack:

Simultaneously like some bird of prey, they fall upon their victim and then release their load of bombs on the target. We can see the bombs very clearly. It becomes a regular rain of bombs, that whistle down on Sedan and the bunker positions. Each time the explosion is overwhelming, the noise deafening. Everything becomes blended together, along with the howling sirens of the Stukas in their dives, the bombs whistle and crack and burst. A huge blow of annihilation.... We stand and watch what is happening as if hypnotized, down below all hell is let loose! At the same time we are full of confidence ... and suddenly we notice that the enemy artillery no longer shoots ... while the last squadron of Stukas is still attacking, we receive our marching orders.

The Stukas fell on the older French *poilus,* on the reinforcements that hadn't had time to dig themselves in, on bunkers that were inadequately prepared, on artillery positions that had been told to hoard their ammunition even though huge stacks of it lay just a few miles away, on men who lacked adequate artillery pieces though enough to equip ten new divisions lay in French warehouses. Under the dives of the Stukas, all of the French frailties combined and were exacerbated. There was virtually no Allied air protection—those few planes that arrived over Sedan that day were so overwhelmed by odds of fifty and a hundred to one that they flew away. The unchallenged Stukas had total freedom to bomb when and where they wished, and under their cover German artillerymen and flak gunners aimed high-velocity 88mm guns at the armored bunkers and began to penetrate and blow them up. For the French, it was a nightmare. As General Ruby later described it:

> The gunners stopped firing and went to ground, the infantry cowered in their trenches, dazed by the crash of bombs and the shriek of the dive-bombers; they had not developed the instinctive reaction of running to their anti-aircraft guns and firing back. Their only concern was to keep their heads well down. Five hours of this nightmare was enough to shatter their nerves, and they became incapable of reacting against the enemy infantry.

As the Stukas waned, the Grossdeutschland began its crossing. The French guns could not point down at a steep enough angle to rake every inch of the riverfront, and despite large losses, the GD men kept coming, kept getting into rubber boats, kept swimming across in full kit. On the far side of the river they destroyed the bunkers with hand grenades. The French fought back, and the GD lost 70 to 80 percent of its men; but, one by one, the bunkers fell. By seven-thirty in the evening, six infantry battalions were in the German bridgehead and some had penetrated to parts of the La Marfée heights. In London, Churchill was about to offer his blood, toil, tears, and sweat; but at Sedan the Germans were in command of the Meuse, though not a single German tank had yet crossed the river.

It was then, at Sedan, that the unexpected but perhaps inevitable break occurred. Just after sunset, as the night closed in and when shapes were most shadowy, an artillery battery commander at Chaumont, a few miles from Sedan, reported German tanks on La Marfée. This false report was not refuted, but was compounded by another from a second artillery man who said that the fighting at nearby Bulson was so heavy that he would have to withdraw before he was encircled. The two reports together engendered a third. Five miles back of Chaumont and Bulson, the artillery commander who received the two front-line reports decided to remove his own command post to the rear. Three points made a line, and the line was withdrawal. As General Ruby described it:

> A wave of terrified fugitives, gunners, and infantry, in transport, on foot, many without arms but dragging their kitbags, swept down the Bulson road. "The tanks are at Bulson," they cried. Some were firing their rifles like madmen.... Officers were among the deserters. Gunners, especially from the corps' heavy artillery, and infantry soldiers ... were mixed together, terror-stricken and in the grip of mass hysteria. All these men claimed actually to have seen tanks at Bulson and Chaumont! Much worse, commanders at all levels pretended having received orders to withdraw, but were quite unable to show them or even to say exactly where the orders had come from.

As the defenders of the Meuse began to stream away from the fortifications, the panic spread and overwhelmed a battalion that tried to get through to the support of the French positions on La Marfee. Some of the French who ran did not stop until they reached Rheims, sixty miles away. Informed of the retreat, Huntziger did little to stop it; he merely ordered his commanders to do what they thought appropriate under the difficult circumstances. Left to their own lights, those commanders withdrew their headquarters to the rear, which also exacerbated the situation.

No commander likes to send bad news to his superior. In the manner of lost military campaigns throughout history, as the reports got passed up the chain of command, General Georges's subordinates tended to underestimate the gravity of the situation. The incident at Houx simply involved a battalion that had got knocked about. There had been pressure at Sedan, but the defenses had held. As the darkness gathered, the reports became more accurate and more urgent; yet at nine in the evening, Georges still felt confident enough to tell Gamelin on the telephone that there had been "un pépin assez serieux," a rather serious snag at Sedan.

That may have been the understatement of the century, but in a curious sense it was also true, for the German bridgehead, without a single tank, could have been wiped out by any large Allied force— either planes or tanks. But during the later hours of the evening the idea began to suffuse through the French command that the pinprick was fatal, as if the German spearhead was a dart covered with poison. It was near midnight when General Georges summoned General André Doumenc, the man who in August had sat with Reginald Drax and Kliment Voroshilov and had watched the dream of a tripartite alliance dissipate. Doumenc found a somber scene at Georges's headquarters in the resort hotel. In the grand ballroom, which had been made into a map room, exhausted and silent staff officers slumped in chairs. The lights were low, the atmosphere reminded him of a wake. Georges, terribly pale, told Doumenc that the front had been pushed in at Sedan, and that the Germans were across the Meuse. Georges began to weep uncontrollably and to say he did not know what could be done. Doumenc comforted him and told him that there were reverses in every war, and that there was still time to recover.

The next day, May 14, was for the Allies the crucial moment, for on that day the German bridgehead had to be wiped out before it was enlarged.

The day started with a small victory. Corap's motorized troops captured forty of Rommel's motorcyclists. The field commander was satisfied with this very small bag and retired back to his own lines. He left untouched Rommel's tanks, which he could have wiped out, whereupon the dashing Rommel led those tanks in an assault on the last major high point before the plains. In his scatter-shot approach toward Onhaye, he blasted an ambulance and other noncombatant vehicles, and then he himself came under heavy artillery fire. When his tank was hit, his driver drove it into a ditch, where it lay exposed to French gunfire. Rommel wrote:

> I had been wounded in the right cheek by a small splinter from the shell which had landed in the periscope. It was not serious though it bled a great deal. . . . At any moment we could expect fire to be aimed at our tank, which was in full view. I therefore decided to abandon it as fast as I could, taking the crew with me. At that moment the subaltern in command of the tanks escorting the infantry reported himself seriously wounded, with the words, "Herr General, my left arm has been shot off." We clambered up through the sandy pit, shells crashing and splintering all around.

In fact, Rommel narrowly escaped death and narrowly avoided being captured by North African colonial troops. His whole assault was on the verge of disaster.

Here was the moment for a strong French counterattack. Corap's Zouaves and Algerian Tirailleurs were among the finest soldiers in the field, and not far away was a major French armored division with 150 tanks. The tank corps had been delayed by the Luftwaffe, which had bombed the railroads, but for the past twenty-four hours it had been less than twenty-five miles from Rommel's bridgehead, awaiting orders. Billotte had at first wanted it to go to help Prioux, but Corap argued he must have it on the Meuse. At midnight it had finally been ordered to the Meuse, but it did not get started for seven hours and then took seven more to cover the twenty-five miles. By the time the French tanks came upon Rommel, they were out of fuel, and by evening Rommel was in Onhaye, and the Zouaves and Tirailleurs, unable to hold without tanks of their own, had been ordered to fall back.

In its midsection the Ardennes forest was as thick and impenetrable as French wishful thinking had made the whole of it out to be.

There Reinhardt had encountered inordinate difficulties before arriving at the city of Monthermé, where the forest fell in a near-straight drop to a wide and fast-flowing reach of the river. Opposite Reinhardt at Montherme, Corap had a very strong force, the 102nd Fortress Division, a regular-army unit of African colonials who were backed up by a half-unit of Indochinese machine-gunners. Even though the French had very little artillery and almost no air cover, thanks to their withering fire the 102nd and their machine-gunners prevented Reinhardt from crossing throughout May 13 and May 14. But no reinforcements came to the 102nd's rescue; they pleaded for antitank mines, or for planes which could have easily knocked the Germans off their precarious positions. Nothing came, but by nightfall Reinhardt was still being held up by what the Nazis considered to be "subhuman" black, brown, yellow, and other nonwhite soldiers.

It was at Sedan that the greatest damage was done on May 14. At nearby Chemery, Huntziger's tanks engaged Guderian's advance units and beat them back, but—as with the tanks farther north—then nothing happened. Unwilling to go for the jugular once initial blood had been spilled, the French did not follow up the success, and a German engineer battalion threw hollow charges under the tank tracks and carriages and beat off the French machines. Then the Germans pushed on and sent as many tanks as possible over their slim engineer-built bridges. The Allies tried to bomb these bridges with everything they had. In the early morning, ten British bombers caught the Germans by surprise, but the targets were so small, and the bombs the planes carried were so lightweight, that the British did little damage. A later second strike of twenty-eight French bombers suffered great casualties. Guderian wrote that they happened to come over about midday, when

> Col.-General von Rundstedt arrived to have a look at the situation for himself. I reported our position to him in the very middle of the bridge, while an air-raid was actually in progress. He asked drily, "Is it always like this here?" I could reply with a clear conscience that it was.

In the afternoon, some two hundred and fifty fighters and seventy-one bombers, what was left of the British and French air forces on the continent after four and a half days of war, arrived over Sedan. Against them the Germans threw up eight hundred fighters, and the very accurate fire of their antiaircraft guns. The Allies attacked in groups of a half-dozen, rather than with their concentrated might, and they were destroyed. The valley of the Meuse became a graveyard for Allied planes. For the RAF, it was the worst day of the war; of its seventy-one bombers, forty did not return. Of the two hundred fifty fighters, about fifty were shot down and a large proportion of the remainder were crippled and limped back to their bases.

After that, the deluge. Frightened by stories of immense concentrations of panzers, French tank units did not attack Guderian's few tanks. Confusion spread. There were rumors of a fifth column. French rifle companies shot up one another; truck drivers ran their vehicles off the road and artillery was abandoned. Soldiers ripped their regimental badges off their uniforms to be less conspicuous to possible German captors and to French officers who tried to stem the tide of deserters.

Then—again—the unexpected but perhaps inevitable happened. For several days Huntziger had faced Guderian, and Corap had faced both Rommel in the north and Reinhardt at Monthermé. The French generals had no air support, and their tank reinforcements had been slowed and delayed until they had seemed virtually useless. General Huntziger remarked to an underling that he would probably always be remembered as "*le vainçu de Sedan,*" the vanquished of Sedan, and took the step that fulfilled his prophecy. Guessing that Guderian's next move would be to outflank the Maginot Line and turn down toward Paris, Huntziger ordered the northern leading edge of his troops to pull back in a pivot on the end of the Maginot Line. It was as if one half of a swinging door had opened—a small crack on the Meuse widened to a gap of fifteen miles. A few hours later Corap compounded Huntziger's error when he ordered the southernmost leading edge of his troops to fall back to the north and away. That opened the other half of the swinging door and added another twenty-five miles to the gap, making a forty-mile hole through which Guderian, Reinhardt, and Rommel poured all of their power.

On May 14, the situation at Rotterdam was desperate. German tanks, parachutists, and seaplane fighters could not take the city; but most of Holland had been overwhelmed, and Queen Wilhelmina and the government were on their way to London. Colonel Scharroo, commander of the Rotterdam garrison, had refused the first German request to surrender. Now a second request came, backed with the threat of a German bomber raid should it be refused. Scharroo said he would have to take up the demand with higher authorities. Counting this as a positive sign, the German commander signaled the Luftwaffe to delay the bombers, but his signal was itself delayed and was only received when the bombers were already in flight and had shut off their radios. Surrender negotiations were in progress when the planes loomed. Desperately, the Germans on the ground sent off red Very flares to call off the raid, but these mingled with Dutch antiaircraft fire and were not seen until half the planes had dropped their bombs. Nine hundred people died, and Rotterdam's oldest section burned to the ground. Two hours later, a broken Colonel Scharroo capitulated; two hours after that, Holland formally surrendered.

At 7:30 A M on May 15, Churchill was awakened to take a telephone call from Reynaud. The premier spoke in English. "We have been defeated. We are beaten; we have lost the battle." Churchill couldn't believe it: "Surely it can't have happened so soon?" "The front is broken near Sedan; they are pouring through in great numbers with tanks and armored cars." Churchill tried to calm Reynaud by recalling the days after March 21, 1918, when the Germans had broken through on the Somme, but the Allies had regrouped and had gone on to victory. Reynaud was beyond such help. "We are defeated; we have lost the battle," he repeated.

Later that morning Churchill learned that Holland had surrendered, that Corap had been relieved of command and the remnants of his army had been divided between Giraud and a newly forming force near Paris, that along the Dyle the Germans had punched holes in the lines of the French First Army. The only bright spot was that British troops had managed to hold their ground everywhere they had been attacked. Not yet comprehending the extent of the German breakthrough or the fact that it was fatal—which Reynaud already believed—Churchill made plans to go over and cheer up the French. It was, he thought, all he could do.

16

The Muddle

"Hurrying Heinz" Guderian had taken pains to ensure that when he crossed the Meuse no orders from above would tell him what to do next. But when he had completed the crossing, he hesitated. Should he wait for reinforcements and consolidate the bridgehead or plunge west without waiting for anything? A subordinate quoted back at him one of Guderian's own slang terms, *"Klotzen, nicht Kleckern,"* the sense of which was to strike concentrated, not dispersed. Guderian ordered two of his divisions west with all speed, and the third to lag slightly to counter a possible French riposte at Sedan. His tanks were set to go when, he later wrote,

> Panzer Group Leader von Kleist ordered a halt to all further advance and to any extension of the bridgehead. I neither would nor could agree to these orders, which involved the sacrifice of the element of surprise we had gained and of the whole initial success that we had achieved. . . . The conversation became very heated and we repeated our various arguments several times. Finally General von Kleist approved of the advance being continued for another 24 hours so that sufficient space could be acquired for the infantry corps that were following.

Had Guderian halted them, the French DLC which was moving up might well have hurt him; by refusing to be ruled by his superior's caution, he managed to escape the French counterattack. Urging his panzers on "until the last drop of petrol was used up," Guderian reached Montcornet at midday on the sixteenth, at the same moment as Reinhardt's tanks. Then he and Reinhardt both advanced farther west, along parallel roads. By evening, Guderian was fifty-five miles past Sedan—and he was again ordered to halt.

The pace of the German advance had made the Führer nervous—Halder and other professionals believed his was the nervousness of the amateur in warfare—and Hitler now wanted Guderian to consolidate. But Halder's OKH intelligence showed that there was no serious threat of a French counterattack, and that the French were trying to consolidate their positions farther west. Halder wrote in his diary, "Picture shows clearly that enemy still not taking any major measures to close the breakthrough gap." Halder wanted Guderian to go on. But Hitler now so totally distrusted OKH that he would not listen to Halder even when he was right.

At a landing field in eastern France on the morning of May 17, a tight-lipped von Kleist stepped out of his plane and berated Guderian for having disobeyed orders. Guderian asked to be relieved of his command. Kleist agreed. The decision was transmitted to higher authorities, and that afternoon Colonel-General Siegmund List arrived and told Guderian not to resign. He explained that the order to halt had come directly from Hitler and could not be contravened. Together, Guderian and List then worked out a ruse which would allow the tank commander to make a "reconnaissance in force," but which would leave his headquarters where it was, far to the rear of the tanks. A further Guderian ruse assured his independence: he arranged to have a wire laid from rear headquarters to a forward one "so that I need not communicate with my staff by wireless and my orders could therefore not be monitored by the wireless intercept units of the OKH and OKW." By nightfall, he was seventy miles from Sedan and determined not to be stopped again.

Rommel also encountered a brief delay. After racing for two days, he reached what he thought was the Maginot Line, though it was actually only a series of antitank obstacles, ditches, and pillboxes. He halted, and during the night his engineers blew up the obstacles. Then, to make up for lost time, Rommel ordered a night march. He said to his men, "We'll do it like the Navy. Fire salvoes to port and starboard." Under a bright moon, Rommel observed:

> The people in the houses were rudely awakened by the din of our tanks, the clatter and roar of tracks and engines. Troops lay bivouacked beside the road, military vehicles stood parked in farmyards and in some places on the road itself. Civilians and French troops, their faces distorted with terror, lay huddled in the ditches, alongside hedges and in every hollow beside the road. We passed refugee columns, the carts abandoned by their owners, who had fled in panic into the fields. On we went, at a steady pace.

Having reached Avesnes by morning, Rommel signaled headquarters for further orders. There were none, so he continued on, his panzers driving "westward through the brightening day with guns silent." When they encountered French soldiers by the roadside, they ordered them to throw down their weapons, and most did.

Some entries from the logbook of Gamelin's Vincennes headquarters chronicle the trauma of May 16:

0430—General Giraud has led the 2nd Armored Division as far as he can and at daybreak will clean up the Marles-Vervins-Montcornet area.

0530—General Dufour telephones. "This morning at 3:30 five good-for-nothings, one of them a general practitioner, two junior doctors and an officer of the 41st Corps (the only survivors) have fled shamefully to the rear. Orders to send them back to the front." Dufour says that those moving toward the rear are people attached to the army: baggage-masters, supplies officers, commissariat officers (many from the reserves) and twelve thousand soldiers on furlough (unarmed).

0720—Gamelin decides to bring up to Paris forty battalions of the state police.

0920—As a result of an error at the 4th Bureau, four *Somua* squadrons of the 1st Mechanized Infantry are at Soigny instead of Mauberge. First Army situation precarious.

0925—There is no liaison left at the Charleroi Canal with the British who are retreating without having received any orders. There is a gap between the 3rd and 4th Corps.

1110—German detachments at Montcornet and Marles.

1150—Impossible to hold on to the Aisne.

1200—No news from General Giraud.

1240—Leopold III is not happy about the idea of re-establishing ourselves on the Charleroi Canal. He does not want to endanger Brussels. Maybe General Billotte will reposition on the Escaut.

1325—[After orders to bomb the Germans who entered Montcornet.] There are some doubts about that armored column at Montcornet. Perhaps it is French, so we must cancel the bombing order.

1350—A large enemy column heading in direction of Laon. . . . Enemy attacks Dinant-Sedan area with 1,600 tanks . . . 1st Armored Division suffered heavy losses . . . its units have dispersed and are unfit for action. Besides we cannot find the commander. . . . Unable to contact General Giraud. [Later it was realized that Giraud had been captured.]

Gamelin's headquarters received a firsthand report of the terrible disintegration of Corap's Ninth Army. Gamelin ordered an ancient gun set up in the yard at Vincennes, and he ordered the cabinets emptied of papers and the walls shorn of maps. These were placed in boxes in preparation for a move farther south. He told Daladier that the French army was "finished."

The situation was desperate as Winston Churchill, John Dill, and General Hastings Ismay arrived at the Quai d'Orsay at 5:30 PM to meet Gamelin, Reynaud, and Daladier. Churchill could see venerable civil servants of the French Foreign Ministry feeding bonfires with documents from wheelbarrows, as more came flying down from the windows above. Gamelin outlined the position of the forces: the "bulge" in front of Sedan, which was getting larger by the minute, was aimed either at the Channel coast or at Paris, and he was not yet sure which roads to defend.

Churchill asked the key question in his so-so-French: "*Ou est la masse de manoeuvre?*" Where is the strategic reserve? Gamelin shook his head, shrugged his shoulders, and uttered one word: "*Aucune,*" there is none.

Churchill was dumbfounded. It was basic military strategy when one held a long line to keep troops in reserve in case that line was broached. What about the hundreds of thousands of men in the Maginot forts? Gamelin said that German bombing of the railroads had made it difficult to transport these men, but he agreed to bring out eight or nine divisions. However, he despaired because of his "inferiority of numbers, inferiority of equipment, inferiority of method."

The French begged Churchill for air cover. That day Churchill had already sent over four more air squadrons; now he asked the cabinet in London for six more. He stressed the "mortal gravity of the hour" and suggested that "It would not be good historically if [the French] requests were denied and their ruin resulted." Near midnight he got the authorization and drove to Reynaud's apartment. There he found the premier in his dressing gown. Daladier, summoned to hear the good news, silently wrung Churchill's hand; he seemed like a drowning man. Reynaud, Daladier, Baudouin, Ismay, Dill, and others listened into the wee hours as Churchill painted a picture of determination. If France were destroyed, if England were levelled, he would direct an air war from Canada against a blasted Europe. Reynaud pronounced himself inspired.

Unfortunately, the ten additional British squadrons were more illusory than real. Based on earlier precedent and policy, the cabinet refused to reduce Britain's at-home fighter complement below twenty-five squadrons, and by this time British air bases in France had been so overrun that only three of the new squadrons could be actually landed in France. The remaining seven had to fly their missions from bases in England, which effectively cut their operating time over the battlefields.

British ground troops had been fighting well; along the Dyle and then along the Charleroi Canal they had held and had retreated only because of the German onslaught along the entire front. Now retreat was becoming more difficult. "The hours are so crowded and follow so fast on each other," wrote Alan Brooke, "that life becomes a blur and fails to cut a groove in one's memory." He, Montgomery, and Harold Alexander suffered

> lack of sleep, irregular meals, great physical exertions of continuous travelling in all directions, rumors, counter-rumors, doubts, ambiguous orders and messages, lack of information on danger-points, and the thousand-

and-one factors that are perpetually hammering away at one's powers of resistance.

Most threatening to an orderly retreat was the immense swell of refugees that clotted the roads and prevented swift and continuous movement of troops.

> They were all haggard-looking, and many women were in the last stages of exhaustion, many of them with their feet tied up with string, and brown paper where their shoes had given out; they were covered with mud from throwing themselves into the ditches every time a plane flew over. There were old men trundling their old wives in wheelbarrows, women pushing prams piled high with all their belongings, and all their faces distorted by fear, a heart-breaking and desperate sight.

Goebbels instructed his propaganda people to "use every means to create a mood of panic in France." Increasing the flood of refugees was high on the list. A secret radio transmitter broadcast a rumor that the Germans' first act in captured towns would be to confiscate bank deposits. This drove listeners to withdraw their money—a sure impetus to panic and flight. When the exodus began, Antoine de Saint-Exupéry was billeted in a small town:

> All the stables, all the sheds, all the barns and garages had vomited into the narrow streets a most extraordinary collection of contrivances. There were new motor cars, and there were ancient farm carts that for half of a century had stood untouched under layers of dust. There were hay wains and lorries, carry-alls and tumbrils.... From door to vehicle, wrapped in bedsheets sagging with hernias, the treasures were being piled in. Together these treasures had made up that greater treasure—a home. By itself each was valueless; yet they were the objects of a private religion, a family's worship. Each filling its place, they had been made indispensable by habit and beautiful by memory.... Fling sacred relics into a heap, and they can turn your stomach.

Saint-Exupéry talked with a woman who with her sister-in-law and seven children was taking to the road. His questions echoed those of the English novelist who had fled Warsaw in September:

> That road easy to drive? A road over which you made two or ten miles a day, stopping dead every two hundred yards? Braking, stopping, shifting gears ... in the confusion of an inextricable jam.... "Better watch your water. Your radiator is leaking like a sieve.... You'll be on the road a week, you know. How are you going to make it?" "I don't know."

He ached as he imagined their car breaking down, then being abandoned, leaving the women and children forlorn by the wayside, perhaps to be machine-gunned by a German plane. They might die, but perhaps not, for "death was a sort of luxury, something like a bit of advice. It was the nip in the hock by which the shepherd dog hurried the flock along."

At Amiens, André Maurois saw the columns where they paused for a moment:

> a torrent of refugees... seated on their bags, on sidewalks, on pavements, they made an immense human carpet worked in dull and lifeless colors. They had emptied the larders of the restaurants, the ovens of the bakeries, the shelves of the groceries, as completely as necrophagous insects clean out a corpse.

Death was on the roads, in the ditches, and especially in the fields, where the bloated corpses of animals and men stank in the fresh spring air. People tied mattresses to the roofs of their cars, and hoped that these would protect them from machine-gun bullets. At first the stolid farmers laughed at the refugees and charged them outrageous prices for produce, drinkable water, and the occasional night of comfort in a barn; then, as the breadth of the disaster grew, the farmers refused everything in the belief that they had to keep their food and water and barns for themselves. Townspeople begged soldiers not to defend their town so that it would not be destroyed. Refugees turned on the French troops and berated them as they retreated or tried to get to the shifting front. They blocked the advance of the newly-created tank force of Colonel Charles de Gaulle.

"There, de Gaulle," General Georges said as he entrusted 150 tanks and some infantry to the lanky officer. "For you who have so long held the ideas which the enemy is putting into practice, here is the chance to act." In de Gaulle's makeshift force, some of the tank commanders had never fired a shot, some of the drivers had only four hours' experience, and the infantry did not know their commanders and had to travel by unarmed bus and without radio communications or air cover.

On May 17, de Gaulle's tanks swept up the road from Laon to Montcornet, shot up some motorcycles and trucks, and captured a few hundred German soldiers. At Montcornet they surprised and chased away some Germans; however, as soon as the French tanks were inside the town, the Germans struck back. With half-repaired tanks, antiaircraft guns, and some artillery, they made life difficult for de Gaulle until the Stukas came and did real damage. Unprotected from air attack, de Gaulle's forces retreated down the road whence they had come, and within twenty-four hours de Gaulle was back where he had started. He had done little to damage Guderian's advance, but in personal terms he had achieved a victory, and this victory was enough to provide the relentless self-propagandist with the beginnings of a legend of battlefield invincibility against heavy odds.

Denis Barlone moved eight hundred horses and fifteen hundred men from Belgium back into France. Bombed out of one town after another, he and his men paused only for short rests—as in Saint-Amand, where ten thousand bottles of good vintages in a famous hotel could not be left for the *boches*. Barlone had no news, no newspapers, no wireless, no electricity, and no air cover. He saw only German planes, never a French one. He could not understand the actions of the high command, and the orders he received were so contradictory as to be often useless. Barlone felt he did not know what was going on in the war; he just received inexplicable orders and was detailed to carry them out.

Some orders he would not carry out, such as the edict which demanded that he shoot all spies and strangers who could not justify their existence or who tried to precipitate a retreat or a panic. "No fuss or bother, merely keep an account of the total number dealt with." It was ridiculous. Barlone heard rumors about changes in the high command.

The rumors were true. Reynaud made the decision to get rid of the two men who had haunted him and France for so long, Daladier and Gamelin. There was no longer time to be delicate about feelings or party politics, for France might fall within days. He asked Maxime Weygand to return from Syria, and Marshal Pétain to return from Spain. Weygand said later that if he had known the true nature of the situation, he would never have agreed to leave Syria; Pétain told Franco before he left Madrid, "My country has been beaten and they are calling me back to make peace and sign an armistice."

On May 18, as the panzers thrust forward almost without interference from French forces, Pétain and Reynaud went to see Georges. His gray-gloved hand moved a chart up and down; he appeared only to be going through the motions as he pointed out the panzer positions. Reynaud was chilled. In the evening he and Pétain went to see Gamelin, and found Daladier also waiting at Vincennes. Gamelin, too, had a chart, and pointed out the situation in his detached, elegant, and controlled manner, as if demonstrating a classroom exercise and not the death throes of his own army. Daladier told friends privately that he thought Gamelin had made a grave mistake by having gone so far into Belgium and Holland.

On May 19, Reynaud announced that he would take over the war and defense portfolios, and that Daladier would take the Quai d'Orsay; Pétain would serve as vice-premier, and Georges Mandel would become minister of the interior. (Goebbels made much of the Jew Mandel taking over in the midst of the crisis.) All of these changes were prelude to the one important change, the sacking of Gamelin. While Gamelin was still thinking about taking control from Georges, just after he had written out in pencil a personal directive on what the armies should do next, he was informed by letter that he would be succeeded by Weygand.

The disciple of Ferdinand Foch replaced the disciple of Joseph Joffre, but not without incident. Weygand saw Gamelin, and they had a strained talk. Gamelin was busy consolidating his position for the history books; Weygand was frigid, unwilling to learn how the disaster had occurred, and slow. His first official act was to cancel Gamelin's last personal order, which had mandated an immediate counterthrust to break up the Germans who were about to reach the Channel coast. If the order had been implemented at once, there was a small chance that it might have altered the headlong rush of the German advance. But it was not implemented, for Weygand wanted first to inspect the northern forces and then to make a plan. As he plotted the inspection tour, German panzers had already reached the Atlantic coast.

On their race to the sea, Guderian and Rommel sped so quickly that they captured intact an English battery which had only blank ammunition, and they overran a British airfield almost before its Hurricanes could take off. British territorial divisions that had been mustered from lines-of-communications troops managed to hold up the German advance somewhat. But by nightfall on the twentieth, Guderian was at Abbeville, and one of his battalions continued through the dark to the very edge of the coast at Noyelles.

All ten panzer divisions were at or near the coast, and reports indicated that sixty Allied divisions were trapped without supplies in a pocket north of the Somme. The news buoyed Hitler. He waxed philosophic to Jodl and Keitel. A peace treaty with France would follow, and it would repay Germany for four hundred years of indignities; after that there would be a peace with England in which the German colonies would be restored to the Reich; Versailles would then be properly avenged. Believing that total victory had already been won, and that the blitzkrieg was over, he began to plot the next phase of the campaign. Yet the destruction of the enemy's forces, the classic Clausewitzian objective which Hitler had himself set, had not been achieved, and in his premature celebration Hitler sowed a seed that would later lead to the BEF's escape from Dunkirk.

On May 21, Weygand sent his car to Abbeville with the intention of following it himself by train, and then he discovered that Abbeville was in German hands. Changing plans, he flew to see Billotte; but Billotte's airfield had been overrun, and the two generals agreed to meet together with Leopold and Gort at Ypres. Gort did not show up; Weygand waited, then outlined a plan to Leopold and Billotte—a plan nearly identical with the one Gamelin had suggested fifty-four hours earlier. "Fresh" French troops south of the Somme would thrust north, while the BEF and Blanchard's First Army would push south; the Belgians would go laterally to the Yser River and cover the gaps left by the BEF's move.

Although it was perhaps already too late for this plan, even further hitches developed. Speaking for King Leopold, van Overstraeten refused to send Belgian troops to the Yser because they would have to leave Belgian soil. Paul Henri Spaak and other Belgian civilian ministers heard this and were apoplectic; they accused van Overstraeten and Leopold of usurping the power of the people's elected representatives. But Leopold, as head of the army, would not yield. Weygand left without having seen Gort or having resolved this crisis. Though planes still flew to Paris, he was persuaded to take a roundabout route by torpedo boat, ship, and train, back to the capital. An hour after Weygand left Ypres, Gort arrived.

Gort had been busy because the British had undertaken—alone—the only significant Allied counterattack of the whole campaign. There was little left of Arras after the Germans had bombed and strafed it, but the city stood athwart many roads and it had been British headquarters in two wars. An attack had been ordered to recover the ground around it. Two BEF divisions would go south and then east, while two French divisions would strike east toward Cambrai; in the process, they would break Rommel's lines. The plan started to fall apart before it began, for Gort could muster only two battalions rather than two divisions, and the French sent signals that they would not be ready at all until the following day. Believing that the attack must come on the twenty-first or that Arras would be completely lost, the BEF attacked virtually alone, except for limited help from General Prioux's fragmented cavalry. With only two makeshift battalions and fewer than a hundred travel-weary tanks, the British achieved spectacular results. The British heavy tanks, the Matildas, shot up a number of the lighter German tanks, and put to flight with (Rommel reported) "signs of panic" an SS division made up of concentration-camp guards. One British unit that got isolated from the main force resorted to subterfuge. They had no antitank weapons and so along one road they placed china plates in a crazy pattern; the German panzers approached, and their puzzled crews got out to investigate, whereupon the British killed them and set the tanks afire.

Rommel himself panicked and reported that five divisions faced him—nearly ten times the actual force. Surrounded, he was once again almost captured before he was able to improvise a defense and an escape. He brought up the trusty 88mm flak guns, which proved to be the only weapons able to halt the Matildas, and by the day's end the British attack had been blunted. It was in the midst of this battle that Gort had found himself summoned to Ypres.

Once there he sat through a depressing meeting with Billotte and the Belgians—and Sir Roger Keyes. Yet, despite their difficulties they worked out a plan: the Belgians would go to the Lys, not the Yser, to release the BEF for a counterattack. Gort did not hold out too much hope for success, but said he would try if the French too were willing. Billotte agreed; he got into a car to go and brief Blanchard, whose army would have to execute the "Weygand maneuver." En route, the car skidded and crashed into a refugee truck, and Billotte was fatally injured. While he lay dying for two days, no one on the French side knew what Blanchard's army was supposed to do in Weygand's plan.

Next day, when Churchill met Weygand at Vincennes, he was enchanted. The general was "brisk, buoyant, and incisive," a welcome change after the aloofness and overveneered manner of Gamelin. In fact, Weygand made an indelible impression on all the civilians and military men who listened to him, starved as they were for a hero who would save the democracies. Weygand outlined a grand sweep. Armies of three countries would block the German advance to the sea, and they would counterattack. The Belgians would go to the Yser and flood the dikes, the new French army in the south would push across the Somme, the BEF would contribute its divisions, the RAF would cover, and "the light enemy units which are trying to cause disruption and panic in our rear between the frontier and the Somme . . . are in a dangerous position and will be destroyed."

It was pure fantasy. The Germans were already at the sea, and the "light enemy units," which were ten panzer divisions, had already broken the back of the Allied defense effort. The Belgians had refused to go to the Yser, there was no new force to speak of south of the Somme, and the BEF could only muster part strength and had only one serviceable Matilda left. Weygand knew all this. Wreathed in false hopes and in wilful ignorance of the facts, he had no plan. But for a time Reynaud, Churchill, Dill, Ismay, and the others believed he had. Gort, Blanchard, and Leopold could have told them Weygand's plan was poppycock, but they were not consulted. Churchill fired off an order to Gort to comply with Weygand's plan—its date of execution now set for the very next day, May 23—and flew back to London satisfied that the French were finally in good hands and that the decisive battle was just about to be fought.

Something decisive was about to happen, but it was not that battle; rather, it was the conjoint effect of two momentous decisions taken in the midst of a massive muddle of command, information, and clashing personalities.

A week earlier, when *Sichelschnitt* sliced through Sedan, Lord Gort had, as a precaution, established temporary supply depots north of the Somme, so that he would not be caught empty-handed as he retreated across Belgium. A few days later he had begun preparations for an evacuation: routes were mapped out, "useless mouths" identified and moved to the ports to embark for England. Gort had hoped these preparations would prove unnecessary, and he had demonstrated the British willingness to continue to fight at Arras.

Gort waited for the French at Arras in vain. Their offensive came a day late and was rendered useless by Rommel's augmented forces. When Churchill's order to execute Weygand's plan arrived, it sent Gort into despair. To implement Weygand's vague and sweeping scheme, he had no specific instructions, no ammunition, and no hope that the French would be able to bear their share of the load; the real thrust would have to come from south of the Somme. Gort signaled his reactions to London and Vincennes. Although Churchill began to get the idea, he nevertheless again instructed Gort to execute the Weygand maneuver, and Alan Brooke wrote in his diary that "nothing but a miracle can save the BEF now." Montgomery, Alexander, and the other officers agreed. Rommel's panzers had all but enveloped the town of Arras; only two roads were still open for a British escape. On the evening of May 23, Gort made his decision: he would disobey the instructions of Weygand and Churchill, and he would get his men out of Arras before they were slaughtered. He told the men at Arras to withdraw fifteen miles to a canal northeast of the city, and he put the BEF on half-rations.

An immediate clamor arose. Reynaud fired off a bitter telegram to Churchill:

> The British army [has] carried out, on its own initiative, a retreat of 25 miles towards the ports at a time when our troops moving up from the south are gaining ground towards the north, where they were to meet their allies. This action of the British army is in direct opposition to the formal orders.... This retreat has naturally obliged General Weygand to change all of his arrangements, and he is compelled to give up the idea of closing the gap and restoring a continuous front. I need not lay stress upon the gravity of the possible consequences.

The British had moved fifteen, not twenty-five miles; the southern army hadn't moved an inch; there was no continuous front—but the French did need a scapegoat. Investigating, Churchill found that Gort had done what he had thought best and the Prime Minister wired Reynaud that Gort would try the Weygand plan but that to hold the lines open to Dunkirk the BEF must keep two divisions between itself and the Germans: "Nothing in the movements of the BEF of which we are aware can be any excuse for the abandonment of the strong pressure of your northward move across the Somme, which we trust will develop."

Gort's decision was one half of the decisive stroke. The other half was a German decision. On May 21, when Rommel got stuck at Arras, the German timetable had begun to unravel. It had been twice held up, for a total of two days, and the British counterattack again brought Hitler's nervousness to the fore. He and OKW took Rommel's difficulties as evidence that the German spearhead had moved too fast, and that a great Allied counterstroke might be about to develop. An entire Guderian panzer division and some of Reinhardt's tanks were diverted to help Rommel. On May 22 and 23 as Rommel and his augmented forces crushed the resistance at Arras, Guderian's weakened panzers besieged Calais and Boulogne but were unable to take either city.

Thus late on May 23, at about the hour when Gort ordered his men to retreat from Arras, von Rundstedt ordered the panzers of Guderian, Reinhardt, and Hoth to halt temporarily twelve miles from Dunkirk, along the Aa and a line of other canals. Boulogne and Calais had not fallen, von Kleist had reported that 50 percent of the tanks were out of commission, and Rundstedt reasoned that he could not be blamed for caution.

Later that evening Göring telephoned Hitler. The time had come, the airman said, for the Luftwaffe to finish off the Allies. Tanks were expensive and would be needed for the sweep down through France, so it would be far better to leave Dunkirk to the less expensive bombs. Moreover, as the army was full of non-Nazis like Brauchitsch and Halder who were against Hitler, the ideologically pure Luftwaffe that had been developed under the Führer's tutelage should strike the final blow. In this manner the victory would be a personal one for Hitler, and not something the Führer would have to share with the generals.

In the morning, Hitler flew to Army Group "A" headquarters at Charleville. He arrived so suddenly that Rundstedt's orderlies barely had time to blow tobacco smoke out the windows and dump liquor bottles into a filing cabinet.

At the Charleville conference the Germans made their worst decision of this phase of the war. The reasons for it have been endlessly debated. Göring's persuasive phone call was one. Another was that Hitler, Jodl, Keitel, and Rundstedt had all served in the Flanders mud and had watched men and machines get stuck in it. Also, Hitler admired the British and perhaps cherished a subconscious wish that they would escape from Dunkirk and maintain their empire. This last argument has lately been rendered doubtful by evidence that suggests that Hitler did not understand that the British were about to evacuate France. Signs of the possible evacuation were all about—a gathering volume of ships off Dunkirk, the increased radio traffic between the BEF and London—but these had been noted only at OKH headquarters, and the advice of Brauchitsch and Halder no longer sat well with the Führer.

The military problem was a matter of hammer and anvil. Originally Rundstedt's "A" group was to be the hammer and his panzers, led by Guderian, Reinhardt, and Hoth were to have smashed the Allies against the immovable anvil of von Bock's Group "B." While the panzers stood at ease within viewing distance of Dunkirk, the hammer and anvil were reversed. Hitler decreed that the "B" group, whose forces were relatively fresh and conventional, would be the hammer and would push the Allies against the anvil of Group "A." However, so that the Luftwaffe would have time to bomb the Allies into submission, the hammer-anvil maneuver was to be delayed one or two days. Hitler retroactively approved Rundstedt's order halting the tanks and extended it another day. He then announced:

> Next goal of operations is the annihilation of the French, British, and Belgian forces. . . . During this operation the task of the Luftwaffe is to break all enemy resistance in the encircled parts and to prevent the escape of the British forces across the Channel.

At Sedan, two decisions had swung open the doors and had let the panzers through; at the edge of the sea two more decisions let a third of a million Allied soldiers slip away from Hitler's grasp.

In 1945, when the war was over, von Rundstedt would shift his decision entirely onto Hitler's back; so would Guderian, who omitted from his memoirs the fact that he had immediately acquiesced in the order to halt the tanks and had, after a day or so, agreed that it had been the correct order. Lord Gort's decision lapsed into almost total obscurity. The BEF commander was awarded no medals and was not celebrated for his foresight or courage. Many others, desiring the limelight, claimed to have saved the BEF.

17

The Miracle

On May 24, 25, and 26, the overcast skies over Dunkirk were almost impenetrable, and during these days the British prepared their escape. Meanwhile, Boulogne and Calais provided rehearsals for what would happen there. Guderian attacked the medieval ramparts of Boulogne, but for two days his weakened forces could not take the town. The French admiral in charge ordered the city abandoned, but his marines refused to obey the order and held out while the cream of England's home troops, Welsh and Irish Guards, crossed the Channel to help defend the city. Their help continued for twenty-four hours, and then under heavy fire the Guards were evacuated. In the confusion the Royal Navy drove away at bayonet point many BEF "lines-of-communications" troops, and mistook French marines for Germans and fired on them. They also sank a blockship at the mouth of Boulogne harbor, which made it impossible for the remaining French defenders ever to get away.

After Boulogne, the British troops at Calais were ordered to fight to the death "for the sake of Allied solidarity," even though the harbor was "of no importance to the BEF." Churchill saw the blunt wireless and sent, through Anthony Eden, a more tactful one:

> Defence of Calais to the utmost is of highest importance to our country as symbolising our continued co-operation with France. The eyes of the Empire are on the defense of Calais, and HM Government are confident you and your gallant regiments will perform an exploit worthy of the British name.

The "eyes of the Empire" may have been those of the only fresh and well-equipped troops left in England, the Canadian First Infantry Division. Gort asked London to send them over to hold Dunkirk's perimeter while his men got out, but the Canadians declined this "theatrical sacrifice."

On May 22, British cryptanalysts finally succeeded in making the Bombe operational, and thereafter could read the German Enigma code settings at will. The range and density of the information thus gained were enormous: the German orders of battle, reports on casualties and troop strengths, precise objectives of advancing units—in short, anything of importance. However, it was essential that the Germans not learn that the British had broken the Enigma, and so the information gained had to be acted on sparingly. British intelligence learned, for example, that an important meeting of four Luftwaffe generals would take place on May 26, but the RAF decided not to risk its planes in an attempt to bomb the meeting place, and intelligence vetoed any such mission lest the Germans suspect how the British had discovered the site.

One piece of Enigma information in this period proved crucial. A radio message corroborated the evidence of the German order to halt which had turned up in some papers lost by a German officer and found by one of Brooke's units. The papers alone might not have been acted upon, for they could have been planted, but in conjunction with the Enigma decrypt, on May 25 they provided Gort with a reason for ignoring an order to join in yet another version of the Weygand maneuver. Henceforth he would devote all his time and energies to evacuating his men. Eden agreed and told Gort, "It is obvious that you should not discuss the possibility of the move [i.e., the evacuation] with the French or the Belgians."

In his London meeting with Reynaud on May 26, Churchill took the same line and said nothing about the evacuation. He suffered through another request for fighters, and bolstered Reynaud against those members of the French cabinet—Pétain, Baudouin—who already were contending that France should seek a separate peace. He assured France of England's commitment to victory; but, moments after Reynaud's departure, he confirmed the Admiralty order: "Operation Dynamo is to commence."

During the Napoleonic Wars tunnels had been cut into the white chalk cliffs of Dover. From the mouths of the tunnels the French coast could be seen clearly. One room in the maze of tunnels, which had originally been designed to house a dynamo, became the headquarters for the operation that directed the removal from Dunkirk. Dynamo's first estimate was that 45,000 BEF troops might be evacuated in two days, but that the rest would have to surrender.

Gort received a signal that it was his "sole duty" to evacuate the BEF; at nearly the same moment Blanchard, who had taken over for Billotte, received an order from Weygand to defend Dunkirk—the French soldiers must not retreat, "animated by a savage desire to fight where they stand until they die." Thus Blanchard did not guess Gort's intention, even though Gort's staff had stocked the beaches near Dunkirk with eighty thousand gallons of drinking water and made many other preparations.

Hitler met with Heinrich Himmler, head of the SS. They discussed what to do with the Poles, Jews, Ukrainians, White Russians, Gorals, Lemkes, and Kashubs in the area that had been Poland. Lack of racial purity, Himmler said, had caused the downfall of the Greek and Roman empires; it must not infect the Third Reich. Himmler proposed tests to extract the "racially valuable elements" from the twenty-three million people of the area, and methods which would turn the remainder into "substandard human beings." The latter would go to school for only four years:

> The aim of this primary school should be to teach the pupil solely: how to count up to a maximum of 500, how to write his name, that it is God's command that he should be obedient to Germans, honorable, industrious, and brave. I regard reading as unnecessary.

If the measures were consistently carried out, in ten years the peoples of Poland would be reduced to a "leaderless labor force, capable of furnishing Germany with casual laborers annually, together with the manpower required for special projects." Eventually the various peoples would "disappear as racial entities." Hitler approved, but told Himmler to make only a limited number of copies of the six-page memorandum he had printed. A few key people must read the document and sign a statement that they had done so; thereafter they must act only on verbal orders and must not quote or refer to the document in orders to their own subordinates. In this manner everyone in the chain of command would have to take some responsibility for extermination, degradation, and the forced migration of peoples. It may also have been at this meeting that Himmler asked Hitler to let the SS unit Leibstandarte Adolf Hitler, the Adolf Hitler Lifeguards, take a decisive part in the action against the Allies.

Sepp Dietrich, a former Hitler bodyguard, and the SS brigade Leibstandarte moved up to the Aa Canal with orders to capture a hill opposite. It was May 25, the order to halt was already a day old, and the Luftwaffe had been grounded by fog during that entire time. While the mass of Guderian's tanks and men still awaited for orders to advance, Dietrich's men crossed the canal, which was a mere thirty yards wide, and moved forward. But British Bren guns and fierce resistance quickly scattered the elite unit. Dietrich and some of his officers sheltered in a drainage ditch until some of Guderian's regular army units went with a certain amusement to their rescue. Later in the day—in part because these units were already across the canal—Hitler rescinded the "halt" order, and the panzers began to roll again.

But half the Luftwaffe was now out of action because of repairs and losses suffered during two weeks of continuous flying; and inclement weather grounded much of the other half. The British had several days to dig in their perimeter defenses and move men along the roads toward evacuation points. Even when planes got through to the beaches, they were ineffective, for the bombs they carried were designed to destroy concrete, not to scatter bodies of troops. However, on the twenty-sixth these same Luftwaffe bombs set ablaze a large tanker in the outer Dunkirk harbor, making entry impossible. They also shattered the lock gates of the inner harbor, so that ships with large drafts could not come close to the town. "Let's hope the Tommies can swim," Göring smugly said to Hitler. The Germans saw no way out of Dunkirk.

May 27, when the evacuation began, became known as "Bloody Monday" at Dunkirk. With clear skies, the Luftwaffe firebombed the town, turning streets into alleys of flame and buildings into ash. The fires raged out of control, often suffocating people who took refuge in cellars. Bombs burst the water mains. A thousand civilians died in the city each day. Meanwhile, the French "Admiral North," Abiral, in his concrete bunker headquarters below street level, tried to prevent the evacuation, under the illusion that the British were there to defend his bastion. By midday the soldiers had been forced out of the town and onto the twenty miles of beaches which surrounded Dunkirk. Peter Hadley recalls this as pure hell:

> The beach was an extraordinary sight. As far as the eye could see it stretched away into the distance, the firm sand of the shore stretching farther back into dunes where the surface was no more than a thin yellow powder interspersed with parched tussocks of coarse grass. And covering this vast expanse, like some mighty antheap upturned by a giant's foot, were the remains of the BEF, some standing in black clusters at the water's edge, waiting for the boats that were to take them to the two or three ships lying off-shore, while others, whose turn had not yet come, or who were too tired to care whether it was their turn, lay huddled together in a disorderly and exhausted multitude.

The beaches were death traps, and were inefficient. So, too, were the rowboats which carried a dozen men at a time to the ships that stood a half-mile out to sea. Salvation called for a better solution—more and larger ships, and a place where they could be tied up.

West and east of the firebombed inferno of Dunkirk town two moles extended. They were built of stone and pilings to let the sea through, and were topped with rickety boards. The east mole stretched almost a mile into the water. It was risky to bring a large ship near it because of the ripping tides, and it was also risky because it made an inviting target for the Stukas—but the risk had to be taken. Just after dark May 27, the first big ship tied up to the east mole and hundreds of men poured aboard. The escape route had finally been evolved. By the end of Day One of Dynamo, two thousand of the BEF lay dead on the beaches and in the town, and only eight thousand had gotten away.

Throughout the next day, the men on the beaches searched the skies, but saw only the Luftwaffe. German planes bombed and broke apart the French transport Côte d'Azur, the British ferry Mona's Queen, and several more ships. Where was the RAF?

It was in violent action further inland. British intelligence jammed Luftwaffe radio frequencies and made the German bombers an easier target for the RAF fighters. The British also used their radar, for Dunkirk was just within its range, though this fact was kept from the French. In many instances squadrons of Spitfires attacked units of about a dozen bombers and sent half of them down in flames or to emergency landings. Luftwaffe Air Corps II's log describes May 27 as a "bad day"; sixty-four men and twenty-three aircraft were reported down: "today's losses exceeded the combined total of the last ten days."

Also out of sight of the beaches was a mass murder, of the sort already commonplace in Poland. It may have been in response to their humiliation at Arras that the SS unit of concentration camp guards took vengeance on the British. At any rate, behind a farmstead wall at Le Cornet Malo they killed eighty-nine British officers, shooting some in the head, caving in the skulls of others with rifle or pistol butts. The SS commander later told a German inquiry that his men had been lured into a British ambush, had beaten off the British, and then had wiped out the enemy's "cowardly methods of combat" in the most expedient way possible.

Also on May 27, the Belgians dropped out of the war. Since the assault on Fort Eben Emael, Belgium's twenty divisions had been fighting a losing battle. Hundreds of thousands of Belgians had been shunted onto the roads; most of the cabinet had fled to France; the list of Belgian cities abandoned to the advancing Germans read like a litany of despair: Brussels, Antwerp, Ghent, Bruges. The twenty divisions had been reduced to less than ten. All semblance of cooperation between the monarchy and the government had ceased. At five in the morning of May 25, Paul Henri Spaak and Hubert Pierlot met with the king. The ministers wanted Leopold to leave the country with them, so that he would not be captured by the Germans and forced to head a puppet government. They wanted a government in exile—as Holland, Poland, and other conquered nations had—and to continue the fight. Leopold disagreed. Should Belgium fall, he would treat with the enemy and hope by his presence to lessen his countrymen's suffering under a Nazi regime. The ministers decided to leave. They all believed Belgium would fall within hours.

Leopold had deep and justifiable grudges against the Allies. Daily his men had been asked to cover British positions during the retreat, and had done so with vigor. (Hitler wrote Mussolini at this time that the Belgians' tenacity was "astonishing.") But when Leopold asked for Allied counterattacks, he was ignored. Leaflets dropped by the Germans told Belgian soldiers, "The war is over for you; your leaders are about to leave by plane." In those leaflets Leopold was accused of abandoning his army. That cut him to the quick, and he countered with a proclamation that "whatever happens, my fate will be your fate." Keyes wrote Churchill:

> I trust that HM Government will not be unduly impressed by the arguments of the Belgian Ministers who, apparently, have had no thought but the continuation of a political regime whose incapacity and lack of authority have been only too apparent during the last fortnight.

Should Leopold leave, Keyes said, the Belgian army's capitulation would be hastened, and the BEF would be more endangered.

"Our front is fraying away," wrote van Overstraeten, "like an old rope that is about to snap." On May 25 and 26, Leopold sent distress signals to the British and French. Early on the twenty-seventh large breaches appeared in the Belgian lines; in anguish, the army's chief of staff wrote, "The army has reached the limit of organized resistance. ... [We succumb] under vastly superior technical means, without either hope, or renewed aid or any solution other than that of total destruction."

Most of the country was in German hands. Inside the "circle of fire" still controlled by the Belgian military were 1.5 million civilians and refugees, plus the soldiers, most of whom were without electricity, running water, and food. Not surprisingly, there was an outbreak of typhus.

Leopold informed Gort and Weygand that he was going to surrender but that he would draw out the process in order to give the Allies as much time as possible. These warnings were received, but were overlooked or possibly even ignored in the heat of battle. In any case, the hopelessness of the Belgian situation had been obvious for a week: Weygand would not have asked the Belgian army to go to the Yser if Belgium could have been defended.

Leopold sent an emissary to find out the German terms. Hitler demanded "unconditional surrender," and Leopold acquiesced. Keyes got out on the last ship. The surrender began on the morning of May 28. Over the next two days, the Belgians gave up as slowly as they could, which delayed in large measure von Bock's advance and gave the British northern flank time to move in and cover some of the perimeter.

But on May 28, Reynaud, Weygand, Spaak, and Gort publicly lambasted Belgium and Leopold. They said the king was a traitor to his own people and to his allies for having taken Belgium out of the war so abruptly and without consultation, and for remaining at home to become a collaborator. Leopold, who had only wished to spare his people added torment and slaughter, had to take all the blame for Belgium's capitulation. It tarnished him for the rest of his life.

Paul Reynaud proposed to Churchill an approach to Italy to keep that country out of the conflict. It was a suggestion fraught with difficulties, and led to a widening of the rift between the two governments. The French were prepared to make some concessions to Italy in the Mediterranean, but Mussolini would surely want something on the order of Malta, Suez, or Gibraltar, all of which were British holdings. Such concessions might keep Mussolini out of the war, or they might give him the chance to suggest his mediating between Germany and the Allies. If that happened, undefeated Britain might be forced to accept what France, which seemed already close to defeat, was willing to agree to. If the BEF were captured at Dunkirk, that would also force a negotiated peace. After three days of discussion, the British cabinet concluded that an approach to Italy could lead straight to a negotiated defeat for England, and so refused to approach Mussolini at all.

The only thing that mattered was to extract the BEF from Dunkirk, not least because they might soon have to defend the British Isles at home. The defenses about Dunkirk were like a beehive: hard on the outside, a maze within the shell, and with a single exit at the bottom of the center. One break in the perimeter could mean the collapse of the entire structure. The Belgian surrender threatened such a break. It would leave an undefended gap of twenty miles between Alan Brooke's divisions north and east of Dunkirk, and the sea. The morning of May 28, Gort met with Blanchard, who said that the First Army, now under Prioux, was worn out and could not fill the gap. Gort ordered Brooke to cover; Brooke acted even before the order was given. His commanders moved with great speed, and aided by the deliberate slowness of the Belgians in the surrender, managed to fill the gap. Gort moved BEF headquarters to a villa at La Panne, which had been King Albert's headquarters during the Great War. It was symbolically important and had the advantage of direct underwater telephone communications with London.

From the night of May 27 to the night of May 31, all three of the German services were stymied, and the evacuation proceeded well. For much of the time the Luftwaffe was grounded by fog and pouring rain. If Göring's men had had clear skies, the evacuation would surely have been a catastrophe; on the one afternoon in this period when it was not hampered by bad weather, the Luftwaffe sank three British destroyers, damaged seven others, and demolished five large passenger ships as they left Dunkirk. The panzers had also been ordered to stop moving on Dunkirk, because the rain had made the marshes more dangerous, and because time was needed to repair damaged tanks before the sweep down to Paris. And after the debacle in Norway, the German navy was in no condition to mount a challenge to the British navy in the Channel.

In queues of twenty or fifty, the soldiers clustered on the moles, policed by Dynamo specialists who enforced discipline at revolver point. Some men crazed by the bombing were shot dead to prevent their endangering the vast enterprise. As the tides shifted, destroyers and passenger ships tied up precariously to the mole. Small boats appeared in fantastic variety: a German launch which had been scuttled at Scapa Flow and then refloated; pleasure yachts; fishing smacks; trawlers, flat-bottomed barges and dredges; a Yangtze River gunboat; a boat manned by teenaged Sea Scouts; Dutch "skoots"; Belgian channel ferries; French vessels, from destroyers to skiffs. Contrary to the later legend that Dunkirk was solely a British operation, French ships took more than 50,000 men across to safety, one out of every seven saved. On May 29, when Abiral and Blanchard at last received orders to assist the evacuation, the French began to help in a big way.

On May 31 in Paris, at a meeting with Reynaud, Churchill was embarrassed to learn that very few French had yet been taken across to England. For Churchill the men of the BEF were "the whole root and core and brain of the British army," and should they be captured or annihilated, England would have an appallingly difficult time re-forming an army, because there would be a serious lack of trained officers. However, if the French got the idea that the British didn't care about French soldiers as well as their own, then France would drop out of the war and England would be left to fight alone. Churchill said that British and French soldiers were to be evacuated together, "bras-dessus, bras-dessous," arm in arm, as comrades.

Alan Brooke had spent every waking moment shuttling between one troop concentration and the next, offering advice, ordering the transfer of units to plug gaps in the line, encouraging, flattering, stiffening spines where necessary. He was immensely tired. One scene haunted him: lunatics freed by the bombing of the Armentières asylum stood by the sides of the roads in their brown corduroy coats, saliva dripping from their mouths. Brooke felt, near Dunkirk, that he too stood just on the edge of sanity. "I had reached a stage when the receptive capacity of my brain to register disaster and calamities had become numbed by successive blows. It is a providence of nature that it should be so, otherwise there would be more mad people in this world."

He continued to choreograph improvisations of defense and retreat. By day his men would stand and fight, by night they would retreat, and by dawn they would again be ready to take up shaky new defensive positions. His genius at improvisation was reinforced by the brilliance of Montgomery, Alexander, and Harold Franklyn (who had commanded the assault at Arras). Each escape was narrow. Chance was everywhere, and death dogged the roads. Often the French units seemed at cross-purposes with the British. But after an eternity, Brooke received a direct order to get himself home, and he caught his first glimpse of the Dunkirk beaches:

A black cloud of smoke soon shrouded the whole beach and was punctuated by vivid flashes as new bombs burst and threw up jets of sand and what appeared to be human bodies, but luckily turned out be greatcoats and clothing abandoned by men who had embarked. . . . We also watched another raid directed against the shipping lying off the beaches, and this time the results were far more serious. One destroyer was hit amidships by a dive-bomber; the bomb must have penetrated into the ammunition magazines, as there was a terrific explosion followed by a column of smoke which mushroomed over the ship. As the smoke cleared, the destroyer had entirely disappeared. Such a sight was not a cheering one for those on the beach awaiting embarkation.

Brooke's last hours at Dunkirk left him with an indelible image: a lunch of chicken, which had been slaughtered so that the Germans would not get it, had to be eaten too near the stench of three dead cows decaying in a yard. Brooke nominated Montgomery to succeed him, and left.

Denis Barlone had no illusions about the unheroic part he had played in the debacle. He commanded one transport division, which didn't engage in combat. Nevertheless he suffered and exulted at each turn of fortune. He had been at the Dyle and at many of the engagements along the line of retreat. The night of May 28, at Lys, he went to the First Army's headquarters to try to obtain definitive orders for the North African Division:

> The exhausted staff officers are rolled up in blankets and sleep on the floor. Those on duty seem depressed. I hear orders given by phone to send a few scattered units out to act as stopgaps and to try and delay, for an hour or two, the closing-in of the infernal circle. . . . The regiments melt away visibly; our division has received orders to hold out at all costs. The 13th Rifles (who made six attacks in eight days) have only 500 men left; nearly all the officers have been killed. . . . While I am there, a staff officer phones instructions to the general in command at Lille to fire all the petrol dumps as the Germans are expected to enter the town tonight.

At midnight Barlone rejoined his retreating column. They ran into a traffic jam of horse-drawn vehicles, motor-hauled machine guns, ambulances, refugee cars and carts. German tanks fired a few rounds at them. The next day Barlone saw British tanks and French infantry battling German tanks and planes. "We fight blindly against an adversary with a hundred eyes, and ten times superior." His unit pressed on, only to discover that the British had blocked the roads so that BEF men could get to Dunkirk more easily. As senior officer, Barlone took command and with a British counterpart worked out an orderly way to get both French and British columns to the beaches—they took parallel roads.

After having traveled for twenty-one hours without unharnessing the horses, his men were a dozen miles from Dunkirk. They passed damaged cars and saw rifles, artillery, and motorized vehicles which had been thrown into ditches or pushed into them to keep the roads clear. His horses were spooked by a German artillery attack; in front of him a wagon and two horses plunged into a canal and entirely disappeared. Barlone dismounted and continued on foot. Along the roads were corpses and scores of wounded calling for help that was nowhere to be found. He walked miles to the dunes of La Panne, where his division was to regroup. Of its original 18,000 men, only 1,250 remained. He looked around the scene:

> The westerly wind beats down the immense columns of grim, black smoke from the flaming oil tanks. Truly this is the suffocating breath of the last judgment. Long sheaves of bright flames shoot up from the huge, burning buildings. Broken bricks and mortar, windows, paving stones dislodged by shells, strew the ground. Immense open spaces stretch farther than the eye can see with only a fragment of wall standing here and there, and the carcasses of the monster cranes in the docks despairingly hold up their great black arms towards a ghastly sky, rent unceasingly by the explosions of the whining shells.

Eventually, Barlone and the small remnant of his North African Division crossed to England.

Dunkirk may have been a miracle, but it was also an inferno from which many thousands did not emerge alive. Men were smothered in foxholes when bombs threw sand over them; they drowned as they waded out into the water to catch boats; they starved; they ate poisoned food; they went mad and were shot; they capsized in overloaded boats then drowned in slicks of oil and blood; they were blown to bits when bombs hit their boats. There were deaths from in-water collisions, from unexpected beachings, from the ceaseless bombing and strafing, from torpedoes fired from German ships based in captured Dutch ports. The Channel and waters near Dunkirk were a navigator's nightmare; boats were wrecked on sandbars, and collided because of missed and misplaced buoys, shoals, and burning wrecks. In the confusion, the dead lay where they fell, or where they washed up on the beaches. Dunkirk was chaos and chance.

But in the last reckoning, Dunkirk was the play of large numbers. On the first day, May 27, fewer than 8,000 men got out. On the second day, May 28, it was 17,000 men; the third day, May 29—when the French began to cooperate and the Luftwaffe was held down by bad weather—47,000, of whom only 655 were French. On the fourth day, May 30, 53,000 got out, of whom 8,000 were French; and on the fifth day, May 31, when 68,000 were evacuated, 14,000 were French. In five days, nearly 200,000 men had been taken across to England. And tens of thousands still waited for ships.

One additional casualty of Dunkirk was the Allied effort at Narvik.

With British, Chasseurs Alpins, Foreign Legionnaires, and Polish troops, the Allies were numerically superior to the Germans in early May, but the attack barely crept along. After the invasion of France, Narvik became less important. As a colonel of the Legion explained to his men:

> What is my aim? To take Narvik. And why take Narvik? For the iron ore, for the anchovies, for the sake of the Norwegians? I haven't the faintest idea. But I shall take Narvik. Between ourselves, I don't think it will be any use, either we blockade the ore by sea, in which case why trouble to take the town? Or we don't blockade it, on account of Sweden, or because Germany has already got plenty of iron in Lorraine, in which case it doesn't make any difference. I don't think I've ever taken part in a more useless campaign. We shan't even get any thanks for our pains, because all the big battles and the big honors will be in France.

Dietl, in command of the Germans at Narvik, was close to giving up the fight. Plans had been laid for his troops to be evacuated to Sweden by the railroad which had already taken out eight hundred German wounded. To the dismay of the surviving troops, the bodies of Germans who had died in the brief encounters with Allied and Norwegian troops had been piled up and thrown into sewers. By May 15, Dietl warned Berlin that he would lose the northern front if reinforcements did not immediately arrive by air; on May 21, he reported that his troops were near rebellion from lack of sleep and continuous fighting.

In ignorance of this, on May 25, the Allies made a decision, mostly at Churchill's urging. He had initiated the Norwegian campaign but now believed it to be a lost cause. The Allies needed every man for the defense of the British Isles and for whatever might come in the second phase of the battle of France. An evacuation was planned.

As with the Belgians at Dunkirk, the Norwegians at Narvik were not made privy to the plans lest they precipitously collapse and endanger the withdrawal. And the Allied troops were told to take Narvik and provide a victory which might simultaneously cheer England and France and allow the Norwegians to control the town after the Allies were gone. The British told the Norwegians that troops were repairing to Tromsö to establish an additional base there; the Norwegians suspected nothing.

On May 28, 25,000 British, French, Norwegian, and Polish troops succeeded in taking Narvik. The town had been plundered and the Germans were gone, so the victory was less than stunning. No sooner had the town been taken than the evacuation began. On June 7, 15,000 men embarked for England, and on June 8 the remaining British forces left. It was only then that Dietl and his men in the hills realized that the Allies had left the area. The Germans regrouped and marched back into Narvik by nightfall on June 8. Two days later, the Norwegian troops who had continued the fight signed an armistice, and Norway was totally under German control.

After the ignominious evacuation, the British had a bad passage home. British intelligence, as cautious with information as Mackesy had been with his troops, sent a series of halfhearted warnings to the Admiralty, capped by one on June 7: "German naval forces in Norwegian waters may in future be associated in any offensive action taken by German units in the North Sea." German intelligence had done far better, and when the British sailed from Narvik the hastily repaired *Gneisenau, Scharnhorst,* and *Hipper* lay in wait. Among them they sank two British destroyers, a troopship, a tanker, an armed trawler, and the *Glorious.* This last was an aircraft carrier which was laden with extra planes because the pilots had been unable to fly them back to England because of lack of fuel. The *Glorious* ignored the early signs of the battle, did not launch the planes so that they might attack the Germans, and was sunk with great loss of life; only forty-three men survived. Neither the *Glorious* nor the other British ships broke radio silence for some time, even though that might have helped save some lives. Later it became known that the ships had kept quiet in order to protect the remainder of the troop-carrying ships, especially the *Devonshire,* which had on board King Haakon, most of the Norwegian Storting, and Norway's gold reserves.

On June 1, the Paris newspapers denounced the British perfidy at Dunkirk in carrying out an evacuation which had rescued the BEF but had abandoned the *poilus;* on the same date, the London papers crowed over the victory at Dunkirk and the end of a successful operation. None of these contentions was the truth. Some 200,000 troops, of whom 25,000 were French, had crossed to England; another 200,000 remained at or near Dunkirk, and the majority were French. The operation was not finished.

Early on the morning of June 1, the fog lifted at Dunkirk, and that event coincided with a three-hour absence of RAF planes, during which time clouds of Stukas and dive-bombers attacked the ships, sinking thirty-one and severely damaging eleven others. Many lives were lost. The German artillery had also moved close enough to shell the beaches and the offshore boats and make shelter an impossibility. Even so, on June 1, 64,000 men were taken across the Channel; for the first time more than half of them (35,000) were French.

On that day also, the French First Army surrendered at Lille, and the RAF lost three planes for every two Luftwaffe planes shot down. As the BEF was almost entirely across and the British troops had nearly all disengaged from the perimeter, Churchill wirelessed to Reynaud that "It is desirable that the embarkation should cease this night." An outraged Reynaud forced Churchill to back down, and the two leaders agreed that troops would henceforth be taken across only under cover of darkness. On June 2, the Luftwaffe did not appear in such great strength as the day before, and the 88mm flak guns did not fire so continuously on the beaches. Later it was learned that both planes and artillery had been withdrawn to be readied for the next phase of the war.

Despite these mitigating factors, there was near disaster as the British bungled nearly every aspect of transporting the French over the routes they had already established for themselves. Code books for communicating with the ships were not made available to the French; some British ships sailed back to England empty even as ten thousand French lined up on the beaches; others went inexplicably to the west mole instead of to the east. In the worst mix-up, part of the Royal Navy attempted to block the port by sinking barrier ships in the harbor, but the vagaries of the tide left enough channels open so that the last rescue ships could get in and out. Reynaud had to prod London continually to keep up the rescue work, threatening that France might be forced to sign a separate peace. From May 29 to 31, an average of 62,000 men a day had crossed the Channel to England. After almost all the British were out, the average dropped markedly. On June 2, it was 30,000, of whom half were French; on June 3, 26,000, of whom 19,000 were French; and on June 4, 29,000, of whom all but six were French. Yet the grand totals were worthy of great respect. In the nine days of Dunkirk, 338,226 men had been carried to safety, and over a third of them, about 120,000 men, were French soldiers.

The Germans entered the blasted town of Dunkirk on June 4. Fires still raged in the streets; ten to fifteen thousand men lay dead in the town, on the beaches, in the waters. Between thirty and thirty-five thousand French soldiers were still on the beaches and in the harbor area. When the French general in charge of Dunkirk asked the Germans to provide food and water for his starving men, the Germans agreed, and the French were taken prisoner. "Where are the English?" the Germans asked. The French said there were none left; the Germans were surprised.

In fact, although the myth had persisted that all the British left France at Dunkirk, there were 140,000 British troops left in France at that time. But they were not at Dunkirk. They were the "lines-of-communications" troops who provided services to both French and English armies, and were stationed in Brittany. Weygand had specifically asked that they remain in France, saying they were vital to the continuation of the Allied fight.

Belgium and Holland had been defeated, Norway was gone, and France had lost 370,000 men dead, wounded, or taken prisoner. The British had lost many men and nearly all their forward equipment, and their only combat-trained soldiers had been removed from the battle. "We must be careful not to assign to this deliverance the attributes of a victory," Winston Churchill said as he addressed Commons on the beautiful evening of June 4. "Wars are not won by evacuations." What happened in Holland, Belgium, and northern France was "a colossal military disaster," which nevertheless contained some lessons for the future:

> The great French army was very largely, for the time being, cast back and disturbed by the onrush of a few thousands of armored vehicles. May it not also be that the cause of civilization itself will be defended by the skill and devotion of a few thousand airmen?

The RAF, Churchill said, had done great work at Dunkirk, and now would defend the British Isles. He made light of Hitler's plan to invade England—Napoleon had thought to invade and had failed. His speech closed with a passage over the composition of which he had shed tears, a passage which embodied all the emotion, intelligence, and persuasive power at his command:

> Even though large tracts of Europe and many old and famous states have fallen or may fall into the grip of the Gestapo and all the odious apparatus of Nazi rule, we shall not flag or fail. We shall go on to the end, we shall fight in France, we shall fight on the seas and oceans, we shall fight with growing confidence and growing strength in the air, we shall defend our island, whatever the cost may be, we shall fight on the beaches, we shall fight on the landing-grounds, we shall fight in the fields and in the streets, we shall fight in the hills; we shall never surrender, and even if, which I do not for a moment believe, this island or a large part of it were subjugated and starving, then our Empire beyond the seas, armed and guarded by the British Fleet, would carry on the struggle, until, in God's good time, the New World, with all its power and might, steps forth to the rescue and liberation of the old.

18

The End in France

Every night between one hundred and two hundred German planes bombed the British Isles. The blitz had begun. Although initially the German bombs did not cause drastic physical damage, their psychological effect was severe, and served to waken England to the reality of a possible invasion. Preparations were made to demolish bridge crossings on the roads from the Channel beaches, and to render potential air landing sites unusable. A million Molotov cocktails and fifty thousand Mills bombs were made. The fifteen tattered divisions of the former BEF were deployed to defend the presumed invasion routes. However, a study undertaken for the cabinet concluded that an invasion by sea could not be prevented, even though the Royal Navy controlled the Channel, and that the chances were better than fair that an invading force could batter its way to London.

In his first message to Roosevelt after becoming prime minister, Churchill had told the president that "the voice and the force of the United States may count for nothing if they are withheld too long," and he asked for forty or fifty old destroyers, several hundred aircraft, steel, and raw materials. He also suggested that Roosevelt continue to send such supplies on credit after British dollar reserves ran out, and he asked that America declare nonbelligerency, rather than neutrality, and give all help to the Allies short of war.

Roosevelt replied that some of Churchill's requests were beyond an American president's authority to grant, but that he would do his best. And the day after he received Churchill's message, he asked Congress for a billion dollars with which to upgrade America's defenses. At the time, the United States could only field 80,000 men and could supply another 400,000. Roosevelt painted a picture of future American defenses which included fifty thousand airplanes—about five times as many as then existed in the entire world. The new situation created by the invasion of France was obvious to everyone, and Congress quickly appropriated the billion dollars and a little more.

As he had warned Churchill, Roosevelt was not able to do as much as he would have liked to help the Allies. He was still hampered by the need for congressional approval, and by isolationists within his own administration. When the debacle began in northern France, Reynaud had asked for equipment, and Roosevelt directed General George C. Marshall to see what he could find. Marshall located half a million rifles and nine hundred 75mm artillery pieces, but the president had great difficulty in getting permission to ship them overseas. He cabled Reynaud that he was doing what he could; he also urged the French premier to take steps to safeguard the French fleet in case of "alluring offers to France" in exchange for the fleet's surrender. Roosevelt firmly believed that if the French fleet were to fall into German hands the safety of the United States would be seriously compromised. Together with the German and Italian fleets, the French ships would give Hitler control of the Atlantic.

On May 31, Roosevelt went back to Congress and asked for another $1.7 billion with which to expand the army to 375,000 men, to rebuild the navy, and to purchase some of those 50,000 planes. This request also met with quick approval.

However, Charles Lindbergh again raised his voice in objection, declaring on the radio that the United States was not in jeopardy, did not need more than ten thousand planes, and that no material aid should go to France or England. Roosevelt said the speech "could not have been better put if it had been written by Goebbels himself. What a pity that this youngster has completely abandoned his belief in our form of government and has accepted Nazi methods because apparently they are efficient." In September and October 1939, most of the country had agreed with Lindbergh's position. Now polls began to show that much of the country agreed with Roosevelt's position. The Old World's crisis had shaken up the New World.

Sometime during the German sweep through northern France—the exact date has never been pinpointed—Franklin Roosevelt made up his mind to run for re-election, for that unprecedented third term. Had the Allies prevailed over Germany, he might have retired, but when it became obvious that the war would go badly for the democracies, he decided to stay on, if he could. At about the same time, a majority of Americans began to feel that if FDR did run they might well vote for him. In the midst of a world crisis, they wanted a firm and recognizable hand at the tiller.

Held up by congressional and Department of the Army tactics, six hundred freight cars filled with 75mm artillery and rifles sat on the New Jersey docks and waited for shipment to France on the morning of June 5, as the panzers surged through France. Weygand ordered several hundred 75mm pieces brought out of French warehouses and told his troops to use them against the advancing panzers as if they were pistols. The troops were to cluster in "hedgehogs" about the country; the front lines were to be the Somme and Aisne rivers. Weygand had no plans for a back-up line should that one be broached. His troops included forty-three divisions, plus another seventeen which were still in the Maginot Line, a few weakened armored units, and about nine hundred aircraft scattered about the many airfields of southern France. De Gaulle pleaded with him to deploy the twelve hundred remaining French tanks in two great clusters, which might be able to break the panzer spearheads, but Weygand refused. He knew he was facing about a hundred German divisions, and said privately he would fight one more battle "for the sake of honor," and would then give in.

And on June 5, Reynaud shook up his government. He finally ousted Daladier completely. The former premier told friends he had done nothing for which he could reproach himself, and would continue to be consoled by the esteem of his sons. Reynaud took over Daladier's post as foreign minister—he and Hélène had once lambasted Daladier for holding the portfolios of defense, war, foreign affairs, and the premiership—and made Baudouin his under secretary. He also appointed his friend, the newly elevated General de Gaulle, to be under secretary of defense. That appointment provoked howls from both Weygand and Pétain. De Gaulle wanted to fight on in France and then from North Africa should continental France be lost, and neither Pétain nor Weygand wished to do so. On June 7, when the French army was still holding back the new German advance, Pétain told the cabinet, "If the present battle is lost, there is nothing left to do but to treat with the enemy."

At first that "present battle" did not go badly for the French. Von Bock, whose troops began the advance on June 5, wrote in his diary that "it seems we are in trouble," and a subordinate described what happened when the Germans advanced on the "hedgehogs."

> In front of us, every village and wood—one might even say every clump of trees—is literally stuffed with guns and defenses; even small artillery detachments can put us under direct fire. Behind us is the glare of a vicious battle where one fights not only for each village, but each house. We are therefore not surprised to find ourselves under fire from all quarters, and one could say, "Nobody knows which is the front and which is the rear."

This situation quickly changed when, avoiding the "hedgehogs," daring to do what was considered impossible—such as crossing a high railroad bridge with a brigade of heavy machines—zigzagging and covering twenty to thirty miles each day, Erwin Rommel's tanks made a shambles of the whole western section of the French defenses. On the third day of the advance, his "Phantom Division" split the French Tenth Army, isolated Rouen, and then turned up the coast. Some days later, Rommel wiped out the defenses of Dieppe and Le Havre, and with only a hundred tanks captured an entire British division and some French units that included twelve generals and forty thousand soldiers.

Rommel's panzers were von Bock's spearhead. The second and eastern half of the German advance was commanded by von Rundstedt. His men started four days later than von Bock's, on June 9, led by Guderian's panzers. By the time Guderian got going, von Bock's infantry were within hailing distance of Paris.

In Paris on June 9, André Maurois could hear almost continuous cannon sounds, and he marveled that the city was still calm:

> We began to read in the papers and to hear on the radio quite unexpected names of places. . . . Was it possible the Germans were only half an hour from us by car, while we were living and working just as usual? We had lunch in the open courtyard of one of the big hotels on the Place Vendôme. There were lots of people at the tables. We went to the cinema: it was nearly full. We saw the attack on Narvik and the Paris raid (of June 3rd, in which Luftwaffe bombs killed many people). The tragedy of last week had already become entertainment.

By late afternoon hundreds of thousands of Parisians began to flee the capital, and by nightfall endless lines of cars streamed south and away from Paris. Within the week the refugee throng would swell to ten million people.

In the high councils, Pétain and Weygand were complaining that the eight months of phony war—and the years of leftist governments—had so weakened the French forces that they were incapable of fighting. On June 9, Pétain came close to demanding that Reynaud seek an armistice. Weygand agreed with Pétain, and so did ministers Baudouin, Camille Chautemps, and Boutillier, all of whom were intimates of Hélène de Portes. On June 10, Reynaud decided the government must abandon Paris; the capital would be declared an open city so that it would not be destroyed. He began the transfer of the government 160 miles south. In the late afternoon of June 10, as he and de Gaulle were about to take to the road, word came that Mussolini had declared war on the Allies.

During the first days of the invasion, Hitler had written Mussolini almost daily letters saying that no one in the world except the Duce could understand what the operations meant, and stressing that the fates of Italy and Germany were linked. Hitler wished to induce Italy to come in and tie down French forces. Mussolini hesitated. Italy had nearly a thousand airplanes, a hundred submarines, and several million men under arms, yet his service chiefs considered the forces to be in sad shape and counseled staying out of the war. But Mussolini said he wanted war; more precisely, he wanted "a few thousand dead in order to be able to sit at the peace conference as a belligerent."

To Roosevelt, who sent three messages asking Italy to remain neutral, Mussolini replied that "Italy is and means to be Germany's ally, and Italy cannot remain absent in the moment when the future of Europe is at stake." He told Hitler he would come in on June 1; busy with Dunkirk, Hitler asked him to wait. Hitler also forbade German staff talks with Italian officers and refused to coordinate German army movements with Mussolini. Thus rebuffed, yet not wanting to be shut out of the action lest the game finish too soon, Mussolini declared war on June 10. An Italian army of thirty-two divisions attacked the Alpine passes and the entry points of the Côte d'Azur. In each place, handfuls of French soldiers brought the Italian advances to a standstill. Hitler joked about the "looting expedition" that passed for Mussolini's war effort.

When Roosevelt learned of the Italian entry into the war, he incorporated a denunciation of it in a speech he was to deliver that very day. But the State Department advised against it, and his political intimates suggested it could alienate Italian-American voters in an election year. He took the phrase out, and then was uncomfortable with himself and put it back in. Addressing a large audience that afternoon, he announced, "On this tenth day of June, 1940, the hand that held the dagger has struck it into the back of its neighbor." The phrase was widely quoted, but the heart and intent of the speech, not so widely quoted at the time, lay in a passage in which Roosevelt revealed his beliefs as to the course the United States must take in the months ahead:

> In our American unity, we will pursue two obvious and simultaneous courses: we will extend to the opponents of force the material resources of this nation; and, at the same time, we will harness and speed up the use of these resources in order that we ourselves in the Americas may have equipment and training equal to the task of any emergency and every defense.

Churchhill understood Roosevelt's signal. After hearing the speech on the radio, he wrote the president, "my heartfelt thanks and those of my colleagues for all you are doing and seeking to do for what we may now, indeed, call the Common Cause."

On the morning of June 11, Churchill received a memorandum from Dudley Pound and Alexander Cadogan on what might happen to the French fleet should France leave the war. If the French took the fleet to North Africa and fought from there, no problems would develop, but if any other solution were to occur, "we should aim at getting the fleet scuttled."

Later that day Churchill and his advisors flew to Briare, near Orléans. The Château du Muguet was now headquarters for the French high command, and according to General Spears, it was a sorry second-rate place which had only one telephone but an array of inconveniences. In the early evening, a cast of characters that could hardly have been bettered by a dramatist sat about a long dining table: Churchill,

Spears, Eden, Dill, and Ismay for England, and, on the French side, Reynaud, Pétain, Weygand, de Gaulle, Georges, and Admiral Jean Darlan, who commanded the French navy. To Spears all the French seemed to have "set white faces, their eyes on the table," except for de Gaulle, who had been on the battlefield and whose face showed some color.

The first item discussed was a joint Anglo-French bombing raid on Genoa, Turin, and Milan, planned for that evening—an early reply to Italy's entry into the war. French intelligence had learned that such a raid would bring reprisals on Lyon and Marseilles, where the raid was to originate, and Reynaud wanted to cancel it. Ismay whispered to Churchill that the British bombers had already left England on their way to link up with the Marseilles-based planes and could not now be recalled. The French were dismayed.

Despite the overall situation, Churchill still saw some hope. He pleaded with the French to continue the fight and perhaps hang on in a "Breton redoubt" on the Brittany peninsula; he promised to keep such a bastion supplied, and said that within a year twenty to twenty-five British divisions would join the French there, at which time they could break out and recapture metropolitan France. Weygand answered that the current position of the French troops was hopeless, and that twenty divisions in a year meant none now. He threatened to resign, a prospect which elated de Gaulle but which was soon scotched. He also reminded Churchill that in the Great War the situation after a German breakthrough had been saved by thirty reserve divisions, but "today I have but one regiment in reserve—and it will be used up tomorrow in the first hour." Georges, whom Churchill had always trusted, confirmed Weygand's realistic estimate.

The conferees slipped into recriminations. "History will say," Reynaud charged, "that the battle of France was lost for lack of planes." "And through lack of tanks," Churchill retorted. "But now is the decisive moment," Weygand shouted. "It is therefore wrong to keep any squadrons back in England!"

"This is *not* the decisive moment," Churchill shouted back. "That moment will come when Hitler hurls his Luftwaffe against Britain. If we can keep command of the air, and if we can keep the seas open, as we certainly shall keep them open, we shall win it back for you."

During dinner, word arrived that the British planes had not taken off from Marseilles. So fearful of reprisals were the citizens that the French air commander had allowed them to drive their cars onto the runways and block the planes from taking off. Over coffee and brandy, Reynaud confided to Churchill that Pétain was soon going to hand in a formal request for an armistice. As Churchill sat with de Gaulle, he had become impressed by the general's determination, and as if to confirm that impression, at bedtime de Gaulle caught Reynaud alone, advised him to get rid of Weygand, and said he was personally going to Brittany that instant to see if a Breton redoubt were possible. He would return late the next day. The next morning, as Churchill, Eden, and Reynaud talked quietly in the garden, the ancient Pétain came slowly toward them. "The old man looks buoyant this morning," Reynaud observed. "There must be some bad news."

During the morning conference, Churchill counseled making a stand at Paris to delay the German advance. The French refused. They saw no point in risking the destruction of their beautiful city, and believed furthermore that it would hardly slow down the Germans. They made no mention of the extent to which the resistance of Warsaw had deflected and delayed the German advance in Poland. Then Churchill asked Darlan to guarantee at least that the Germans would never get the French fleet. "There is no question about that," Darlan avowed. "It would be contrary to naval tradition and to honor."

The British party returned to London, where Churchill told the cabinet his inescapable conclusion: that it was time for England to divorce her fate from that of France.

France was crumbling quickly. Rommel and his panzers continued to clean up the coast; Hoth advanced on Paris after taking Rouen; Guderian spearheaded an attack on the rear of the Maginot Line. In many areas the German panzers traveled as if they were on maneuvers, dozens of miles a day. French unit commanders had virtually no communication with the high command once it left Vincennes, and the great hordes of French soldiers who still had weapons and were capable of fighting were uncoordinated, undirected, and thus could not stem the tide. Many, unable to find either a place or a reason to fight, took to flight. Tens of thousands fled south, along with ten million refugees. One of these soldiers was Hans Habe, a Hungarian novelist who had fought for France near Sedan and in other hopeless encounters. He wrote:

> You could catch the smell of the earth, the smell of a good June rain, the smell of sweating horses, the smell of the starched white blouses of the peasant girls. And then your eyes turned back to the flood of limping soldiers, trying in vain to look like men in the presence of the fleeing women. You saw children screaming desperately or still as death; officers' cars blowing their strident horns and trying to open a path; bright cavalry uniforms on nervous, weary horses; wagons with their sleeping drivers; cannon without ammunition; the whole disordered funeral procession of a disintegrated army.... Thousands of soldiers hobbled along the highway, and out of their pockets hung bottles, women's shoes, neckties, ribbons, toys. A Negro soldier was carrying three or four women's corsets. The ribbons hung down and twisted around his legs. Baby carriages rolled along, bearing champagne, cognac, shirts, clocks, umbrellas, coffee mills.... The witches' sabbath increased in horror and absurdity. Since every town and village offered new luxuries, the officers in fleeing cars threw overboard

the loot from the last town to make room for the new merchandise. . . . The best things that the best men of France, the peasants of this peasant country, had created in the sweat of their brow, were thrown on the road and trampled on. Champagne, the product of hundreds of years of diligence and skill, flowed in the ditches.

It was through such scenes that de Gaulle fought his way to Brittany and returned to the government's headquarters by the evening of June 12 to learn that during the day Reynaud had been battered by Weygand's and Pétain's demands for an armistice. When de Gaulle excitedly reported that a Breton redoubt was feasible, Reynaud agreed to move the government to Quimper, near Brest. From there the British could help transfer a half-million men, airplanes, the navy, and the government to North Africa. As Reynaud was still talking with de Gaulle, his door was flung open by a furious Hélène de Portes.

"What is this ridiculous joke about going to Quimper?" she asked, "Are you anxious to make a fool of yourself? I certainly don't propose to go and sleep in Breton four-poster beds. If you want to go to Quimper, go by yourself." Hélène called Baudouin, who told Reynaud that German troops were already in Brittany and that the move was impractical. Reynaud caved in; there would be no Breton redoubt, and the plan to remove to North Africa took a giant step toward oblivion.

Hélène continued to hammer at Reynaud. She broke up several of his conferences. An urgent cable was found crumpled up in her bed, and Spears was amazed to see her in a dressing gown over bright red pajamas, directing traffic outside Reynaud's château. As Reynaud met with Churchill, she sat outside the room and importuned Baudouin to "tell Paul we must give up, we must make an end to it."

Finally, Reynaud, harassed by Hélène and outvoted by his colleagues, asked Churchill to release France from the common cause and "allow her to conclude a separate peace." Churchill's initial reaction was to refuse vehemently, but he at last agreed to withhold judgment until Reynaud had made one last appeal to Roosevelt. The premier cabled the president that "the last hour had come" and renewed his plea for the United States to intervene in the war. Only if that occurred, Reynaud said, could he persuade his own government to continue the fight.

In the interim before receiving this cable, Roosevelt replied to an earlier one from Reynaud:

> I am personally impressed by your declaration that France will continue the fight on behalf of democracy even if it means slow withdrawal even to N. Africa and the Atlantic. It is most important to remember that the French and British fleets continue the mastery of the Atlantic and other oceans. Also to remember that vital materials from the outside world are necessary to maintain all armies.

And he promised that the United States would redouble its efforts to speed supplies to France. In the superheated atmosphere of the day, Churchill characterized this cable as coming "as near as possible to a declaration of war," and wanted to make it public in the hope that it would inspire the French to fight on. But Roosevelt now refused permission, saying bluntly that his message "was in no sense intended to commit and did not commit this government to military participation in support of Allied governments." To do more, Roosevelt told intimates, might result in the destruction of his own authority. The president wished to continue his efforts to persuade the Reynaud government to fight on from North Africa, but the man on whom he had relied to influence Reynaud had not accompanied the government as it fled south.

That man was United States Ambassador William C. Bullitt. When, at eight in the morning of June 14, the German armies began flooding into Paris, and German MPs with red discs on their batons directed traffic near Notre Dame and on the boulevards, French policemen with white batons stood idly by. The Paris police had been ordered by the civilian authorities to stay on guard in order to prevent chaos. Weygand and Pétain feared a Communist takeover of Paris, a prospect more alarming to them than that of the Germans in control of the city. After all, the Germans had occupied Paris in 1870 and had threatened it in the Great War, and Paris had survived. But the city had to be formally surrendered, and—in the absence of the government—this task fell to Ambassador Bullitt. Over the violent objections of Cordell Hull, as well as those of Roosevelt, the ambassador had chosen to stay behind in the city he loved. He believed it would be cowardly to flee, and the fact that his place as an ambassador was at the side of the government did not shake his belief. So Bullitt stayed in Paris and handed the city over to the Germans, while in the south Reynaud was desperate for allies who could help him persuade his colleagues in the cabinet to go to North Africa, and while President Roosevelt sought in vain to find ways to persuade the French to fight on.

Reynaud declared himself in favor of the "Dutch solution"—the military would capitulate while the government went overseas—and he moved the government further south, to Bordeaux. But Weygand said he would not leave metropolitan France, and Pétain saw Weygand's refusal as support for his own position, in favor of total capitulation. On the morning of June 16, it seemed finally that the British had agreed to allow the French to negotiate and conclude a separate peace with the Germans—but on one condition: "provided but only provided [a cabinet telegram said] that the French fleet is sailed forthwith for British harbours pending negotiations."

Abruptly, and briefly, a diversion in the intent was created by the arrival of a proposal for a Franco-British union. If the two countries became one, France would not have to capitulate: the French government could sit in London and the war could go on. Jean Monnet, Ambassador Corbin, Leo Amery, Desmond Morton (then Churchill's secretary), and de Gaulle were among the proposal's ardent supporters. There would be common citizenship and the pooling of resources. Apprised of the proposal, Reynaud thought it wonderful and vowed to fight to the death for it. He prepared to do so in his own cabinet. But Hélène de Portes had seen the proposal as it was being typed, and had stirred up the opposition. When Reynaud introduced it, one opponent said, "We have no intention of becoming a dominion of the British Empire." Mandel retorted, "Would you rather be a German district than a British dominion?" The answer came back: "Yes, better a Nazi province. At least we know what that means."

The proposal died, and the cabinet voted, fourteen to ten, to seek an armistice. Reynaud said he would resign. President Alfred Lebrun spent the afternoon crying on his sofa; he then had to decide whether or not to accept Reynaud's resignation. The head of the Senate and the head of the Chamber of Deputies both advised him to reappoint Reynaud, get rid of Pétain, and move the government to North Africa. But Lebrun refused; he said France required a policy which would save lives now that the battle had been lost.

"In that case," Reynaud disparagingly told him, "I can't form a government. If you want such a policy, go and ask Marshal Pétain." Lebrun took Reynaud at his word. When he approached Pétain, he was amazed to learn that the marshal had in his briefcase a list of ministers for a new cabinet. By a half-hour after midnight, Baudouin, the new foreign minister, asked through the Spanish government for Germany's armistice terms.

Late in the evening, as Spears went to a meeting, a tall figure stepped out of the shadows and intercepted him. It was de Gaulle, convinced that he must get to London and there rally Frenchmen to continue the fight, and equally sure that Weygand was about to arrest him here. The two cooked up a plan. In the morning, de Gaulle accompanied the British general to the airport; at takeoff, after waving goodbye to Spears and an associate, he moved forward to shake their hands, and they lifted him bodily onto the already-moving plane. After landing in Jersey, the officers went into a canteen and ordered coffee. When it came, de Gaulle grimaced. It was tea. This, wrote Spears, "was his first introduction to the tepid liquid which, in England, passed for either one or the other. His martyrdom had begun."

On June 17, Pétain broadcast his sad message to the French: "It is with a broken heart that I tell you today it is necessary to stop fighting." But in the field the battles did not quite stop. Nor had Germany given France any terms. In London, de Gaulle persuaded Churchill and the cabinet to allow him to broadcast a message to those Frenchmen who wanted to continue the fight, and on the evening of June 18 he told France that while the leaders of the government had sued for peace, he, for one, did not believe all had been lost. France stood not alone, but with the might of the British Empire and of the United States' industrial resources behind her:

> The outcome of the struggle has not been decided by the Battle of France. This is a World War.... The destiny of the world is at stake. I, General de Gaulle, now in London, call on all French officers and men who are at present on British soil, or may be in the future, with or without their arms ...to get in touch with me. Whatever happens, the flame of French resistance must not and shall not die!

This broadcast thrust de Gaulle into the limelight. He wanted to broadcast again the following night, but Alexander Cadogan of the British Foreign Office managed to see an advance text of his projected speech and was horrified. De Gaulle intended to announce that the French government, having capitulated, no longer represented the will of France, and that a new government had been formed in London with himself at its head. The British cabinet could hardly allow de Gaulle to bring off a *coup d'etat* over the BBC airwaves, and they forced him to tone down his language. Even so, it was clear to all that, having brought the tall Frenchman over from Bordeaux, England now had a problem as well as a promise on its hands.

Hitler ordered his armies to race as far as they could before a cease-fire could take effect, specifically to take Strasbourg in the Alsace, and Cherbourg on the coast. And he would not sit down with the French until he had met with Mussolini. When he did, the Duce demanded Toulon, additional French territory, and the French fleet. He also wanted to be on hand when Hitler humiliated the French. Hitler refused on all counts. At roughly the same time, Roosevelt announced that Republicans Frank Knox and Henry L. Stimson would enter his cabinet; with this one stroke he eliminated isolationists Harry Woodring and Charles Edison from his inner circle and sent confusion through the Republican convention that was just starting.

On the Brittany coast near Cherbourg, the recently knighted Alan Brooke played out the last act of the British presence on the continent, taking charge of 140,000 lines-of-communications troops. Most were in disarray, though some had been formed into combat units and had hindered the German advance. Also at Brooke's disposal was a superbly equipped Canadian division. But when Pétain asked the French to lay down their arms, it seemed as if there was nothing left of France worth defending—and so Brooke missed a chance to destroy Rommel's exhausted forces. Instead he supervised one last evacuation, but this one held little glory. Several ships were bombed or sunk on the way back to England, and many lives were lost.

On June 18, the British public learned that France had asked for an armistice. "Thank God we're now alone," the king said privately, echoing the sentiments of many of his subjects. The slant to the future was emphasized in an anonymous and posthumous letter from an airman to his mother published in that morning's London *Times*. The young airman wrote that the job of defending the British Isles was to him of "the greatest importance," and was a job he had carried out

> to the utmost of my ability. No man can do more, and no one calling himself a man could do less. . . . My death would not mean your struggle has been in vain. Far from it. It means that your sacrifice is as great as mine. Those who serve England must expect nothing from her; we debase ourselves if we regard our country as merely a place in which to eat and sleep. . . . Today we are faced with the greatest organized challenge to Christianity and civilization that the world has ever seen, and I count myself lucky and honoured to be the right age and fully trained to throw my full weight into the scale. . . . The life of one man can only be justified by the measure of his sacrifice. We are sent into this world to acquire a personality and a character to take with us that can never be taken from us. Those who just eat and sleep, prosper and procreate are no better than animals if all their lives they are at peace. . . . With the final test of war I consider my character fully developed. Thus at my early age my earthly mission is already fulfilled and I am prepared to die with just one regret and one only—that I could not devote myself to making your declining years more happy by being with you; but you will live in peace and freedom and I shall have directly contributed to that, so here again my life will not have been in vain.

19

Signals

In 1918, Foch and Weygand had handed the Allied armistice terms to the defeated Germans in a railroad car on a siding in the forest of Compiègne north of Paris. Hitler insisted that the French receive his armistice terms in the same railroad car at the same spot. Weygand, Pétain, and the rest of the French high command would not attend the ceremony. They turned over the onerous task of receiving the terms to General Huntziger and two middle-ranking officers of the navy and air force, all of whom were aghast when they found out where the ceremony was to take place.

Hitler, Hess, Göring, Ribbentrop, Raeder, Keitel, and Brauchitsch led the German delegation. On the crystal clear day of June 21, swastika-ornamented cloths were draped over the monuments commemorating the 1918 signing. But somehow those who had prepared the site in the forest had neglected to cover a great granite block bearing an inscription: "Here on the eleventh of November 1918 succumbed the criminal pride of the German people." From fifty yards away, William Shirer, who was observing the ceremony through binoculars, saw Hitler's face as he read it:

> It is afire with scorn, anger, hate, revenge, and triumph. He steps off the monument and contrives to make even this gesture a masterpiece of contempt. He glances back at it, contemptuous, angry—angry, you almost feel, because he cannot wipe out the awful, provoking lettering with one sweep of his high Prussian boot. He glances slowly around the clearing, and now, as his eyes meet ours, you grasp the depth of his hatred. But there is triumph there, too—revengeful, triumphant hate.

Hitler preceded the other Germans into the railroad car, and the French followed. Huntziger saw that Hitler was seated where Foch had sat in 1918; the Germans had researched and rehearsed every detail.

For twelve minutes Hitler sat stiffly while Keitel read out a preamble which the Führer himself had written:

> Germany does not intend to give the armistice terms or negotiations the character of an abuse of such a gallant enemy . . . [but rather] to make possible the dawn of a new peace whose primary element will be the rectification of all the brutal injustices inflicted on the German Reich.

Before the actual terms were read out, Hitler, to the strains of "Deutschland über Alles," left the car and the clearing. He was followed by Göring, Hess, Ribbentrop, then the service chiefs, and last of all by Brauchitsch. Keitel stayed to read the terms and to hand them to the French. Charles Huntziger had been instructed to break off the talks if the Germans asked either for the surrender of the fleet or the right to occupy any colonial territory. Having received the terms, the French went into a small nearby tent to discuss them.

"I had of course taken the necessary steps to ensure that we could unobtrusively listen in to their telephone conversations," Keitel later wrote. Huntziger telephoned the terms to Weygand, who in turn told Pétain that they were "harsh but not dishonoring." After attempting to change some of the terms, Huntziger signed at 8:50 PM on Saturday, June 22. Keitel announced, "It is honorable for the victor to do honor to the vanquished," and the military men all stood in silence for a minute in a salute to the fallen, and then it was over.

At dawn the next morning, in company with his two favorite intellectuals, Speer and sculptor Arno Breker, as well as armed guards and aides, Hitler took a whirlwind tour of Paris. A third of the population had fled the city, and in the early morning the streets were deserted; the motorcade sped along unhindered and unobserved past palaces and churches Hitler had heretofore seen only in his art and history books. Inside the Opéra, his favorite building, he displayed an intimate knowledge of architectural details. Speer wrote that he went "into ecstasies about its beauty, his eyes glistening with an excitement that struck me as uncanny." He also tried to tip the guard who showed him about, but the man refused money. They went past the Madeleine, down the empty Champs Elysées, and across the river to the Eiffel Tower and to Napoleon's tomb at Les Invalides. Looking down into the vault, Hitler reverently bared his head, but he was dissatisfied: "They have made a big mistake . . . you should look up to Napoleon, feeling small by the very size of the monument." Speer was amazed to find Hitler uninterested in the Place des Vosges, the Louvre, the Palace of Justice, the stained-glass windows of Sainte-Chapelle but fascinated by the church of Sacre Coeur on the heights of Montmarte. There Hitler stood and gazed at the dome while early churchgoers recognized and ignored him. In the evening, he told Speer to push hard on the plans to remake Berlin, so that when the renovation was completed, "Paris will be only a shadow. . . .

Berlin is to be given the style commensurate with the grandeur of our victory."

Like most of the 120,000 other evacuated French soldiers, Denis Barlone returned to France soon after Dunkirk. He stayed briefly in a hospital, and then sought his regiment's new quarters. But before he got back into the fighting, it was over. There were rumors that the air force had gone to Oran, that thirty ships a day were transferring troops from Bordeaux, that Pétain had talked the army into defeat when it had not yet been crushed. He observed:

> The behavior of civilians towards officers has already undergone a notice-able change. During the last few days they have been treated with a marked lack of respect. The people, embittered by defeat, do not distin-guish between those officers who, on the whole, have fought admirably, sustaining grievous losses, and the High Command, which as I see it, has not been able to fulfil its task.... Our High Command has learned noth-ing, understood nothing, and had no information about the preparations, the capacity and tactics of the enemy, despite the campaigns in Poland and Norway.... No one can understand why the French Army was not em-barked; if 335,000 men could be saved ... at Dunkirk, one or two million fighting men could have embarked for Algeria and England.

Barlone did not hear de Gaulle's historic first broadcast, but when he learned of it he was convinced that de Gaulle had the backing of the British government. The high command disowned de Gaulle and pub-licly relieved him of his command, and announced that French soldiers who went to London to enlist would be considered deserters. Not want-ing to be considered a deserter, Barlone did not take an early opportu-nity to embark from Bayonne, and then he regretted it.

Pétain replied to de Gaulle's broadcasts: the peasants, he said met-aphorically, must continue to toil even though a hailstorm passed through their fields. Barlone was outraged: "Can one compare the di-saster of our beloved land to a simple hail-storm of no consequence?" Night after night he listened to de Gaulle's "energetic and engaging words ... his dignified and proper attitude ... a moving speech [that] came from a burning heart." As soon as de Gaulle was officially recog-nized by the British government as the leader of all the French on Brit-ish soil—which meant he could legitimately recruit troops—Barlone made his decision: no matter how long it might take him, he would work his way to England and enlist with de Gaulle and the Free French.

After the armistice, France was divided in two. In the north, the conquered provinces became a part of the Reich. In the south a nomi-nally independent country remained, under the leadership of Pétain, with Vichy as its capital. The Germans treated the Vichy government as the only legitimate power in France, and would negotiate only with Pétain and his cohorts. One of the worst provisions of the armistice—protested by Huntziger but to no avail—was that the French were to hand over to the conquerors all the German and Austrian refugees. The French fulfilled this demand with bureaucratic thoroughness, thereby condemning to death thousands who might have escaped.

Leo Lania was in a French open-air internment camp when the armistice was signed. On June 19, the camp was formally placed under the Red Cross, but the Germans started to move in anyway. Lania was not going to die in Buchenwald or Dachau; he knew too much about those places to let himself be taken prisoner by the Nazis. He and a handful of other refugees escaped from their camp, and for weeks they hid in caves, traveled down mined beaches, coaxed or stole bicycles, ate crusts of bread or nothing at all. They underwent many hardships and narrow escapes as they crossed through the German zone down into the French zone, and along the whole thousand miles to Marseilles—but they were never once betrayed by the French peasants. For Lania, after all he had been through, that was a measure of saving grace from his adopted country.

Ruth Andreas-Friedrich and her circle of Berlin intellectuals were shocked by the victories in the West. They had put their hopes in France, and now they worried about England—and about themselves, trapped inside a Germany they detested:

> Put out the flags, take in the flags. Every window, every gable, every tower, all in a sea of swastika'd flags. Order for display of flags: "As of today, for a period of one week." Ringing of churchbells: three days. Once again Christian tongues have to join in praising the bloody victory of arms. ... Paris fell last Friday. When the report came in over the radio, employees of the paper were all at lunch in the canteen.... "Hurrah," comes a shout from a corner. Everyone winces. "Hurrah!" again, but this time with noticeably less authority. One of our scrubwomen has jumped up, grabbed her glass, and is cheering, "Long live the Führer!" Icy silence at every table.

It was going to be a long time before the tide turned, a long time indeed. Those who intended to resist would have to go underground. It would be the only way to survive.

At each successive victory in France and the Low Countries Wilhelm Prüller's eyes grew moist "for joy and pride in the Wehrmacht's accomplishments." When the armistice was announced he was so "utterly happy" he could hardly write in his diary—not because the war was over, but because Germany had triumphed. On the occasion of his wife's "first anniversary of motherhood" he wrote in the diary an apostrophe to German women:

> How many *Kameraden* who gave up their lives in this gigantic, decisive

battle died with the word *"Mutter"* on their lips. . . . You mothers have a national responsibility in war. . . . Be unswerving in the holy belief in this our rightful cause, be never wavering in your confidence in our dearly beloved Führer, be proud that your sons may take part in this, the greatest war in history. Be overjoyed if you may be permitted to sacrifice them for *Volk, Reich, und Führer.* Be honest and true, German mothers!

Else Wendel and her sister Erna talked of a recent celebration in East Prussia when a new gauleiter was installed. Erna and her boss, a kindly Austrian, were ordered to organize the workers in their nursery for a reception. "This will be about the most useless hour in my whole life," her chief laughed. And indeed it was—interminable songs, presentation of flowers, a red carpet. When the new gauleiter arrived, the ceremony went off "according to the book," and then they collapsed into their seats. The nursery chief lit a cigarette, only to be lambasted for such a breach of protocol by a high party official "with all the air of an insulted god." The party man insisted that the chief stop smoking immediately or take the consequences. The chief decided to continue smoking and was soon fired. Erna commented,

> Do you know what my chief said as he left? This is only the beginning of a very bad end. The top jobs are falling more and more to men who know less and less, the very scum indeed. All you have to do today is kneel down and worship Hitler—you don't want any other qualifications for your job of work at all.

"If it's really like that," Else responded, "then the whole thing will crash."

In Poland the western invasion brought firing squads to those who had waited in the first *Todesborn,* and death from typhoid, dysentery, and pneumonia to the Jews within the barbed wire of Lublin. Plans were made to remove the remainder of the Jews in Lublin to larger ghettos and to send some to Auschwitz to replace construction workers who had died.

On a rainy morning all the Jews of Lask were assembled in the main square, and two were hanged. Sala Kaminska and her mother, who watched that event, were all that remained of their family. During the winter Aunt Mina had nearly frozen to death, and then gangrene had taken her off; Sala's brother had been abducted by the conquerors. The women were sent out daily to the fields to do farm work. At night, for diversion, the Germans sometimes staged mass disrobings of the Jewish women, and at other times searched the houses for them. One evening they came to Sala's apartment. She hid in a cubicle beneath a trap door. Red-haired and green-eyed, she had grown prettier despite the privations, and now had a woman's body. She listened in terror as the Germans beat her mother because they could not find her. When the Nazis were gone, Sala emerged and was transfixed at the sight of her mother. Next day she gave herself up to the men who had searched for her. She would do what she must to ensure that she and her mother would survive.

It was almost over now, this time of violence and soiled honor, of incessant talk and dissembling stances, of flawed victories and ignoble defeats. Soon enough there would be total war. There remained but a few strokes, a few signals to be sent and received.

In June 1940, Stalin placed twenty-two Russian divisions on the German border of what used to be Poland; he forbade publication in *Izvestia* and *Pravda* of articles on the war; he completed the military occupation of Lithuania, Latvia, and Estonia; he demanded that Finland demilitarize the strategic Aaland Islands which could control the Baltic; he established diplomatic relations with Yugoslavia; he mobilized the Soviet economy for war by lengthening the work day and by introducing more severe discipline into the factories; and he further accelerated the reorganization of the Red Army.

He also received in Moscow Sir Stafford Cripps, head of a new British trade delegation, as Britain's ambassador to the Soviet Union. Cripps was a radical leftist and a friend of Churchill's. Shortly after he arrived, Molotov left his calling card at the British embassy on the occasion of the birthday of King George VI. It was the first time since the Revolution that a high Russian official had done so.

Stalin also pressured Rumania. In the spring, Hitler had tried to force King Carol closer to the Nazi camp. Carol sent four million boys and girls out into the fields to sow millions of dollars' worth of wheat to be sold at a loss to Germany. He also eased restrictions on the pro-Nazi Iron Guard and replaced a pro-Allied foreign minister with a pro-German one; finally, on June 21, Carol assumed totalitarian powers and stationed troops on Rumania's border with Russia.

On June 26, Molotov handed a note to the Rumanian minister in Moscow. It demanded the return to the Soviet Union within twenty-four hours of Bessarabia and "the part of Bukovina which, in the composition of population, is historically and linguistically bound up with the Soviet Ukraine." In a panic, Carol appealed to Hitler for help. Hitler looked again at the secret protocol to the Nazi-Soviet pact, and was incensed to discover that, through a blunder of Ribbentrop's, it referred not only to Bessarabia, but also implied that the Soviets had access to whatever territories they wanted in the Balkans. He advised Carol to yield. Without German military assistance, the Rumanian army could not long withstand the Red Army, and four days later, the Red Army occupied Bessarabia and Bukovina with tanks and blossoming parachutes in a lightning strike. The next day a hundred German bombers landed in Rumania; a press release said they had been promised previously in conjunction with other war supplies. Rumania's orientation toward Berlin was now complete, and the bombers were Hitler's sign to Stalin that he had gone far enough.

In less than a year, and mostly without bloodshed—except in Finland—Stalin had extended Soviet control over Lithuania, Latvia, Estonia, part of Finland, part of Poland, and part of Rumania; he had received enormous quantities of war supplies from Germany and yet he had retained control over rail routes which were Germany's main access to foreign oil; he had effectively placed checks on the further expansion of both Germany and Italy in the Balkans, and he had once again established ties with Germany's enemy, England.

Paul Reynaud and Hélène de Portes drove from Bordeaux toward a vacation house in Saint-Maxime. Hélène had sent ahead to Spain luggage which contained several million dollars in secret government funds, gold, and jewelry. She suggested that Reynaud drive to take his mind off his worries. Moments after he took the wheel, the car went into a ditch; Hélène's heavy suitcase flew from the back to the front of the car and broke her neck. She died instantly. Reynaud suffered minor injuries. The two men with Hélène's luggage were apprehended in Spain on an informant's tip, and were returned to France to stand charges. In deep mourning, his head swathed in bandages, Reynaud came to Vichy to briefly defend the men; he said they had not known what they carried. In the summer, Reynaud was arrested and taken to prison.

At about the same time, Georges Mandel and Edouard Daladier sat aboard a ship moored in Casablanca harbor. If he had not been a Jew, Mandel said, he would have seized the reins of government at once, at home. With Daladier, he now planned to form a government in North Africa. They worked on a proclamation announcing their intention. Lord Gort had been recently appointed governor of Gibraltar, and he flew to Casablanca to meet with the former ministers. But the French governor at Casablanca refused Gort permission to see them, believing them to be traitors. He confiscated their proclamation and sent them back to Pétain. Soon Daladier and Mandel, too, were in a Vichy prison.

Hitler had hoped to sign a peace treaty with England, and had made no real plans for war with the British Empire. He had only forty-five landing craft available for an invasion of the British Isles, and no complete or detailed plan for an invasion. German troops had been demobilized or given leave. Despite the protestations of Marshal Göring, whose pilots were bathing in French champagne, air superiority over the British Isles had not been established. Yet Hitler's advisers kept nagging him to get to work on England, and at long last, on July 2, he issued a less-than-forthright directive: "The Führer has decided:

That a landing in England is possible, providing that air superiority can be attained and certain other necessary conditions fulfilled. The date of commencement is still undecided. All preparations to be begun immediately."

Both Roosevelt and Churchill agreed in late June that the French fleet was the key to the continuation of the war. Whether Hitler invaded England or not, if the Axis held the French fleet it could control the Mediterranean and could savage the Atlantic shipping lanes. If the French fleet fell into German hands, Roosevelt might have to bring the stronger American fleet back from Hawaii and into the Atlantic to supplement the weak Atlantic force and to protect the United States' east coast—which would leave the Pacific open to the Japanese and which might prove equally disastrous. Churchill knew England's survival now depended on the supplies coming by ship from the overseas dominions and from the United States. And he needed to send an unmistakable signal to Roosevelt, Stalin, Hitler, and Mussolini that England was prepared to fight to the death and would never surrender.

Despite continued assurances from Pétain, Weygand, and Darlan that the French fleet would be scuttled and would never be handed over to Germany, the British cabinet could not be sure what would happen. The armistice directed that fleet to be decommissioned in French ports. But, as Churchill wrote to FDR, "Have you considered what offers Hitler may choose to make to France? He may say, 'surrender the fleet intact, and I will leave you Alsace Lorraine,' or alternatively, 'If you do not give me your ships I will destroy your towns.'" How could the British cabinet believe that Germany would stand by and let France control her own ships in French ports, when those ships might so easily be used by the Axis against England? Over the objections of nearly all junior and senior British naval officers and those of many in the cabinet, Churchill conceived a plan to deal with the French fleet, which was concentrated in three places. One was Portsmouth, England, a second was Alexandria, and the third, the most important, was Mers-al-Kabir in Oran, Algeria.

On the evening of July 2, the cabinet finally swung around to Churchill's position, but the prime minister himself wept before he sent a cable to Admiral James Somerville ordering him to proceed from Gibraltar with "Force H" and to persuade the French at Mers-al-Kabir to surrender or to neutralize their ships: "You are charged with one of the most disagreeable and difficult tasks that a British Admiral has ever been faced with, but we have complete confidence in you and rely on you to carry it out relentlessly."

Somerville's force included the *Hood*, which was considered the most powerful ship afloat, the carrier *Ark Royal*, two battleships, two cruisers, and eleven destroyers. At Mers-al-Kabir, Admiral Gensoul had the mighty *Dunkerque*, the very modern battle cruiser *Strasbourg*, two battleships, seven cruisers, four submarines, and a torpedo boat—in themselves a not inconsiderable force.

It was broiling hot on July 3 as the British force ran legs to sea outside the harbor of Mers-al-Kabir, which was fairly jammed with French ships. Somerville dispatched Captain Cedric Holland, a former naval attaché in Paris, to see Gensoul. The French admiral would not allow Holland aboard the *Dunkerque* and insisted that he talk on a barge in mid-harbor with a flag lieutenant named Dufay. The two junior men did the dirty work. Holland presented four drastic alternatives: the French could sail with the British against the Axis; they could transfer the ships under British armed guard to the French West Indies; they could turn over the ships to the British; or they could, within six hours, scuttle them. Should all these alternatives be rejected, Somerville had been told to use whatever force was necessary to sink the French ships and to render them useless to the enemy. Holland conveyed all this to Dufay, who relayed it back to Gensoul. As the day wore on, the tragic proportions of the gathering storm became obvious to the two junior men. At its heart was the fact that the French did not trust the British, and that the British, although willing to trust the French, could not believe that the Germans would allow the French to keep their ships intact and inoperative for the duration of the war.

Late in the torrid afternoon, Gensoul finally saw Holland in person and informed him that the first shot fired by a British ship would be "tantamount to a declaration of war." Holland beseeched the French admiral to yield to *force majeure*. At Alexandria and at Portsmouth that was concurrently happening. Gensoul could not agree. He had received permission to sail for the West Indies, but he could not do so "under British guns" in a British convoy, because "I have my code of honor." Holland felt the two sides were not far apart and that, given time, a compromise might be effected—but there was no time left. He told Gensoul that the British also had a code of honor, and had now to do their duty. When Holland bade Dufay farewell in mid-harbor, both were weeping.

For the next ten minutes the harbor became an inferno: hundreds of rounds of shells were fired, geysers shot thirty stories into the air, black oil flamed the waters, men boiled in steam and were struck through with steel splinters. Former allies killed one another. The *Provence* cracked apart and capsized; the *Bretagne* went down; the *Mogador* was exploded by its own depth charges; the *Dunkerque* was stove in and ran aground. Only the *Strasbourg* managed to escape across the Mediterranean. It was a bloody and decisive encounter: at Mers-al-Kabir and in an ensuing action, 1,297 French sailors died and 351 were wounded.

The message of brutality and determination produced strong reactions everywhere. Germany sent her largest bomber strike yet against the British Isles. In France, an outraged Darlan wanted to mount punitive expeditions against British African and Middle East possessions, and Pétain sent some bombers against Gibraltar and talked of declaring war. But war was not declared, because France was impotent. In Rome, Ciano noted in his diary that the action at Mers-al-Kabir "proves the fighting spirit of His Britannic Majesty's fleet is quite alive," and observed that the dejected Mussolini could do nothing about it. Stalin told intimates that the British had done what was necessary, and his admiration for them increased. He also noted that the Germans had no riposte with which to answer the British action. He continued to train his armies hard, while he kept up his trading with Hitler.

In Washington, Ambassador Lord Lothian wrote to Roosevelt, "You will see that Winston Churchill has taken the action in regard to the French fleet which we discussed and you approved." In London, when Churchill spoke to Commons about what had happened at Oran, he received a rousing ovation, and the country rallied behind him. There were no second thoughts. In the next several weeks Churchill consolidated his leadership of the country; he became the colossus, the voice of democracy, and England aligned herself behind him.

And with his new height, Churchill reached out more and more to the United States. His correspondence with Roosevelt became more frequent, and warmer. On his end, Roosevelt, too, grew in influence and stature. Once nominated by his party, he seemed certain of reelection, and began to use his regenerated political power to loosen the strings of American aid. He found the forty destroyers Churchill had sought, edged the United States closer to becoming the "arsenal of democracy."

Hitler, too, assimilated the message of Oran, and in the next few weeks came to a fundamental decision which, in the manner of the growing Atlantic alliance between Churchill and Roosevelt, would shape the whole future course of the war and the world. He turned over the task of bringing England to her knees to Göring and the Luftwaffe; surely the heir must be able to finish the task of humiliating a small island. But whether England was conquered now or not, Hitler knew a greater enemy lay in wait—his true enemy, the one he had always dreamed of conquering. Stalin had been encroaching in the Baltic and the Balkans; he must be stopped. German reports showed that the Red Army had been remarkably weak in Finland, which was encouraging. Now was not the time to strike at Russia, for it would take a minimum of ten weeks in which to prepare a campaign and to transfer troops to the eastern frontier, which would put the date for an invasion into October. Hitler did not intend to get caught, as Napoleon had been, in the snows of the Russian winter. He would wait out the cold weather of 1940, but by the spring of 1941 he would be entirely ready to invade Russia.

Sources
Bibliography
Notes
Index

Sources

The many volumes of *Trial of the Major War Criminals before the International Military Tribune*, and the earlier *Nazi Conspiracy and Aggression* (TMWC and NCA) are culled from the Nuremberg materials, and are the major sources of information about Germany in this era. On foreign policy, I have used extensively the volumes of *Documents on German Foreign Policy* (DGFP), *Documents on British Foreign Policy* (DBFP), and *Foreign Relations of the United States* (FRUS), and secondarily the British *Blue Book* and the French *Livre Jaune*, which describe the events leading to the war. A major source for France is the eleven-volume set of documents and testimony given to the parliamentary inquest, *Les Evénements survenus en France de 1933 à 1945*.

Other publications of official papers used include Roosevelt's *Complete Press Conferences*, his *Speeches*, and the *Parliamentary Debates, House of Commons*. I have made continual use of the Polish *Black Book*, published in the West after the defeat of Poland, which documents German acts. I have referred to the daily accounts of *The New York Times*, the London *Times*, *Le Matin*, *Le Figaro*, and the weekly accounts of contemporaneous large-circulation magazines such as *Life*, *Illustrated London News*, and *Match*. For recent scholarship I have used the issues of *Revue d'Histoire de la Deuxieme Guerre Mondiale*.

The British cabinet and war cabinet papers are now in the Public Records Office in London, for the most part, though some remain sealed, as do some important papers in France. Perhaps in 1990 they will provide some surprises. I have had access to the Franklin D. Roosevelt collection at Hyde Park, New York, the vast storehouse of German and American records in the National Archives in Washington, and have used the collections at the New York Public Library and the New York University Library.

In the bibliography I have listed books in translation, where available, and have listed American publishers by name and foreign publishers by location. In the notes, references are made by key words and quotations within the chapters. For the sake of brevity, I have not repeatedly listed the published volumes, papers, or daily and weekly sheets cited above.

Bibliography

Arthur E. Adams, *Stalin and His Times*, Holt, Rinehart & Winston, 1972.

Margery Allingham, *The Oaken Heart*, London, 1941.

Wladyslaw Anders, *An Army in Exile*, Macmillan, 1949.

Ruth Andreas-Friedrich, *Berlin Underground*, Holt & Co., 1947.

Anonymous, *My Name is Million*, Macmillan, 1940.

A. Armengaud, *Batailles Politiques et Militaires Sur l'Europe*, Paris, 1948.

Sidney Aster, *1939: The Making of the Second World War*, Simon & Schuster, 1973.

Joan Bright Astley, *The Inner Circle*, London, 1971.

Thomas A. Bailey and Paul B. Ryan, *Hitler vs. Roosevelt: The Undeclared Naval War*, Free Press, 1979.

Hanson W. Baldwin, *The Crucial Years, 1939–1941*, Harper & Row, 1976.

Sybil Bannister, *I Lived under Hitler*, London, 1957.

Noel Barber, *The Week France Fell*, Stein & Day, 1976.

A. J. Barker, *Dunkirk: The Great Escape*, McKay, 1977.

Denis Barlone, *A French Officer's Diary*, translated by L. V. Cass, Macmillan, 1943.

Paul Baudouin, *Private Diaries*, London, 1948.

Jozef Beck, *Dernier Rapport*, Neuchatel, 1951.

Patrick Beesly, *Very Special Intelligence*, London, 1977.

Cajus Bekker, *Hitler's Naval War*, translated by Frank Ziegler, Doubleday, 1974.

_____ , *The Luftwaffe War Diaries*, translated by Frank Ziegler, Doubleday, 1948.

P. M. H. Bell, *A Certain Eventuality*, London, 1974.

Charlotte Beradt, *The Third Reich of Dreams*, translated by Adriane Gottwald, Quadrangle, 1969.

Michael R. Beschloss, *Kennedy and Roosevelt: The Uneasy Alliance*, Norton, 1980.

S. Payne Best, *The Venlo Incident*, London, 1950.

Nicholas Bethell, *The War Hitler Won*, Holt, Rinehart & Winston, 1972.

Ursula Bloom, *The Log of No Lady*, London, 1940.

John Morton Blum, *From the Morgenthau Diaries: Years of Urgency*, Houghton-Mifflin, 1965.

Gunther Blumentritt, Von Rundstedt, London, 1952.
Willi A. Boelcke, ed., Secret Conferences of Dr. Goebbels, Dutton, 1970.
Joseph Borkin, The Crime and Punishment of I. G. Farben, Macmillan, 1978.
Theodor Broch, The Mountains Wait, St. Paul, Webb, 1943.
Ewart Brooks, Prologue to a War, London, 1966.
Arthur Bryant, The Turn of the Tide, Doubleday, 1957.
Alan Bullock, Hitler: A Study in Tyranny, Harper & Row, 1971.
James MacGregor Burns, Roosevelt: The Lion and the Fox, Harcourt, Brace, 1956.
Angus Calder, The People's War, Pantheon, 1969.
Peter Calvocoressi and Guy Wint, Total War, Penguin, 1972.
Hadley Cantril, editor, Public Opinion, 1935-1946, Princeton University Press, 1951.
Mark Lincoln Chadwin, The Warhawks, Norton, 1970.
Camille Chautemps, Cahiers Secrètes de l'Armistice 1939-1940, Paris, 1960.
Allen F. Chew, The White Death, Michigan University Press, 1971.
Winston S. Churchill, The Second World War: vol. 1, The Gathering Storm; vol. 2, Their Finest Hour, Houghton-Mifflin, 1948-9.
Ciano's Diary, edited by Malcolm Muggeridge, London, 1947.
J. A. Cole, Lord Haw-Haw. London, 1964.
Basil Collier, The Second World War: A Military History, Morrow, 1967.
Richard Collier, Duce: Viking, 1971.
————, 1940: The Avalanche, Dial, 1979.
J. R. Colville, Man of Valour, London, 1972.
Ian Colvin, The Chamberlain Cabinet, Taplinger, 1971.
Patrick S. Cosgrave, Churchill At War: Alone, 1939-1940, London, 1974.
Geoffrey Cox, The Red Army Moves, London, 1941.
Birger Dahlerus, The Last Attempt, London, 1948.
Robert Dallek, Franklin Delano Roosevelt and American Foreign Policy, 1932-1945, Oxford University Press, 1979.
David J. Dallin, Soviet Russia's Foreign Policy, 1939-1942, translated by Leon Dennen, Yale University Press, 1942.
Brian Davis, German Forces 1939-1940, London, 1976.
Lucy S. Dawidowicz, The War against the Jews, Holt, Rinehart & Winston, 1975.
Len Deighton, Blitzkrieg, Knopf, 1980.
Maja Destrem, L'Été 39, Paris, 1969.
Wallace R. Deuel, People under Hitler, Harcourt, 1942.
Harold C. Deutsch, The Conspiracy against Hitler in the Twilight War, University of Minnesota Press, 1968.
Robert A. Divine, The Illusion of Neutrality, University of Chicago Press, 1962.
Alexander Donat, The Holocaust Kingdom, Holt, Rinehart & Winston, 1965.
André Doumenc, Histoire de la 9e Armée, Grenoble, 1945.
L. F. Ellis, The War in France and Flanders, London, 1953.
Eloise Engle and Lauri Paananen, The Winter War, Scribner's, 1973.
A. Fabré-Luce, Journal de la France, Paris, 1946.
Ladislas Farago, The Game of the Foxes, McKay, 1971.
T. R. Fehrenbach, F.D.R.'s Undeclared War, McKay, 1967.
Herbert Feis, The Road to Pearl Harbor, Princeton University Press, 1950.

Laura Fermi, *Mussolini*, University of Chicago Press, 1961.

Janet Flanner, *Paris Was Yesterday*, Viking, 1972.

Thomas Foley, *I Was an Altmark Prisoner*, London, 1940.

François Fonvieille-Alquier, *The French and the Phoney War*, translated by Ed Ashcroft, London, 1973.

Saul Friedlander, *Prelude to Downfall*, translated by Aline B. and Alexander Werth, London, 1967.

Willi Frischauer and Robert Jackson, *The Altmark Affair*, Macmillan, 1975.

George H. Gallup, *The Gallup Poll, 1935–1971*, vol. 1, Random House, 1972.

Maurice Gamelin, *Servir*, 3 vols., Paris, 1946.

Charles de Gaulle, *War Memoirs*; vol. 1, *The Call to Honour*, translated by Jonathan Griffin, London, 1955.

André Géraud (Pertinax), *The Gravediggers of France*, Doubleday, Doran, 1944.

A. Goutard, *La Guerre des Occasions Perdues*, Paris, 1956.

Michael Gibson, *Russia under Stalin*, Putnam's, 1972.

Martin Gilbert, *Churchill: The Prophet of Truth, 1922–1939*, Houghton-Mifflin, 1977.

———, *Final Journey*, Mayflower, 1979.

Ian Grey, *Stalin: Man of History*, Doubleday, 1979.

Eric Grove, *German Armour 1939–40*, London, 1976.

Richard Grunberger, *The 12-Year Reich*, Holt, Rinehart & Winston, 1971.

Heinz Guderian, *Panzer Leader*, London, 1952.

Hans Habe, *A Thousand Shall Fall*, translated by Norbert Gutterman, Harcourt, Brace, 1941.

Peter Hadley, *Third Class to Dunkirk*, London, 1944.

John McVickar Haight, *American Aid to France*, Atheneum, 1970.

Franz Halder, *Kriegstagebuch*, Stuttgart, 1962.

Oron J. Hale, *The Captive Press in the Third Reich*, Princeton University Press, 1964.

Carl J. Hambro, *I Saw It Happen in Norway*, Appleton-Century, 1940.

Nicholas Harman, *Dunkirk: The Necessary Myth*, London, 1980.

Tom Harrison, *Living through the Blitz*, Penguin, 1976.

Joseph C. Harsch, *Pattern of Conquest*, Doubleday, 1941.

Nevile Henderson, *Failure of a Mission*, Putnam's, 1940.

Marc Hillel and Clarissa Henry, *Of Pure Blood*, McGraw-Hill, 1976.

Stanley Hilton, "The Welles Mission to Europe, February–March, 1940: Illusion or Realism?" *Journal of American History*, June 1971, vol. LVIII.

F. H. Hinsley, with E. E. Thomas, C. F. G. Ransom, and R. C. Knight, *British Intelligence in the Second World War*, vol. 1, London, 1979.

J. L. Hodson, *Through the Dark Night*, London, 1941.

Heinz Höhne, *The Order of the Death's Head*, translated by Richard Barry, Coward, McCann & Geoghegan, 1969.

Alistair Horne, *To Lose a Battle: France, 1940*, Little, Brown, 1969.

Harold L. Ickes, *The Secret Diary of Harold L. Ickes*: vol. 1, *The Inside Struggle*, and vol. 3, *The Lowering Clouds*, Simon & Schuster, 1954, 1955.

Edmund Ironside, *The Ironside Diaries*, London, 1962.

David Irving, *Hitler's War*, vol. 1, Viking, 1977.

———, *The War Path*, Viking, 1978.

————, editor, Breach of Security, 1968.

Max Jakobson, The Diplomacy of the Winter War, Harvard University Press, 1961.

Brian Johnson, The Secret War, London, 1978.

Louis de Jong, The German Fifth Column in the Second World War, London, 1956.

David Kahn, Hitler's Spies, Macmillan, 1978.

Basil Karslake, 1940: The Last Act, London, 1979.

Wilhelm Keitel, In the Service of the Reich, translated by David Irving, Stein & Day, 1966.

George F. Kennan, Russia and the West under Lenin and Stalin, Little, Brown, 1961.

Arthur Koestler, Scum of the Earth, London, 1941.

Nikita Khrushchev, Khrushchev Remembers, translated by Strobe Talbott, Little, Brown, 1970.

William L. Langer and S. Everett Gleason, The Challenge to Isolation, vol. 1, Harper, 1952.

Leo Lania, The Darkest Hour, Houghton-Mifflin, 1941.

Pierre Lapie, With the Foreign Legion at Narvik, translated by Anthony Merryn, London, 1941.

Joseph P. Lash, Roosevelt and Churchill, 1939–1941, Norton, 1976.

Jacques de Launay, Histoires Secrètes de la Belgique, Paris, 1975.

Pierre Lazareff, Deadline, translated by David Partridge, Random House, 1942.

Gottfried Leske, I Was a Nazi Flier, Dial, 1941.

Basil H. Liddell Hart, The German Generals Talk, Morrow, 1948.

————, History of the Second World War, Putnam's, 1970.

Francis L. Loewenheim, Harold D. Langley, and Manfred Jonas, eds., Roosevelt and Churchill: Their Secret Wartime Correspondence, 1975.

John Lukacs, The Last European War, Doubleday, 1977.

Eino Luukanen, Fighter over Finland, London, 1963.

Donald McIntyre, Narvik, London, 1959.

Iain MacLeod, Neville Chamberlain, London, 1961.

William Manchester, Arms of Krupp, Little Brown, 1968.

Erich von Manstein, Lost Victories, London, 1958.

Arthur Marder, "Winston Is Back," The English Historical Review, Supplement 5, London, 1972.

André Maurois, Tragedy in France, translated by Denver Lindley, Harper & Bros., 1940.

Henri Michel, The Second World War, vol. 1, Praeger, 1975.

Lars Moën, The Iron Heel, Lippincott, 1941.

Leonard Mosley, On Borrowed Time, Random House, 1969.

————, The Reich Marshal, Doubleday, 1974.

J. L. Moulton, The Norwegian Campaign of 1940, London, 1966.

Vyaschlev Oreshin, The Diary of Politruk Oreshin, London, 1941.

Mollie Panter-Downes, London War Notes, Farrar, Straus & Giroux, 1971.

Roger Parkinson, Peace for Our Time, McKay, 1971.

————, Summer, 1940, McKay, 1977.

Sala Pawlowicz, with Kevin Klose, I Will Survive, Norton, 1962.

Richard Petrow, The Bitter Years, Morrow, 1974.

Oscar Pinkus, *The House of Ashes*, World, 1964.
Leon Poliakov, *Harvest of Hate*, Holocaust Library, 1979.
Dudley Pope, *The Battle of the River Plate*, London, 1956.
Wilhelm Prüller, *Diary of a German Soldier*, Coward, McCann, 1963.
Curt Reiss, editor, *They Were There*, Putnam's, 1944.
Rémy, *The 18th Day*, translated by Stanley R. Rader, Everest, 1978.
Paul Reynaud, *In the Thick of the Fight*, London, 1955.
Erwin Rommel, *The Rommel Papers*, London, 1951.
Elspeth Rosenfeld, *The Four Lives of Elspeth Rosenfeld*, London, 1965.
Stephen W. Roskill, *The British Navy at War, 1939-1945*, vol. 1, London, 1960.
Walter S. Ross, *The Last Hero: Charles A. Lindbergh*, Harper & Row, 1976.
Vivian Rowe, *The Great Wall of France*, Putnam's, 1961.
General Ruby, *Sedan, Terre d'Epreuve*, Paris, 1948.
Antoine de Saint-Exupéry, *Pilote de Guerre*, Paris, 1942.
Paul Schmidt, *Hitler's Interpreter*, London, 1951.
Albert Seaton, *Stalin As Warlord*, London, 1976.
Max Seydewitz, *Civil Life in Wartime Germany*, Viking, 1945.
William L. Shirer, *Berlin Diary*, Knopf, 1942.
_____ , *The Rise and Fall of the Third Reich*, Simon & Schuster, 1960.
_____ , *The Collapse of the Third Republic*, Simon & Schuster, 1969.
Robert Sobel, *The Origins of Interventionism*, Bookman Associates, 1960.
Mikhail Soloviev, *My Nine Lives in the Red Army*, McKay, 1955.
Edward Spears, *Assignment to Catastrophe*, 2 vols., London, 1954.
Albert Speer, *Inside the Third Reich*, Macmillan, 1970.
Väinö Tanner, *The Winter War*, Stanford University Press, 1957.
A. J. P. Taylor, *The Second World War*, Putnam's, 1975.
_____ , *English History 1914-1945*, Oxford University Press, 1965.
Telford Taylor, *Munich: The Price of Peace*, Doubleday, 1979.
_____ , *The March of Conquest*, Simon & Schuster, 1958.
Laurence Thompson, *1940*, Morrow, 1966.
Robert S. Thompson, *Pledge to Destiny*, McGraw-Hill, 1974.
Fritz Thyssen, *I Paid Hitler*, London, 1941.
P. Tissier, *The Riom Trial*, London, 1942.
E. S. Turner, *The Phoney War*, St. Martin's, 1961.
Warren Tute, *The Deadly Stroke*, Coward, McCann & Geoghegan, 1973.
Johan Waage, *The Narvik Campaign*, London, 1964.
Robert G. L. Waite, *The Psychopathic God*, Basic Books, 1977.
Walter Warlimont, *Inside Hitler's Headquarters*, London, 1964.
Oliver Warner, *Marshal Mannerheim and the Finns*, Helsinki, 1967.
Bernard Wasserstein, *Britain and the Jews of Europe, 1939-1945*, London, 1979.
Sumner Welles, *The Time for Decision*, Harper, 1944.
Else Wendel, *Hausfrau at War*, London, 1957.
Robert Wernick, *Blitzkrieg*, Time-Life, 1976.
Maxime Weygand, *Recalled to Service*, London, 1952.
Richard J. Whalen, *The Founding Father*, NAL, 1964.
F. W. Winterbotham, *The Ultra Secret*, Harper & Row, 1974.
Elizabeth Wiskemann, *The Rome-Berlin Axis*, London, 1966.

Notes

1. Parties

World's Fair, various newspapers; hot-dog story, *NYT* 10/13/80; polls: Cantril, Gallup; neutrality defeat, Dallek, Burns; bet you an old hat, Blum; *la grande semaine:* Flanner, Destrem, Lazareff, Géraud, Fabré-Luce; Luka party, Reynaud: Lazareff; parade, *Illustrated London News*; Morton letter, Gilbert 1; visit to Maginot, Spears 1, Churchill 1; Pétain testimony, Rowe; what was remarkable, Churchill 1; Göring party, Mosley 1; kisses, *Life*; Dahlerus/Göring, *Last Attempt*; Ivan the terrible, Grey; Bukharin, Grey; purges, Kennan, Seaton; Pasternak to Ilya Ehrenburg, and Stalin speeches, Grey.

2. Pact with the Devil

Trilateral talks, Shirer 2, 3; Chamberlain letter, MacLeod; Voroshilov, *NCA*; Berghof description, Irving 2, Speer; near collapse, I have them: Speer; Aug. 22 speech, *TMWC*, Shirer 2, Irving 3 (Lukacs says evidence may have been doctored); Roosevelt note, *FRUS*; Berle comment, Dallek; not prostitutes, Collier 1; no precedent, Fermi; Reynaud disliked him, Shirer 3; three questions, *Evénements*; cabinet room description, Colvin; Aug. 22 London meeting, Aster, Bethell, *Blue Book*; intercepts, Irving 3; Henderson war fever, Irving 2; Weizsäcker diary, Deutsch; Ribbentrop joke, Mosley 1; death knell, hero of myth, last act, Speer; Stalin like you, Shirer 2; Poland: Beck, Taylor 1; Rosenfeld, *Four Lives*; Ruth Andreas-Friedrich, *Berlin Underground*; Prüller, *Diary*; von Fritsch diary, Irving 2; Reichschancellery description, shiver and shake, Speer; pledge himself personally, Henderson; clandestine H. Wilson meetings, Irving 2; asked Keitel, *In the Service*; inform you in advance, *DGFP*; Hitler to Göring, Mosley 2.

3. Last Days of Silence

Intelligence, Irving 2 & 3. Bekker 1; Bötticher, in Friedlander; FDR letter, *FRUS*; *L'Action Française* editorial, in Shirer 3; Daladier letter in *DGFP*: Italian forces need, *DGFP*; Attolico added demand, Irving 3; Ciano observed, *Diary*; U-boats, U-boats, Dahlerus; statistical analyses, Deutsch; Keitel distrusted,

270

In the Service; Hitler and deputies, Irving 2; Oster and opposition, Deutsch; Beck resignation, Taylor 1; Barlone, *French Officer's Diary*; Lania, *Darkest Hour*, and Koestler; Paris is dim, Destrem, Fabré-Luce; Warsaw, golden corn, *Million*; Kaminskas, Pawlowicz, *I Will Survive*; Bannister, *I Lived under Hitler*; fortified by champagne, Henderson; Himmler's diary, in Irving 2; yes or no, Henderson; Halder game-plan, *Kriegstagebuch*; Henderson-Lipski, Shirer 2; cabinet proceedings, Aster, Colvin; Goerdeler telegram, in Bethell; Schmidt, *Hitler's Interpreter*; Henderson, *Failure*; wouldn't take the call, Shirer 2; Dahlerus, *Last Attempt*, Mosley 1 and 2; Beck telegram, *Dernier Rapport*; intercepted telegram, Irving 3; too late, Shirer 2; Gleiwitz: Höhne, Farago, Mosley 1; slammed phones, Irving 2; Shirer and Murrow, Shirer 1.

4. The Silesian War

Vormann's instructions, Irving 2; practice raids, Bekker 2; opposing forces and strategies, Liddell Hart 2, Basil Collier; A. J. P. Taylor 1, Telford Taylor 2, Shirer 2; Rydz pointed out, Bethell; von Richtofen and Dilley, in Bekker 2; Göring radioed, Bekker 2; first day descriptions from newspaper dispatches; Göring says Poles are hiding, Bekker 2; vitiated acts of bravery, Anders; Prüller, *Diary*; Guderian, *Panzer Leader*; Vormann diary, Irving 2; events in England, Colvin, Cosgrave, Bethell, Aster; Chamberlain sick at heart, MacLeod; von Thoma, in Liddell Hart 1; Beilitz: G. W. Klein, *All But My Life*; Everything that I have worked for, *PD*; Eden, in Bethell; Churchills, in Cosgrave; Hitler's orders and *Athenia*, Bekker 1, Irving 2; Fireside Chat, *Speeches*; Raeder, in Bekker 1; Kordt-Weizsäcker, in Deutsch; Ruth Andreas-Friedrich, *Berlin Underground*.

5. The Death of Poland

Awoke, Irving 1; Guderian-Hitler, *Panzer Leader*; Halder, *Kriegstagebuch*; Bydgoscz, *Black Book*; Heydrich and Keitel, in Höhne; Anders, *Army in Exile*; Kutrzeba, in Wernick; shrill whine, Pinkus; three panics, Csokor, *A Civilian in the Polish War*; questions, *Million*; Amery and Kingsley-Wood, Spears 1; Wilhelmshaven raid, Bekker 1 and 2; BEF crosses, Bryant, Colville; Barlone, *French Officer's Diary*; Gamelin offensive, *Evénements*; von Rundstedt in Blumentritt; CIGS did not object, Shirer 3; communiqués in *Evénements*; amazed at no real attack, *TMWC* and Deutsch; lost track of forces, Blumentritt; propaganda maneuver, Höhne; Kutrzeba and Bortnowski: Anders, Beck, Bekker 2, Shirer 2; Reinhardt, in Bekker 2; Allingham, *The Oaken Heart*; Ironside reports, *Diaries*, Bethell; Gamelin reports, Shirer 3 and *Evénements*; von Briesen to Hitler, and adjutant's notes, Irving 1; Kaminska, Pawlowicz, *I Will Survive*, as well as Pinkus, Höhne, and *Black Book*; Prüller, *Diary*; searing agony, *Million*; Blaskowitz, in Bekker 2; oversight or design, Irving 1; *Pravda*, cited in Bethell; game was up, Beck, Bethell, Irving 1; *Courageous*, Roskill, Churchill 1; Gdynia observed, Shirer 1; Hitler irrepressible, Irving 1.

6. Beginnings

FDR-Kennedy, Beschloss; Bullitt, Dallek; neutrality fight, Dallek, Fehrenbach, Burns; Lindbergh, Ross; polls, Gallup and Cantril; savagely to Lindbergh, Ross; destroyers and neutrality patrol, Bailey and Ryan; quitted in pain, Churchill 1; Roskill, *The White Ensign*; Churchill decisions, ideas, and Godfrey observation,

Marder; letter from Chamberlain, FDR correspondence, Lash; NYT 10/2/39 on Churchill; floodings, Life; secret protocol, NCA; Estonia, Dallin, Bethell, Grey; Enigma, in Cosgrave; Soloviev, My Nine Lives; Oreshin, Diary; Prüller, Diary; gullible Ribbentrop, Shirer 2; Halder and Heydrich, Höhne; Blaskowitz and Ulex, Deutsch; dog and rabbit, other killings, Black Book; Kaminska, I Will Survive, with added material from Pinkus; Rosenfeld, Four Lives; dreams, from Beradt; Bannister, I Lived under Hitler; London impressions: Turner, Calder, Harrison; Bloom, Log of No Lady; feelers, Irving 1; Davis episode, Friedlander, Dallek, Irving 1, Mosley 2; look at Warsaw, Shirer 1; von Leeb, in Deutsch.

7. Winds of Change

October 10 speech, NCA, Irving 1, Shirer 2; internment camps, Koestler; Meslay, Lania; Barlone, Diary; Armengaud, Batailles Politiques, Gamelin, Goutard, Horne; Prien, Bekker 1; politically fatal, Churchill 1; Firth of Forth raid, Bekker 2; bold strokes, Roskill; Brauchitsch-Halder, interview with Halder by Deutsch; three alternatives, Kriegstagebuch; opposition stalwart is Grosscurth, in Deutsch; City of Flint, Bailey and Ryan, Dallek; Nelson, Bekker 1; coup attempt: Deutsch, Shirer 2, Irving 1, TMWC.

8. The War of Words

Oster-Sas, Deutsch; Leopold and Wilhelmina, Rémy; Belgian defenses: Horne, Shirer 3, Rémy, Rowe, Taylor 2; conversations with French, Gamelin; Kordt, Deutsch; Hitler advances speech, Irving 1; Rommel, in Irving 1; Venlo incident: Best, Farago, Kahn, Höhne, Irving 1, Bullock; telegram from Gestapo, Farago; propaganda, Fonvieille-Alquier, Cole; Goebbels, Secret Conferences, Shirer 2; effects on French, Fonvieille-Alquier; Else Wendel, Hausfrau at War; Ruth Andreas-Friedrich, Berlin Underground; all we want is peace, Wendel; Göring's attitude, Mosley, Irving 1; secret training, NCA, Irving 1; Oslo Report, Hinsley; rights revokes, Calder, Turner; Mass Observation, Harrison; some obscurity, Turner; more money paid and blockade effective, A. J. P. Taylor 2; Thames shut, Johnson, Churchill 1; Doric Star, Foley, Pope, Frischauer and Jackson; Graf Spee battles, Pope, Roskill; Langsdorff wires for instructions, Irving 1, Bekker; end of Graf Spee, Pope; Columbus, Bailey and Ryan.

9. Christmas in Finland

Soviet-German cooperation, Bethell, Black Book, Grey; negotiations, Jakobson, Tanner, Engle and Paananen; tale of heroism, Warner; attack on Helsinki, Chew; moral foundation, Shirer 1; many thrusts, Jakobson, Chew, Engle, Cox; Oreshin Diary; Kalevala and jokes, Chew, Engle and Paananen; Mannerheim and the line, Warner; Aldridge column, NYT 12/25/39; Finnish relief, Sobel; Voroshilov-Stalin, Khrushchev Remembers; Mussolini letter, Fermi, Irving 1; Lublin, in Gilbert 2, Black Book, Poliakov, Wasserstein; Hitler at Christmas, Irving 1; A. J. Liebling, in They Were There; King George's speech, poetry chase, L. Thompson.

10. A Plane Crashes

Reinberger crash, Bekker 2, Rémy, Shirer 3, Mosley 2; Hitler rage, Irving 1;

soothsayer, Mosley 2; contradicted by intelligence, Irving 1; revising the plan, Manstein, Deighton, Horne, Shirer 2, Guderian, Irving 1; Rommel promotion, *Papers*; Quisling to Raeder, Petrow, Brooks; euthanasia, Irving 1, Harsch, Seydewitz; wildest fantasy letter, Deutsch; Blaskowitz report, Höhne, Deutsch; Hlond's report, *Black Book*, Gilbert 2, Poliakov; *Todesborn*, Borkin, Irving 1, Höhne; *Lebensborn*, Hillel and Henry, Seydewitz, Grunberger; Himmler dream, Höhne; Gort, Colville, Bryant; invitation, Rémy, Horne; Gamelin's plans, *Servir*, Horne, Shirer 3, Deighton, Taylor 2; Georges, in Horne; Pretelat, in Rowe, Horne, Doumenc; Corap's men, Doumenc, Bryant; boredom, Barlone, Shirer 3; soldiers' worries, Fonvieille-Alquier; production figures, *Evénements*, Horne, Reynaud; Daladier accident, Géraud; Supreme War Council, *Evénements*, Horne, Shirer 3, Cosgrave, Marder, Thompson.

11. Residue of Fortune

Litchfield and Churchill memo, Marder; "White Rabbit," Cosgrave; many angles of criticism, Marder; Brooke told Dill, Bryant; U-33 capture, Hinsley; Haw-Haw, Cole; *Altmark* affair, Frischauer and Jackson, Roskill, Petrow, Foley; Hitler and *Altmark*, Irving 1; Falkenhorst, Petrow; Stalin's negotiations, Shirer 2; Soloviev, *Nine Lives*; Oreshin, *Diary*; Jakobson, *Diplomacy of the Winter War*; Luukanen, *Fighter over Finland*; Helsinki decision, Jakobson, Chew, Engle and Paananen, Tanner; Daladier and Reynaud, Géraud, Shirer 3, Reynaud; Tanner, *Winter War*; Jakobson, *Diplomacy*.

12. Mission to Nowhere

Appeals and moral embargo, Divine, Langer and Gleason, Dallek, Fehrenbach; powder puffs, in Sobel; Sobel, *The Origins of Interventionism*; battle of Washington, Haight, Blum; Woodring, in Haight; Morgenthau diary, Blum; Welles's trip, Hilton; Ciano, in Welles; ponderous and other descriptions, Welles, *The Time for Decision*; told a friend, Hilton; Welles and Ribbentrop, Schmidt; Hitler to Welles, *Decision*; food restrictions, Fonvieille-Alquier; accusers of Daladier, Shirer 3, Géraud; Reynaud, *In the Thick*, Horne, de Gaulle; influential groups, de Gaulle, *Memoirs*; Welles, in *Decision*; Hitler to Mussolini, *DGFP*, Irving 1; Rome rumor, Welles's bluff, Hilton; Mussolini dream, Fermi; did not mention Norway, Irving 1; Goebbels, Boelcke, *Secret Conferences*; Molotov, in Dallin; float dynamite charges, Collier 2; Reynaud in council, *In the Thick*; *Evénements*, Géraud, Horne, Shirer 3, Polish documents, Hilton, Dallek; Goebbels, Boelcke, *Secret Conferences*.

13. Norwegian Adventure

Plans for Norway, Irving 1, Petrow, *NCA*; German naval actions, Bekker 1; Ironside to Gamelin, Marder; Daladier and delay, Géraud; no lack of information, Hinsley; Chamberlain speech, Churchill 1; British actions, Brooks, McIntyre, Petrow, Roskill; Denmark, Petrow; German naval actions, Bekker 1; Quisling, Petrow, Irving 1; Narvik, Bekker 1, Broch, R. Collier 2; Dietl greeting, R. Collier 2; Dietl to Broch, *The Mountains Wait*; Warburton-Lee, Roskill; eleven transports, Irving 1; panic in Berlin, Bekker 1, Deutsch, Irving 1, Petrow, Shirer 2; Jodl comment, Brauchitsch refusal, Irving 1.

14. Preparations

Soviet actions, Dallin; sweeping reform, Grey; Churchill's difficulties, Cosgrave, Marder, Roskill; de Wiart, "Mauriceforce" and "Sickelforce," L. Thompson, Petrow; captured units, Irving 1; de Wiart signaled, Brooks, McIntyre; Keyes incident, Marder; Norwegians bitter, Petrow; Mackesy's timidity, Cosgrave, Marder; Roosevelt's plans, Lash, Burns; poll, Gallup; more dead than alive, Wendel; GD regiment, Deighton; VP2623, Hinsley; Brooke and Dill, Bryant; Barlone, *Diary*; Corap and Huntziger troops, Doumenc, Goutard, Ruby, Horne, Deighton; Maurois, *Tragedy in France*; Weygand luncheon, Rémy; Hélène de Portes, Géraud, Horne; French intelligence, Horne, Shirer 3, Hinsley; French had more, Deighton; indictment, Géraud, Reynaud, Shirer 3; British reckoning, L. Thompson, R. Collier 2, Spears 1, Churchill 1, Shirer 2, Marder; speeches, PD, tea party, L. Thompson, Collier 2; Prüller, *Diary*; matador's cloak, Manstein, Deighton, Horne, Shirer 2; tank rider, in Horne; train ruse, Irving 1.

15. The Invasion of the West

Reward, Irving 1; Eben Emael, Deighton, Rémy; parachutists, Bekker 2; Leske, *I Was a Nazi Flier*; Rotterdam attack, Bekker 2; no fifth column, de Jong; resignations withdrawn, Reynaud, Gamelin; martial air, in Horne; limit air activity, *Evénements*; BEF moves up, Ellis; Hodson, *Through the Dark Night*; shock at the Dyle, Bryant; Hitler wept, Keitel; Giraud drew no conclusions, Goutard; Belgians outfought Germans, Rémy; tank battle, Grove, Horne; Churchill's day, L. Thompson, Cosgrave; walking with destiny, Churchill 1; could have done nothing, Churchill 2; new cabinet, Churchill 2, Spears 1; speech in Commons, Spears 1; not too late, R. Collier 2; considered the Ardennes impenetrable, Deighton, Manstein, Guderian; Rommel, *Papers*; French did not believe, Goutard, Doumenc; groups of unsaddled horses, Ruby; Rommel's actions, *Papers*, Deighton; Guderian's actions, *Panzer Leader*, Horne, Shirer 3; Meuse badly held, Goutard, Doumenc, Ruby, Horne; high command full of talk, Horne; wargame orders, Guderian, Deighton; panzer sergeant description, Horne; Ruby, *Sedan*; GD regiment, Horne, Deighton, Wernick; Ruby, *Sedan*; underestimates of the situation, Horne; Doumenc, *Histoire*; Rommel, *Papers*; tank corps awaiting orders, Horne; Sedan, Ruby, Goutard; Guderian, *Panzer Leader*; confusion spread, Ruby, Shirer 3; Huntziger remarked, Horne; Rotterdam, Bekker 2; call from Reynaud, Churchill 2.

16. The Muddle

Guderian, *Panzer Leader*; Führer nervous, Irving 1; Halder, *Kriegstagebuch*; Hitler distrusted OKH, Irving 1; von Kleist berated Guderian, *Panzer Leader*; Rommel, *Papers*; Vincennes logbook, Rémy; Churchill actions, Churchill 2; Reynaud's apartment, Horne, R. Collier 2, Churchill 2, Baudouin; 10 squadrons illusory, Horne, Deighton; Brooke, Bryant; Goebbels, *Secret Conferences*; St.-Exupéry, *Pilote de Guerre*; Maurois, *Tragedy in France*; death on the roads, Habe, Maurois; de Gaulle, *Memoirs*; de Gaulle at Montcornet, R. Thompson, Horne; Barlone, *Diary*; Pétain and Weygand comments, Shirer 3; gray-gloved hand, Reynaud; Daladier said nothing, Shirer 3; Gamelin directive, *Servir*; Weygand canceled it, *Recalled to Service*; British territorial division, Karslake; news buoyed Hitler, Irving 1, Keitel; Ypres meeting, Horne, Rémy, Weygand;

Spaak apoplectic, Rémy; Gort had been busy, Colville, Ellis, Deighton; Rommel panicked, Deighton, Bekker 2; Gort at Ypres, Colville, Ellis; description of Weygand, Churchill 2; light enemy units, Horne; Gort's precautions, Colville; Alan Brooke, Bryant; Reynaud telegram, Churchill 2; spearhead moved too fast, Irving 1, Halder, Liddell Hart 1; von Rundstedt ordered halt, Blumentritt, Irving 1; Göring telephoned, Mosley 2, Irving 1; Charleville conference, Irving 1, Horne, Deighton, Guderian, Manstein, Blumentritt, Liddell Hart 1.

17. The Miracle

Boulogne and Calais, Harman; defense of Calais, Churchill 2; Bombe and Enigma, Hinsley, Colville, Bryant, Winterbotham; Eden told Gort, Rémy; tunnels, Barker; animated by savage desire, in Harman; Hitler and Himmler, Höhne, Irving 1; half the Luftwaffe out, Bekker 2; Hadley, *Third Class to Dunkirk*; east mole, Barker; Luftwaffe figures, Bekker 2; Le Cornet Malo, Harman; Belgium out of the war, Rémy, Horne, Shirer 3; approach to Italy, Bell; Dunkirk defenses, Colville, Bryant; panzers ordered to stop, Irving 1; German navy in no condition, Bekker 1; Dunkirk small boats: Barker, Harman, R. Collier 2; *brassus*, Churchill 2; Brooke, Bryant; Barlone, *Diary*; Dunkirk figures, Harman; Legion colonel, Lapie; Narvik evacuation, Waage, Petrow; halfhearted warnings, Hinsley; German naval actions, Bekker 1; RAF figures, Parkinson 2; British bungled, Harman; 140,000 left, Karslake; speech in Commons, Churchill 2.

18. The End in France

Blitz, preparations, cabinet study: Parkinson 2; Roosevelt-Churchill, Loewenheim, Lash; Marshall located, Haight; cabled Reynaud, *FRUS*; Lindbergh, Lash, Ross; polls began to show, Gallup, Cantril; sat on docks, Haight; Weygand, *Recalled to Service*; de Gaulle, *Memoirs*; Pétain, in Shirer 3; von Bock and subordinate, in Horne; Rommel's actions, *Papers*; Karslake, *Last Act*; Maurois, *Tragedy*; high councils, *Evénements*; Mussolini enters the war, Wiskemann, Fermi, Irving 1; Mussolini to FDR, *FRUS*; Hitler forbade staff talks, Irving 1; Roosevelt denunciation, Lash; memo from Dudley Pound, Bell; Briare: Spears 2, Churchill 2, Barber, Shirer 3, Bell, de Gaulle, Reynaud, Géraud; traveled as if on maneuvers, Guderian; Hans Habe, *A Thousand Shall Fall*; Quimper and Hélène, Géraud, Baudouin, Barber; Roosevelt cables, *FRUS*, Loewenheim, Lash; Bullitt, Barber; Franco-British union, Bell; Reynaud-Lebrun, Reynaud; de Gaulle escape, Spears 2; de Gaulle speeches, Bell, R. Thompson; Hitler ordered race, Irving 1; last act, Karslake, Bryant; Thank God, Parkinson 2; letter, *LT* 6/18/40.

19. Signals

Armistice, Shirer 1, Shirer 3, Horne, Irving 1, Keitel; Hitler's tour, Speer, Wernick; Barlone, *Diary*; refugees, Koestler, Lania; put out flags, *Berlin Underground*; Prüller, *Diary*; Wendel, *Hausfrau*; Poland, *Black Book*, Höhne, Gilbert 2; Sala, *I Will Survive*; Stalin's actions, Dallin, Grey; King Carol, R. Collier 2; Molotov note, Dallin; Hélène's death, Géraud, Shirer 3, Horne; Daladier and Mandel, Géraud, Shirer 3, Horne; Hitler had no plans, Irving 1, Bekker 1, Mosley 2; Roosevelt and Churchill agreed, Lash, Loewenheim, Tute; Churchill wept, R. Collier 2; Mers-al-Kabir, Tute, Bell, R. Collier 2; worst bombing raid, Parkinson 2; reaction to raid, Bell; Hitler's fundamental decision, Irving 1.

Intrepid, 149
invasion of the West, 195–222
air battles in, 203, 206, 209
airborne strikes in, 195, 196, 197
Allied Plan D in, 197–200, 204–210, 218
Allied retreat from Sedan in, 210–224, 233
Ardennes forest battle in, 201–204
bombing of civilians in, 196–197
British counterattack in, 220–222
commencement of, 195–210
Dunkirk evacuation in, 219, 222–238
fifth column stories in, 197, 210
Gembloux Gap tank battle in, 199–200, 205
German advance in, 212–224
German plans for, see Plan Yellow
German sweep to Atlantic coast in, 219
refugees in, 216–217
Sedan battle in, 205–210, 211
Weygand maneuver in, 219–222
Iron Duke, 97
Ironside, Sir William Edmund, 18, 63, 67, 92, 143, 169, 180, 183
Ismay, Hastings, 214, 215, 221, 244
Italy:
Allied campaign in, 244
Allied dissension on, 231, 244
in Anti-Comintern Pact, 16
as German ally, 242–243
in Pact of Steel, 22–23
Roosevelt and, 22, 158–160, 242–243
Russia seen as threat to, 22
unpreparedness of, 22–23

Jakobson, Max, 151–152, 154
Japan, 15
in Anti-Comintern Pact, 16
in peace treaty with Russia, 73
in war with Russia, 15, 21
Jews, 13, 143
in France, 35, 39, 161
in German labor camps, 88
in Germany, 28–29, 90, 111
in Poland, 28, 56, 89–90
in Polish concentration and death camps, 127, 136, 255
Jodl, Alfred, 168, 176, 223
Joffre, Joseph, 23
Johnson, Louis, 158
Joyce, William ("Lord Haw-Haw"), 147–148

Kalevala, 124
Kallio, Kyosti, 155
Kamenev, L. B., 15, 16
Kaminska, Sala, 40–41, 70–71, 89–90, 255–256
Kapurthala, Princess of, 6

Keitel, Wilhelm, 32, 61, 67, 94, 168, 176, 199, 223, 251, 252
Kennedy, Joseph P., 79
Keyes, Sir Roger, 138, 179–180, 188, 198, 220, 230
Khrushchev, Nikita, 126
Kleist, Ewald von, 205, 212, 213, 223
Klops, Dutch policeman, 107–108
Knox, Frank, 80, 249
Kollontay, Alexandra, 151–152
Königsberg, 173
Kordt, Erich, 37, 59, 106–107
assassination of Hitler planned by, 106
Kutrzeba, General, 61, 68, 70, 72
Kuusinen, O. W., 122, 123, 125, 152

Landon, Alf, 80
Langsdorff, Hans, 117–120
Lania, Leo, 38–39, 65, 95, 254
Latvia, 17, 21, 86, 256–257
Laval, Pierre, 143, 161–162, 163, 186
League of Nations, 125
Lebrun, Albert, 6, 162, 186, 248
Leeb, Wilhelm von, 93, 98, 99
Lenin, V. I., 15, 16
Leopold III, king of the Belgians, 104–106, 199, 214, 219–220, 221
Gamelin's defense plan accepted by, 106
in negotiations with Allies, 138
surrender by, 229–230
Leske, Gottfried, 196–197
Lewis, John L., 92, 181
Liebling, A. J., 128
Lindbergh, Charles A., 80–81, 240
Lindsay, Martin, 188
Lippmann, Walter, 156
Lipski, Jósef, 43, 45
List, Siegmund, 213
Litchfield, J. S., 145
Lithuania, 17, 21, 85, 86, 256, 257
Litvinov, Maksim, 17, 20
Lloyd George, David, 188–189
London Daily Herald, 84
London Daily Mail, 84
London Daily Telegraph, 84
London Times, 147, 250
"Lord Haw-Haw," 147–148
Lossberg, Bernhard von, 176
Lothian, Lord, 260
Ludendorff, Erich, 98
Luftwaffe:
Dunkirk evacuation and, 227–228, 229, 231, 236
Göring's vaulting ambitions for, 112–113
in invasion of West, 195, 196, 199, 203, 205, 223
in Norwegian campaign, 169, 172, 179, 180
Royal Navy as target of, 97

CPSIA information can be obtained
at www.ICGtesting.com
Printed in the USA
LVHW110955180422
716424LV00010B/121